1351

LOCI CRITICI

PASSAGES ILLUSTRATIVE OF CRITICAL THEORY AND PRACTICE FROM ARISTOTLE DOWNWARDS

SELECTED, PARTLY TRANSLATED, AND ARRANGED WITH NOTES

BY

GEORGE SAINTSBURY, M.A. Oxon., Hon. LL.D. Aberd.

PROFESSOR OF RHETORIC AND ENGLISH LITERATURE IN THE UNIVERSITY OF EDINBURGH

—•▸◂•—

1351

GINN AND COMPANY
BOSTON · NEW YORK · CHICAGO · LONDON
ATLANTA · DALLAS · COLUMBUS · SAN FRANCISCO

The Athenæum Press

GINN AND COMPANY · PRO-
PRIETORS · BOSTON · U.S.A.

PREFACE

The present volume is one of the most strictly practical purpose, and its compiler lays claim to nothing beyond mere "porter's work" — except in the one point, not common to all porters, of having perceived that the work was needed. During the last few years the study of Rhetoric — long disused almost entirely in England,[1] and pursued with somewhat altered intent in America — has been revived to some extent in the former country, and to a very large extent, I am informed, in the latter. In particular, so far as England is concerned, the recent institution of Honours Schools of English Literature in the newer Universities almost necessarily involved the direction of study to the history and principles of criticism. I was enabled, some eight or nine years ago, to take part in the institution of such a School in the Victoria University, and a little later to undertake the charge of one which had been just formed at Edinburgh by my honoured predecessor, Professor Masson, and by his and my colleague, Mr. Gregory Smith, Lecturer in English at that University.

The resumption of rhetorical-critical studies, however, brought with it, in the changed circumstances of education, a new and very real difficulty. In the old days of rhetorical teaching, every student knew Latin with more or less thoroughness; and in the sixteenth and seventeenth centuries most knew some Greek. This last tongue has become disastrously strange at the present day to many — probably to the large majority — of the students likely to "take" English: while I fear it would be sanguine to expect that all of them should read Latin with the current ease which enables a man to extract the meaning of his author without formal

---

[1] In Scotland the institution of the Chair which I have now the honour to hold, and of others later, kept it alive, or should have done so, from the very period when it was most failing.

"construing." Hence, what are, and always must be, the texts
and scriptures of the subject — Aristotle, Longinus, Quintilian, and
others — have to be sought in translations.

Moreover, even supposing that these translations were in all
cases easily attainable in entirely satisfactory forms, there is the
further difficulty that they, with the modern authorities on the
matter, form a small library, with which it is rather unreasonable
to expect that the ordinary student will provide himself, and with
which, as a matter of fact, he most certainly does not. I have
myself found this a very real difficulty in eight years' actual practice ; and from the very first of these years I have meditated the
production (if necessary privately and at my own expense, seeing
that, for a time at least, the sale was not likely to tempt publishers
in England) of something like this book. Recently, however, in
conversation with an American friend who was *du métier* (Professor
Gayley of the University of California), I found that there was
likely to be a larger demand in America, and my present publishers, on the matter being represented to them, offered, with great
kindness and spirit, to take the work in hand.

The principle of the book is to give nothing more than the actual
text (with such annotation as may be barely necessary to comprehension) of the passages which experience has shown me to be
most useful for the purpose, from ancient writers, from Dante,
from a few Renaissance critics of the formative period, and from
English critics of the Elizabethan age and onwards. I have only
in a few cases drawn on writers in the modern foreign languages
— first, because it was very important not to make the book too
big ; and secondly, because the *matter* of their criticism (which is
here alone important) can, in almost every case, be perfectly well
exhibited out of English stores. The passages chosen from the
enormous bulk at hand are such as may best illustrate the *general*
drift of criticism in modern Europe, with a few exceptions and
singularities. In giving this matter I have taken as much pains as
I could to abstain, as a rule, from expressing any opinions of my
own except on points of bare interpretation. All argumentative
matter — all deduction, adjustment, application — is left to the
teacher, who will, by using the book, have his hands left free and

his time saved for this very purpose. Anybody who — studying without a teacher or for other reasons — wants my opinions, not in my fatigue-jacket as compiler but in a somewhat statelier uniform, may find them in my *History of Criticism;* anybody who does not want them will seldom be troubled with them here.

The passages selected are, as has been said, those which I have myself found either indispensable or most useful. I have taken the advice of some of the best available authorities on the subject; but if any expert reader detects *lacunæ* or superfluities, he will oblige me by letting me know of them. The exclusion of living writers and of very modern critical phases is deliberate; and it can be but barely necessary to say that there is no intention of giving " Beauties of Criticism." In the case of Aristotle I have, to save time and labour (or rather under the idea of doing so, for I am by no means sure that it was not the more troublesome process of the two) adapted (in each case with many changes) Twining's version of the *Poetics* and the old " Oxford " one of the *Rhetoric;* adding in the former case, by the kindness of my colleague, Professor Butcher, some variants from his own admirable work, and in the latter, by the similar courtesy of Bishop Welldon, some from his version of the *Rhetoric.* The translations of Dionysius, Longinus, Quintilian, and Dante, as well as all the shorter translated extracts, are entirely my own. Their chief aim is at the utmost possible *closeness.*[1]

GEORGE SAINTSBURY.

EDINBURGH, July, 1903.

---

[1] The notes indicated by *numbers*, 1, 2, etc., are mine ; those asterisked belong to the originals.

[In the present edition a few misprints and minor oversights of impression have been corrected. G. S.]

CONTENTS

BIBLIOGRAPHICAL NOTE

A connected commentary on these passages, and on much else, will be found in the editor's above-mentioned *History of Criticism* (Edinburgh and London, in three volumes, 1900–1904), with full references to other authorities on the whole subject; the following list is confined to critical editions of the actual works excerpted, where the contexts may be sought, and further elucidation obtained, by those who have interest and time.

ARISTOTLE, *Poetics.*

> Butcher, S. H., *Aristotle's Theory of Poetry and Fine Art*, Third Edition, London 1902.

> *Rhetoric.*

>> (Greek only in text, but with a practically complete translation in notes) Cope, E. M., 3 vols., Cambridge 1878 (with a fourth but earlier volume of Introduction, *ibid.* 1868), ed. J. E. Sandys.

>> (English only) Welldon, J. E. C., London 1886.

DIONYSIUS OF HALICARNASSUS.

> *Rhetorical Works*, (Greek) ed. Reiske, vols. 5 and 6, Leipsic 1775.

> *Three Literary Letters*, (Greek and English) Roberts, W. R., Cambridge 1901.

LONGINUS, *On the Sublime.*

> (Greek and English) Roberts, W. R., Cambridge 1899.

> (English only) Havell, H. R., London 1890.

QUINTILIAN, *Institutes of Oratory.*

> (Latin) Leipsic 1820.

> (English) Watson, J. (Bohn's Classical Library).

DANTE, *De Vulgari Eloquio [Eloquentia].*

> (Latin) Rajna, P., Florence 1896, or Moore, E., in *Dante's Works*, Oxford 1897.

> (English) Ferrers-Howell, H. C., London 1890.

> In all cases of doubtful reading Dr. Prompt's facsimile of the Grenoble MS. (Venice 1892) has been compared.

It has not seemed necessary to indicate editions, etc., of the authors from whom the shorter passages are taken, or of modern works. Such indications, if wanted, will be found in the *History of Criticism* above cited. For an almost complete bibliography of critical literature, see Gayley and Scott, *Literary Criticism*, Boston 1899.

LOCI CRITICI

I

ARISTOTLE (384–322 B.C.)

1. THE POETICS

(This book, which is incomplete, deals very fully with Tragedy, slightly with Epic, and scarcely at all with other literary kinds.)

CHAPTER I.— THE NATURE AND KINDS OF POETRY

My design is to treat of Poetry in general, and of its several species; to enquire what is the proper power[1] of each — what construction of plot is essential to a good Poem — of what, and how many, parts each species consists; with whatever else belongs to the same enquiry: which I shall consider, beginning at the beginning, in the order of nature.

Epic poetry, tragedy, comedy, dithyrambics, as also, for the most part, the music of the flute and of the lyre — all these are, in the most general view of them, imitations; differing, however, from each other in three respects, according to the different means, the different objects, or the different manner of their imitation.

For, as men, some through art and some through habit, imitate various objects by means of colour and figure, and others, again, by voice; so, with respect to the arts above mentioned, Rhythm, Words, and Melody are the different means by which, either single or variously combined, they all produce their imitation.

---

[1] Twining, " effect "; Professor Butcher, " essential quality." (In future notes these translators will be indicated by the letters T. and B.) Perhaps δύναμιν here would be best rendered by " *virtue.*"

1

For example, in the imitations of the flute and the lyre, and of any other instruments capable of producing a similar effect — as the syrinx, or pipe — melody and rhythm only are employed. In those of dance, rhythm alone, without melody; for dancers, by rhythm applied to gesture, express manners, passions, and actions.

The art which imitates by words alone, either prose or verse — the latter being either composed of various metres, or confined, according to the practice hitherto established, to a single species — is hitherto nameless.[1] For we have no general name which would comprehend the mimes of Sophron and Xenarchus and the Socratic dialogues; or poems in iambic, elegiac, or other metres, in which the epic species of imitation may be conveyed. Custom, indeed, connecting the poetry or making with the metre, has denominated some elegiac poets, i.e., makers of elegiac verse; others, epic poets, i.e., makers of hexameter verse; thus distinguishing poets, not according to the nature of their imitation, but according to their common use of metre. For even they who compose treatises of medicine or natural philosophy in verse are denominated poets: yet Homer and Empedocles have nothing in common, except their metre; the former, therefore, justly merits the name of poet, while the other should rather be called a physiologist[2] than a poet.

So, also, though any one should choose to convey his imitation in every kind of metre promiscuously, as Chæremon has done in his *Centaur*, which is a medley of all sorts of verse, we must call him a poet. — But of these distinctions enough.

There are, again, other species of poetry which make use of all the means of imitation, — rhythm, melody, and verse. Such are the dithyrambic, pastoral, tragedy, and comedy: with this difference,

---

[1] Here comes in the first important difference of text and translation. The older texts, which Twining followed, generally read ἐποποιία at the beginning of the sentence, and it was doubted whether λόγοις ψιλοῖς could mean "prose" or whether it meant "uncouth" verses. The addition of ἀνώνυμος, from the old Arabic version, completely changes, and seems beyond doubt to establish, the sense.

[2] In the Greek sense: "physicist" rather, according to the arbitrary modern limitation of "physiology."

however, that in some of these they are employed all together, in others separately. And such are the differences of these arts with respect to the means by which they imitate.

Chaps. II-V contain remarks in more detail on the subject of Chap. I, which may be thus summarized : Imitation may be either of the actual, or, as in the case of tragedy, of something better than the actual, or, as in the case of comedy, of something worse. It may also differ as to its *manner:* adopting narration or action or a mixture of the two. The delight in it is congenital; and the pursuing of this delight has led to the discovery of the various kinds of poetry, and of the various kinds of verse appropriated to them. Iambic is best suited to drama, because it is the most *conversational* metre. Comedy is inferior to tragedy in subject, and also in age. Epic is not inferior in subject, but differs from it in uniformity of metre, and in the fact that tragedy, *as a rule*, does not go much beyond a day's time, while epic is unlimited. As for the parts, *all those of epic are found in tragedy: not all those of tragedy in epic.* The important textual passages of these chapters are the following :

The Origin of Poetry

Poetry, in general, seems to have derived its origin from two causes, each of them natural.

1. To imitate is instinctive in man from his infancy. By this he is distinguished from other animals, that he is of all the most imitative, and through this instinct receives his earliest education. All men likewise naturally receive pleasure from imitation. This is evident from actual experience : for we contemplate with pleasure, and with the more pleasure the more exactly they are imitated, such objects as, if real, we could not see without pain; as the figures of the meanest and most disgusting animals, dead bodies, and the like. And the reason of this is, that to learn is a natural pleasure, not confined to philosophers, but common to all men; with this difference only, that the multitude partake of it in a more transient and compendious manner. Hence the pleasure they receive from a picture : in viewing they learn, they infer, they discover, what every object is; that this, for instance, is such a particular man, etc. For if we suppose the object represented to be something which the spectator had never seen, his pleasure, in that

case, will not arise from the imitation, but from the workmanship, the colours, or some such cause.

2. Imitation, then, being thus natural to us, and, secondly, Melody and Rhythm being also natural (for as to metre, it is plainly a species[1] of rhythm), those persons in whom originally these propensities were the strongest were naturally led to rude and extemporaneous attempts, which, gradually improved, gave birth to Poetry.

COMEDY

Comedy, as was said before, is an imitation of characters inferior, not with respect to every sort of vice, but to the ridiculous only, as being a subdivision of turpitude or deformity, since it may be defined to be a fault or deformity of such a sort as is neither painful nor destructive. A grotesque mask,[2] for example, is something ugly and distorted, but not from pain.

The successive improvements of Tragedy, and the respective authors of them, have not escaped our knowledge; but those of Comedy, from the little attention that was paid to it in its origin,[3] remain in obscurity. For it was not till late that Comedy was authorized by the magistrate, and carried on at the public expense; it was at first a private and voluntary exhibition.

EPIC AND TRAGEDY

Epic poetry agrees so far with Tragic as it is an imitation of great characters and actions by means of verse[4]; but in this it differs, that it makes use of only one kind of metre throughout, and that it is narrative. It also differs in length; for Tragedy endeavours, as far as possible, to confine its action within the limits

[1] So T.; B., better, "sections." Even this does not perhaps fully explain μόρια, "limbs," "organized parts." The relation of "rhythm"—the general mass out of which the more definitely organized metre is taken—is referred to *infra.*

[2] T., "face," no doubt wrongly. B. takes it of the actual comic mask of the stage.

[3] B., "because it was not taken seriously."

[4] T., "words," the original text being doubtful. The version adopted above seems to give the best and most probable sense; but it may have been "words in verse."

of a single revolution of the sun, or nearly so ; but the time of Epic action is indefinite.   This, however, at first, was equally the case with Tragedy itself.

Of their constituent parts, some are common to both, some peculiar to Tragedy.   He, therefore, who knows about good and bad Tragedy knows also about Epic ; for all the parts of the Epic poem are to be found in Tragedy ; not all those of Tragedy in the Epic poem.

CHAPTER VI. — THE DEFINITION AND CONSTITUTION OF TRAGEDY

Of the species of poetry which imitates in hexameters, and of comedy, we shall speak hereafter.   Let us now consider Tragedy, collecting first, from what has been already said, its true and essential definition.

TRAGEDY, THEN, IS AN IMITATION OF SOME ACTION THAT IS SERIOUS, ENTIRE, AND OF SOME MAGNITUDE — BY LANGUAGE. EMBELLISHED AND RENDERED PLEASURABLE, BUT BY DIFFERENT MEANS IN DIFFERENT PARTS — IN THE WAY, NOT OF NARRATION, BUT OF ACTION, EFFECTING THROUGH PITY AND TERROR THE CORRECTION AND REFINEMENT OF SUCH [1] PASSIONS.

By pleasurable language I mean a language that has the embellishments of rhythm, melody, and metre.   And I add, by different means in different parts, because in some parts metre alone is employed — in others, melody.

Now, as Tragedy imitates by acting, the Decoration, in the first place, must necessarily be one of its parts ; then the *melopœia*, or Music, and the Diction ; for these last include the means of tragic imitation.   By Diction, I mean the metrical composition.   The meaning of *melopœia* is obvious to every one.

Again : Tragedy being an imitation of an action, and the persons employed in that action being necessarily characterized by their Character and Thought (since it is from these that actions themselves derive their character), it follows that there must also be Character

---

[1] B. prefers to give τῶν τοιούτων the restricted sense, which it undoubtedly sometimes has, of "these."

and Thought as the two causes of actions, and, consequently, of all success or ill success.[1] The imitation of the action is the Plot[2]; for by Plot I now mean the contexture of incidents. By Character I mean whatever marks the characters of the persons; by Thought whatever they say, whether proving anything or delivering a general sentiment, etc.

Hence, all Tragedy must necessarily contain six parts, which, together, constitute its peculiar character, or quality — Fable, Character, Diction, Thought, Decoration, and Music. Of these parts, two relate to the means, one to the manner, and three to the object of imitation. And these are all. These specific parts, if we may so call them, have been employed by most poets, and are all to be found in almost every tragedy.

But of all these parts the most important is the combination of incidents. Because Tragedy is an imitation, not of men, but of Action — of life, of happiness; for unhappiness consists in Action, and the very end [of life] is Action of a certain kind, not quality.[3] Now, men's Character constitutes their quality; but it is by their actions that they are happy, or the contrary. Tragedy, therefore, does not imitate Action for the sake of imitating Character, but in the imitation of Action that of Character is of course involved; so that the Action and the Plot are the end of Tragedy; and the end is of principal importance.

Again: Tragedy cannot subsist without Action; without Character it may. The tragedies of most modern poets have this defect [4] —

[1] T., much more widely and less aptly, " of the happiness or unhappiness of all men."

[2] T., in accordance with the habit, still not quite disused, of the 17th and 18th centuries, "Fable "; and for " Character," " Manners." " Sentiments," his equivalent for " Thought," has not the same excuse of at least literal fidelity to the Greek. But διάνοια is a difficult word to translate, and even " Thought " is not quite satisfactory.

[3] The meaning is quite clear, but the text is confused, there being no apparent reason why " happiness " should appear alone in the first clause, and " unhappiness " in the second. One way is to repeat each: the other (now preferred), to turn them out altogether, repeat " of life " as bracketed above, and make it run simply " of action, of life; and life consists in action, and its end, etc."

[4] i.e., of *not* giving character.

a defect common, indeed, among poets in general. As among painters also, this is the case with Zeuxis, compared with Polygnotus; the latter excels in the expression of Character. There is no such expression in the pictures of Zeuxis.

Further: suppose any one to string together a number of speeches in which Character is strongly marked, the Language and the Sentiments well turned — this will not be sufficient to produce the proper effect of Tragedy; that end will much rather be answered by a piece defective in each of those particulars, but furnished with a proper Plot and contexture of incidents. Add to this, that those parts of Tragedy by means of which it becomes most interesting and affecting are parts of the Plot: I mean Revolutions and Discoveries.[1] As a further proof, adventurers in tragic writing are sooner able to arrive at excellence in the language and the manners than in the construction of a plot, as appears from almost all our earlier poets.

The Plot, then, is the principal part — the soul, as it were — of tragedy, and Character is the next in rank. For Tragedy is an imitation of an Action, and through that principally of the agents. Just as in painting, the most brilliant colours, spread at random and without design, will give far less pleasure than the simplest outline of a figure.[2]

In the third place stands Thought. To this part it belongs to say such things as are true and proper, which in the dialogue[3] depends on the political and rhetorical arts; for the ancients made their characters speak in the style of political and popular eloquence, but now the rhetorical manner prevails.

Character is whatever manifests the disposition of the speaker. There are speeches, therefore, which are without manners or character, as not containing anything by which the propensities or aversions of the person who delivers them can be known.[4] Thought

---

[1] B., "Reversal" and "Recognition." These are perhaps better, but the old words have become part of the accepted language of criticism.

[2] The great Italian commentator and critic, Castelvetro, transposed this sentence back so as to come after "contexture of incidents."

[3] B., "in the case of oratory." This is certainly more in the usual sense of the Greek ἐπὶ τῶν λόγων: but the older rendering seems to suit the context rather better.

[4] The text is rather uncertain here.

comprehends whatever is said, whether proving anything affirm-
atively or negatively, or expressing some general reflection, etc.

Fourth in order is the Diction — that is, as I have already said,
the expression of the sentiments by words, the power and effect of
which is the same, whether in verse or prose.

Of the remaining parts the Music is the greatest embellishment.
The Decoration has also a great effect on the soul, but, of all the
parts, is most foreign to art and least germane to poetry; for the
power of tragedy is felt without representation and actors, and
the production of the decorations depends more on the art of the
mechanic than on that of the poet.

CHAPTERS VII–XIII. — THE PLOT: ITS NATURE AND CHARACTER

VII. 1–5

These things being thus defined, let us go on to examine in what
manner the Plot should be constructed, since this is the first and
most important part of tragedy.

Now, we have defined tragedy to be an imitation of an action that
is complete and entire, and that has also a certain magnitude; for a
thing may be entire and a whole, and yet not be of any magnitude.

(1) BY ENTIRE I MEAN THAT WHICH HAS A BEGINNING, A MIDDLE,
AND AN END. A beginning is that which does not necessarily suppose
anything before it, but which requires something to follow it. An
end, on the contrary, is that which supposes something to precede
it, either necessarily or probably, but which nothing is required to
follow. A middle is that which both supposes something to precede and requires something to follow. A properly constructed
plot, therefore, is not at liberty to begin or end anyhow, but
must conform to these definitions.

(2) Again: whatever is beautiful, whether it be an animal,[1] or
any other thing composed of different parts, must not only have

---

[1] There is a very important difference of opinion here whether the Greek
word ζῷον means as usual "an animal" (or rather, "living organism") or else
"the *picture* of such an organism." The discussion of this question lies outside
our scope. B. adopts the "picture" version.

those parts arranged in a certain manner, but must also be of a certain Magnitude; for beauty consists in magnitude and order. Hence it is that no very minute animal can be beautiful; for the survey of it is confused, being made in a nearly indistinguishable time. Neither, on the contrary, can one of a prodigious size be beautiful; because, as all its parts cannot be seen at once, the whole (the unity of object) is lost to the spectator: as it would be, for example, if he were surveying an animal ten thousand stadia long. As, therefore, in bodies, animal and other, a certain magnitude is requisite, but that magnitude must be such as to present a whole easily comprehended by the eye, so in the plot a certain length is requisite, but that length must be such as to present a whole easily comprehended by the memory.

The rest of the chapter is less important, dealing with the length or size of the fable or plot from special points of view.

VIII, WHOLE. THE UNITY OF ACTION

A plot is not One, as some conceive it to be, merely because the hero of it is one. For numberless events happen to one man, many of which are such as cannot be connected into one event; and so, likewise, there are many actions of one man which cannot be connected into any one action. Hence appears the mistake of all those poets who have composed "Herculeids," "Theseids," and other poems of that kind. They conclude that because Hercules was one, so also must be the plot of which he is the subject. But Homer, among his many other excellences, seems also to have been perfectly aware of this mistake, either from art or genius. For when he composed his *Odyssey*, he did not introduce all the events of his hero's life — such, for instance, as the wound he received upon Parnassus; his feigned madness when the Grecian army was assembling, etc. — events not connected, either by necessary or probable consequence, with each other: but he comprehended those only which have relation to one action: for such we call that of the *Odyssey*. And in the same manner he composed his *Iliad*.

As, therefore, in other mimetic arts, one imitation is an imitation of one thing, so here the plot, being an imitation of an action, should be an imitation of an action that is one and entire, the parts of it being so connected, that if any one of them be either transposed or taken away, the whole will be destroyed or changed. For whatever may be either retained or omitted, without making any sensible difference, is not part of a whole.

IX. 1–9

It appears, further, from what has been said, that it is not the Poet's province to relate such things as have actually happened, but such as might have happened — such as are possible, according either to probable or necessary consequence.

For it is not by writing in verse or prose that the Historian and the Poet are distinguished; the work of Herodotus might be versified, but it would still be a species of history, no less with metre than without. They are distinguished by this — that the one relates what has been, the other what might be. On this account POETRY IS A MORE PHILOSOPHICAL AND A MORE SERIOUS THING THAN HISTORY: FOR POETRY IS CHIEFLY CONVERSANT ABOUT GENERAL [1] TRUTH, HISTORY ABOUT PARTICULAR. In what manner, for example, any person of a certain character would speak or act, probably or necessarily — this is general; and this is the object of Poetry, even while it makes use of particular names. But what Alcibiades did, or what happened to him — this is particular truth.

With respect to Comedy, this is now become obvious; for here the poet, when he has formed his plot of probable incidents, gives to his characters whatever names he pleases, and is not, like the iambic poets, particular and personal.

Tragedy, indeed, retains the use of real names; and the reason is, that what we are disposed to believe we must think possible. Now, what has never actually happened we are not apt to regard as possible; but what has been is unquestionably so, or it could not have been at all. There are, however, some tragedies in which one

---

[1] B., "universal," which is far better in itself, and would be better altogether, if "general" had not been the general rendering and had not exercised a great — and positively disastrous — historical influence. It was on this that 18th century critics based their doctrine that poetry must be "general," understanding the word not as equivalent to "universal" but to "conventional."

or two of the names are historical, and the rest feigned. There are even some in which none of the names are historical — such is Agathon's *The Flower;* for in that all is invention, both incidents and names, and yet it pleases. It is by no means, therefore, essential that a poet should confine himself to the known and established subjects of tragedy.   Such a restraint would, indeed, be ridiculous, since even those subjects that are known are known comparatively but to few, and yet are interesting to all.

From all this it is manifest that a Poet should be a poet, or Maker, of plots rather than of verses, since it is imitation that constitutes the poet, and of this imitation actions are the object. Nor is he the less a poet though the incidents of his fable should chance to be such as have actually happened; for nothing hinders, but that some true events may possess that probability and possibility, the invention of which entitles him to the name of poet.

This chapter is completed by remarks on episodic plots (which are condemned), etc. X divides plots into " simple," *i.e.*, without revolution or discovery, and " complex," with one or both. XI defines and illustrates these things. XII is a probably spurious, and at any rate purely technical, list of the names given to the divisions of the tragedy. Then follow three chapters which are the very kernel or, if another metaphor be preferred, cream of the whole.

CHAPTER XIII. — THE TRAGIC 'AMAPTIA OR FRAILTY

The order of the subject leads us to consider, in the next place, what the poet should aim at, and what avoid, in the construction of his plot; and by what means the purpose of Tragedy may be best effected.

Now, since it is requisite to the perfection of a tragedy that its plot should be of the complicated, not of the simple kind, and that it should imitate such actions as excite terror and pity (this being the peculiar property of the tragic imitation), it follows evidently, in the first place, that the change from prosperity to adversity should not be represented as happening to a virtuous character; for this raises disgust rather than terror or compassion. Neither should the contrary change, from adversity to prosperity, be exhibited in a vicious character: this, of all plans, is the most opposite to the genius of tragedy, having no one property that it ought to have; for it is neither gratifying in a moral view, nor affecting, nor terrible. Nor, again, should the fall of a very bad man from prosperous to adverse fortune be represented: because, though such a subject may be pleasing from its moral tendency, it will produce neither pity nor terror. For our pity is excited by misfortunes undeservedly suffered, and our terror by some resemblance between the sufferer and ourselves. Neither of these effects will, therefore, be produced by such an event.

There remains, then, for our choice, the character between these extremes: THAT OF A PERSON NEITHER EMINENTLY VIRTUOUS OR JUST, NOR YET INVOLVED IN MISFORTUNE BY DELIBERATE VICE OR VILLAINY, BUT BY SOME ERROR OF HUMAN FRAILTY[1]; and this person should also be some one of high fame and flourishing prosperity. For example, Œdipus, Thyestes, or other illustrious men of such families.

Hence it appears that, to be well constructed, a plot, contrary to the opinion of some, should be single rather than double; that the change of fortune should not be from adverse to prosperous, but the reverse; and that it should be the consequence, not of vice, but of some great frailty, in a character such as has been described, or better rather than worse.

These principles are confirmed by experience, for poets, formerly, admitted almost any story into the number of tragic subjects; but now the subjects of the best tragedies are confined to a few families — to Alcmæon, Œdipus, Orestes, Meleager, Thyestes, Telephus, and others, the sufferers or the authors of some terrible calamity.

The most perfect tragedy, then, according to the principles of the art, is of this construction: whence appears the mistake of those

---

[1] δι' ἁμαρτίαν τινά. It is in this place especially important to refer to Professor Butcher's exhaustive examination of the word ἁμαρτία, op. cit. p. 311 sq. Generally speaking, it means in A's mouth (1) a fault through avoidable, but more or less excusable, ignorance; (2) one incurred through passion, etc., without deliberate evil purpose. The far-reaching character of this remark has been more and more recognized. There is greater difference of opinion whether, in what follows, A. does or does not lend unlucky countenance to the "neo-classic" idea that the tragic hero must be a person of "rank and fashion."

critics who censure Euripides for this practice in his tragedies, many of which terminate unhappily; for this, as we have shown, is right. And, as the strongest proof of it, we find that upon the stage and in the dramatic contests such tragedies, if they succeed,[1] have always the most tragic effect; and Euripides, though in other respects faulty in the conduct of his subjects, seems clearly to be the most tragic of the poets.

I place in the second rank that kind to which some assign the first: that which is of a double construction, like the *Odyssey*, and also ends in opposite ways, for the good and for the bad characters. That this passes for the best is owing to the weakness of the spectators, to whose wishes the poets accommodate their productions. This kind of pleasure, however, is not the proper pleasure of tragedy, but belongs rather to comedy, for there, if even the bitterest enemies, like Orestes and Ægisthus, are introduced, they quit the scene at last as friends, and nobody is killed.

CHAPTER XIV. — TERROR AND PITY — THE 'OIKEIA 'ΗΔΟΝΗ OR SPECIAL PLEASURE

Terror and pity may be raised by the Decoration; but they may also arise from the circumstances of the action itself, which is far preferable and shows a superior poet. For the plot should be so constructed, that, without the assistance of the sight, its incidents may excite horror and commiseration in those who hear them only; as would be the case with one hearing the story of the *Œdipus*. But to produce this effect by means of the decoration is less artistic and needs more "mounting." As to those poets who make use of the decoration in order to produce, not the terrible, but the monstrous only, their purpose has nothing in common with that of tragedy. FOR WE ARE NOT TO SEEK FOR EVERY SORT OF PLEASURE FROM TRAGEDY, BUT FOR THAT ONLY WHICH IS PROPER TO THE SPECIES.[2]

Since, therefore, it is the business of the tragic poet to give that pleasure which arises from pity and terror, through imitation, it is

---

[1] So T.; B., better, "if they are well represented."

[2] The second great utterance of the context.

evident that he ought to produce that effect by the circumstances of the action itself.[1] Let us then see of what kind those incidents are which appear terrible or piteous.

Now, such actions must, of necessity, happen between persons who are either friends or enemies, or indifferent to each other. If an enemy kills, or purposes to kill, an enemy, in neither case is any commiseration raised in us except for the actual suffering. The case is the same when the persons are neither friends nor enemies. But when such disasters happen between friends — when, for instance, the brother kills or is going to kill his brother, the son his father, the mother her son, or the reverse — these, and others of a similar kind, are the proper incidents for the poet's choice. The received tragic subjects, therefore, he is not at liberty essentially to alter; as of Clytæmnestra dying by the hand of Orestes, and Eriphyle by that of Alcmæon; but it is his province to invent other subjects, and to make a skilful use of those which he finds already established. What I mean by a skilful use I proceed to explain.

The tragic action may be perpetrated knowingly and intentionally, as was usual with the earlier poets, and as Euripides, also, has represented Medea destroying her children. It may, likewise, be perpetrated by those who are ignorant, at the time, of the connection between them and the injured person, which they afterwards discover; as by Œdipus, in Sophocles. There, indeed, the action itself is outside the drama: the *Alcmæon* of Astydamas, and Telegonus in the *Ulysses Wounded*, furnish instances within the tragedy. There is yet a third way, where a person upon the point of perpetrating, through ignorance, some dreadful deed, is prevented by a sudden discovery.

Beside these there is no other way. For the action must of necessity be either done or not done, and that either with knowledge or without. But of all these ways, that of being ready to execute, knowingly, and yet not executing, is the worst; for this is, at the same time, shocking and yet not tragic, because it exhibits no disastrous event. It is, therefore, never, or very rarely, made

---

[1] B., "that this quality must be impressed upon the incidents." So better, I think, for ἐμποιητέον.

use of. The threat of Hæmon to kill Creon in the *Antigone* is an example.

Next to this is the actual execution of the purpose. To execute, through ignorance, and afterwards to discover, is better : for thus there is nothing shocking, while the discovery is striking.

But the best of all these ways is the last. Thus, in the tragedy of *Cresphontes*, Merope is about to slay her son, but discovers him and does not. In the *Iphigenia* the sister in the same manner discovers her brother; and in the *Helle* the son discovers his mother at the instant when he was going to give her up. On this account it is that the subjects of tragedy, as before remarked, are confined to a small number of families. For it was not to art, but to fortune, that poets applied themselves to find incidents of this nature. Hence the necessity of having recourse to those families in which such calamities have happened.

Of the arrangement of the incidents, and of the kind of which the story should be, enough has now been said.

CHAPTER XV. — CHARACTER

With respect to Character four things are to be aimed at by the poet. First and principally, it must be good. Now, character belongs, as we have said before, to any speech or action that manifests a certain disposition; and it is good as this is good. This holds in each kind; a woman or a slave may be good, though, in general, women are perhaps inferior, and slaves altogether bad. The second requisite of Character is propriety. There is a manly character of bravery and fierceness which cannot, with propriety, be given to a woman. The third requisite is verisimilitude[1]; for this is a different thing from their being good and proper, as above described. The fourth is consistency; for even though the model of the poet's imitation be some person of inconsistent character, still that person must be represented as consistently inconsistent.

[1] T., "resemblance" ; B., "truth to life." I am not quite satisfied with either of these terms, or with my own, for ὅμοιον, which (see commentary in B. at passages noted in his index) usually means in the *Poetics* "the quality of a man *like ourselves*," "*average* humanity."

We have an example of character unnecessarily bad in the character of Menelaus in the tragedy of *Orestes ;* of improper and
unbecoming manners in the lamentation of Ulysses in *Scylla,*
and in the speech of Melanippe; of inconsistency in the *Iphigenia
at Aulis ;* for there the Iphigenia who supplicates for life has no
resemblance to the later one.

In the character, as in the plot, the poet should always aim,
either at what is necessary, or at what is probable; so that such a
character shall appear to speak or act, necessarily or probably, in
such a manner, and this event to be the necessary or probable consequence of that.   Hence it is evident that the *dénouement* also of a
plot should arise out of the plot itself, and not depend upon
Machinery,[1] as in the *Medea,* or in the incidents relative to the
return of the Greeks, in the *Iliad.*   The proper application of
Machinery[1] is to such circumstances as are extraneous to the
drama; such as either happened before the time of the action, and
could not, by human means, be known; or are to happen after, and
require to be foretold; for to the Gods we attribute the knowledge
of all things.   But nothing improbable[2] should be admitted in the
incidents of the plot; or, if it cannot be avoided, it should, at least,
be confined to such as are without the tragedy itself; as in the
Œdipus of Sophocles.

And since Tragedy is an imitation of our betters, we should
follow the example of skilful portrait painters; who, while they
express the peculiar lineaments, and produce a likeness, at the
same time improve upon the original.   And thus, too, the poet,
when he imitates passionate men (or indolent, or others of a similar
kind), should draw them as they are, but reasonably attractive[3] : as
Achilles is drawn by Agathon and by Homer.   These things the
poet should keep in view; and, besides these, whatever relates

[1] B., more completely for modern readers, "the *Deus ex Machina.*"

[2] B., "irrational," more literally.

[3] B., "should preserve the type and yet ennoble it."   I have tried to keep
still closer to ἐπιεικεῖς, but have followed him, as he has followed Mr. Bywater,
in omitting two words, παράδειγμα σκληρότητος — "an example of hardness" —
which make no sense unless something is added.   T., retaining (and doing some
violence to) them, has "draw an example approaching rather to a good than to
a hard and ferocious character."

to those senses which have a necessary connection with poetry; for here, also, he may often err. But of this enough has been said in the treatises already published.

CHAPTERS XVI–XXII. — DETAILS AND MISCELLANEA ON TRAGEDY

XVI illustrates " discovery " from different Greek tragedies in a manner not very relevant for *general* critical purposes, and is perhaps spurious.

XVII. 1–2. CAUTIONS AS TO STAGE PROBABILITY

The Poet, both when he plans and when he writes his Tragedy, should put himself as much as possible in the place of a spectator; for by this means, seeing everything distinctly, as if present at the action, he will discern what is proper, and no inconsistencies will escape him. The fault objected to Carcinus is a proof of this. Amphiaraus had left the temple. This the poet, for want of conceiving the action to pass before his eyes, overlooked; but in the representation the audience were disgusted and the piece condemned.

In composing, the poet should even, as much as possible, be an actor[1]; for, by natural sympathy, they are most persuasive and affecting who are under the influence of actual passion. We share the agitation of those who appear to be truly agitated; the anger of those who appear to be truly angry. Hence it is that poetry demands either great natural quickness of parts or an enthusiasm allied to madness.[2] By the first of these we mould ourselves with facility to the imitation of every form; by the other, transported out of ourselves, we become what we imagine.[3]

[1] B., "should work out his play, to the best of his power, with appropriate gestures."

[2] Lit., "Poetry is either of a genius or a madman, for of these the first are plastic and the others out of themselves." This, which follows Plato, is itself the origin of the doctrine of *furor poeticus*, which the pseudo-Aristotelian critics of the 16th–18th centuries took such pains to combine with that of Sense, Nature, and Reason.

[3] The extraordinary *capacity* of expression in Greek is perhaps shown in these two sentences better than almost anywhere. The whole from " Hence " to " imagine " occupies in the Greek sixteen words only, the gist lying in five. There are forty-six in T. and thirty-eight in B.

The rest of the chapter is practical on the arrangement of plot and episode.

XVIII explains the terms δέσις and λύσις, the intertwining and *dénouement* of the plot:

Every Tragedy consists of two parts — the Complication and the *Dénouement*.[1] The Complication is often formed by incidents supposed prior to the action, and by a part also of those that are within the action; the rest form the *Dénouement*. I call Complication all that is between the beginning of the piece and the last part, where the change of fortune commences; *Dénouement* all between the beginning of that change and the conclusion.

This is followed by rather desultory observations on the conduct of these operations by different poets, but the following is important:

The Chorus should be considered as one of the persons in the drama; should be a part of the whole and a sharer in the action, not as in Euripides, but as in Sophocles. As for other poets, their choral songs have no more connection with their subject than with that of any other tragedy; and hence they are now become detached pieces, inserted at pleasure; a practice first introduced by Agathon. Yet where is the difference between this arbitrary insertion of an ode and the transposition of a speech, or even of a whole episode,[2] from one tragedy to another?

XIX approaches, and XX and XXI discuss, the subject of *Diction:* but the first is vague, and the other two consist of trivial and probably spurious grammatical observations. XXII reads in a more likely fashion, but does little more than repeat the doctrine of the *Rhetoric, v. inf.*, on κυρία and ξένα, with remarks (again similar) on the value, and the danger, of metaphor. It is important that Aristotle, in the teeth of Wordsworth's future theory, holds that prosaic and familiar language is mainly appropriate to "iambic," *i.e.*, satiric, verse.

---

[1] T., "Development"; B., "unravelling," but with *dénouement* as an alternative. This word is now practically naturalized; but "complication" is a little awkward. It might not be ill boldly to install "knotting" (Chaucer uses "knot" for "plot") and "unknotting" as the English equivalents for Greek *desis* and *lusis*.

[2] B., probably better, "act." The double sense of the word is sometimes rather troublesome.

CHAPTER XXIII AND PART OF XXIV.— THE EPIC

With respect to that species of Poetry which imitates by Narration and in verse,[1] it is obvious that the plot ought to be dramatically constructed, like that of tragedy, and that it should have for its subject one entire and perfect action, having a beginning, a middle, and an end. So that, forming like an animal[2] a complete whole, it may afford its proper pleasure, and will not in its construction be like history, which necessarily treats not of one action, but of one time, and of all the events that happened to one person, or to many, during that time — events, the relation of which to each other is merely casual. For, as the naval action at Salamis and the battle with the Carthaginians in Sicily were events of the same time, unconnected by any relation to a common end or purpose, so also, in successive events, we sometimes see one thing follow another without being connected to it by such relation. And this is the practice of the generality of poets. Even in this, therefore, as we have before observed, the superiority of Homer's genius is apparent — that he did not attempt to bring the whole war, though an entire action with beginning and end, into his poem. It would have been too vast an object, and not easily comprehended in one view ; or had he forced it into a moderate compass, it would have been perplexed by its variety. Instead of this, selecting one part only of the war, he has from the rest introduced many episodes — such as the catalogue of the ships, and others — by which he has diversified his poem. Other poets take for their subject the actions of one person, or of one period of time ; or an action which, though one, is composed of many parts. Thus the author of the *Cypriacs* and of the *Little Iliad*. Hence it is that the *Iliad* and the *Odyssey* each of them furnish matter for one tragedy, or two at most; but from the *Cypriacs* many may be taken, and from the *Little Iliad* eight or more, as the Contest for the Armour, Philoctetes, Neoptolemus, Eurypylus, the Begging of Ulysses, the Spartan Women, the Fall of Troy, the Sailing of the Fleet, Sinon, and the Trojan Women.[3]

---

[1] So the MS., ἐν μέτρῳ. B., very ingeniously, ἑνὶ μέτρῳ, " in a single metre." It has been usual to read ἐν ἑξαμέτρῳ " in hexameter verse," and so T.

[2] See note *supra*, p. 8.   [3] Some omit these two last.

Again, the Epic Poem must also agree with the tragic as to its kinds — it must be simple or complicated, ethic or pathetic. Its parts also, setting aside music and decoration, are the same, for it requires revolutions, discoveries, and disasters, and it must be furnished with proper sentiments and diction, of all which Homer gave both the first and the most perfect example. Thus, of his two poems, the *Iliad* is of the simple and pathetic kind, the *Odyssey* complicated (for it abounds throughout with discoveries) and ethic. Add to this, that in diction and thought he has surpassed all poets.

The rest of XXIV deals with the points in which Epic *differs from* Tragedy. Its scale is much larger, but need not be so large as that of the "ancients" [ἀρχαίων]. This larger scale admits of episodes and avoids the monotony which besets tragedy. [This is an important confession.] "Heroic" metre has been justified by experience. Nobody has succeeded with any other. The epic poet should very seldom appear *in propria persona*. He has the advantage over the Tragedian in being able to introduce not merely the Wonderful but the Irrational — because his actors are not seen. But both " SHOULD PREFER PLAUSIBLE IMPOSSIBILITIES TO IMPROBABLE POSSIBILITIES." This is one of the greatest critical dicta of the whole book. And " POETIC CHARM CAN MAKE ABSURDITY IMPERCEPTIBLE."

CHAPTERS XXIV TO END.—ADDENDA ON POETIC CRITICISM

The treatise, as we have it, ends with a consideration of critical objections to poetry, and a critical comparison of Tragedy and Epic. The first is rather disappointing. A. gives five possible lines of criticism — tending to fix on the work criticised Impossibility, Irrationality, Moral Hurtfulness, Self-contradiction, and Artistic Error: and supplies twelve categories of reply. But he busies himself almost wholly with material objections — to the description of spears set point upwards (said to be an actual Illyrian custom), or else verbal criticisms (change accent, breathing, or punctuation, etc.). In fact, the passage is rather desultory and rather peddling. The comparison of Epic and Tragedy rises higher. After defending the latter from the charge of appealing to a vulgar taste — that for gesture — and expressly vindicating its charm as merely *read*, A. goes on (XXVI. 4) :

And Tragedy *is* superior because it possesses all that Epic possesses ; it might even adopt the metre : and to this it makes no inconsiderable addition in the music and the decoration; by which the pleasure is rendered most distinct. It has also this distinctness as well in reading as in representation. Moreover, it attains the end of its imitation in a shorter compass; for the concentrated effect is more pleasurable than when weakened by diffusion through a long extent of time, as the *Œdipus* of Sophocles, for example, would be if it were drawn out to the length of the *Iliad.*

Further, there is less unity in epic imitation, as appears from this — that any epic poem will furnish matter for several tragedies. For, supposing the poet to choose a fable strictly one, either his poem, if proportionably contracted, will appear curtailed, or, if extended to the usual length, it will become washy. . . .[1] The *Iliad*, for example, and the *Odyssey* contain many such subordinate parts, each of which has a certain magnitude and unity of its own; yet is the construction of those poems as perfect, and as nearly approaching to the imitation of a single action, as possible.

If, then, Tragedy be superior to the Epic in all these respects, and also in its work as an art (for each art ought to afford, not any sort of pleasure, but only that laid down for it), it evidently follows that Tragedy, as it attains more effectually the end of the art itself, must deserve the preference.

---

[1] After this there is an apparent gap in the sense which it does not seem possible to supply shortly. T. has, " If, on the other hand, we suppose him to employ several fables — that is, a fable composed of several actions — his imitation is no longer strictly One." B., more wisely, accepts the gap. Perhaps, after all, it is more apparent than real. The [epic] action of the *Iliad* and *Odyssey* is *not* washy *being epic:* it *would be* washy in *tragic* form.

II

ARISTOTLE

2. THE RHETORIC

(The first two books of the *Rhetoric* have little or nothing to do with Criticism, being wholly occupied with the subject as the "Art of Persuasion," and with the methods of effecting that persuasion most valuable to the orator in court or public assembly — especially the dispositions of the hearers, and the probable circumstances of cases or causes. The Third Book, however, deals with the Style (or Diction) and with the Arrangement of a speech; and so, incidentally, with these matters in regard to all literary composition in prose. This Book therefore becomes of almost the highest critical importance.[1])

BOOK III. CHAPTER I. — STYLE (AND DELIVERY?)

As there are three points which ought to be handled respecting a speech; one, as to the sources out of which will arise means of persuasion; a second, respecting the *style*; a third, how we ought to *arrange* the *parts* of a speech, — on the subject of the means of persuasion we have already spoken. . . . It follows that we treat of the subject of Style : for the mere being in possession of what one ought to say is not enough; but it is moreover necessary that we deliver it as we ought; and this contributes much to give the speech *quality*.[2]

[1] The following translation is based upon the old "Oxford" version with very considerable alterations by the present editor. The Greek text used is generally Cope's, and a few variants of version will be given from him and from Bp. Welldon, *op. cit.* These scholars will be referred to as C. and W.

[2] Lit., "to make it appear of a certain kind." C., "character"; W., "a certain colour."

Now that which by its nature is first, was, conformably to nature, investigated the first; *viz.*, whence these things derive their persuasive efficacy : next to this was the disposition of them in the speaking : and thirdly [arose an enquiry] of the greatest consequence, but which never yet has been handled, on the subject of Delivery. For this was introduced into tragedy and the public recitations at a late period, since at first the poets used themselves to sustain the dialogue in their tragedies. It is therefore plain that some such power exists in relation to Rhetoric, as well as to Poetry; of which [as connected with the latter art] Glauco the Teian, and some others, have treated. And it depends on the voice, as to how we ought to manage it in reference to each several passion : when, for instance, we should employ a loud, when a low, and when a moderate pitch of voice; and on the manner in which we should employ its tones, *viz.*, the acute, the grave, and the intermediate; and on certain rhythms in reference to each. For the points, in reference to which men conduct these enquiries, are three, *viz.*, the loudness of the voice, the fitness of its tones, and its rhythm. Now these proficients bear away nearly all the prizes in the disputations; and as in the other contests the actors now produce a greater effect than the poets, so likewise do they in civil causes, owing to the depravity of states. There is not yet however any "Art" compiled respecting these points, since even the subject of Style was brought forward at a late period, and, if rightly conceived of, it [1] appears a vulgar sort of thing. But as the whole subject of rhetoric has reference to opinion, we should pay attention to it, as to a matter not of moral obligation, but of practical necessity. For mere justice seeks no further in speeches than neither to vex nor to charm; since the rule of right is, that the contest be carried on by means of the facts themselves. So that, except the proof, all the rest is superfluous;

---

[1] Some would limit these slighting remarks to "elocution" in its limited modern sense, *i.e.*, mere *delivery*. So W. who translates — italicizing, however, to show that the word is not in the text — "and *declamation* is thus popularly considered, and indeed is rightly supposed, to be something vulgar." The original — text and context — makes this possible rather than (to me) probable ; but it is certain from the whole chapter that Aristotle had not thoroughly cleared up his mind on the difference between the two senses of "elocution."

but it is notwithstanding, as has been stated, a point of great moment, in consequence of the weak judgment of the auditor. The subject of style, however, has some necessary though trifling claim on our attention in all kinds of teaching; for the expressing one's self in this or that way does make a difference with a view to exhibiting the subject clearly, though not to so great a degree [as is generally supposed].[1] All these points are however mere idea, and have a reference to the auditor; wherefore it is that no one teaches geometry in such a style.

This art then, be it introduced when it may, will produce the same effect as that of acting. And some, to a small extent, have already made an effort to treat of it; Thrasymachus, for instance, on *the excitement of compassion*. Again, the being qualified for delivery is a gift of nature, and rather outside the province of art; the subject of style, however, is clearly reducible to an art. Wherefore rewards are bestowed in turn on those who are proficients in this, just as they are on those rhetoricians [who claim] on the ground of delivery; for written orations influence more by means of their style than through their thought.[2]

Now the poets, as was natural, began to make a stir upon the subject at first; for words are imitations, and the voice, of all our parts, is the most imitative; on which account also these arts were constructed, both that of recitation, and that of acting, and others too. But as the poets, though what they said was very frivolous, appeared to acquire their reputation by means of their style, on this account the first style [of rhetoric] was formed on that of poetry — witness the style of Gorgias; and even at the present time the majority of ignorant people fancy that such orators speak most finely. This, however, is not the case, but the style of poetry and that of prose are distinct, and the result shows it; for not even the writers of tragedy themselves any longer employ the same turn of diction. But just as they have passed from trochaic to iambic metre,

[1] Observe that, even if the former passage of slight be limited to *delivery*, this certainly is not; though A. veers back thereto presently.

[2] Here, as in the *Poetics*, the older translators rendered διάνοια "sentiment"; and here, as there, it is not easy to get a single English equivalent. C., "thought or intellectual part"; W., "thought" simply.

because the latter is most like prose of all the other metres, so have they also relinquished all those terms which are foreign to the style of conversation, although the early writers used to embellish [their works] with these, and even at the present day they are employed by those who write in heroic metre. Wherefore it is ridiculous to imitate the tragedians, who in their own case no longer employ that turn of diction.

So that it is evident that we need not discuss with minuteness all points soever which it is possible to treat of under the head of style, but so many only as belong to such an art as we are speaking of: the other part of the subject has been spoken of in my treatise on Poetry.

CHAPTER II.—DICTION, STAPLE AND UNFAMILIAR (METAPHOR)

Let this then have been discussed: and let excellence of style be defined to consist in its being clear (a sign of which is this, that the diction, unless it make the sentiment clear, will not effect its purpose), and neither low, nor above the dignity of the subject, but suitable; for the style of poetry indeed is not low, yet it is not becoming in prose.

Of nouns and verbs those which are in general use [1] produce the effect of clearness; to prevent its being low, and to give it ornament, there are other words which have been mentioned in the *Poetics*. A departure [from ordinary acceptations] causes language to appear more dignified; for men are affected in respect of style in the very same way as they are towards foreigners and citizens. On which account you should give your phrase a *foreign* air; for men are admirers of things out of the way, and what is an object of admiration is pleasant. Now in verse, there are many things which produce this effect, and *there* are suitable, because both the subject and the person stand more apart [from ordinary life]. In prose, however, we must use fewer, for the subject is less exalted: since

---

[1] κύρια. C., "proper," which, however, too much suggests the sense of the French *mot propre.* ὀνόματα κύρια are "standard," "staple," "authorized" words, neither vulgar nor "out-of-the-way." W., "proper *or usual.*"

even in that art were a slave, or a youth, or one speaking of mere trifles to "talk fine," it would be rather unbecoming; but here too [as in poetry] the rule of good taste is, that your style be lowered or raised according to the subject. On which account we must escape observation in doing this, and appear not to speak in a studied manner, but naturally. For a natural style tends to persuade, the other does the very reverse; because people put themselves on their guard, as though against one who has a design upon them, just as they do against loaded wine. . . .[1]

As however nouns and verbs are [the materials] of which the speech is made up, and as nouns admit so many species as have been examined in the Poetics, out of the number of these we must employ but sparingly, and in very few places, exotic and compound words, and those newly coined. Where they may be employed I will state hereafter: the reason of the restriction has been mentioned, *viz.*, because they remove your style from that of common life more than is consistent with good taste. Words however of *ordinary* use,[2] and in their *original acceptations,* and *metaphors,* are alone available in the style of prose: a proof [that this is the fact, is] that these are the only words which *all* persons employ; for everybody carries on conversation by means of *metaphors,* and words in their *primary sense,* and those of *ordinary use.* Therefore it is clear that points of good style are striking [" foreign "] effect, and the concealment of art, and clearness.

The latter part of the chapter deals with *Metaphors* and (with a cross reference to the *Poetics*) insists on their being (1) analogically appropriate, (2) adjusted in point of subject to the purpose of exalting or degrading as the case may be, (3) euphonious, (4) not too far-fetched, (5) derived from beautiful objects.

---

[1] Illustrations, not entirely clear, and therefore omitted, follow as to the acting of Theodorus and the style of Euripides.

[2] κύρια as before.

CHAPTER III. — FRIGIDITY

Frigidity,[1] as dependent on the style, consists in four points. In the use of compound words ; like Lycophron, where he says, " the many-visaged heaven," and " the mighty-topped earth," and " the narrow-gladed [2] shore." And as Gorgias used the expression, " a beggarly-mused flatterer," and " the forsworn and downright-truly-sworn." [3] Or like Alcidamas, [who talks of] " the soul replete with anger, and the visage waxing fire-coloured." Again, " he supposed their zeal would be completion-working " ; and " he settled a completion-working persuasiveness of speech "; and " the azure-hued level of the main." For all these expressions, by reason of their being compounded, appear poetical.

This, then, is one cause : also the employment of strange terms [4] is one ; as when Lycophron calls Xerxes, " prodigious hero," and Sciron, " baneful man," or Alcidamas, when he says " gambollings [5] in poetry," and " nature's surquedry," [6] and " whetted by unrestrained rage of soul."

A third description of Frigidity consists in the employment of epithets either too long, or out of place, or too frequent; for in poetry,

[1] This word, though the only possible equivalent for the Greek ψυχρότης, is not satisfactory. The quality referred to is described in English by different adjectives and substantives for its different subvarieties : — " tinsel," " fustian," " poor," " claptrap." Generally speaking, it may be said to be that which intends to produce excitement, enthusiasm, sense of the sublime or striking, *and fails*. The ancients were more afraid of this, and disliked it more, than any other fault ; and the remarks, both of Aristotle at one end and of Longinus at the other, may seem, even to rather severe modern critics, excessive in their severity. C. and W. translate ψυχρά " faults of taste," which seems to me rather too wide.

[2] Spenser (*F. Q.*, III. 4. xxi. 5) uses " glade " of the coast passage between sea and cliff ; and I have thought it allowable here for στενοπόρον.

[3] Greek κατευορκήσαντας : the double compound seems to be objected to. W., " forsworn and forever-sworn."

[4] γλώτταις : these are the *verba insolentia* of divers Latin cautions — the ῥήματα ἔκφυλα of Lucian.

[5] ἄθυρμα : apparently an obsolete or purely poetical word for " amusement." C. suggests " toy " or " gaud " ; W., " baubles."

[6] ἀτασθαλία : the favourite Homeric word for " insolent crime." C., *outrecuidance;* W., " retchlessness."

indeed, it is becoming enough to say "white milk"; in prose, however, it is rather bad taste. Also, should there be a superabundance, it is telltale and makes it evident that the whole is a mere made-up thing [1]; this, however, you may occasionally avail yourself of, since it produces a departure from the ordinary style, and renders the diction foreign. Yet ought we to aim at the mean; for a too free indulgence in the licence does more harm than speaking carelessly; for the one is not good, the other is bad. Hence it is that the writings of Alcidamas appear frigid; for he employs epithets not as the seasoning, but as the food, with such profusion does he scatter them, and those both too long, and where the meaning is self-evident.

A long list of criminal examples from Alcidamas follows; but as almost every one would, *ut supra*, require the citation of the original Greek and a note, they are omitted. The most striking instances of A's prudery are the objections, under the fourth head of improper metaphor, to this same Alcidamas for calling philosophy " a rampart of the laws " (or, as some say, " an outpost against the laws ") and the *Odyssey* " a fair mirror of human life."

CHAPTERS IV–V.— SIMILES, "PURITY"

In Chap. IV, A. states the obvious differences and resemblances between Simile and Metaphor. In V, handling the important subject of " Purity," he is at first a little rudimentary and grammatical, but ends with four important cautions, that style must be (1) easy to read and understand, (2) not of ambiguous punctuation, (3) not mixed in expression, (4) not too much parenthesized.

CHAPTERS VI–IX.— ELEVATION, PROPRIETY, RHYTHM.
LOOSE AND PERIODIC STYLE

The following expedients contribute to Elevation [2] of the style, *viz.*, — the employing the definition instead of the noun; saying

---

[1] Perhaps " that it *is* poetry." W., "show it to be *simple* poetry."

[2] This, like Frigidity, is not quite satisfactory for the Greek. ὄγκος means " bulk accompanied by weight." Perhaps " importance," as used in artistic slang, comes nearest. C. translates " dignity or amplification "; W., "dignity" only.

for instance, not " a circle," but " a plane superficies, whose circumference is at all points equidistant from the centre." The reverse, however, *viz.*, the use of the noun instead of the definition, contributes to abruptness.

Again, if the matter be indelicate or unbecoming ; using the noun, if the indelicacy be in the definition ; or the definition, if it be in the noun.

Also, the illustration of the subject by metaphor and epithets, guarding, however, against what savours of poetry. And the putting what is but single as many, a thing which the poets do. . . .[1]

The practice of Antimachus, too, is of service, *viz.*, speaking of what is not in the subject,[2] . . . as he does in celebrating the hill Teumessus.

Propriety, or the Becoming, comes next.

Style will possess the Becoming, if it be expressive at once of feeling and character, and in proportion to the subject-matter.[3]

Chap. VIII, on *Rhythm*, is of extreme and permanent importance for the *fact* of the stress laid on that ornament. But the details would be hardly intelligible to any but Greek scholars. The main precept is that prose style " must neither possess *metre* nor be destitute of *rhythm*." Chap. IX deals at some length with the distinction between "loose" and "periodic" style, familiar in all modern composition-books.

[1] An illustration is here omitted, and some prescriptions for doubling the article, etc., which apply to Greek only.

[2] Unfortunately A. gives only the first line, which is a reference, but not an illustration. Antimachus was often ranked next to Homer. The proceeding referred to is common in all poetries; and the editor of C., Dr. Sandys, has well illustrated it by the famous descriptions of Paradise in the *Odyssey*, Lucretius, Lactantius, and the Anglo-Saxon *Phœnix*.

[3] This important definition is illustrated and commented in the original after a fashion prejudicially but inevitably affected by the *oratorical* purpose — the consideration how the *audience* will be affected. Elaborate and unusual words are only to be used when the speaker or writer is excited, or intends to arouse excitement.

CHAPTERS IX–XII. — FIGURES

This subject, so fertile after a fashion in later hands, is dealt with rather incidentally by A. He has, as we have seen, already referred to *Metaphor* and *Simile;* and his examples of Frigidity, Elevation, etc., would certainly have been "figured out" by the later rhetoricians. He now devotes some space to the subject, though hardly as a separate heading, beginning in the middle of Chap. IX (the earlier part of which deals generally with Ornament and once more with Metaphor) with *Antithesis,* mainly as a special ornament of Periodic style. From this he goes to *Parisosis,* "Balance," and to *Paromœosis,* in which he includes both Alliteration and Homœoteleuton, as well as repetition or play on the word. In X he partly returns and partly continues, dealing yet again with *Metaphor, Simile,* and *Antithesis,* while adding in *Personification* and *Hyperbole, Paronomasia,* etc. The most important observations in these two chapters are given below. Chap. XII is a valuable caution against confusing style proper to speech with style proper to writing, and styles proper to different kinds of speech with one another.

X. 1. To make witty [sparkling, elegant] and brilliant [striking, effective] sayings is the lot of the man of genius or of the thoroughly trained man; to expound them is the business of this treatise.[1]

X. 6. [To secure vividness of style] three things are to be aimed at, metaphor, antithesis, and actuality.[2]

XI. 1–3. Thus, then, "sparkle" results, as has been said, from analogous metaphor, and from the production of a visual image setting the thing actually before the eyes; but we must now explain what "before the eyes" means, and how men must do to bring it about. I mean that whatsoever carries the sense of actuality brings things before our eyes. . . . As Homer also constantly

---

[1] This dictum is again an example of A's pregnancy. C. takes seven English adjectives to express ἀστεῖα καὶ εὐδοκιμοῦντα, and the word which I have rendered "expound" (lit., "show") appears to have the force of "analyze and exhibit in their sources." W's "clever and popular sayings" is probably the closest possible version of the Greek.

[2] I venture to prefer this for ἐνέργεια, both to the old rendering "personification" and to C. and W's "vividness of representation." What A. means by it is expanded below.

makes the inanimate alive by metaphors and is in all cases[1] famous
for producing actuality, as here :

> Again to the plain rolled the shameless stone,

and "the arrow *flew*," and "*burning* to fly thither," and [of spears]
"they stood in the ground longing to gorge with flesh," and "the
point rushed exulting through his breast." For in all these cases
the things seem *actual* from being made *living*.

XII. 1. It must not escape us that a different Style is appropriate to each different Kind. A man must not write as he speaks
in debate, nor a politician as does a barrister. A man should
know both; for one implies the art of speaking correct Greek, and
the other that of leaving nothing compulsorily unexpressed which
one wishes to communicate to others, as happens to those who
do not know how to write. The style of literature is the most
exact, that of debate the most declamatory ; and of this [the debating
style] there are two kinds, the ethical and the pathetic [the appeal
to character and the appeal to passion].

In the observations which follow it is pointed out that the "epideictic"
style of Oratory, *i.e.*, that of speeches composed to be delivered as "lec-
tures," not to the Public Assembly or in the Law Courts, is nearest to
that of Literature.

CHAPTERS XIII–XIX. — ARRANGEMENT

The last division of the book, that on *Taxis* or arrangement, has
necessarily less to do with general Criticism than the two earlier parts.
Most of it purely concerns the advocate.

[1] This translation of ἐν πᾶσι is Professor Butcher's, who agreed with C. ("in
all of them") and W. ("always") in taking πᾶσι as neuter and referring to the
examples, when I consulted him on the possibility of rendering ἐν πᾶσι . . .
εὐδοκιμεῖ "is universally renowned." Against these legions one fights not.

III

FRAGMENT OF SIMYLUS ON THE CONDITIONS OF LITERARY ACHIEVEMENT

(Simylus was a poet of the Middle Comedy who flourished about 355 B.C. The fragment which follows only exists in the *Florilegium* of Stobæus, nearly a thousand years later. Some have chosen to see in it a mere description of the difficulties of an Athenian dramatist in getting his pieces put on the stage. But clearly this would go only to the intention of the writer; and it is not the intention of the writer, but the significance of the writing, which is of importance to posterity. In any case it is probably a very early, and certainly a very remarkable, " conclusion of the whole matter " as to Literature.)

Neither nature without art, nor again art unassociated with nature, is sufficient to any one for any accomplishment. And when these two are brought together in one, it is still needful to add appliances and means [lit., the *choragia* or official provision of chorus, etc.], love of the task, practice, a suitable occasion, time, and a judge [or critic] able to grasp what is said. For by whichsoever of these a man is deserted, he comes not to the end of his purpose. Nature, will, pains, method — make poets good and wise: number of years brings them nothing but old age.

IV

DIONYSIUS OF HALICARNASSUS (50–7 B.C.)

CRITICAL EXCERPTS AND AXIOMS

I. THE STUDY OF STYLE

For since study of literature [1] generally is so to say twofold — of the thoughts and of the words, whereof the one part has to do most with the matter, the other with the form, of speech [2] — and, since all who try to speak *or write* well pay equal attention to both these branches of investigation, the division of knowledge which leads to facts and the wise management of them is slow and hard *to master* for the young, and rather an altogether crushing burden to beardless boys. For it is the business of a mature intelligence — nay, the knowledge of it is more suitable to an age already disciplined by grey hairs, — growing by much study of books and things, by much experience and bringing together of things suffered by ourselves and others. But the study of the glories and beauties of style is wont to flourish along with youthful years. For all young minds are in a flutter over bellettristic elegance, conceiving an unreasoning, and as it were inspired, impulse towards it. But they have need of much and careful teaching and guidance if they are not to pour out any unsuitable words that come upon their tongues, nor to heap phrases together higgledy-piggledy, but to use a

---

[1] Here and elsewhere — it may be well to repeat — the meanings of " speech " and " literature " were probably both, at least in some degree, present even to the writer's mind. They are certainly both important for *us*.

[2] The opposition of πρακτικὸς and λεκτικὸς is common enough, and usually easy to translate. Here, however, without stretching the latter a little, it is hard to avoid apparently tautologous repetition (for there is repetition which is not tautologous).

selection of pure and genuine words, and arrange them in composition providing a mixture of dignity and sweetness.

He will himself attempt to supply the want of a treatise on such Composition and follow it by one on *The Choice of Words.*

De Comp. Verb. i.

II.   THE SOURCES OF BEAUTY

And what is the head and front of my argument ? That with the
conjunction of letters comes the varied composition of syllables,
and with the composition of syllables the omniform nature of words,
and with the harmonious arrangement of words comes Literature in
its many kinds.   So that it is necessary that the phrase be beautiful in which there are beautiful words, and that of beautiful words
beautiful syllables and letters be the causes, and a charming style
must result from what charms the ear.   And just so the particular
differences of words and syllables and letters, by which the character
and the passions and the dispositions and the deeds of persons,
and all thereto appertaining, are set forth, must acquire their
properties from the first foundation of the letters.

Ibid. xvi (p. 96, ed. Reiske).

III.   THE IMPORTANCE OF RHYTHM IN PROSE

My reasons for making these remarks [*on the character of certain
feet*] are as follows:—for I have not undertaken to discuss the
subject of rhythm and metre idly, but of necessity.   Through
rhythms that have nobility, and dignity, and greatness, composition
itself becomes dignified, and firm, and magnificent; but by mean
and paltry ones it loses greatness and dignity, whether the rhythms
be taken by themselves, or arranged conjointly and symphonically.
Therefore, if we can succeed in composing our style of all the best
rhythms, we shall have all we can pray for ; but if we are forced
to mix the worse with the better (as generally happens — for
chance decides the imposition of names on things) we must dispose

them with heed to the rules of art, and smuggle our inanities under cover of beautiful composition, giving ourselves fearless licence. For no rhythm whatever is banished[1] from unmetred composition any more than from that in metre.

Ibid. xviii (pp. 111–112 Reiske).

IV. THE SUPREMACY OF VARIETY

That style is best of all which has most reliefs and changes of harmony, — when part is arranged in period and part loosely ; when one period is composed of many clauses and another of fewer; when of the clauses themselves this is short and that long, this aiming at nervous intensity, that more languid, a third rigidly close to the sense; when the rhythms are different, the figures of all kinds; and when the very tensions and intonations of the voice vary so as to cheat weariness by their multiplicity.

Ibid. xix (p. 133 Reiske).

V. THE UPSTART ASIATIC STYLE

For in the times before us classical and philosophic Rhetoric was put down, pelted with mud, and subjected to gross insults. It began to lose breath and flesh about the death of Alexander of Macedon ; and towards our own day it was within a little of utter disappearance. But another kind of rhetoric, slipping into its appointed place, intolerable in its theatrical impudence, dissolute, without tincture of philosophy or any other liberal study, stealthily deluding the ignorance of the vulgar, not merely outwent the first in wealth and luxury and fulness of outward seeming, but drew to itself those civic honours and eminences which philosophical Rhetoric ought to have had. And vulgar it was and offensive ; and it made Greece like unto the households of debauchees and worthless wretches. For as in these the free and virtuous wife

---

[1] Reading ἀπελαύνεται as in R.'s note ; ἀπολαύεται, the reading of his text, would make nonsense of this striking dictum.

sits mistress of nothing that is really hers, while a brainless con-
cubine, bringing ruin to the life of the house, thinks to rule it
all, and insults and browbeats the wife — so in every city, and
(which was the worst evil of all) even not least in those best
instructed, the classical, the native Attic Muse, had taken an
unhonoured place, being driven from her proper goods, while some
Lycian, or Phrygian, or Carian baggage, imported yesterday or the
day before from some purlieu of Asia, thought herself worthy to
direct the affairs of Grecian cities, chasing her rival from public business — the dunce banishing the philosopher, the wanton expelling
the chaste.

De Oratoribus Antiquis, Preface.

VI. CRITICISM OF PLATO

(This and the following are given, not as specimens of infallible criticism, but as examples of criticism, vigorous and acute from its own point
of view, and such as we have too seldom from ancient writers.)

Plato's style aims at being a mixture of the two kinds, the lofty
and the plain: but it is not equally happy in the two respects.
When it practises plain and simple and unadorned phrase, it is
singularly pleasant and agreeable to men.   For it becomes bright
and pellucid enough in all conscience, like the clearest of fountains,
and it is also exact and subtle beyond any other of the like kind.
It keeps to usual words, and practises perspicuity, disdaining
plastered-on ornament.   The *patina* of its classical antiquity gently
and by stealth overruns it, giving a bloom of cheerfulness and
vigour and beauty ; as if from fragrant meadows, a sweet breeze of
odour is wafted from it, and its fluency is no more mere prattle
than its ornateness is theatrical.   But when, as it often does, it
rushes headlong into verbosity and fine writing, it does itself much
injustice.   For it then shows lack of charm, faults of Greek, even
coarseness of texture : it darkens clearness and turns it into
obscurity, it makes the meaning drag by wiredrawing it ; and when
terseness is required, it pours forth tasteless circumlocutions to
show off copiousness of vocabulary.   Nay, despising ordinary

language, and that which is in common use, it goes in quest of the manufactured, the foreign, the archaic. But it is most tempest-tossed in the use of Figures — for it is excessive in epithets, unseasonable in metonymies, rough and neglectful of analogy in metaphors, swaddled in allegories long, numerous, ill-proportioned, and out of place. Unseasonably also, and in a puerile manner, it luxuriates in poetical figures (particularly in those of Gorgias [1]) which produce the uttermost disgust: and "in such things he has much of the mystery-monger," as Demetrius Phalereus and many others have said; for "not mine the story."

This half apology — the last words are Euripidean — is followed by a more elaborate one explaining the grounds of D's objection to P's ornater passages. He thinks (Longinus knew better, *v. inf.*) that P. "should have guarded against any censure," and almost blushes as he repeats the philosopher's own confession that he is occasionally "dithyrambic." D. thought well enough of his criticism to quote it at length from his *De Admiranda Vi Demosthenis*, where it first appears, in his letter to Cn. Pompeius, § 2. He does the same (making some alterations) in the corresponding section of his second letter to Ammæus, with the following criticism on Thucydides, which had first appeared in his formal *Judgment* of the greatest of Greek historians.

VII. CRITICISM OF THUCYDIDES

For Thucydides, coming after him [Herodotus] and the others formerly mentioned, and taking a synoptic view of the merits which each of them possessed, set himself to introduce into historical practice a new kind of style, neither wholly prose nor completely metrical, but something common to and compounded of both. In his choice of words he proceeds by adopting a figurative, precious,[2] archaic diction, instead of that common and usual with the men of his time; in his expressions,[3] in which he especially wished to differ from[4] his predecessors, by taking the greatest possible trouble with them. Now he makes a sentence out of a word; now he compresses a sentence into a word; now again he turns a verbal

[1] See Aristotle, *supra*, and Longinus, *infra*.
[2] Or, "foreign."
[3] Or, "construction."
[4] Or, "excel."

form into a noun, or makes a noun a verb.   He turns the uses of
these parts of speech themselves upside down, so that a proper
name becomes common, actives become passive, and *vice versa*.[1]   He
confounds the natures of the plural and the singular ; and predicates
them of one another, also conjoining masculine with feminine,
feminine with masculine and neuter, in such a way that the natural
sequence is destroyed.   He twists the cases of nouns and parti-
ciples now to the thing signified away from the form of the phrase,
now the other way ; and he abuses conjunctions and prepositions, and
the connections that set out the power of words, just as if he were
a poet.   You will find innumerable expressions in him travestied,
by changes of person and confusions of tense and metaphorically
topical meanings, into the likeness of solecisms ; and as many in
which things and persons change places, in which the multiplicity
of parentheses puts off the sequence of his enthymemes and his
deliverances of thought, together with incorrectness, complexity,
hardness to unravel, and all their kind.   You will find also many
theatrical figures in him — the *parisoses*, etc., in which Gorgias and
others of his contemporaries revelled.   His most obvious and characteristic endeavour is to put the most meaning in the fewest words,
to compress many thoughts in one, and to leave the hearer in
expectation of more.   Whence the brief becomes the obscure.   To
sum up : there are four organic constituents of the style of Thucydides, poetical vocabulary, variety of figures, a rough harmony,
a rapid narration.   Its " colours " are sinewiness, pungency, compression, austerity, weight, intensity, the power of striking awe,
and above all that of moving the passions generally.

[1] I think Professor Rhys Roberts is right in substituting the text of the *Judgment* here for that in the *Letter*, which is confused or tautologous.

V

PHILOSTRATUS ON IMAGINATION

(Philostratus (A.D. 170?–250?) wrote much of divers kinds. The following passage — generally acknowledged to be the oldest *locus* for "Imagination" in the full modern sense — occurs in his *Life* of the philosopher-charlatan Apollonius of Tyana (vi. 19), and is put in his mouth.)

Imagination, a wiser craftsmistress than Imitation, has done this. For Imitation will fashion what she sees, but Imagination what she has not seen, supposing it according to the analogy of the Real. Moreover, a sudden shock will put Imitation's hand out, but not Imagination's. For *she* will proceed undisturbed to what she has, by supposition, set before her, and conceived.

VI

LUCIAN (A.D. 125?–210?) ON PRECIOUS AND ECCENTRIC STYLE

(Conclusion of the *Lexiphanes*.)

If then you wish to obtain a real reputation for your speeches among people at large, fly from, and turn your back on, all such stuff as this. Begin with the best poets, and read them with a tutor; then go to the orators, and, after feeding yourself with them, proceed in due season to the works of Thucydides and Plato, having also taken much exercise in graceful comedy and the tragic stateliness. For when you have culled all the fairest flowers from

these, you will be something of a man of letters [*or* "orator"][1];
whereas now you have unconsciously made yourself like unto the
work of the image makers in the market place, smeared with
vermilion and blue outside, but inwardly of crumbling clay. . . . But
above all I bid you remember not to imitate the worst tricks of
modern sophists, and, as it were, nibble at and chew them as you do
now; but to tread them under foot and imitate the classical models.
Neither let the windflowers of speech beguile you; but, like an
athlete in training, accustom yourself to solid nourishment. Above
all, sacrifice to the Graces and to Perspicuity, whom you have
utterly deserted. Say "Avaunt!" to bombast and magniloquence
and spite and snorting and shrieking and nagging at others' work
and thinking that you will be first if you rail at everybody else.
Moreover, this is not the least but the greatest of your faults, that
you do not first prepare the *meaning* of your phrase and then ornament it with words and names, but, if you take a fancy to some
outlandish term which you have found or yourself invented, you
try to tack a meaning on to it, and think yourself injured if you
cannot stuff it in somewhere, even if it be superfluous to the subject
of discourse.[2]

[1] In Greek, especially in this later Greek, "orator" and "man of letters,"
"literature" and "speeches," are often used almost convertibly.

[2] The story is actually told of the late M. Paul de Saint-Victor, that he used,
when sitting down to write, to put words that had struck his fancy at intervals
over the sheet, and write his matter in and up to them.

VII

LONGINUS (A.D. 213 ?–273)

(Whether the treatise Περὶ Ὕψους (or, as it is traditionally and perhaps necessarily but inexactly translated, *On the Sublime*) was actually written by the rhetorician Longinus, who acted as a kind of prime minister to Queen Zenobia of Palmyra, and was put to death by the Emperor Aurelian, need not be here discussed. There is no MS. of it older than the 10th century, and no certain reference to it older than the 13th. It was published in the middle of the 16th by Robortello, was not very much noticed at first, acquired immense, if sometimes strangely perverted, authority during the 17th and 18th, was a little neglected during the Romantic movement, but for some time past has been increasingly studied. The author, whoever he was, begins with some unfavourable criticism on a former handling of his subject by a certain Cæcilius, and proceeds (I. 4) as follows :)

In writing to you, good friend, who are well skilled in culture, I need hardly premise in many words that Sublimity is a certain consummateness and preëminence of phrase, and that the greatest poets and prose writers gained the first rank, and grasped an eternity of fame, by no other means than this. FOR WHAT IS OUT OF THE COMMON LEADS AN AUDIENCE, NOT TO PERSUASION, BUT TO ECSTASY [*or* "transport"]. The startling effect of the Wonderful always and everywhere has the better of the merely persuasive and the merely pleasing ; for to be persuaded depends, as a rule, on ourselves, but this other quality applies irresistible authority and force, and gets the better of all hearers. Inventive skill, orderly disposition of matter, we see struggling to appear as the effect, not of this or that thing, but of the whole tissue of the work in letters. But the Sublime, shooting forth at the nick of time, scatters everything like a levin bolt and shows the whole power of the author [orator] at once.

II–IV

This chapter begins with a discussion of the sempiternal question, how far "rules" can compass the Sublime and other artistic excellences. Longinus takes the obvious and most satisfactory — if still unsatisfactory — line that Nature must *supply*, but that Art can and should *regulate*. The passage, however, breaks off in the middle, and two leaves of the MS. are totally lost. It begins again abruptly with a quotation (identified for us by one of the late references above noticed) from the *Orithyia* of Æschylus.

"And let them stop (?) the long flash of the furnace! For if I can spy one hearth-holding spark, I will twist a curly torrent [of wind, or flame?] till I set the very roof in a blaze, and burn it to a cinder. And I have not yet sung my noblest song."[1]

To this L. — thereby no doubt commending himself to the 18th century — wholly objects as παρατράγῳδον, "sham-tragic": and in Chaps. III and IV of our text he proceeds to stigmatize στόμφος, ("bombast," "mouthing"), τὸ οἰδεῖν ("tumidity"), χαῦνοι ("swellings"), τὸ μειρακιῶδες ("boyishness"), ψυχρότης ("frigidity," *v. sup.*), τὸ κακόζηλον ("affectation"), and τὸ παρένθυρσον ("the thrusting in of the Bacchic thyrsus where it is not required," "sham enthusiasm"). He produces numerous examples of these various forms of the false-Sublime, not merely from tragedians and poets, but from prose-writers, especially from the historian Timæus, and even from Herodotus and Xenophon. From these sometimes dubious examples he generalizes, with admirable sense, in the following chapters, which must be given whole.

V–VI

All these undignified things grow as a fungus on letters, owing to one single reason — that quest after novelty in thought which leads our folk of to-day so mad a dance (περὶ ὃ δὴ μάλιστα κορυβαντιῶσιν οἱ νῦν). For good and evil generally come to us from the

---

[1] This is obviously from a sort of boast of his powers by Boreas, Orithyia's lover. I used to think, in common with the usual translators, that the fine phrase πλεκτάνην χειμάρροον referred to the licking, twisting tongue of *flame*. But now, it seems to me better to take it of the curling bellows-blast of *wind*, wherewith Boreas boasts himself able to revive, for destructive purposes, the spark which men have tried to curfew.

same source.   As beauty and height, aye, and fascination of rendering, are contributory to the successful arrangement of composition,
so these very things are the beginnings and understructure, not
merely of felicity, but of its opposite.   So is it with paraphrase, and
hyperbole, and the use of the plural[1]: but we shall show the
dangers of this later.   We must now investigate, and suggest a
way of escaping, the vices that alloy the sublime.   (VI) And there
is such a way, O my friend, if, above all, we could achieve a clear
understanding and critical knowledge of the true Sublime.   Yet
this is hard to catch; FOR THE JUDGMENT OF LITERATURE IS THE
FINAL AFTER-GROWTH OF MUCH ENDEAVOUR : nevertheless, to give,
as it were, the word of command, one may perhaps diagnose these
matters somewhat in this way.

In Chap. VII, L. considers further the difference of the true and false
Sublime, and decides that the best criterion of the true is, that it produces the effect of transport not once only, but again and again, on intelligent and experienced readers of the most different circumstances.   For,
he says,

Our souls are somehow naturally exalted by the true Sublime ;
and, as if rearing or prancing [*lit.*, taking a prancing elevation,
γαῦρον ἀνάστημα, the adjective being specially used of a skittish
horse], are filled with joy and exultation, as if themselves had
produced what they hear.

VIII enters upon the *sources* of sublime expression: perhaps it would
have obviated an objection if L. had said " the *forms* which this expression
takes," or "the *ways* in which it is attainable."   They are, first, weighty
and solid thought; secondly, intense passion; (both of which are, as a
rule, congenital); thirdly, Figures; fourthly, diction or phrase ; and
fifthly, distinguished composition.   Cæcilius is blamed for having omitted
passion, which L. thinks of the very first importance :

I should cheerfully lay it down that there is nothing so eloquent
as real passion, standing where it ought, in enthusiastic *afflatus* of
inspired madness, and filling the phrase with a sort of Delphic
rapture.

[1] I should like to translate τὰ πληθυντικά "pleonasm," but the above is the
orthodox rendering.

IX

These "sources" are then discussed seriatim, and with examples —
greatness of thought [formerly ἀδρεπήβολον, now μεγαλοφυές] still holding
pride of place. A very remarkable passage refers to Moses, "the legislator of the Jews, not the first comer," and his "Let there be light"; but
most of the favourable instances are taken from Homer. And then follows, in the shape of a comparatively unfavourable criticism of the *Odyssey*,
one of the most capital and characteristic passages of the whole, as illus-
trating the Classical distrust of, and distaste for, the Romantic, and the
comparatively low estimate of manners and character.

Yet he shows in the *Odyssey* (a matter to which we must give
attention for many reasons) that, when a great nature is now in its
decline, the love of the mythical is a senile characteristic. For that
he took the *Odyssey* as his *second* subject of composition, is clear
both from many other reasons and because he puts in scraps of the
tale of Troy as episodes of the *Odyssey;* nay, from his even bestow-
ing on his heroes epitaphs and dirges, as if devised beforehand.
For the *Odyssey* is nothing but an epilogue of the *Iliad* [*Od.* iii.
109–111 quoted]. For the same reason, I suppose, in the case of
the *Iliad*, written at the top of his inspiration, he has made the
whole body of the story dramatic and combative, that of the *Odyssey*
narrative for the most part, as is proper to old age. Whence, in the
Odyssey, one might liken Homer to the setting sun, whose greatness
remains, divorced from its intensity. For he does not here keep
the tone equal to that of the Trojan pieces, nor maintain his
heights equally, impatient of collapse or bathos, nor preserve the
steady profusion of redoubled passions, nor yet the qualities of
rapid transition, of practical reality,[1] of fertile images drawn from
truth. But, as if the Ocean were withdrawing into itself and leaving
the shore bare within its own bounds, there is shown the ebb of
greatness, and a mind wandering in the mythical and the incredible.
And when I say this, I do not forget the storms in the *Odyssey*, and
the Cyclops episode, and some other things. I speak of old age, but
of the old age of Homer. Yet everywhere the fabulous has the

---

[1] πολιτικόν, "statesmanlike," "keeping close to the actualities of war and
politics and life generally."

better of the practical. And I have digressed thus in order to show
how easily the noblest natures in their decline turn aside to twaddle
— such as the winds in the wine-skin, and the herd of Circe (the
"weeping piglings" as Zoilus called them), and Zeus as the nestling
of the doves, and the ten days' fast on the wreck, and the incredible
slaughter of the suitors. For what else can we call these things
but dreams — if in truth dreams of Zeus himself ? And it is worth
remarking on the *Odyssey*, in the second place, that you may observe
how this decline of passion, in great poets and prose-writers, relieves
itself in character-drawing [*or* manners-painting]. For the accurate
observations of life and manners in and about Odysseus' palace
amount to a kind of comedy of manners.

In X, L. returns to his investigation of the " sources," or contributory
elements, of Sublimity. He quotes (and in so doing has most fortunately
saved for us) the great ode of Sappho to her beloved, as an example of
" selection and combination" of striking traits. And he follows this up
with divers other examples, favourable and unfavourable. He then passes,
in XI and following chapters, to the rhetorical Figure (or rather method)
called *auxesis* — the common English rendering of which, " Amplification,"
is not very instructive. He himself defines it (just before another of
the long and annoying gaps in the MS.) after a fashion suggestive of, and
beyond doubt suggesting, the favourite method of Burke, as —

Filling in the subject from all analogous and relevant [1] parts and
topics, strengthening the general arrangement by dwelling on these—

Unluckily another gap in the MS. occurs here; and when it ceases, we
find ourselves in the midst, apparently, of a comparison between Plato and
Demosthenes, which almost immediately shifts into one between Demosthenes and Cicero. This is fortunately complete, and is of the utmost
value, Greek writers as a rule, whether from pride or for some other reason,
avoiding the treatment of Latin literature.

It seems to me (if we as Greeks may be allowed to know anything about the matter) that there is in the same way a cross-
difference [2] between Cicero and Demosthenes in their altitudes.

---

[1] ἐμφερομένων is usually translated "constituent." I prefer to interpret it in
accordance rather with the usual meaning of the adjective ἐμφερής.

[2] παραλλάττει, where I take the preposition to suggest that the eminence of D.
in one respect is made up by that of C. in another.

For the latter has usually a rugged loftiness, Cicero a voluminous effusion. Our man, in his ability at once to set on fire and hurry along everything with his force, his swiftness, his vigour, and his intensity, may be likened to a meteor or thunderbolt, while Cicero is like an all-embracing conflagration, devouring and consuming in every direction, having a mighty reserve of flame distributed now hither now thither, and maintaining itself by successive reinforcements. You Romans are better judges of appeal here. But the special moment of the Demosthenic high-strung sublimity is that of intensity and violent passion, where the hearer is to be utterly carried out of himself ; of the Ciceronian, volume, where he is to be saturated with commonplaces, and perorations, and digressions, and descriptions and show-passages of all kinds.   For the [Ciceronian] style is suitable to these, and to history, and natural history, and not a few other kinds.

XIII returns to Plato, and, praising him for his combination of ease and sublimity, diverges again to recommend as a " source " of the sublime the " imitation and emulation " — μίμησις καὶ ζήλωσις — of great prose-writers and poets.   This is an important passage because, though in itself quite sound and carefully distinguishing " imitation " from " theft " — μίμησις from κλοπή [v. inf. on Vida] — it shows us how the confusion was reached later.   But the next chapter (XIV) supplies what should have been a full antidote to any possible bane.

It will be good then for us to body forth mentally, when we are at work on something that needs sublimity of thought and expression, how Homer would have said it, how Plato, or Demosthenes, or in history Thucydides, would have given it exaltation.   For these great figures, presenting themselves to us on high as objects of emulation, will somehow or other raise our souls to the imagined standard.   It will be still better if, in addition, we set a sketch before our minds of how Homer and Demosthenes would have been affected, as actual hearers or readers of what we have said.   For it is trying ourselves really high to suppose such a tribunal, such a theatre, for our own work, and to stand a mock audit[1] of our writings with such hearers for judges and assessors.   It will spur you

---

[1] Reading πεπαῖχθαι as usual, I think this version may do.

on yet more, if you add further "How will my writing strike each next age?" And if any one be made, in the very fact of this, fearful of speaking, as it were, to audiences beyond his own life and time,[1] the conceptions of such a one's mind must be, so to say, unfinished and blind abortions, not accomplished to the point of posthumous fame-worthiness.

At the beginning of Chap. XV Longinus excites our hopes by mentioning φαντασίαι, "fancies," "images," which he says some also call εἰδωλοποίιαι, "fictions of the mind," as "especially useful in furnishing" Sublimity and its congeners. We find, however, very quickly, that he is not speaking of "imagination" in the full modern sense, but only of description so vivid that the writer "seems actually to see what he describes and to place it before the eyes of his readers" or hearers. And the chapter, which is a long one, contains numerous examples of this feat from the Greek poets and prose-writers. L. then turns once more to the subject of Figures: and for nearly the whole of no less than seventeen chapters, XVI–XXXII, devotes himself to them, or some of them, never indeed indulging in the puerile multiplication and hairsplitting which is too common and of which Quintilian speaks scornfully, but sometimes descending to a lower level than that of general Criticism. Some very important and striking passages must, however, be excerpted from this part of the book.

XVII. i. Somehow or other Figures naturally fight on the side of Sublimity, and in turn receive a wonderful reinforcement from it. A Figure looks best when it escapes one's notice that it *is* a Figure.

XXVIII. i; XXIX. i. No one, I think, will doubt that Periphrasis is a source of Sublimity. For as in music the dominant note is more sweetly brought out by accompanying trills and harmonies [2] — so periphrasis often harmonizes with the main thing said, and gives it symphonic order to a great extent, especially if it is not blatant and discordant but sweetly attempered. . . . Yet

[1] The meaning of the original here is a little ambiguous, and I have thought it better to leave it so than to incline the English to one side or the other. The Greek may refer to shrinking (with the characteristic Hellenic fear of Nemesis) from the attempt to speak to posterity; or it may admit the lower interpretation of prudential reluctance to speak above the heads of the actual readers.

[2] I am no musician myself, and even those who know both Greek and music are often at much variance in "combining their information." But this version of παραφώνων and κύριος φθόγγος at least falls in logically with the context.

periphrasis is a risky, a particularly risky business, if it be not exactly handled ; for it is apt to fall into feebleness and to smell of triviality and the windbag.

XXX. But, since thought and style in literature are for the most part intertwined and mutually enfolded, let us go on to consider any part of style that may be left. That the selection of proper and magnificent words has a wonderfully seductive and caressing effect on readers — that all speakers and writers make it their chief study, inasmuch as it confers upon literature, as it were on the fairest sculpture, grandeur, beauty, *patina*,[1] weight, strength, force, and what not — inasmuch as it puts, as it were, a living voice in the work — it were idle to urge upon the intelligent. FOR IN FACT BEAUTIFUL WORDS ARE THE VERY AND PECULIAR LIGHT OF THE MIND. Yet high language is not for indiscriminate use ; for to put great and dignified words on petty trifles would be like putting a tragic mask on a baby. But in Poetry and Hi[story ?][2] . . .

Come, then, let us catch some really spotless writer, free from all possible reproach! Is it not worth while to thrash the whole question out on this same point, which is the better in prose and poetry, grandeur amid some shortcomings, or moderate correctness free from all positive unsoundness and lapse ? Yes, moreover, and whether the greater *number* or the higher *quality* of excellences should bear the bell in literature ? For these things are germane to an enquiry about the Sublime, and by all means to be decided. Now I know perfectly well that the highest natures are the least faultless. A mind bent on absolute accuracy will run the risk of littleness, and in mighty genius, as in great wealth, there will be some things missed or slighted. It may even be unavoidable that low

[1] The much prized "bloom" of age on bronze. Those translators who do not give its special sense to εὐπίνεια deprive their readers of the chief link with sculpture.

[2] This inestimable passage is broken by one of the longest and most lamentable gaps (four leaves). When the text begins again, we find ourselves in a discussion, interesting but a little *meticulous*, on Metaphors and their allowable number, character, etc. L. takes occasion by this to object to his predecessor Cæcilius for ranking the "faultless" Lysias above the "often faulty" Plato. And then in XXXIII he proceeds to a really valuable discussion of "faultlessness" itself.

and middle natures, never setting all to the touch or aiming at the summit, remain as a rule free from danger, while great things totter through their very greatness. Nor, in the second place, am I ignorant that, in everything human, the faults are most conspicuous, and that the memory of slips abides uneffaced, while that of beauties speedily fades. But while I have myself noted not a few such slips in Homer and others of our greatest; while I am not in the least pleased with these; and while I nevertheless call them not so much wilful errors as chance oversights of *incuria*, casually introduced by the heedlessness of genius; yet I think, none the less, that the major excellences, even if not uniformly present, should always carry the election for their greatness of thought, if for nothing else.

L. proceeds to illustrate this from Greek authors, preferring, as greater though less faultless, Homer to Apollonius and (less reasonably?) Theocritus, Archilochus to Eratosthenes, Sophocles to Ion, Pindar to Bacchylides, and — at some length in the whole of Chap. XXXIV — Demosthenes to Hyperides. A brief return to the comparison of Plato and Lysias at the beginning of XXXV introduces the following admirable outburst.

What then was seen by those godlike ones, who, yearning after the greatest achievement of literature, made light of undeviating accuracy? Besides much else, *this* — that Nature set us men apart as no vile or lowborn animals, but, introducing us into life and the universal Cosmos, as into a great assembly, to be at once spectators of all its displays and most emulous competitors in them, she inspired our souls with an irresistible and eternal love of all that is great and, as it were, diviner than ourselves. Wherefore neither does the whole world suffice for the intellectual survey and process of human enterprise, but our daring thoughts frequently overpass the bounds of circumstance. And if a man will consider life in its whole circuit, and see how superabundantly it is furnished with what is extraordinary, and beautiful, and great, he shall soon know for what we were born. Hence are we naturally drawn to admire, not the petty streamlets, though they be clear and of good use, but the Nile and the Danube and the Rhine, and the Ocean most of all. Nor are we more awed by the flamelet of our own creation, even

though its light be steady, than by the heavenly fires, darkened as
they often are; nor do we think it worthier of wonder than the
craters of Etna, whose eruptions fling out from the abyss rocks and
masses, and sometimes vomit rivers of earthborn and absolute fire.
In fine of all — the Useful and the Necessary are to man easily
enough accessible; but that which is beyond his expectation is the
object of his Wonder.

After, in the beginning of XXXVI, making a slight return upon, or *résumé*
of, the above passage (which contains the remarkable words " Grandeur,
in literature at any rate, is never dissociated from use and profit " and
" Writers of this kind are above what is mortal. . . . Sublimity lifts
them near the mighty thought of God "), L. redescends into details
about faults and failures, reiterating, however, the preference for even
" faulty " grandeur. XXXVII is a mere fragment initiating a last discussion of Simile ; and in XXXVIII we find ourselves in the middle of one
on Hyperbole. Isocrates is especially censured for " puerile " amplification ;
examples of defensible though extreme hyperbole being produced, on the
other hand, from Thucydides and Herodotus.

XXXIX then passes to the fifth " tributary of the Sublime," namely,
rhythm.

Not only [*says L.*] is Harmony a natural cause of persuasion
and pleasure to men, but it is also a wonderful instrument of
high and passionate eloquence. [*If flute and harp have such
well-known power, being mere bastard imitations of human effort,*]
shall we not think that literary composition, being, as it were, a
harmony of the language natural to man, and capable of seizing
not merely his ears but his soul — exciting myriad ideas of words,
thoughts, and deeds, of beauty and melody, all born with and bred
up in us — and with the mixture and variety of its own tones
communicating the actual passion of the speaker to the souls
of those about him — yea, bringing the audience into communion
of being with him, and building phrase on phrase into a majestic
edifice — shall we not hold that, by this very means, it bewitches
us and disposes us to elevation, and dignity, and sublimity,
and all that itself contains, exercising universal royalty over
our minds?

The chapter concludes with an example of harmonic arrangement from Demosthenes, which, of course, is only intelligible in the Greek. XL proceeds, in the same way, to deal with "composition" proper ; that is to say, the arrangement of words, clauses, and sentences, again with examples at least sometimes subject to the same drawback. XLI consists, on the other hand, of cautions against unsuitable and "niggling" rhythm ; XLII of similar but briefer warning against excessive conciseness; and XLIII of attacks on "pettiness" in certain passages of Herodotus and Theopompus, in reading which a former inability to sympathize with the horror of "Frigidity" may recur to modern readers. And then comes the last actual chapter (the MS. is incomplete as well as gapped), which is too famous, and too representative of a certain not ignoble drift of criticism, not to be given whole.

There remains, however, my dear Terentianus, (I shall not hesitate to make the postscript for the sake of your love of learning) the clearing up of a certain point, which one of our philosophers has just discussed. "It is surprising to me," he says, "and no doubt to many others, how many natures there are in our time, admirably persuasive and statesmanlike, keen and versatile, and especially happy in attractive eloquence, how few and rare are those really sublime and grand. So world-wide a dearth of [great] literature cramps our life.[1] Are we to give faith to the common cant that democracy is the kind nurse of sublimity, and that mighty men of letters flourish and die with it ? For they say that freedom has the might to cherish and encourage the thoughts of the magnanimous, and that with it there is disseminated eager mutual emulation, and the thirst for fame and supremacy. Moreover, by the prizes open in republics the soul-gifts of orators are periodically practised and whetted, and as it were burnished; and naturally shine free as the state itself. But now," he continued, "we seem to have learnt from infancy that subserviency is the law of life,[2] being from our tenderest years of thought all but swaddled in its manners and customs, and having never tasted that most beautiful and fertile fountain of eloquence, Freedom — so that we turn out

[1] I think this is at least possible for ἐπέχει τὸν βίον, and much more characteristic than the common rendering "prevails in our age."
[2] Lit., "to be child-instructed in a just slavery."

merely sublime in Courtiership. Therefore it was," he said, "that while all other faculties fall to the lot of servants, no slave was ever an orator; for in him there is always an eruption of the lack of free speech, the symptoms of the house of bondage and of buffetings. 'For the day of slavery,' says Homer, 'takes away half our virtue.' As then," said he, "if one may believe what is said, the cases in which pygmies or dwarfs are kept not merely prevent the growth of those shut in them, but thin them down by the bonds cast round their bodies, so all servitude, even if it be most justly exercised, has been rightly called a cramping-case of the soul and a public house of bondage."

But I took him up and said, "It is very easy, my good friend, and extremely human, to blame what actually exists. But take care lest it be not the settled peace of the world which spoils great natures, but much rather the boundless riot which keeps hold on our lusts, and not less the passions which garrison our life now, and harry and ravage it from top to bottom. For covetousness, wherewith we are all deeply afflicted, and love of pleasure, lead us captive, nay, one might say, plunge our lives, like ships, crews and all in the depths — love of money causing meanness, and love of pleasure being the ignoblest of all diseases. Nor can I, after much thought, discover how it is possible for us, if we overvalue (or, to speak in the truest way, deify) boundless wealth, to refuse the entrance of our souls to the evils that are wealth's congeners and come in its train. For, as men say, there follows unmeasured and intemperate wealth, closely allied and with equal step, Lavish Expenditure, and when Wealth has opened the doors of cities and houses the other makes its way in and abides there. And in due time, say the wise, these build nests in the lives of men, and, swiftly setting about childmaking, beget Show, and Pomp, and Luxury — no bastards they, but true-born offspring. And if any suffer these children of Wealth to grow up, *they* produce inexorable tyrants of the soul — Insolence, and Lawlessness, and Lack of Shame. These things must needs be so; and the men [in such a case] will no longer look upwards nor care for fame, but in the round of such occupations accomplish, little by little, the ruin of their lives, while the greatnesses of the soul diminish and wither, and sink below emulation, while they fix inordinate admiration on the mortal parts of themselves and neglect the augmentation of the immortal parts. For the judge with greasy palm can never judge freely and soundly on questions of justice and decency — to the bribe-taker his own side must always seem decent and just. And when the arbiters of the whole life of each of us are bribes and legacy-hunting — when each of us buys gain, from no matter what source, at our soul's price, enslaved by lust — can we then, in such a plague-stricken spoiling of life, think that there is left any free and unbribed judge of great and ever-lasting things, or that any is not canvassed to his destruction by the lust of gain ? . . ." Finally, I said that among the idle outgoings of our actual genius is that nonchalance in which all of us (save a few) spend our lives — taking no trouble and undertaking nothing save for praise or pleasure, instead of for what is worth emulation and honour.

The piece ends, once more abruptly, with the introduction of a lost treatise on the Passions.

VIII

HORACE (65–8 B.C.)

THE EPISTLE TO THE PISOS, OR ART OF POETRY

(It has seemed best to deal with this famous document — the traditional and influential importance of which cannot possibly be exaggerated, though its intrinsic critical value may be much more disputable — by a mixture of abstract and literal translation. The italics represent the former, and also occasional insertions for clearness' sake; the Roman text contains the latter. I have used the text of the Dean of Lincoln, Oxford 1900.)

If a painter chose to combine a human head and a horse's neck, and to clothe limbs brought together from all sorts of bodies with varied plumage — to make what is a lovely woman above end hideously in a black fish-tail below — you would laugh when he exhibited his work, would you not, friends? Believe me, O Pisos, that such a picture will find its match in a book where, as in a sick man's dreams, the forms are idly fictioned, so that neither head nor foot belongs to a single kind. *But surely, you will say,* "Painters and poets have always had an equal right to dare anything?" I know it; and I grant and claim the privilege by turns. *But inconsistent things must not be joined :* the purple patch *at certain places must not be laid on without cause, and a poet must not quit his type at pleasure.* Let the work be what you like, provided it has simplicity and unity. Too many of us poets are deceived by a fallacious appearance of correctness — while I try to be terse I become obscure; the quest of smoothness leads to the failure of nerve and spirit; if a man aims at grandeur he becomes turgid — if he plays too much for safety, and fears a storm, he grovels. In seeking to do conjuring feats of variation on a single theme, there is danger of exhibiting a dolphin in the woods, in the floods a wild boar. The

very desire to avoid faults produces fault if art be lacking. . . .
Choose, O ye men of letters, a subject suited to your strength, and
meditate long what your shoulders can bear, and what they cannot.
He who suits his matter to his powers will never lack eloquence
or *ordonnance.*[1] Now the virtue and beauty of this ordonnance is,
unless I mistake, that it makes a man say *now* what ought *now*
to be said, and postpone the rest for the present.

Let[2] the author of a projected poem use subtlety and caution in
the contexture of his words, and set before him the following things
to choose and to avoid. You will be thoroughly successful if an
ingenious context gives a new sense to an old word. If it is really
necessary to give fresh expression to something recondite you may
coin words unknown to the ancients, and the licence, moderately
exercised, will be confirmed. *After illustration and repetition of the
same doctrine, he lays down the general rule as follows:* Many words
will revive which are now in abeyance, while those now in honour
will give way, as usage — with which the arbitrament and right and
law of speaking rests — shall decide.

*This dictum as to "usage" seems to suggest to the poet a fresh
application of it to versification, and he explains, at considerable
length, how the metres appropriate to epic, elegiac, satiric, and other
poetry have been settled once for all and must not be changed; how*
a comic matter refuses to be set forth in tragic verse, *and how con-
trariwise even tragic heroes* in poverty and exile cast aside their
yard-long verbiage and their swelling pride *of language if they
wish to touch the spectators. Many famous critical aphorisms are
scattered about this part of the piece, as,* " It is not sufficient for poems
to be finely written : they must please "; " If you wish me to weep,
you must first yourself express real sorrow "; *etc. As throughout,
the drift is always towards Consistency, Proportion, Order; and the
passage culminates in the famous exhortation to* " keep to the type," *to*
follow tradition or else make things consistent with themselves, *to
represent* Achilles *as* active, passionate, inexorable, keen ; Medea
fierce and indomitable, *etc., etc.* If you put a novelty on the stage,
and dare to invent a new personage, let it be kept throughout true

---

[1] This word, a favourite with Dryden, should be restored.
[2] Taking Bentley's order of ll. 45, 46.

to its first appearance and consistent to itself. It is difficult to give proper expression to common things;[1] and you will have more chance of success in dramatizing the *Iliad*, than if you be the first to put forth something "new and original." You may make your own use of *such* public material, provided that you neither tread the old and hackneyed round once more, nor stick to mere word for word rendering, nor, in your imitation, thrust yourself into tight places where you have no business, either in decency or in craftsmanship. Neither should you begin, as did a cyclic poet once upon a time, " I will sing the fortune of Priam and the far-famed war." What can this undertaker produce worthy of such an opening? How far better he who makes no inept attempt: "Tell me, Muse, of the hero who, after the capture of Troy, saw the manners and cities of many men." *He* aims not at following flash and crash with smoke, but at blowing his smoke into flame. *Divers Homeric traits of merit are then noticed — the restriction to a reasonable scope, the* constant hastening to the end, the hurrying of the reader into the midst of matters as if they were well-known, *the relinquishment of unpromising topics, the constant* CONSISTENCY. *To this beloved virtue Horace then once more returns, insisting that boys shall be boys, gamesome, unthrifty, and so forth, the old avaricious, slow,* praisers of the times when they were young, *etc. The poet-critic returns and returns to this " carefulness of the type."*

Then he shifts again. The theatre proceeds either by action, or by narration of action. Things heard affect the soul less vividly than what is put before the faithful eyes, and what the spectator administers to himself. But you will not bring on the stage what ought to be done behind the scenes, and you will keep out of sight much which can be presently narrated. Let not Medea slaughter her sons in public, nor wicked Atreus cook the human joint, nor Procne be turned into a bird, Cadmus into a snake. If you show me anything of this kind, I disbelieve it, and feel disgust. Nor let

---

[1] It is still more difficult to be certain of the exact bearing of this famous phrase ; and the interpretation most in accordance both with the usual meaning of the words and with general critical truth (" It is hard to give individual expression to what is common property as thought ") does not perhaps fit most obviously into the context.

a play which aims at being in demand, and at holding the stage, be longer or shorter than five acts; nor let gods intervene unless on a worthy occasion; nor let a fourth personage intrude his observations. *The office of the chorus is then described and defended; and the traditional origins, gradual elaboration, and various kinds of the Greek drama are set forth with considerable detail. Even metrical minutiœ of the best-known kind* — "a long syllable following a short is called an iamb," etc. — *are not disdained; but in all there is a constant repetition, in cleverly varied forms, of the cries, "Imitate! Keep the type! Observe propriety!" And at last we have the famous injunction,* Let the Greek patterns be never out of your hands by night or day. *This leads to yet another digression, or retrogression, to the history of the Greek theatre itself, with a fresh return to Latin. It is impossible to clear this part — or indeed the whole — from the charge of incompleteness and desultoriness; but striking and valuable passages are nowhere wanting for long. Of such are, the praise of those Latin dramatists who* dared to quit the footsteps of the Greeks, and to celebrate the ways of home, either in the statelier (*prœtexta*) or the more familiar (*togata*) form; *the anxious recommendation of* the labour of the file; *the modest pretence merely to* discharge the function of the whetstone, which can make steel sharp, though itself unable to cut; *the supreme motto or maxim, so eagerly accepted by the neo-classic criticism of the 17th–18th centuries* — OF WRITING WELL RIGHT THINKING (*sapere*) IS THE BEGINNING AND THE FOUNT; *the scorn of* verse devoid of meaning and tuneful trifles; *the second capital dictum* — POETS WISH EITHER TO INSTRUCT, OR TO DELIGHT, OR TO COMBINE THE TWO; *the renewed caution* — Let what is imagined for the sake of giving pleasure keep as close as possible to actual fact; *and the exaltation of the poet who* mixes the pleasant and the useful *as having* carried every point.

Then some mitigations are allowed. When a poem is generally brilliant, not mine be it to be offended at a few blots, the result of negligence or of human frailty. — The good Homer nods *a little below, and the immortal* as painting is, so is poetry *follows, though in the original context it is limited to the necessity of viewing both now near and narrowly, now farther off and at large. A little later comes the famous* Gods and men and columns (*the columns on which new poems were posted*) forbid the existence of minor (*or* "middling") poets. *More in the same vein follows: cautions to do nothing* in the teeth of Minerva, to keep a poem for nine years *before publication, inasmuch as* a voice once let loose comes not back again. *Illustrations of a somewhat desultory kind ensue — praises of the poets of old — a diversion to the ever vexed question* whether a praiseworthy poem is the result of nature or of art? *Horace, as might be expected, answers, Of both; but lays special stress on cultivation of talent.*

The remainder of the poem is chiefly occupied, at what may seem very disproportionate length, with directions for taking the criticism of friends (using great care that it be competent and serious); and the actual conclusion is half ironical.

IX

PETRONIUS (*fl. c.* A.D. 60)

A. ON DECLAMATION[1]

These things might be tolerable if they really opened a path to eloquence. As it is, by the bombast of the matter and the idle clatter of the phrase, men gain simply this : that, when they actually come into court, they think they have been transported to another world. And I believe that schoolboys become such utter dunces for the very reason that they neither hear nor see any of the usual actualities of life, but pirates standing on the shore with chains ready, and tyrants ordering sons by edict to cut off their fathers' heads, and oracular responses in time of plague bidding the sacrifice of three or more maidens, and scraps of phrase drugged with honey and poppy and sesamum. Those who are bred in such an atmosphere can no more keep their senses unaffected than those who live in the kitchen.[2] Excuse me, but you declamation-mongers have been the ruin of eloquence ; for, by fostering all this sham of light and empty sound, you have enervated and made to totter the

[1] The "Declamation," or set artificial speech, not only formed a very great part of school and university education among the Romans, but was actually resorted to by grown men, to keep in full play those oratorical powers which were of so much importance in business and politics. The examples which, some of them *in extenso*, we possess under the name of Quintilian, and the very curious declamatory miscellanies (as we may call them) of Seneca the Elder, show that the attacks of Petronius (which are repeated by the satirists from Persius onwards) were not ill-deserved.

[2] Lit., "those who are nourished amid such things can no more have good taste than those who live in the kitchen good smell." A satisfactory rendering is made difficult by the fact that, in English, the verbs "taste" and "smell" have both the active and the passive sense, while in Latin *sapere* has both and *olere* only the passive.

body of oratorical speech.   Youth were not yet kept a-declaiming
when Sophocles and Euripides devised their styles.   The private teacher had not spoilt good wits when Pindar and the
nine lyric poets thought shame merely to follow Homer.   And,
not to cite poets only, I certainly do not find that Plato or
Demosthenes went through this training.   The ripe but maiden
Muse of oratory, so to speak, is not blotched in countenance nor
bloated in form, but shoots up in natural beauty.   Of late this
windy and unruly loquacity migrated from Asia to Athens, and, as
it were, blasted with a pestilential star the magnanimous aspirations of youth.   Simultaneously, true eloquence has halted and
been struck dumb as the system became corrupt.   Who has since
come near the fame of Thucydides — of Hyperides ?   Not even verse
has shown the colours of health ; every style, as if fed on the same
food, has failed to reach a hale old age.

Satyricon i. 2.

B. ON POETRY

Many young men have fallen into a mistake about poetry.   For
when any one has arranged a verse metrically, and has woven in
words a somewhat tender [1] conceit, he thinks forthwith that he is
free of Helicon.   Thus lawyers and statesmen have often sought
the quiet ways of verse as a happy port of refuge, thinking it
easier to "build a rhyme" than to adorn an argument with flashing
phrase.   But neither does the nobler breast love mere vanity, nor
can the mind conceive or yield its fruit unless it be flooded with
a mighty torrent of letters.   We must, so to speak, flee from all
commonness of diction, and take words remote and afar from the
vulgar, that we may have the benefit of *Odi profanum*, etc.   We
must also take care that no *sentences* [2] project, as though forced out

[1] *Teneriorem* may here have the literal sense, as of a love-poem ; or it may
mean "more delicate," "more fantastic" than would suit prose.

[2] These "sentences," or γνῶμαι, which make a very great figure in the
rhetorical treatises of the ancients, originally meant moral axioms, etc., inter-
spersed to give weight and dignity to the speech.   As these things, however,
were usually expressed with particular care, or, as we say, "sententiously,"
the word got to be applied to what the French call *pointes* — "conceits," plays
on words, "purple patches," etc., in general.

of the body of the style; but that they make the verse glow with
enwoven colour, as Homer shows us, and the Lyrists, and the Roman
Virgil, and the curious felicity of Horace.   For the rest either saw
not the path that leads to true Poesy, or, seeing, feared to tread
it.   Whoso, forsooth, attacks the mighty task of a *Civil War*,
unless he be full of letters, will fall under the burden.   For it is
not a question of putting together the mere facts (which historians
will do much better) in verse.   But the free spirit must be
hurried through difficulties, and the ministry of the gods, and
a fabulous torment of sentences, so that it may appear rather the
vaticination of a frenzied mind than a trustworthy discourse,
scrupulously according to evidence.[1]

[1] This not very easy passage was seized upon, by the 17th century more particularly, and elaborated into a whole code of "revolutions," "machinery,"
"poetic fury," "poetic diction," and the like, for the Heroic Poem.   The chief
crux is *fabulosum sententiarum tormentum*, in which (probably at least) *fabulosum* refers to the supposed necessity of bringing in as much mythological matter
as possible, *sententiarum* is employed as above, and *tormentum* repeats the
doctrine that the phrase used must not be facile and ordinary.   But there
are other possibilities, especially of allusion and side-glance; the whole is
emphatically a text for the student to ponder and for the teacher to expound.

Ibid. § 118.

X

QUINTILIAN (A.D. 35?–96?)

I. FAULTS AND FIGURES

It is often hard to distinguish faults from Figures of speech.

Inst. Or. I. v. 5.

II. THE DUTIES OF THE TEACHER IN LITERARY[1] CRITICISM

But to point out merits, and, where chance shall require it, faults, is the special and proper duty of his profession and undertaking as a Master of Eloquence. . . . After setting forth the case on which the oration to be read was written (for what is said there will be thus better understood), let him occupy himself with everything notable either in the *invention* or in the *style;* with the method of conciliating the judge in the proem; with the lucidity, terseness, persuasiveness, of the setting forth, the design here and there, and the concealment of artifice — for art in this matter wholly consists in being imperceptible except to the artist. Then he must point out what foresight there is in the disposition, how subtle and unremitting is the argument, how powerful the excitement, how seductive the coaxing, what keenness there is in the attack, what urbanity in the humorous passages, how the writer sways the passions, and captures the heart, and makes the mind of the jury follow what he says. There must be pointed out the propriety, ornament, sublimity of the diction; the praise due to amplification, or compression, as the case may be; the speciousness of

[1] With the usual caution as to *Oratory* and *Literature.*

the metaphors; the figures; the smooth and polished, yet virile, composition.

Ibid. II. v. 5–9.

III. USE AND BEAUTY

True beauty is never divorced from utility.

Ibid. VIII. iii. 11.

IV. OF CONCEITS[1]

There are two parties in reference to Conceits, the one paying almost sole attention to them, the other condemning them altogether. I agree wholly with neither. If such things come too thick, they get in each other's way; as in all crops, ground or tree, nothing can grow to full size if it has no room. Nor in a picture, where there is no shading or valuing, does anything stand out; so that artists who put several objects in one painting keep them apart, lest the shadows should fall on them. The practice also makes the style "cut-up"; for each conceit stands by itself, and there is really a fresh beginning after it. So that the phrase is wanting in continuity, and, being, as it were, made up not of members but of single bits, has no structural unity, inasmuch as these parts, rounded off and separated on all sides, have no mutual dependence. Besides this, the complexion of the writing is, so to say, sprinkled with spots, bright indeed if you like, but too many and too different. Nay, though purple stripes in their proper place give brightness to a dress, no one would look well in sheer motley. Wherefore, though such things may seem, to a certain extent, to give brilliancy and distinction, yet it would be better to call such flashes not pure flame, but sparks mixed with smoke. They would not even be

---

[1] Difficult as it is to render many of the technical terms of Greek and Latin rhetoric into English, there are few more difficult words among these than γνώμη, *sententia*. We keep (as is noted elsewhere) something like the meaning in our adjective and adverb "sententious-ly," but have lost it in "sentence." "Conceit," in a half-archaic sense, comes near; "epigram" is rather farther off; the French *pointe* comes between the two. The "sentence" is really *any* brief detachable and quotable phrase which is particularly *striking*, either as phrase or as thought.

visible, if the whole composition were luminous — even as in
sunlight the very stars cease to be seen. Nor can incessant and
insignificant attempts at elevation, from their uneven and broken
nature, obtain the admiration due to sublimity, while they lose the
pleasantness of level ground.

Ibid. VIII. v. 25–29.

V. ON COMPOSITION, OR DELIBERATE CULTIVATION OF STYLE

I am not ignorant that there are some who would shut out all
care for *Composition*, who contend that mere unpolished speech,
just as it comes, is not only more natural but even more manly. . . .
(*After using what has been called in England " the woad argument "
about going back to wood-dwelling and wild-beast-skins, Q. joins closer
issue.*)   But that is most natural which nature permits to be done
in the best way possible.   How can anything be firmer when
it is in disorder than when it is bound fast together and well
arranged ? . . .   As the flow of rivers is stronger in a sloping bed,
which interposes no obstacle, than when the waters are broken by,
and struggle with, obstacles of rock, so is style which is connected,
and flows with full force, better than that which is broken and
interrupted.   Why then should men think that vigour is impaired
by beauty, when nothing is ever at its full power without art, and
beauty is art's constant companion ? . . .

If, then, there is a certain secret force even in inarticulate harmonies, this force in eloquence must be most vehement.   As it
makes a difference in what words the sense is expressed, so does
it in what composition the words themselves are contextured and
brought to a conclusion.   Nay, some things not great in thought
and little set off by delivery, are made acceptable by this sole
excellence; while if a man will take to pieces, and alter in order
of words, anything that he thinks written with force, or sweetness,
or grace, — all these qualities will be found to have disappeared.

Ibid. IX. iv. 3–14.

VI. ON PROSE RHYTHM

(A cento, or rather mosaic, from *Inst. Or.* IX. iv. 52–end. Some general remarks on metre and rhythm have preceded.)

And even metrical feet are so frequently found in prose-writing that in it actual verses of all kinds often escape us without our perceiving them ; while, on the other hand, there is nothing written in prose which cannot be redacted into some kind or other of verses or at least fragments of verse. . . . Nay, Cicero frequently says that all prose consists in numbers, and has been blamed for it by some, as if he had bound prose down to (*fixed*) rhythms. . . . But prose *will* condescend to finger-beats. Cicero himself knew this perfectly well, and often assures us that he is seeking what is *numerous*, with the intent rather that the composition shall not be without rhythm, which would be ignorant and clownish, than that it should be definitely rhythmical, which is the business of poetry. Just as we care neither to be called professional athletes nor to be thought ignorant of gymnastics.

But the even accomplishment effected by feet is in want of some name ; and what can be better than " number," and " prose " (*lit.*, " oratorical ") " number " ? . . .

However, the chief business in this matter is to know what word will square best in each particular place ; and he will be the best composer who does this [1] only with a view to composition. But the arrangement of feet in prose is much more difficult than in verse : first, because a verse is contained in a small compass, while prose often takes much wider sweeps ; and then, because verses resemble each other and run off on one system, while unless prose is varied in composition it both offends by sameness and is convicted of affectation. Indeed, the whole body, or if I may so say the whole course, of prose is pervaded by number ; and we cannot even speak except in longs and shorts, the materials of feet. (*After giving very special directions for attention to number at the close, and at the beginning, of periods, Q. goes to various details.*)

---

[1] It has been usual to desiderate a *non* here ; I am not so sure that it is wanted.

That an entire verse should appear in prose is the ugliest fault of all; even in part it is inelegant, especially in the end or beginning of a period. (*Of this many examples, both Latin and Greek, are given.*) But this whole subject has been handled by no means with the idea that prose, which ought to have sweeping and fluent motion, should dawdle itself into dotage [*consenescat*] in measuring feet and weighing syllables. For this would be the part of a wretched creature, occupied on the infinitely little. Nor could one who exhausted himself in this care, have time for better things; if, abandoning the weight and despising the beauty of *things*, he were to "tessellate words and worm phrases into each other," as Lucilius says. The heat will be cooled, the rush checked, as finikin *manège*-riders break the pace of horses into mincing step. . . .

The best judge of good composition is the ear — which feels what is full, has a sense of want at what is incomplete, is hurt by the rugged and soothed by the smooth, provoked by contortion and satisfied by straightforwardness, which detects lamenesses at once, and is disgusted at redundancy and verbiage. (*Very minute directions for the accommodation of rhythm and delivery to each other, and to the subject and kind of composition, are given; but towards the end Q. repeats his cautions against a finikin smoothness.*)

On the whole, however, if I must say it, I should prefer the composition to be hard and rough, rather than, as so many now are, effeminate and enervated. For every day we grow more wanton in skipping measures, as if to a pitchpipe. Nor will any system be so good that it may be continually adopted and go always on the same feet. For it is a kind of versifying to subject all writing to the same measure; and this is not only clear affectation (which has to be most of all guarded against), but creates disgust through its sameness and satiety. The sweeter it is, the sooner its sweetness perishes, and he who is seen to be busied on it loses grasp of persuasion, and of the passions and all the emotions, nor will any juryman who thinks him occupied therewith believe, or be sorry, or be wroth, at his instance. (*Looser composition, therefore, is to be designedly intermixed, but not to excess: and*) The chief business is to dissemble art; so that numbers may seem to flow of their own accord, not to be fetched and forced into service.

VII. THE CHOICE OF READING

But before I speak of individuals, it will be well to make some general observations on differences of opinion. Some think that only the ancients ought to be read — they consider that nowhere else is there a natural eloquence, a virile vigour; while others rejoice in our modern wantonness and refinement, and in all the tricks of composition to please the ignorant vulgar. Even of those who wish to follow correctness in speaking, some think true and sound Atticism to consist in terseness, simplicity, and as few departures as possible from ordinary diction; some are attracted by more ambitious efforts of mind, by rapid motion, by fulness of elevation and spirit; while there are no few lovers of a style smooth, and polished, and carefully arranged. Of these differences I shall speak more at length hereafter (*v. inf.*, §§ IX and XII, *to which this is a kind of introduction*).

VIII. JUDGMENT OF SENECA

(Quintilian's survey of Greek and Roman literature is of the first interest; but it is rather too long as a whole, and in parts too scrappy and summary, to be given in full here. The judgment of his elder contemporary Seneca, with which it concludes, is the fullest and most instructive item in it. But Q's critical attitude — and in part that of the ancients generally — is illustrated powerfully by his missing in Apollonius Rhodius all qualities but "even mediocrity"; by the patronizing dismissal of Theocritus as "admirable in his own way," but merely "rustic" and "shrinking from the city"; by his omission of Sappho altogether, and his more than half-rebuke to Alcæus for writing love-poems; by his slighting treatment of Lucretius as "difficult" though "elegant," and of Catullus as simply "bitter.")

I have deliberately postponed notice of Seneca in every department of eloquence, because of the opinion falsely but commonly entertained of me — that I regard him with hostility. Now this has come about while I have been striving to bring back, to a severe critical standard, a style of oratory corrupt and debased by every fault. At that time [*i.e.*, when I began] Seneca was almost the only author in the hands of youth. Nor did I attempt to wrest him from them altogether; but I would not allow him to be set above better men, whom he was incessantly attacking for the reason that, being conscious how much his style differed from theirs, he despaired of pleasing those who were pleased by them. But those who studied him rather liked than copied him; and diverged from him as much as he had fallen below the ancients. For it would have been positively desirable that they should be equals, or even fair seconds, to him. But they liked only his faults, and merely tried to copy, each what he could, from him; after which their boast of speaking in his style was merely a disgrace to Seneca himself. For the rest, he had many and great merits : a ready and copious wit, a great deal of erudition, much knowledge of facts — in which point, however, he was sometimes led astray by those whom he had commissioned to make research for him. Also there was hardly any department of studies that he did not handle; for there are extant speeches of his, and poems, and letters, and dialogues. He was not a very exact student of philosophy, but a capital attacker of faults. There are many brilliant conceits [1] in him; much of him is worth reading for its morality. But the greater part of his style is corrupt, and all the more dangerous that it abounds in pleasing faults. One could wish that he had written from his own wit, but under another's judgment. For if he had disdained some things, if he had not set his heart on littleness, [2] if he had not fancied himself indiscriminately, if he had not broken up solid matter in trifling conceits, — he would have the approval, rather of the agreement of the learned, than of the affection of boys. But, even as he is, he is to be read by the robust and those confirmed by severer studies, if only that critical judgment may be exercised on him in either direction. Much in him, as I have said, is to be approved, much even to be admired; but we must take care to select, as I would that he had done himself. For a nature which achieved whatever it chose, was worthy to choose better things than it did.

Ibid. X. i. 125–131.

[1] See caution above.
[2] *Parum* is not often used in this way, but it makes good sense.

IX. OF WRITING BETTER THAN YOU CAN

About this I remember that the famous Julius Secundus, my contemporary, and, as is well known, my familiar friend, a man of wonderful eloquence, yet of infinite laboriousness, told me a saying of his uncle's. This was Julius Florus, the very chief of Gaul in eloquence, which he long practised there, an orator among few anywhere, and worthy of his relationship. Now he, by chance seeing Secundus, who was still busy with his studies, looking downcast, asked him why he was so dejected. The young man made no secret of it, that for three days he had been unable, with all his pains, to hit upon an opening for a subject set him to write upon — which was not only a present annoyance to him, but made him despair of the future. Then Florus smiled and said: " Pray, do you want to speak [write] better than you can ? "

Ibid. X. iii. 12–14.

X. DIVISION OF STYLES — ATTIC, ASIATIC, AND RHODIAN

From of old there has been the famous division of Attic and Asiatic writers — the former being reckoned succinct and vigorous, the latter inflated and empty. In those there was to be nothing superfluous, in these a lack of nothing so much as of judgment and measure. Some, such as Santra,[1] think that this came about because, as the Greek tongue spread little by little among the neighbouring states of Asia, folk who were not yet sufficiently accomplished in it were ambitious of eloquence, and so at first began to express periphrastically what might have been signified directly, and then held on in the same path. But I think that the different natures of speakers and audiences produced the difference of style, inasmuch as the Attics, polished in form and clear of head, could not endure inanity and redundancy; the people of Asia, in other ways more given to boasting and bombast, were likewise puffed up with a vainer conceit in speaking. And soon those who arranged this division added a third kind — the

[1] A grammarian elsewhere quoted but not otherwise known.

Rhodian — which they would have to be a sort of mean and blend of the two. Writers of this class are neither terse, like the Attics, nor prolix after the Asian fashion. So that they seem to have something of their race and something of their master; for Æschines, who chose Rhodes for his place of exile, brought thither Athenian studies, which, as crops degenerate in alien soil and under a foreign sky, blended the Attic taste with that of the foreigner. The Rhodians are held to be somewhat tame and slack, but not quite feeble — resembling neither crystal fountains, nor turbid torrents, but calmly flowing pools.

Ibid. XII. x. 16–19.

XI

In the immediate sequel, Q., while preferring the Attic style as a matter of course, judiciously observes that there are many *kinds* of Attic, and protests, with one of the not too frequent touches of irony which season his book, against the restriction of the "odour of thyme" [the herb of Hymettus] to those who "dribble the stream through the pebbles," *i.e.*, who observe an affected simplicity and absence of ornament. Then he turns to one of the most interesting points in the whole treatise,

A COMPARISON OF GREEK AND LATIN STYLE

Latin eloquence, while it clearly resembles, and is in fact a scholar of, Greek in invention, disposition, judgment, and other similar points, scarcely admits imitation of Greek in the strictly *elocutionary* [1] direction. For, to begin with, it is much harsher in sound. (*He gives a large number of minute instances of this — the lack of the Greek υ and φ,* [2] *the snarling sound of* fr, *the want of the digamma or* w, *the ugliness of the terminations* m, b, d, *the harsh accentuation.*) And thus Greek speech is so much more charming than Latin, that our poets, whensoever they want a verse to be attractive, deck it with Greek words. What is still more serious,

---

[1] Using "elocution," as 18th century writers still used it, to mean not "delivery," but everything pertaining to *diction*.

[2] He does not *name* these, and some have imagined the second to be ς: but this suits the context less, though there are difficulties both ways.

many things with us have no recognized names, so that we are
driven either to metaphor or to periphrasis; and even in those
things which have been named, our poverty of synonyms keeps us
in the same round, while *they* have a supply not merely of different
words, but even of different dialects.

Wherefore, if any shall demand from us Latins that famous
grace of the Attic eloquence, let him provide us with the same
attractive quality and an equally copious supply of vocabulary.
If this be refused us, we shall adjust our meaning to the words
we have, and not blend an excessive subtlety of matter with a
stoutness, not to say grossness, of words, lest the merits of both
disappear in the confusion. For, the less we are helped by our
language, the better fight we must make in originality of matter.
We must extract for ourselves meanings of sublimity and variety.
We must work on all the emotions, and lighten our style with
brilliant metaphor. We cannot have so much grace; let us excel
in strength. In subtlety we yield; but let us be weightier. *They*
can make surer of exact propriety; let *us* have the advantage of
fulness. The genius of the Greeks, even in its minor examples,
has ports open to it alone; let us spread, whenever we can, an
ampler canvas, and bid a mightier wind fill our sails. But we
must not always keep to the high seas — we must coast now and
then. *They* can glide here over any shallows; but *I* shall find a
channel, perhaps not so much deeper, in which my skiff will not
touch the bottom.

Nor if the Greeks manage these subtler and closer-hauled matters
better, and if in them alone[1] we must admit defeat — as, for instance,
we do not attempt to compete in comedy,— are we to give up even
this department altogether. We must do what we best can; and
we *can* be equal in judicious management of matter, while we
must supply our intrinsic lack of graceful words by seasonings from
outside.

Ibid. XII. x. 33–38.

[1] Others take *solo* as from *solum*, "on this ground."

XII. OTHER CLASSIFICATIONS OF STYLE

After divers remarks — among which occurs the all-important statement, containing the validation of the claims of the *Institutes* as a document of literary criticism, TO ME GOOD SPEAKING AND GOOD WRITING
APPEAR TO BE ONE AND THE SAME THING — Q. approaches his conclusion
thus :

There is yet another tripartite division, whereby the kinds, even
of good[1] speaking, may be distinguished.   For one is plain,[2] which
the Greeks call ἰσχνόν; another grand and robust, which they call
ἁδρόν; the third some call the mean between the two, others
" florid," from the Greek ἀνθηρόν.   (*The special uses of these various
kinds in oratory are then noted.*)
But style is by no means tied down to these three forms.   For
as there is a *tertium quid* between the " thin " and the " stout," so
there are subdivisions of these two, and blends and middle terms
of these subdivisions.   There is something more pregnant, and
something plainer, than the plain ; something slacker, and something
more forcible, than the forcible : as the level style either rises to
the sublimer or sinks to the plainer ranges.   And so there are
almost innumerable kinds, distinguished from each other by some
tendency ; just as we hold that the four winds blow generally from
four cardinal points, though there are many between them, and
some even peculiar to special places of land and water.   (*These, as
before, will all be suitable to the orator at one time or another.*)
For they are grossly deceived who think that the most popular
kind of speaking, and that likely to be most applauded, is a vicious
and corrupt style, which gives itself excessive licence of speech,
or wantons in puerile conceits, or is turgid with excessive bombast,
or revels in idle commonplaces, or glitters with flowers of speech
which fall at the lightest touch, or takes violence for sublimity, or
rants under the pretext of freedom.   That such styles do please
many I neither deny nor wonder. . . .   When anything said in a
manner out of the common falls on the ears of the uninstructed,

[1] Taking *etiam recte* with *dicendi*.   Others take it with *discerni*.

[2] Latin *subtile;* but among the many senses of this word "plain " is included,
and is here necessitated by the Greek.

no matter of what sort it be, provided that they cannot hope to do the like themselves, it has their admiration, nor undeservedly — for even to do this is not easy. But such things fade and die when compared with better. . . . Such light shines only this side of the sun. In fine, many approve what is bad, none disapproves what is good.

Ibid. XII. x. 58, 66–67, 73–76.

XI

A. GELLIUS ON VIRGIL'S "ETNA"

(This stricture, partly repeated almost verbatim in Macrobius, shows,
first, a criticism of definite *passages* not very common in the ancients, and,
secondly, that horror of the *excessive* which dominates "classical" criticism.
It forms Bk. xvii. ch. 10 of the *Noctes Atticæ*, a most interesting and constantly imitated miscellany of the middle second century after Christ.
(Gellius *fl. c.* 150; Macrobius *fl. c.* 400.))

I remember that the philosopher Favorinus,[1] when in the heat of
the year he had retired to his host's villa at Antium, and we had
come from Rome to see him, discussed Pindar and Virgil somewhat
in this way : " Virgil's friends and associates," said he, " in their
memorials of his genius and character, say that he was wont to
observe that he produced verses after the manner and fashion of a
she-bear.   For, as this beast produces its cub unformed and unfinished, and afterwards licks the product into shape and figure ; so
the results of his wits were at first rough-hewn and uncompleted,
but afterwards, by rehandling and fashioning them, he gave them
lineaments and countenance.   Now," said he, " the facts prove that
this quick-witted poet spoke with as much truth as frankness.
For those things which he left polished and perfected — those on
which he put the last touch of his censorship and his choice —
rejoice in the full praise of poetical loveliness ; but those of which
he postponed the recension, and which could not be finished owing
to the interposition of Death, are by no means worthy of the name
and judgment of this most elegant of poets.   And so, when he was in
the grasp of sickness, and felt the approach of death, he earnestly
begged and prayed of his dearest friends that they would burn the
Æneid, to which he had not yet sufficiently put the file.

[1] Favorinus, or Phavorinus, was a philosopher of Hadrian's time, who enjoyed
a great reputation, and was the friend not merely of Gellius, but of Plutarch,
Herodes Atticus, and other persons of distinction.   All his works are lost.

"Now among those passages which seem to have been most in need of rehandling and correction, that on Mount Etna holds the chief place. For, while he wished to vie with the verses of the old poet Pindar on the nature and eruptions of this mountain, he wrought such conceits and such phrases that in this place he has out-Pindared Pindar himself, who is generally thought to indulge in too exuberant and luxuriant rhetoric. To put you yourselves" (he continued) " in the position of judges, I will repeat, to the best of my memory, Pindar's verses on Etna. . . . (*The passage will be found in* Pyth. i. 40–50, *that which follows in* Æn. iii. 570 sqq.)

"Now listen to Virgil's verses, which I would rather call 'begun' than 'made.' . . .

"Now, in the first place," said he, "Pindar, paying more attention to truth, says what is the fact — what usually happens there and what is seen with eyes — that Etna smokes by day and flames by night; but Virgil, while he laboriously seeks out noisy sounding words, confuses the seasons without any distinction. And the Greek said clearly enough that fountains of fire belched from the bottom, and rivers of smoke flowed, and twisted yellow volumes of flame rolled to the shore of the sea, like fiery snakes. But this good man of ours, by choosing to interpret 'a burning stream of smoke' 'a black cloud smoking with pitchy gusts and [glowing] ashes,' has heaped things together coarsely and without moderation, and has harshly and inaccurately translated what the other called 'fountains' into 'globes' of flame. Again, when he says that it 'licks the stars,' he has made an empty and idle exaggeration. Moreover, what he says about the black cloud, etc., is indescribable, and almost incomprehensible. For things which glow are not usually black or smoking — unless he has very vulgarly and improperly used the word *candente* of ash merely hot, not fiery and shining. For *candens* is said of the brightness, not the heat. But as for the stones and the rocks being belched and flung up, and the very same ones anon being 'liquefied,' and groaning, and being 'conglomerated in air' — all this was neither written by Pindar nor ever heard in speech, and it is the most monstrous of all monstrosities,"

XII

BOETHÍUS (*c.* 470–*c.* 524 A.D.) ON POETRY

I have thought it worth while to give this short extract from the *De Consolatione,* not merely because the book itself was an oracle to the whole of the Dark and Middle Ages, but because it expresses a critical — or uncritical — view of literature proper, which was almost orthodox during that period, and which, derived ultimately from Plato and strongly supported by the Fathers of the Church, had to be seriously combated by the defenders of Letters at the Renaissance, from Boccaccio downwards. The passage is from nearly the beginning of the prose of the book. The philosopher actually starts with a poem which he represents as dictated to him by the Muses in his prison. Then appears Wisdom.

But when she saw the Muses of poetry standing by my couch, and dictating words to accompany my wailings, she was a little moved; and, flashing her eyes fiercely, "Who," cried she, "has permitted these wantons of the theatre to have access to this sick man; not to soothe his pains with any remedies, but to feed them with sweet poison? These are they who, with the barren thorns of passion, kill the fertile crop of reason's fruit, and do not free men's minds from disease, but familiarize them with it. Nay, if, as ye were wont, ye had deceived some profane one with your blandishments, I might take it less ill, for our business would suffer naught in him. But shall ye delude *this* man, nourished in Eleatic and Academic studies? Avaunt rather, ye Sirens ever sweet to destruction, and leave him to be nursed and healed by *my* Muses." Whereat the bevy, thus rebuked, cast their eyes sadly on the ground, and, confessing their shame by their blushes, sadly crossed the threshold.[1]

---

[1] Later (ii. Prose 1) Rhetoric fares a little, but only a little, better than Poetry. "Let there be present then," says Wisdom, "the persuasion of rhetorical sweetness, which then only goes in the right path, when it does not desert *my* laws."

XIII

DANTE (1265–1321)

DE VULGARI ELOQUIO

I. WHAT THE VULGAR TONGUE IS: AND OF ITS NOBILITY

But since it is for each branch of study, not to prove the existence of its subject, but to open and expound that subject, we say,
to cut the matter short, that what we call the Vulgar Tongue is that
to which infants, when they first begin to distinguish sounds, are
accustomed by those about them. Or, still more shortly, we call
that the Vulgar Tongue which, without any rules at all, we get by
imitating our nurses. We have also another secondary speech,
which the Romans called *grammatica*.[1] This secondary speech the
Greeks have, and others; but not all. Yet few come to familiarity
with this, because we can be schooled and disciplined in it only by
much time and assiduous study. Moreover, of these two the Vulgar
is the nobler, both because it was the first employed by the human
race, and because the whole world enjoys the use of it, though it be
divided into various speeches and vocabularies, and also because it
is natural to us, while the other is rather to be looked upon as
artificial. And of this nobler one it is our intention to treat.

Bk. I ch. i ll. 17–41, ed. Oxon.

---

[1] There is a certain difficulty — arising partly from the mention of *Græci et
alii* here, and partly from the comparison of this passage with others — in being
certain whether Dante means by this word simply "Latin," or the higher and
more literary form of *any* language, refined by study of "grammar" proper,
rhetoric, etc.

II. THE QUALITIES OF AN ILLUSTRIOUS VULGAR

After his general exordium, D. first sketches — rapidly, but with surprising accuracy, all things considering — the tongues of Europe generally, and then successively narrows his consideration to the Romance tongues, and of these to Italian. He next considers the Italian dialects at some length ; and decides that none of them — not even Tuscan — deserves the position of standard by itself, and as it is. And then he goes on :

Since we have hunted through the woods and fields of Italy without coming up with the panther[1] of our quest — let us, in order to find her, conduct the investigation in a more scientific manner, that by methodic effort we may thoroughly include in our nets the beast everywhere scented and everywhere[2] seen in glimpses. So, taking up our hunting gear again, we say that in every class of things there must be some one point by which all the members of the class are compared and weighed — and from this we take the common measure of all.   I. xvi. 1–12.

Some rather scholastic illustrations follow, and then he proceeds.

Now the noblest points of our Italian (" Latin ") sayings and doings are not the exclusive property of any Italian state, but common to all ; and among these we can now distinguish that Vulgar Tongue which we hunted above, the scent of which lies in every state, but her abiding lair in none. This may be more evident in one than in another, just as the pure Divine principle of being is more evident in a man than in a beast ; in an animal than in a plant ; in

[1] Many mysterious qualities and symbolisms were attributed by mediæval bestiaries to the panther ; but Dante here (save for his possible reference to its " sweet breath " below in *redolentem*) is probably only thinking of its *beauty* and *rarity*.

[2] I am as sure as I can be, on such a point, that Dr. Moore is right in extending the *ubique et ū* of the MSS. into the natural repetition of the first word. Dr. Rajna and others conjecture *necubi, nec usquam*, etc., so as to reverse the sense, " scented but not even glimpsed." This is neither necessary nor probable. D. does not say that the beast has never been *seen*, but that we have never " come up with it " — *adinvenimus*. His very argument below is that it *has* been seen — though obscurely and entangled in the crowd.

a plant than in a mineral; in a mineral than in fire; in fire than
in earth. . . .   And so, having caught what we sought, we say that
the Illustrious, Cardinal, Aulic,[1] and Curial Vulgar Tongue in Italy
("Latium") is that which belongs in reality to all Italian towns,
and in appearance to none — which is the measure, standard, and
point-of-comparison for all the municipal vernaculars of the country.

Ibid. l. 39–end.

III. THE APPLICATION OF THE ILLUSTRIOUS VULGAR TO POETRY

Having in his First Book established the existence and qualities of an
Illustrious Vernacular, Dante proceeds in his Second to examine its application to Italian Poetry with regard to Subject, Diction, and Metre.   On
the last head the remarks are necessarily of local and particular interest
chiefly.   Those in reference to the other two — but especially to Diction —
are of such far-reaching importance that a *catena* of the chief of them will
hardly yield to any piece in this book in that respect, if rightly considered.
Contrast, especially, the citations from Wordsworth *infra*.

We confess, first of all, that the Italian ("Latin") Illustrious
Vernacular is to be fitly employed both in prose and in verse.
But because it is more usual for prose-writers to take it from poets
[than vice versa]; and because poetry remains a standing example
to prose-writers and not the contrary, inasmuch as certain things
seem to give the primacy to verse — therefore let us shape our song
in connection with what is itself metrical [*i.e.,* "let us begin with
poetry"].   II. i. 3–12.

Wherefore, if suitability has respect to worth . . . it is clear
that good things will suit the worthy, better the worthier, and the
best the worthiest.   And since speech is not a less instrument to

---

[1] I prefer this to "Courtly," because the latter makes an apparent confusion
with "Curial," and because "Aulic" (in connection with "councillor," etc.) is
good recognized English for "belonging to the *Palace.*"   This Dante explains to
be his meaning, as he does that of *Curiale* to be "suitable to a Court of Justice,
and arrived at by judicial processes of balancing and selection."   "Cardinal"
it is, of course, as being the centre — the hinge — on which all the dialects turn ;
and "Illustrious" because of its beauty and dignity.

our thought than a horse is to a soldier, and as the best horses suit
the best soldiers, the best speech, as we have said, will suit the best
thoughts.   But thoughts cannot be best save where there is knowledge and wit; therefore, the best speech only suits those in whom
wit and knowledge are found.
                                                                    Ibid. 56–71.

After, in Chap. II, deciding that the best *subjects* are *salus*, *Venus*, *virtus*
(that is to say, Self-preservation (= Arms or War), Love, and Virtue in the
double sense of Philosophy and Religion) and in III allotting the order of
dignity in *form* to the *Canzone*, the *ballade*, and the sonnet, Dante proceeds
in IV *sq.* to explain the characteristics and constituents of the best poetry.

Poetry is nothing else than a rhetorical fiction musically
arranged.[1]
                                                                 II. iv. 19, 20.

Now we appear to use the tragic (*he has just explained this to
mean no more than "higher"*) style, when with Weight of Meaning[2] there accords as well Magnificence of Verse,[3] as Elevation of
Style,[4] and Excellence of Vocabulary.[5]

The Weightiest Meanings having been already indicated in the classi-
fication — Safety, Love, Virtue, — and the most Magnificent Verse having
been, in Chap. V, decided to be the *hendecasyllable* — actually the staple
Italian line, — Dante proceeds to Construction ("Style") and Diction.
Of the former he distinguishes four kinds, more easily recognizable in
themselves than in his Latin examples of them, while translation inevitably
puts these still more out of knowledge.   The four are, (1) The "insipid"
or "tasteless," which merely states matter with no art; (2) the "merely
tasteful," which arranges the expression in grammatical order of composition, but no more; (3) the "tasteful and elegant" (*venustus*), which
adds some rhetorical graces; and (4) the "tasteful, elegant, and elevated"
(*excelsus*), which belongs to real masters of style ("Illustrious dictionists"
—*dictatores*).   This last is to be sought for.   And then the matter of
the little treatise which is of general interest culminates in the following

---

[1] As is natural, some have wished to see in this a notion on Dante's part that
all poetry must be actually *sung*.   There is, however, not the slightest justification
for this in the context.   "Music" here clearly means "metrical harmony."
Cf., who will, the *Convito* I. vii.

[2] *Gravitas Sententiæ.*   [4] *Constructionis Elatio.*
[3] *Superbia Carminum.*   [5] *Excellentia Vocabulorum.*

monumental chapter on Poetic Diction — or, as it has been called, the "Chapter of the Sieve." Its own diction is sometimes rather hard to translate succinctly and satisfactorily; but its own conclusion is none the less surely justified, "Let what has been said suffice to a generous intelligence." It has, however, been thought permissible to annotate a little more freely than usual, in order to bring out the meaning.

The division of our progress next in order demands illustration of the proposition that only grand[1] words are worthy to hold office under exalted style. So let us protest, first of all, that it is by no means the least task of the reason to distinguish words, inasmuch as a great many varieties of them can be found. Some words are childish, some womanish, some manly; and of this latter class some are rustic ("sylvan"), some urban; and of those which we call urban, we feel some to be combed and slippery, some shaggy and rumpled.[2] Of these, the combed and the shaggy are those which we call grand; but the slippery and the rumpled are those which sound superfluously.[3] . . . You must therefore look to it, reader, how carefully it behoves you to sift words, in order to get together excellent ones. For if you consider the Illustrious Vernacular, which, as was said above, poets in the vulgar tongue must use when they write in a high style (*tragice, v. sup.*), you will only allow the noblest words to be left in your sieve. In which number you can by no means admit "childish" words, because of their familiarity, such as *mamma*[4] and *babbo, mate* and *pate;* nor "womanish" ones, because of their effeminacy, as *dolciada* and *placevole;* nor rustic

[1] *Grandiosa.* The somewhat unfavourable sense of this actual word in English does not necessarily exist in other languages, *e.g.*, French; but it seems better to avoid it here.

[2] So the MS. Some (whom I am rather surprised to find that Dr. Moore follows) twist the pairs, to suit what follows, reading *pexa et hirsuta, lubrica et reburra.* But surely there is no justification for this, even the apparent gain being unreal, while the first yoking is unintelligible. The terms were certainly in one case (*pexa*), and perhaps in others, already usitate. *Reburra* (*cf.* French *à rebours*) is "brushed or growing *the wrong way.*"

[3] This may seem odd for *lubrica* — but it probably signifies excess of mere sound *in either direction,* that of smoothness or that of roughness.

[4] It is necessary to keep the Italian words, because it is on their actual sound that D. lays most stress.

words, for their roughness, as *gregia*[1] and others ; nor the slippery and rumpled among urban words, as *femina* and *corpo*.   So you will see that only the combed and shaggy urban words remain to you — for these are the noblest, and are members of the Illustrious Vernacular.

Now we call those " combed " which are trisyllabic or very nearly so,[2] without aspirates, without acute or circumflexed accent, or double *z*'s and *x*'s, without the collocation of two liquids, or the position of a liquid immediately after a mute — and which leave the speaker's lips, as it were, with a certain sweetness, as *amore, donna, disio, virtute, donare, letizia, salute, securitate, difesa*.   And we call " shaggy " all words, besides these, which appear to be either necessary or ornamental constituents of the Illustrious Vernacular.   By " necessary," we mean those for which we cannot substitute others — monosyllables like *sì, vo, me*, etc., interjections, and many others. By " ornamental," we mean all polysyllables which when mixed with " combed " words make a beautifully harmonious conjunction, although they may have [the discords above mentioned].

Dante then adds instances, extending to the giant *sovramagnificentissima-mente*, and hints that he should have no objection even to *onorificabilitudinitate* (once in its Latin form dear to schoolboys !) if it were not actually *too* long for a hendecasyllabic line.   Of course his remarks, in the latter part of the above, are adjusted to the requirements of " beautiful words " *in Italian;* but the principle of the " beautiful word " itself applies, no less of course, to any language, and it is here laid down as it never had been before, and has seldom been since.

DANTE — APPENDIX

CRITICAL PASSAGES FROM OTHER WORKS

(These few and short passages are added because they have sometimes been thought to clash with, or at least to modify, the tenor of the *D. V. E.* They will mislead no one who remembers the *many-sidedness* of literature, and therefore of the criticism of literature, and they may be useful as a reminder of this.)

---

[1] For this Latin-Italian dislike to collocations with *r, v. sup.*, Quintilian, p. 70, on *fr.*   They are far from unpleasing to an English ear.

[2] *i.e.*, such as *donna*, where the play of the voice on the double *n* adds, and *letizia*, where the confluence of the *ia* subtracts. something like a syllable.

a. (*The Virtues of Latin.*) Latin is enduring and incorruptible —the vulgar tongue is unstable and corruptible. . . . Latin can express many conceptions which the vulgar tongue cannot. . . The vulgar tongue follows custom, Latin methodic rule.

Convito i. 5.

In this passage Dante promises the *D. V. E.*, but uses expressions given above which seem to conflict with the later book. The contradiction is, however, only superficial. He had evidently, at the time of writing the *Convito*, not fully elaborated his idea of the *Illustrious* Vernacular ; though, even here, he asserts " a natural love of our own tongue." The other commendations of Latin are *ad hoc* — special, not general.

After this he proceeds to show that, *for his actual purpose*, Latin would have been *un*suitable. And so the book which exalts Latin is written in the vernacular; the book which exalts the vernacular in Latin! Which things are an open allegory.

b. (*The Destructiveness of Translation.*) Moreover, be it known to all, that nothing harmonized by the laws of music (*v. sup., Definition of Poetry*) can be translated from its own tongue into another without breaking all its sweetness and harmony.

Ibid. i. 7.

c. (*Form and Letter.*) The exposition of the *letter* of the work is nothing but the setting forth of its form.

Taken from the highly scholastic remarks on the *Commedia* in the *Epistle to Can Grande* (ed. Moore, Epist. x. ll. 285–287), which, by the way, is not universally admitted as genuine.

d. (The *dolce stil nuovo.*) "I am one who note when Love inspires, and proceed to signify what he says within me." "O brother, now I see," said he, " the knot which restrained the Notary, and Guittone, and myself, from reaching the sweet new style that I hear. I perceive well how your pens go closely after the dictator, which certainly did not happen to (?) ours. And he who sets himself to look beyond (or to go beyond ?) sees no more from the one style to the other."

Purg. xxiv. 55–62.

This passage, in which the interlocutor is Bonagiunta of Lucca (who had written in the local dialect, not in the "Illustrious"), is complicated in its difficulty by various readings. I have followed here the text of Mr. A. J. Butler, and have not gone far from his translation — indeed, it is not easy to alter this while keeping to the Italian. *Dittator* is *probably* Love — but not, I think, necessarily; nor do I see, as I believe some have seen, an antidote to the (presumed) bane of the great praise of *words* in the *D. V. E.* Bonagiunta, I imagine, is simply admitting, in himself and the other predecessors of Dante, the old wish "to write better than you can" (*v. sup.* p. 69) — to be unnatural and distorted in conception, instead of expressing what naturally occurs to you in the best way possible. Those who do this, he says, lose their way between one style and the other, — "do not see from" this to that.

XIV

SELECTIONS FROM THE ITALIAN CRITICS OF THE SIXTEENTH CENTURY

The Italian critics of the 16th century, or at least of its three later quarters, founded criticism anew, and taught it to all Europe, though by no means as teachers who thoroughly understood what they taught, or even what they meant to teach. Accepted with almost implicit docility up to Milton's time, they gave way in the later 17th century to the far shallower school of French "neo-Classics," which was represented by Boileau; and, until quite recently, they have been very little studied. The first attempt at synoptic consideration of them was in Mr. Joel Elias Spingarn's *Literary Criticism in the Renaissance* (New York and London 1899); and the Fourth Book of the present editor's *History of Criticism* (vol. ii; Edinburgh 1902) is very mainly occupied with them. The original texts are unfortunately, in not a few cases, rather difficult of access.

A. VIDA (1527) ON THE NECESSITY OF STEALING

Come then, all ye youths ! and, careless of censure, give yourselves up to STEAL and drive the spoil from every source ! Unhappy is he (for such have often been found) who, rashly trusting to his own strength and art, as though in need of no external help, in his audacity refuses to follow the trustworthy footsteps of the ancients, abstaining, alas ! unwisely from plunder, and thinking to spare others. O vain superstition ! O care unhallowed by Phœbus ! Not long do such men prosper — often they outlive their own works, and, unpraised, lament their short-lived offspring before their own death, and living see the funeral of their fame. How [deeply] could they wish to have spared their idle labour and to have learnt other arts from their parents ! Often I love to play on ancient phrase, and utter some far other thought in the same words. Nor will any wise man care to blame my self-confessing thefts — thefts

85

open and to be praised and approved by our children's children.[1]
So far be it from me to wish to hide my stolen goods, and conceal
my plunder, from any fear of the penalty of infamy !

Poet. Lib. iii (vol. i pp. 178–179 in Pope's *Selecta
Poemata Italorum*, London 1740).

B. DANIELLO (1536). THE FUNCTIONS OF POETS AND POETRY

The Poet expresses, with all gravity and jucundity, many things
which the Philosopher is wont, in his disputations, to treat with
few and slight words.

Painting is a tacit and dumb Poetry ; Poetry, a speaking picture.
As the imitation of the painter is done with the stylus, and the
pencil, and a diversity of colours, so is that of the Poet with tongue
and pen, with numbers and harmonies.

I speak of mingling true things with false and feigned, because
the Poet is not bound, like the Historian, to describe things as
they actually are and have happened, but (to make them) such as
they *ought to have been.*[2]   *Poetica* pp. 19, 25, 41 (Venice 1536).

C. MINTURNO (1559). THE THREE FUNCTIONS OF THE POET

It will be the business of the poet so to speak in his verses that
he may teach, that he may delight, that he may *move.*[3]

De Poeta Lib. ii p. 102 (Venice 1559).

---

[1] Vida, to do him justice, was no false prophet. Nearly half a score generations, to all but the end of the 18th century, emphatically endorsed the
"Gospel of Plunder," from the Ancients, so unblushingly and enthusiastically
preached in these lines.

[2] These pronouncements are of course drawn straight from the ancients.
But they are important as appearing in one of the very earliest *Poetics* written
in any modern European vernacular.

[3] The two first of these *dicta* were hackneyed ever since Horace, if not
earlier — the last, if not exactly new, had seldom been formulated side by side
with them. It is of the greatest importance as embodying the Longinian
doctrine of "transport," *v. sup.*, but may have been directly suggested by
the remarks of Cicero and others on the function of the *orator*.

D. SCALIGER, J. C. (1561). THE CONNECTION OF THE POET AND HIS VERSE

The name of the poet is not, then, as men have thought, drawn from his being a "maker" in the sense of using fiction, but from his being a maker of verses.[1]   *Poet.* I. ii (p. 6, ed. 2, *s. l.* 1581).

E. CASTELVETRO (1570). THE THREE UNITIES

But it is evident that, in tragedy and in comedy, the plot ("Fable") contains one action only, or two that by their interdependence can be considered one . . . not because the fable itself is unsuited to contain more actions than one, but because the space of time, of twelve hours at most, in which the action is represented, and the strait limits of the place in which it is represented likewise, do not permit a multitude of actions.[2]

Poetica d' Aristotele, Part. Princ. iii, *Particell.* vi (p. 179, ed. 2, Basle 1576).

The five texts just given represent the trend of that "classic," or "neoclassic," criticism which was the principal and victorious element in the Italian writings. The next two give samples of those "thoughts of the morrow" which, neglected at the time, come to their own later.

F. CINTHIO GIRALDI (1554). THE LIBERTY OF ROMANCE

This may show that the laws given by Aristotle do not extend save to the poems which *are* concerned with a single action ; and

---

[1] On this immortal question, which Scaliger decides in his usual peremptory fashion, the Renaissance was no more at one than other times.

[2] There has been some controversy on the point whether Scaliger or Castelvetro is entitled to the first formulation of the hard and fast Trinity of Unities in Drama. I have no doubt that Castelvetro deserves the honour, or dishonour, whichever it be. But there is the further difficulty of deciding between the rather numerous passages in which Castelvetro himself necessarily (his book being not an original and substantive treatise, but a commentary on Aristotle) refers to the subject. I think the above is on the whole the most cardinal. It will be observed that the critic, instead of laying, as his author had laid, stress almost entirely on the Unity of *Action*, positively subordinates it to those of Time and Place, on the former of which A. had touched slightly, and on the latter not at all.

that all the poetic compositions which contain deeds of heroes (*e.g.*, *Romances*) are *not* included within the limits which A. has set to the poets who write single-action poems.[1]

> *Discorso dei Romanzi*, vol. i p. 26 of *Scritti Estetici di C. G.*,
> ed. Daelli (Milan 1864).

G. PATRIZZI (1586). "NOTHING *NECESSARILY* DEPENDS ON THE SUBJECT"

Let us pass to a universal and true conclusion — that the matter comprised in science, in art, in history, can be a convenient subject for poetry and poems PROVIDED THAT IT BE POETICALLY TREATED.[2]

> *Della Poetica, La Deca Disputata*, Lib. viii p. 175 (Ferrara 1586).

[1] This contention was urged by Cinthio (the famous novelist) with a special and limited object — that of freeing Ariosto, and the other Italian romance-writers, from the objections brought by severe "classical" censors. It evidently, however, contains the germ of a much wider and more audacious Declaration of Independence. "Kinds which the Ancients knew not, are free from the Ancients' laws."

[2] This bombshell, mine, Samson's tug, or whatever else it may be best called — at least from one point of view of the effect of an admission of its truth on the edifice of classical criticism reared by the skill of many great ones, for two thousand years and more, from Aristotle to Mr. Matthew Arnold — seems to have passed almost unnoticed at the time, and for long afterwards. It is even not quite clear whether Patrizzi (Patrici or Patricio) himself entirely realized its effect, and that of the *Deca Istoriale*, or historic survey of poetic products, which accompanied his *Deca Disputata*. But it must be quite clear, as well to those who agree with the opinion, as to those who do not, that the allowance of *any* subject "which can be poetically treated" makes the treatment, the form, and not the subject itself, the matter of first importance; while historical consideration tends to negative the doctrine of fixed kinds, in form itself. But for the moment the other was the winning side; and, when it came to be the losing, men like Cinthio and Patrizzi had been long forgotten and did not even then receive their due at once.

XV

SELECTIONS FROM THE EARLIER ELIZABETHAN CRITICS

A. WILSON (1553). AGAINST INKHORN TERMS [1]

Among all other lessons this should first be learned, that we never affect any strange inkhorn terms, but so speak as is commonly received; neither seeking to be overfine, nor yet living overcareless, using our speech as most men do, and ordering our wits as the fewest have done. Some seek so far for outlandish English, that they forget altogether their mothers' language. And I dare swear this, if some of their mothers were alive, they were not able to tell what they say; and yet these fine English clerks will say they speak in their mother tongue, if a man should charge them with counterfeiting the King's English. Some far-journeyed gentlemen, at their return home, like as they love to go in foreign apparel, so they will powder their talk with oversea language. He that cometh lately out of France will talk French-English, and never blush at the matter. Another chops in with English Italianated, and applieth the Italian phrase to our English speaking, the which is as if an orator that professeth to utter his mind in plain Latin, would needs speak poetry, and far-fetched colours of strange antiquity. The lawyer will store his stomach with the prating of pedlars. The auditor, in making his account and reckoning, cometh in with *sise sould* and *cater denere* for 6s 4d. The fine courtier will talk nothing but Chaucer. The mystical wise men and poetical clerks will speak nothing but quaint proverbs and blind allegories, delighting

---

[1] This setting of the face against anything like " precious " or unusual diction was the attitude alike of Wilson and his more famous friends Cheke and Ascham. It may be said to be the main characteristic of this, the earliest English critical school.

much in their own darkness, especially when none can tell what they do say. The unlearned or foolish fantastical that smells but of learning, (such fellows as have seen learned men in their days) will so Latin their tongues that the simple cannot but wonder at their talk, and think surely they speak by some revelation. I know them that think Rhetoric to stand wholly upon dark words, and he that can catch an inkhorn word by the tail, him they count to be a fine Englishman and a good rhetorician.

Art of Rhetorique, ed. 2, London 1563, fol. 82 *v.*–83 *r.*

B. GASCOIGNE (1575). NOTES ON VERSE MAKING

The first and most necessary point that ever I found meet to be considered, in making of a delectable poem, is this, to ground it upon some fine invention. For it is not enough to roll in pleasant words, nor yet to thunder in *Rym, ram, ruff,* by letter (quoth my master Chaucer) nor yet to abound in apt vocables or epithets, unless the invention have in it also *aliquid salis.* By this *aliquid salis* I mean some good and fine device, shewing the quick capacity of a writer; and where I say some *good and fine invention*, I mean that I would have it both fine and good. For many inventions are so superfine, that they are *Vix good.* And again many inventions are good, and yet not finely handed. . . .

If I should undertake to write in praise of a gentlewoman, I would neither praise her crystal eye, nor her cherry lip, etc. For these things are *trita et obvia.* . . .

Your invention being once devised, take heed that neither pleasure of rhyme nor variety of device, do carry you from it; for as to use obscure and dark phrases in a pleasant sonnet is nothing delectable, so to intermingle merry jests in a serious matter is an *Indecorum.*

Gascoigne then passes to the subject of Prosody proper, which it was high time to treat in English. He gives special caution against irregular verse and against inversion of accent such as Treasùre for Treasure — a fault very common in Wyatt and too common in Surrey. He laments, but admits, that English has been reduced to the iambic foot.

Commonly nowadays in English rhymes (for I dare not call them English verses [1]) we use none other order than a foot of two syllables, whereof the first is depressed or made short, and the second elevate or made long; and that sound or scanning continueth throughout the verse. We have used in times past other kinds of metres; as for example this following:

> No wight in the world, that wealth can attain,
> Unless he believe that all is but vain.

Also our father Chaucer hath used the same liberty in feet and measures that the Latinists do use. . . . And surely I can lament that we are fallen into such a plain and simple manner of writing that there is none other foot used but one. . . .

Unconscious of the coming salvation, through the drama, by the readmission of trisyllabic feet, Gascoigne, like a good patriot, tries to make the best of his actual Sparta, and gives very sensible cautions as to unnatural inversion of the order as well as of the accent of words, etc. He objects to polysyllables — it is curious that there has been a kind of see-saw in our history between this objection and the other to monosyllables —; exhorts men to beware of rhyme without reason; to be moderate in figures; not to hunt the letter [alliterate] to death; to eschew strange words but not be " too easy "; to keep English order and composition; to use but not abuse that " shrewd fellow " poetical licence. And then he delivers himself on the pause, in a passage which must be given at length because, though the opinion expressed hampers English poetry terribly, and was fortunately set aside by writers so different as Shakespeare and Milton, it infested English criticism for the greater part of the next two centuries and has found defenders — notably Dr. Guest — in the nineteenth.

There are also certain pauses or rests in a verse which may be called *caesures*, whereof I would be loath to stand long, since it is at discretion of the writer, and they have been first devised (as should seem) by the Musicians; but yet thus much I will adventure to write, that in mine opinion, in a verse of eight syllables, the pause will stand best in the midst; in a verse of ten it will best be placed at the end of the first four syllables; in a verse of twelve in the midst. In verse of twelve in the first and fourteen in the second,

---

[1] Apparently because the word would too much suggest *Latin* verses, with their licence of substitution.

we place the pause commonly in the midst of the first, and at the end of the first eight syllables in the second. In Rhythm Royal it is at the writer's discretion, and forceth not where the pause be until the end of the line.

Note that Gascoigne's opinion is sensibly mitigated by his allowance of " discretion " generally, and specially in rhyme royal, while the directions for " pausing" the Alexandrine and fourteener [" Poulter's measure "] come to little more than a recognition of the fact that this measure is much better arranged as the quatrain of six, six, eight, six. The rest of his little treatise is occupied with a short account of this and other stanzas, and of couplet measures, including " riding rhyme " — the Chaucerian couplet.

C. SIDNEY (1581 ?). APOLOGY FOR POETRY

THE ANTIQUITY AND NOBILITY OF POETRY[1]

I will give you a nearer example of myself, who (I know not by what mischance) in these my not old years and idlest times, having slipt into the title of a Poet, am provoked to say something unto you in the defence of that my unelected vocation; which if I handle with more good will than good reasons, bear with me, sith the scholar is to be pardoned that followeth the steps of his Master. And yet I must say, that as I have just cause to make a pitiful defence of poor Poetry, which, from almost the highest esti-mation of learning, is fallen to be the laughing-stock of children; so have I need to bring some more available proofs : sith the former is by no man barred of his deserved credit, the silly latter hath had even the names of Philosophers used to the defacing of it, with great danger of civil war among the Muses.

[1] These prologues of general defence of Poetry, against what we may call the Puritan-Platonic impeachments of it, were almost a regulation with the Italian critics. Sidney undoubtedly followed these ; though whether he is here so directly indebted to one in particular (Minturno) as Mr. Spingarn thinks, may be doubtful. This Italian influence and that classical one of the objection to the unusual word, with a belief in the Unities, etc., chequer curiously his romantic and poetic ardour, and are specially interesting as *preceding* the great poetic and dramatic burst which carried his spirit farther and dropped the letter of his cautions.

And first, truly to all them that professing learning inveigh against Poetry may justly be objected, that they go very near to ungratefulness, to seek to deface that, which in the noblest nations and languages that are known, hath been the first lightgiver to ignorance, and first Nurse, whose milk by little and little enabled them to feed afterwards of tougher knowledges : and will they now play the Hedgehog, that being received into the den, drave out his host ? or rather the Vipers, that with their birth kill their Parents ? Let learned Greece, in any of her manifold Sciences, be able to shew me one book before *Musæus, Homer,* and *Hesiodus:* all three nothing else but Poets. Nay, let any history be brought, that can say any Writers were there before them, if they were not men of the same skill, as *Orpheus, Linus,* and some others are named : who, having been the first of that Country that made pens deliverers of their knowledge to their posterity, may justly challenge to be called their Fathers in learning : for not only in time they had this priority (although in itself antiquity be venerable), but went before them as causes, to draw with their charming sweetness the wild untamed wits to an admiration of knowledge. So as *Amphion* was said to move stones with his Poetry to build Thebes ; and *Orpheus* to be listened to by beasts, indeed stony and beastly people : so among the Romans were *Livius Andronicus,* and *Ennius ;* so in the Italian language, the first that made it aspire to be a Treasurehouse of Science were the Poets *Dante, Boccace,* and *Petrarch ;* so in our English were *Gower* and *Chaucer.*

After whom, encouraged and delighted with their excellent foregoing, others have followed, to beautify our mother tongue, as well in the same kind as in other Arts. This did so notably shew itself, that the Philosophers of Greece durst not a long time appear to the world but under the masks of Poets. So *Thales, Empedocles, Parmenides* sang their natural Philosophy in verses : so did *Pythagoras* and *Phocylides* their moral counsels : so did *Tyrtæus* in war matters, and *Solon* in matters of policy : or rather, they being Poets did exercise their delightful vein in those points of highest knowledge, which before them lay hid to the world. For that wise *Solon* was directly a Poet it is manifest, having written in verse the notable fable of the Atlantic Island, which was continued by *Plato.*

And truly, even *Plato*, whosoever well considereth, shall find, that in the body of his work, though the inside and strength were Philosophy, the skin as it were and beauty depended most of Poetry; for all standeth upon Dialogues, wherein he feigneth many honest Burgesses of Athens to speak of such matters, that, if they had been set on the rack, they would never have confessed them. Besides, his poetical describing the circumstances of their meetings, as the well ordering of a banquet, the delicacy of a walk, with interlacing mere tales, as *Gyges'* Ring, and others, which who knoweth not to be flowers of Poetry did never walk into Apollo's Garden.

SACRED POETRY

Among the Romans a Poet was called *Vates*, which is as much as a Diviner, Fore-seer, or Prophet, as by his conjoined words *Vaticinium* and *Vaticinari* is manifest : so heavenly a title did that excellent people bestow upon this heart-ravishing knowledge. And so far were they carried into the admiration thereof, that they thought in the chanceable hitting upon any such verses great fore-tokens of their following fortunes were placed. Whereupon grew the word of *Sortes Virgilianæ*, when by sudden opening *Virgil's* book, they lighted upon any verse of his making : whereof the histories of the Emperors' lives are full : As of *Albinus* the Governor of our Island, who in his childhood met with this verse :

Arma amens capio nec sat rationis in armis:

and in his age performed it. Which although it were a very vain and godless superstition, as also it was to think that spirits were commanded by such verses, — whereupon this word charms, derived of *Carmina*, cometh, — so yet serveth it to shew the great reverence those wits were held in. And altogether not without ground, since both the Oracles of *Delphos* and *Sibylla's* prophecies were wholly delivered in verses. For that same exquisite observing of number and measure in words, and that high flying liberty of conceit proper to the Poet, did seem to have some divine force in it.

And may not I presume a little further, to shew the reasonable-ness of this word *Vates?* And say that the holy *David's* Psalms are a divine Poem? If I do, I shall not do it without the testimony of great learned men, both ancient and modern. But even the name Psalms will speak for me, which, being interpreted, is nothing but songs: then that it is fully written in metre as all learned Hebricians agree, although the rules be not yet fully found: lastly and principally, his handling his prophecy, which is merely poetical. For what else is the awaking his musical instruments; the often and free changing of persons; his notable *Prosopopœias*, when he maketh you as it were, see God coming in his Majesty; his telling of the Beasts' joyfulness, and hills leaping, but a heavenly poesy, wherein almost he sheweth himself a passionate lover of that unspeakable and everlasting beauty to be seen by the eyes of the mind, only cleared by faith? But truly now having named him, I fear me I seem to profane that holy name, applying it to Poetry, which is among us thrown down to so ridiculous an estimation: but they that with quiet judgments will look a little deeper into it, shall find the end and working of it such, as, being rightly applied, deserveth not to be scourged out of the Church of God.

LYRIC

Is it the Lyric that most displeaseth, who with his tuned Lyre, and well accorded voice, giveth praise, the reward of virtue, to virtuous acts; who gives moral precepts, and natural Problems; who sometimes raiseth up his voice to the height of the heavens, in singing the lauds of the immortal God? Certainly I must confess my own barbarousness, I never heard the old song of *Percy* and *Douglas*, that I found not my heart moved more than with a Trumpet: and yet is it sung but by some blind Crowder, with no rougher voice than rude style: which being so evil apparelled in the dust and cobwebs of that uncivil age, what would it work trimmed in the gorgeous eloquence of *Pindar?* In *Hungary* I have seen it the manner at all Feasts, and other such meetings, to have songs of their Ancestors' valour; which that right Soldier-like Nation thinks the chiefest kindlers of brave courage. The incomparable *Lacedæmonians* did not only carry that kind of Music ever with them to the field; but even at home, as such songs were made, so were they all content to be the singers of them, when the lusty men were to tell what they did, the old men what they had done, and the young men what they would do. And where a man may say, that *Pindar* many times praiseth highly victories of small moment, matters rather of sport than virtue : as it may be answered, it was the fault of the Poet, and not of the Poetry ; so indeed the chief fault was in the time and custom of the Greeks, who set those toys at so high a price, that *Philip* of *Macedon* reckoned a horse-race won at *Olympus* among his three fearful felicities. But as the inimitable *Pindar* often did, so is that kind most capable and most fit to awake the thoughts from the sleep of idleness, to embrace honourable enterprises.

ENGLISH POETRY AND DRAMA

Chaucer undoubtedly did excellently in his *Troilus* and *Cressid;* of whom, truly I know not, whether to marvel more, either that he, in that misty time, could see so clearly, or that we, in this clear age, walk so stumblingly after him. Yet had he great wants, fit to be forgiven in so reverent antiquity. I account the *Mirror of Magistrates* meetly furnished of beautiful parts ; and in the Earl of Surrey's *Lyrics* many things tasting of a noble birth, and worthy of a noble mind. The *Shepherd's Kalendar* hath much Poetry in his Eglogues : indeed worthy the reading if I be not deceived. That same framing of his style to an old rustic language I dare not allow, sith neither *Theocritus* in Greek, *Virgil* in Latin, nor *Sannazar* in Italian, did affect it. Besides these, do I not remember to have seen but few (to speak boldly) printed, that have poetical sinews in them. For proof whereof let but most of the verses be put in Prose, and then ask the meaning ; and it will be found, that one verse did but beget another, without ordering at the first what should be at the last : which becomes a confused mass of words, with a tingling sound of rhyme, barely accompanied with reason.

Our Tragedies, and Comedies (not without cause cried out against), observing rules neither of honest civility nor of skilful Poetry, excepting *Gorboduc* (again, I say, of those that I have seen), which notwithstanding, as it is full of stately speeches and well sounding

Phrases, climbing to the height of *Seneca* his style, and as full of notable morality, which it doth most delightfully teach, and so obtain the very end of Poesy; yet in truth it is very defectious in the circumstances: which grieveth me, because it might not remain as an exact model of all Tragedies. For it is faulty both in Place and Time, the two necessary companions of all corporal actions. For where the stage should always represent but one place, and the uttermost time presupposed in it should be, both by *Aristotle's* precept and common reason, but one day: there is both many days, and many places, inartificially imagined. But if it be so in *Gorboduc*, how much more in all the rest? where you shall have *Asia* of the one side, and *Afric* of the other, and so many other under-kingdoms, that the Player, when he cometh in, must ever begin with telling where he is; or else, the tale will not be conceived. Now ye shall have three Ladies walk to gather flowers, and then we must believe the stage to be a Garden. By and by, we hear news of shipwreck in the same place, and then we are to blame, if we accept it not for a Rock. Upon the back of that, comes out a hideous Monster, with fire and smoke, and then the miserable beholders are bound to take it for a Cave. While in the meantime, two Armies fly in, represented with four swords and bucklers, and then what hard heart will not receive it for a pitched field?

Now, of time they are much more liberal. For ordinary it is that two young Princes fall in love: after many traverses, she is got with child, delivered of a fair boy; he is lost, groweth a man, falls in love, and is ready to get another child, and all this in two hours' space: which how absurd it is in sense, even sense may imagine, and Art hath taught, and all ancient examples justified: and at this day, the ordinary Players in Italy will not err in. Yet will some bring in an example of *Eunuchus* in *Terence*, that containeth matter of two days, yet far short of twenty years. True it is, and so was it to be played in two days, and so fitted to the time it set forth. And though *Plautus* hath in one place done amiss, let us hit with him, and not miss with him.

But they will say, how then shall we set forth a story, which containeth both many places, and many times? And do they not know, that a Tragedy is tied to the laws of Poesy, and not of History? not bound to follow the story, but having liberty, either to feign a quite new matter, or to frame the history to the most tragical conveniency. Again, many things may be told which cannot be shewed, if they know the difference betwixt reporting and representing. As for example, I may speak (though I am here) of *Peru*, and in speech digress from that to the description of *Calicut:* but in action, I cannot represent it without *Pacolet's* horse : and so was the manner the Ancients took, by some *Nuncius* to recount things done in former time, or other place.

Lastly, if they will represent an history, they must not (as *Horace* saith) begin *Ab ovo:* but they must come to the principal point of that one action, which they will represent. By example this will be best expressed. I have a story of young *Polydorus* delivered for safety's sake, with great riches, by his Father *Priamus* to *Polymnestor* king of *Thrace*, in the Troyan war time. He after some years, hearing the overthrow of *Priamus*, for to make the treasure his own, murdereth the child : the body of the child is taken up by *Hecuba;* she the same day findeth a sleight to be revenged most cruelly of the Tyrant. Where now would one of our Tragedy writers begin, but with the delivery of the child? Then should he sail over into *Thrace*, and so spend I know not how many years and travel numbers of places. But where doth *Euripides?* Even with the finding of the body, leaving the rest to be told by the spirit of *Polydorus*. This need no further to be enlarged, the dullest wit may conceive it.

But besides these gross absurdities, how all their Plays be neither right Tragedies, nor right Comedies: mingling Kings and Clowns, not because the matter so carrieth it: but thrust in Clowns by head and shoulders, to play a part in majestical matters, with neither decency nor discretion. So as neither the admiration and commiseration, nor the right sportfulness, is by their mongrel Tragicomedy obtained. I know *Apuleius* did somewhat so, but that is a thing recounted with space of time, not represented in one moment: and I know, the Ancients have one or two examples of Tragicomedies, as *Plautus* hath *Amphitryo*. But if we mark them well, we shall find that they never, or very daintily, match

Hornpipes and Funerals. So falleth it out, that, having indeed no right Comedy, in that comical part of our Tragedy we have nothing but scurrility, unworthy of any chaste ears: or some extreme shew of doltishness indeed fit to lift up a loud laughter and nothing else: where the whole tract of a Comedy should be full of delight, as the Tragedy should be still maintained in a well raised admiration.

But our Comedians think there is no delight without laughter: which is very wrong, for though laughter may come with delight, yet cometh it not of delight, as though delight should be the cause of laughter. But well may one thing breed both together. Nay, rather in themselves they have as it were a kind of contrariety: for delight we scarcely do, but in things that have a conveniency to ourselves or to the general nature: laughter almost ever cometh of things most disproportioned to ourselves and nature. Delight hath a joy in it, either permanent or present. Laughter hath only a scornful tickling. For example, we are ravished with delight to see a fair woman, and yet are far from being moved to laughter. We laugh at deformed creatures, wherein certainly we cannot delight. We delight in good chances, we laugh at mischances; we delight to hear the happiness of our friends or Country, at which he were worthy to be laughed at, that would laugh; we shall contrarily laugh sometimes, to find a matter quite mistaken and go down the hill against the bias, in the mouth of some such men, as for the respect of them, one shall be heartily sorry, yet he cannot choose but laugh; and so is rather pained, than delighted with laughter. Yet deny I not, but that they may go well together; for as in *Alexander's* picture well set out, we delight without laughter, and in twenty mad Antics we laugh without delight: so in *Hercules*, painted with his great beard and furious countenance, in woman's attire, spinning at *Omphale's* commandment, it breedeth both delight and laughter. For the representing of so strange a power in love procureth delight: and the scornfulness of the action stirreth laughter.

But I speak to this purpose, that all the end of the comical part be not upon such scornful matters, as stirreth laughter only: but, mixt with it, that delightful teaching which is the end of Poesy.

And the great fault even in that point of laughter, and forbidden plainly by *Aristotle*, is, that they stir laughter in sinful things; which are rather execrable than ridiculous : or in miserable, which are rather to be pitied than scorned.   For what is it to make folks gape at a wretched Beggar, or a beggarly Clown ; or, against law of hospitality, to jest at strangers, because they speak not English so well as we do ?   What do we learn ?   Sith it is certain

> Ni habet infelix paupertas durius in se,
> Quam quod ridiculos homines facit.

But rather a busy loving Courtier, a heartless threatening *Thraso;* a self-wise-seeming schoolmaster; an awry-transformed Traveller : these if we saw walk in stage names, which we play naturally, therein were delightful laughter, and teaching delightfulness : as in the other, the Tragedies of *Buchanan* do justly bring forth a divine admiration.   But I have lavished out too many words of this play matter.   I do it because, as they are excelling parts of Poesy, so is there none so much used in England, and none can be more pitifully abused.   Which like an unmannerly Daughter, shewing a bad education, causeth her mother Poesy's honesty to be called in question.

D. PUTTENHAM (?) (after **1584**, licensed **1588**)

A SURVEY OF ENGLISH POETRY [1]

It appeareth by sundry records of books both printed and written, that many of our countrymen have painfully travailed in this part; of whose works some appear to be but bare translations, other some matters of their own invention and very commendable, whereof some recital shall be made in his place, to the intent chiefly that their names should not be defrauded of such honour as seemeth due to them for having, by their thankful studies, so much beautified

---

[1] The *Art of English Poesy*, which appeared in 1589, is anonymous, but is usually attributed to George Puttenham.   Whoever wrote it, it is an interesting and (with some crotchets and deficiencies) a sensible book, being, moreover, much fuller than any other up to its time.   This passage is perhaps (*v. inf.*) the first attempt, certainly the best early attempt, to survey the subject historically, and slips may therefore be easily pardoned in it.

our English tongue, as at this day it will be found our nation is in nothing inferior to the French or Italian for copy of language, subtlety of device, good method and proportion in any form of poem, but that they may compare with the most, and perchance pass a great many of them. And I will not reach above the time of King Edward III, and Richard II, for any that wrote in English metre; because before their times, by reason of the late Norman Conquest, which had brought into this realm much alteration both of our language and laws, and therewithal a certain martial barbarousness whereby the study of all good learning was so much decayed, as long time after no man or very few entended [*i.e.,* "understood"] how to write in any laudable science; so as beyond that time there is little or nothing worth commendation to be found written in this art.

And those of the first age were Chaucer and Gower, both of them as I suppose, knights. After whom followed John Lydgate the Monk of Bury; and that nameless who wrote the Satire called *Piers Plowman.* Next him followed Harding the chronicler: then in King Henry VIII's time Skelton (I wot not for what great worthiness) surnamed the Poet Laureate. In the latter part of the same king's reign sprung up a new company of courtly makers, of whom Sir Thomas Wyatt the elder, and Henry, Earl of Surrey, were the two chieftains. Who having travelled into Italy, and there tasted the sweet and stately measures and style of the Italian poesy, as novices newly crept out of the school of Dante, Ariosto, and Petrarch, they greatly polished our rude and homely manner of vulgar Poesy from that it had been before, and for that case may justly be said the first reformers of our English metre and style. In the same time, or not long after, was the Lord Nicholas Vaux, a man of much facility in vulgar makings. Afterward in King Edward VI's time came to be in reputation, for the same faculty, Thomas Sternhold, who first translated into English certain psalms of David, and John Heywood the epigrammatist, who, for the mirth and quickness of his conceits, more than for good learning that was in him, came to be well benefited by the king. But the principal man in this profession at the same time was Master Edward Ferris, a man of no less mirth and felicity that way, but of much more skill and magnificence in his metre, and therefore wrote for the most part to the stage in Tragedy and sometimes in Comedy or Interlude, wherein he gave the king so much good recreation, as he had thereby many good rewards.   In Queen Mary's time flourished above any other Dr. Phaer, one that was well learned and excellently well translated into English verse heroical certain books of Virgil's *Æneidos*.   Since him followed Master Arthur Golding, who with not less commendation, turned into English metre the *Metamorphosis* of Ovid ; and that other Doctor who made the supplement to those books of Virgil's *Æneidos* which Master Phaer left undone. And in Her Majesty's time that now is are sprung up another crew of courtly makers, Noblemen and gentlemen of Her Majesty's own servants, who have written excellently well : as it would appear if their doings could be found out and made public with the rest. Of which number is first that noble gentleman Edward, Earl of Oxford, Thomas, Lord of Buckhurst, when he was young, Henry, Lord Paget, Sir Philip Sydney, Sir Walter Raleigh, Master Edward Dyer, Master Fulk Greville, Gascoigne ["Gascon"], Breton ["Britton"], Turberville, and a great many other learned gentlemen whose names I do not omit for envy, but to avoid tediousness, and who have deserved no little commendation.

But of them all particularly this is mine opinion, that Chaucer, with Gower, Lydgate, and Harding for their antiquity, ought to have the first place : and Chaucer as the most renowned of them all for the much learning that appeareth to be in him above any of the rest.   And though many of his books be but bare translations out of the Latin and French, yet are they well handled, as his books of *Troilus and Cressid*, and the *Romaunt of the Rose* whereof he translated but one half (the device was John of Meun's a French poet).   The *Canterbury Tales* were Chaucer's own invention, I suppose, and [w]here he sheweth more the natural of his pleasant wit, than in any other of his works ; his similitudes, or comparisons, and all other descriptions are such as cannot be amended.   His metre heroical of *Troilus and Cressid* is very grave and stately, keeping the staff of seven, and the verse of ten ; his other verses of the *Canterbury Tales* be but riding rhyme, nevertheless very well becoming the matter of that pleasant pilgrimage in which every man's part is played with much decency. Gower, saving for his good and grave moralities, had nothing in him highly to be commended, for his verse was homely and without good measure, his words strained muchdeal out of the French writers, his rhyme wrested, and his inventions small subtlety. The applications of his moralities are the best in him; and yet those many times very grossly bestowed, neither doth the substance of his works sufficiently answer the subtlety of his titles. Lydgate, a translator only and no deviser of that which he wrote, but one that wrote in good verse. Harding, a poet epic or historical, handled himself well according to the time and manner of his subject. He that wrote the satire of *Piers Plowman*, seemed to have been a malcontent of that time, and therefore bent himself wholly to tax the disorders of that age, and specially the pride of the Roman clergy, of whose fall he seemeth to be a very true prophet. His verse is but loose metre, and his terms hard and obscure, so as in them is little pleasure to be taken. Skelton, a sharp satirist, but with more railing and scoffery than became a Poet Laureate; such among the Greeks were called *Pantomimi*, with us buffoons, altogether applying their wits to scurrilities, and other ridiculous matters. Henry, Earl of Surrey, and Sir Thomas Wyatt, between whom I find very little difference, I repute them as before, for the two chief lanterns of light to all others, that have since employed their pens upon English Poesy. Their conceits were lofty, their styles stately, their conveyance cleanly, their terms proper, their metre sweet and well proportioned, in all imitating very naturally and studiously their master, Francis Petrarcha. The Lord Vaux his commendation lieth chiefly in the facility of his metre, and the aptness of his descriptions such as he taketh upon him to make, namely in sundry of his songs, wherein he sheweth the counterfeit action very lively and pleasantly.

Of the later sort I think thus — That for Tragedy, the Lord of Buckhurst and Master Edward Ferris, for such doings as I have seen of theirs do deserve the highest price; the Earl of Oxford and Master Edwards of Her Majesty's Chapel for Comedy and Interlude. For eclogue and pastoral poesy, Sir Philip Sydney and Master Chaloner, and that other gentleman who wrote the late *Shepherd's*

Calendar. For ditty and amorous ode I find Sir Walter Raleigh's vein most lofty, insolent, and passionate; Master Edward Dyer for elegy most sweet, solemn, and of a high conceit; Gascoigne for a good metre and for a plentiful vein; Phaer and Golding for a learned and well corrected verse, specially in translation clear and very faithfully answering their authors' intent. Others have also written with much facility, but more commendably perchance if they had not written so much nor so popularly. But last in recital and first in degree is the Queen our Sovereign Lady, whose learned, delicate, noble Muse easily surmounteth all the rest that have written before her time or since, for sense, sweetness, and subtlety, be it in Ode, Elegy, Epigram, or any other kind of poem heroic or lyric, wherein it shall please her Majesty to employ her pen, even by as much odds as her own excellent estate and degree exceedeth all the rest of her most humble vassals.

Art of English Poesy, Bk. I ch. xxxi.

<h3 style="text-align:center">E. WEBBE (1586)</h3>

<h4 style="text-align:center">SPENSER [1]</h4>

Wherefore I doubt not equally to adjoin the authority of our late famous English poet, who wrote the *Shepherd's Calendar*, where, lamenting the decay of poetry, at these days, he saith most sweetly to the same —

> Then make thee wings of thine aspiring wit,
> And whence thou camest fly back to Heaven apace, etc.

Whose fine poetical wit, and most exquisite learning, as he showed abundantly in that piece of work, in my judgment inferior neither to the works of Theocritus in Greek, or Virgil in Latin, whom he narrowly imitateth; so I nothing doubt, but if his other works were common abroad, which are I think in the close custody of certain his friends, we should have of our own poets, whom we might match in all respects with the best. And among other his works whatsoever, I would wish to have the sight of his *English*

---

[1] These are only specimens of Webbe's enthusiasm for Spenser, to whom he returns again and again.

Poet, which his friend "E. K." did once promise to publish, which whether he performed or not, I know not. If he did, my hap hath not been so good as yet to see it.[1]   *Discourse* p. 23, ed. Arber.

This place have I purposely reserved for one, who if not only, yet in my judgment principally, deserveth the title of the rightest English Poet that ever I read; that is, the author of the *Shepherd's Calendar*, intitled to the worthy gentleman Master Philip Sydney. Whether it was Master Sp. or what rare scholar in Pembroke Hall soever, because himself and his friends, for what respect I know not, would not reveal it, I force not greatly to set down. Sorry I am that I cannot find none other with whom I might couple him in this catalogue, in his rare gift of Poetry; although one there is, though now long since seriously occupied in graver studies (Master Gabriel Harvey). Yet as he was once his most special friend and fellow-poet, so because he hath taken such pains, not only in his Latin poetry, for which he enjoyed great commendations of the best both in judgment and dignity in this realm, but also to reform our English verse, and beautify the same with brave devices, of which I think the chief lie hid in hateful obscurity; therefore will I adventure to set them together as two of the rarest wits and learnedest masters of Poetry in England. Whose worthy and notable skill in this faculty, I would wish, if their high dignities and serious businesses would permit, they would still grant to be a furtherance to that reformed kind of poetry, which Master Harvey did once begin to ratify. And surely in mine opinion, if he had chosen some graver matter and handled with but half the skill which I know he could have done, and not poured it forth at a venture as a thing between jest and earnest, it had taken greater effect than it did. For the other gentleman, if it would please him and his friends to let those excellent poems whereof I know he hath plenty, come abroad, as his *Dreams*, his *Legends*, his *Court of Cupid*, his *English Poet*, with other, he should not only stay the rude pens of myself and others, but also satisfy the thirsty desires of many which desire nothing more than to see more of his rare inventions.   *Ibid.* pp. 35, 36.

---

[1] Neither, alas! hath the hap of posterity been better.

AGAINST RHYME[1]

I know no memorable work written by any Poet in our English speech, until twenty years past; where, although learning was not generally decayed at any time, . . . yet surely that Poetry was in small price among them it is very manifest and no great marvel. For even that light of Greek and Latin poets which they had, they much contemned as appeareth by their rude versifying, which of long time was used (a barbarous use it was!) wherein they converted the natural property of the sweet Latin verse, to be a bald kind of rhyming, thinking nothing to be learnedly written in verse, which fell not out in rhyme — that is, in words whereof the middle word of each verse should sound alike with the last, or, of two verses, the end of both should fall in the like letters as this:

(*Examples of Leonine and other rhyming in Latin given*)

This brutish poetry, though it had not the beginning in this country, yet so hath it been affected here, that the affection thereof would never — nor, I think, ever will — be rooted up again: — I mean this tinkerly verse which we call rhyme. Master Ascham saith, that it first began to be followed and maintained among the Huns and Gothians, and other barbarous nations, who, with the decay of all good learning, brought it into Italy. From thence it came into France, and so to Germany, at last conveyed into England by men, indeed of great wisdom and learning, but not considerate nor circumspect in that behalf.

Ibid. p. 30.

---

[1] Webbe follows this outburst (to be accounted for in him and others by their fancy for the doggerel "classical metres" which certain Cambridge scholars, Watson, Drant, and Ascham himself, had let loose on English) with a not very well-informed survey (which appeared before Puttenham's), placing (as indeed Puttenham had done) *Piers Plowman* after Lydgate, complimenting Lydgate himself on the superiority of his style to his matter, etc.

XVI

BEN JONSON

(The *general* critical position of Jonson rests not so much on the Italians — though partly on them — as on the classical originals of Italian teaching, especially the Latins of the Silver Age. He is thus distinctly "neo-classic" in general tone, but his intensely English idiosyncrasy causes important variations. That he is the first *great* English critic is scarcely matter of opinion. The best edition of his *Discoveries* (from which the following passages are taken) is the separate one of Professor Schelling of Philadelphia: but the Latin headings which are given here will identify the passages (in the absence of a very desirable numbering) in any edition.)

ELOQUENTIA

Eloquentia. — Eloquence is a great and diverse thing: nor did she yet ever favour any man so much as to become wholly his. He is happy that can arrive to any degree of her grace. Yet there are who prove themselves masters of her, and absolute lords; but I believe they may mistake their evidence: for it is one thing to be eloquent in the schools, or in the hall; another at the bar, or in the pulpit. There is a difference between mooting and pleading; between fencing and fighting. To make arguments in my study, and confute them, is easy; where I answer myself, not an adversary. So I can see whole volumes dispatched by the umbratical doctors [1] on all sides. But draw these forth into the just lists; let them appear *sub dio*, and they are changed with the place, like bodies bred in the shade; they cannot suffer the sun or a shower, nor bear the open air; they scarce can find themselves, that they were wont to domineer so among their auditors: but indeed I would no more choose a rhetorician for reigning in a school, than I would a pilot for rowing in a pond.

[1] The "private teacher" of Petronius, *v. sup.*, p. 60.

CENSURA DE POETIS

(cum seq.)

Censura de poetis. — Nothing in our age, I have observed, is more preposterous than the running judgments upon poetry and poets; when we shall hear those things commended and cried up for the best writings which a man would scarce vouchsafe to wrap any wholesome drug in: he would never light his tobacco with them. And those men almost named for miracles, who yet are so vile that if a man should go about to examine and correct them, he must make all they have done but one blot. Their good is so entangled with their bad as forcibly one must draw on the other's death with it. A sponge dipped in ink will do all:

> Comitetur Punica librum
> Spongia.

Et paulo post,

> Non possunt . . . multæ,
> . . . . . una litura potest.

Yet their vices have not hurt them; nay, a great many they have profited, for they have been loved for nothing else. And this false opinion grows strong against the best men, if once it take root with the ignorant. Cestius, in his time, was preferred to Cicero, so far as the ignorant durst. They learned him without book, and had him often in their mouths; but a man cannot imagine that thing so foolish or rude but will find and enjoy an admirer; at least a reader or spectator. The puppets are seen now in despite of the players; Heath's epigrams and the Sculler's poems have their applause. There are never wanting that dare prefer the worst preachers, the worst pleaders, the worst poets; not that the better have left to write or speak better, but that they that hear them judge worse; *Non illi pejus dicunt, sed hi corruptius judicant.* Nay, if it were put to the question of the water-rimer's works, against Spenser's, I doubt not but they would find more suffrages; because the most favour common vices, out of a prerogative the vulgar have to lose their judgments and like that which is naught.

Poetry, in this latter age, hath proved but a mean mistress to such as have wholly addicted themselves to her, or given their names up to her family. They who have but saluted her on the by, and now and then tendered their visits, she hath done much for, and advanced in the way of their own professions — both the law and the gospel — beyond all they could have hoped or done for themselves without her favour. Wherein she doth emulate the judicious but preposterous bounty of the time's grandees, who accumulate all they can upon the parasite or fresh-man in their friendship; but think an old client or honest servant bound by his place to write and starve.

Indeed, the multitude commend writers as they do fencers or wrestlers, who, if they come in robustiously and put for it with a deal of violence, are received for the braver fellows; when many times their own rudeness is a cause of their disgrace, and a slight touch of their adversary gives all that boisterous force the foil. But in these things the unskilful are naturally deceived, and judging wholly by the bulk, think rude things greater than polished, and scattered more numerous than composed. Nor think this only to be true in the sordid multitude, but the neater sort of our gallants; for all are the multitude, only they differ in clothes, not in judgment or understanding.

DE SHAKESPEARE NOSTRAT.

De Shakespeare nostrat. — I remember the players have often mentioned it as an honour to Shakespeare, that in his writing, whatsoever he penned, he never blotted out a line. My answer hath been, " Would he had blotted a thousand," which they thought a malevolent speech. I had not told posterity this but for their ignorance, who chose that circumstance to commend their friend by wherein he most faulted; and to justify mine own candour, for I loved the man, and do honour his memory, on this side idolatry, as much as any. He was, indeed, honest, and of an open and free nature; had an excellent fancy, brave notions, and gentle expressions, wherein he flowed with that facility that sometime it was necessary he should be stopped. "*Sufflaminandus erat*," as Augustus said of Haterius. His wit was in his own power; would the rule of it had been so too. Many times he fell into those things, could not escape laughter, as when he said in the person of Cæsar, one speaking to him : "Cæsar, thou dost me wrong." He replied : "Cæsar did never wrong but with just cause"; and such like, which were ridiculous. But he redeemed his vices with his virtues. There was ever more in him to be praised than to be pardoned.

INGENIORUM DISCRIMINA

Ingeniorum discrimina. — It cannot but come to pass that these men who commonly seek to do more than enough may sometimes happen on something that is good and great; but very seldom : and when it comes it doth not recompense the rest of their ill. For their jests, and their sentences, which they only and ambitiously seek for, stick out, and are more eminent, because all is sordid and vile about them ; as lights are more discerned in a thick darkness than a faint shadow. Now, because they speak all they can, however unfitly, they are thought to have the greater copy; where the learned use ever election and a mean, they look back to what they intended at first, and make all an even and proportioned body. The true artificer will not run away from Nature as he were afraid of her, or depart from life and the likeness of truth, but speak to the capacity of his hearers. And though his language differ from the vulgar somewhat, it shall not fly from all humanity, with the *Tamerlanes* and *Tamer-chams* of the late age, which had nothing in them but the scenical strutting and furious vociferation to warrant them to the ignorant gapers. He knows it is his only art so to carry it, as none but artificers perceive it. In the mean time, perhaps, he is called barren, dull, lean, a poor writer, or by what contumelious word can come in their cheeks, by these men who, without labour, judgment, knowledge, or almost sense, are received or preferred before him. He gratulates them and their fortune. An other age, or juster men, will acknowledge the virtues of his studies, his wisdom in dividing, his subtlety in arguing, with what strength he doth inspire his readers, with what sweetness he strokes them; in inveighing, what sharpness; in jest, what urbanity he uses; how he doth reign in men's affections; how invade and break in upon them, and make their minds like the thing he writes. Then in his elocution to behold what word is proper, which hath ornament, which height, what is beautifully translated, where figures are fit, which gentle, which strong, to show the composition manly; and how he hath avoided faint, obscure, obscene, sordid, humble, improper, or effeminate phrase; which is not only praised of the most, but commended, which is worse, especially for that it is naught.[1]

DOMINUS VERULAMIUS. SCRIPTORUM CATALOGUS

(cum seq.)

Stili eminentia. — It is no wonder men's eminence appears but in their own way. Virgil's felicity left him in prose, as Tully's forsook him in verse. Sallust's orations are read in the honour of story, yet the most eloquent Plato's speech, which he made for Socrates, is neither worthy of the patron nor the person defended. Nay, in the same kind of oratory, and where the matter is one, you shall have him that reasons strongly, open negligently; another that prepares well, not fit so well. And this happens not only to brains, but to bodies. One can wrestle well, another run well, a third leap or throw the bar, a fourth lift or stop a cart going: each hath his way of strength. So in other creatures — some dogs are for the deer, some for the wild boar, some are fox-hounds, some otter-hounds. Nor are all horses for the coach or saddle, some are for the cart and panniers.

De claris oratoribus. — I have known many excellent men that would speak suddenly to the admiration of their hearers, who upon study and premeditation have been forsaken by their own wits, and no way answered their fame; their eloquence was greater than

---

[1] For the original of much of this last passage, see Quintilian, *sup.*, p. 62. Observe how Ben silently transfers the whole from the orator to the writer.

their reading, and the things they uttered better than those they knew; their fortune deserved better of them than their care. For men of present spirits, and of greater wits than study, do please more in the things they invent than in those they bring. And I have heard some of them compelled to speak, out of necessity, that have so infinitely exceeded themselves, as it was better both for them and their auditory that they were so surprised, not prepared. Nor was it safe then to cross them for their adversary, their anger made them more eloquent. Yet these men I could not but love and admire, that they returned to their studies. They left not diligence, as many do, when their rashness prospered; for diligence is a great aid, even to an indifferent wit; when we are not contented with the examples of our own age, but would know the face of the former. Indeed, the more we confer with the more we profit by, if the persons be chosen.

Dominus Verulamius. — One, though he be excellent and the chief, is not to be imitated alone; for never no imitator ever grew up to his author; likeness is always on this side truth. Yet there happened in my time one noble speaker who was full of gravity in his speaking; his language, where he could spare or pass by a jest, was nobly censorious. No man ever spake more neatly, more pressly, more weightily, or suffered less emptiness, less idleness, in what he uttered. No member of his speech but consisted of his own graces. His hearers could not cough, or look aside from him, without loss. He commanded where he spoke, and had his judges angry and pleased at his devotion. No man had their affections more in his power. The fear of every man that heard him was lest he should make an end.

Scriptorum catalogus. — Cicero is said to be the only wit that the people of Rome had equalled to their empire. *Ingenium par imperio.* We have had many, and in their several ages (to take in but the former *seculum*) Sir Thomas More, the elder Wyatt, Henry Earl of Surrey, Chaloner, Smith, Eliot, B[ishop] Gardiner, were for their times admirable; and the more, because they began eloquence with us. Sir Nico[las] Bacon was singular, and almost alone, in the beginning of Queen Elizabeth's times. Sir Philip Sidney and Mr. Hooker (in different matter) grew great masters of wit and

language, and in whom all vigour of invention and strength of judgment met. The Earl of Essex, noble and high; and Sir Walter
Raleigh, not to be contemned, either for judgment or style; Sir
Henry Savile, grave, and truly lettered; Sir Edwin Sandys, excellent in both; Lo[rd] Egerton, the Chancellor, a grave and great
orator, and best when he was provoked; but his learned and able,
though unfortunate, successor is he who hath filled up all numbers, and performed that in our tongue which may be compared or
preferred either to insolent Greece or haughty Rome. In short,
within his view, and about his times, were all the wits born
that could honour a language or help study. Now things daily
fall, wits grow downward, and eloquence grows backward; so
that he may be named and stand as the mark and ἀκμή of our
language.

De augmentis scientiarum. — I have ever observed it to have
been the office of a wise patriot, among the greatest affairs of the
State, to take care of the commonwealth of learning. For schools,
they are the seminaries of State; and nothing is worthier the study
of a statesman than that part of the republic which we call the
advancement of letters. Witness the care of Julius Cæsar, who,
in the heat of the civil war, writ his books of *Analogy,* and dedicated
them to Tully. This made the late Lord S[aint] Alban entitle his
work *Novum Organum;* which, though by the most of superficial
men, who cannot get beyond the title of nominals, it is not penetrated nor understood, it really openeth all defects of learning
whatsoever, and is a book

Qui longum noto scriptori porriget ævum.

My conceit of his person was never increased toward him by his
place or honours. But I have and do reverence him for the greatness that was only proper to himself, in that he seemed to me ever,
by his work, one of the greatest men, and most worthy of admiration, that had been in many ages. In his adversity I ever prayed
that God would give him strength; for greatness he could not want.
Neither could I condole in a word or syllable for him, as knowing
no accident could do harm to virtue, but rather help to make it
manifest.

POESIS ET PICTURA

Poesis et pictura. — Poetry and picture are arts of a like nature, and both are busy about imitation. It was excellently said of Plutarch, poetry was a speaking picture, and picture a mute poesy. For they both invent, feign, and devise many things, and accommodate all they invent to the use and service of Nature. Yet of the two the pen is more noble than the pencil; for that can speak to the understanding, the other but to the sense. They both behold pleasure and profit as their common object; but should abstain from all base pleasures, lest they should err from their end, and, while they seek to better men's minds, destroy their manners. They both are born artificers, not made. Nature is more powerful in them than study.

DE STILO. PRÆCIPIENDI MODI

De stilo, et optimo scribendi genere. — For a man to write well, there are required three necessaries — to read the best authors, observe the best speakers, and much exercise of his own style. In style, to consider what ought to be written, and after what manner, he must first think and excogitate his matter, then choose his words, and examine the weight of either. Then take care, in placing and ranking both matter and words, that the composition be comely; and to do this with diligence and often. No matter how slow the style be at first, so it be laboured and accurate; seek the best, and be not glad of the forward conceits, or first words, that offer themselves to us; but judge of what we invent, and order what we approve. Repeat often what we have formerly written; which beside that it helps the consequence, and makes the juncture better, it quickens the heat of imagination, that often cools in the time of setting down, and gives it new strength, as if it grew lustier by the going back. As we see in the contention of leaping, they jump farthest that fetch their race largest; or, as in throwing a dart or javelin, we force back our arms to make our loose the stronger. Yet, if we have a fair gale of wind, I forbid not the steering out of our sail, so the favour of the gale deceive us not. For all that we invent doth please us in the conception of birth, else we would never set it down. But the safest is to return to our judgment, and handle over again those things the easiness of which might make them justly suspected. So did the best writers in their beginnings; they imposed upon themselves care and industry; they did nothing rashly : they obtained first to write well, and then custom made it easy and a habit. By little and little their matter showed itself to them more plentifully; their words answered, their composition followed; and all, as in a well-ordered family, presented itself in the place. So that the sum of all is, ready writing makes not good writing, but good writing brings on ready writing. Yet, when we think we have got the faculty, it is even then good to resist it, as to give a horse a check sometimes with a bit, which doth not so much stop his course as stir his mettle. Again, whither a man's genius is best able to reach, thither it should more and more contend, lift and dilate itself; as men of low stature raise themselves on their toes, and so ofttimes get even, if not eminent. Besides, as it is fit for grown and able writers to stand of themselves, and work with their own strength, to trust and endeavour by their own faculties, so it is fit for the beginner and learner to study others and the best. For the mind and memory are more sharply exercised in comprehending another man's things than our own ; and such as accustom themselves and are familiar with the best authors shall ever and anon find somewhat of them in themselves, and in the expression of their minds, even when they feel it not, be able to utter something like theirs, which hath an authority above their own. Nay, sometimes it is the reward of a man's study, the praise of quoting another man fitly ; and though a man be more prone and able for one kind of writing than another, yet he must exercise all. For as in an instrument, so in style, there must be a harmony and consent of parts.

Præcipiendi modi. — I take this labour in teaching others, that they should not be always to be taught, and I would bring my precepts into practice, for rules are ever of less force and value than experiments ; yet with this purpose, rather to show the right way to those that come after, than to detect any that have slipped before by error. And I hope it will be more profitable; for men do more

willingly listen, and with more favour, to precept, than reprehension.   Among divers opinions of an art, and most of them contrary
in themselves, it is hard to make election; and, therefore, though
a man cannot invent new things after so many, he may do a
welcome work yet to help posterity to judge rightly of the old.   But
arts and precepts avail nothing, except Nature be beneficial and
aiding.   And therefore these things are no more written to a dull
disposition, than rules of husbandry to a barren soil.   No precepts
will profit a fool, no more than beauty will the blind, or music the
deaf.   As we should take care that our style in writing be neither
dry nor empty, we should look again it be not winding, or wanton
with far-fetched descriptions: either is a vice.   But that is worse
which proceeds out of want, than that which riots out of plenty.
The remedy of fruitfulness is easy, but no labour will help the
contrary.   I will like and praise some things in a young writer
which yet, if he continue in, I cannot but justly hate him for the
same.   There is a time to be given all things for maturity, and
that even your country husbandman can teach, who to a young
plant will not put the pruning-knife, because it seems to fear the
iron, as not able to admit the scar.   No more would I tell a green
writer all his faults, lest I should make him grieve and faint, and
at last despair.   For nothing doth more hurt than to make him so
afraid of all things as he can endeavour nothing.   Therefore youth
ought to be instructed betimes, and in the best things; for we hold
those longest we take soonest, as the first scent of a vessel lasts,
and the tinct the wool first receives.   Therefore a master should
temper his own powers, and descend to the other's infirmity.   If
you pour a glut of water upon a bottle, it receives little of it; but
with a funnel, and by degrees, you shall fill many of them, and
spill little of your own; to their capacity they will all receive and
be full.   And as it is fit to read the best authors to youth first,
so let them be of the openest and clearest, as Livy before Sallust,
Sidney before Donne.   And beware of letting them taste Gower
or Chaucer at first, lest, falling too much in love with antiquity,
and not apprehending the weight, they grow rough and barren in
language only.   When their judgments are firm, and out of danger,
let them read both the old and the new; but no less take heed

that their new flowers and sweetness do not as much corrupt as the others' dryness and squalor, if they choose not carefully. Spenser, in affecting the ancients, writ no language; yet I would have him read for his matter, but as Virgil read Ennius. The reading of Homer and Virgil is counselled by Quintilian as the best way of informing youth and confirming man. For, besides that the mind is raised with the height and sublimity of such a verse, it takes spirit from the greatness of the matter, and is tincted with the best things. Tragic and lyric poetry is good too, and comic with the best, if the manners of the reader be once in safety. In the Greek poets, as also in Plautus, we shall see the economy and disposition of poems better observed than in Terence and the later [qu. Greek poets], who thought the sole grace and virtue of their fable the sticking in of sentences, as ours do the forcing in of jests.

Præcept[a] element[aria]. — It is not the passing through these learnings that hurts us, but the dwelling and sticking about them. To descend to those extreme anxieties and foolish cavils of grammarians, is able to break a wit in pieces, being a work of manifold misery and vainness, to be *elementarii senes.* Yet even letters are, as it were, the bank of words, and restore themselves to an author as the pawns of language. But talking and eloquence are not the same: to speak, and to speak well, are two things. A fool may talk, but a wise man speaks; and out of the observation, knowledge, and the use of things, many writers perplex their readers and hearers with mere nonsense. Their writings need sunshine. Pure and neat language I love, yet plain and customary. A barbarous phrase hath often made me out of love with a good sense, and doubtful writing hath [w]racked me beyond my patience. The reason why a poet is said that he ought to have all knowledges is, that he should not be ignorant of the most, especially of those he will handle. And indeed, when the attaining of them is possible, it were a sluggish and base thing to despair; for frequent imitation of anything becomes a habit quickly. If a man should prosecute as much as could be said of everything, his work would find no end.

De orationis dignitate. — Speech is the only benefit man hath to express his excellency of mind above other creatures. It is the instrument of society; therefore Mercury, who is the president of language, is called *deorum hominumque interpres.* In all speech, words and sense are as the body and the soul. The sense is as the life and soul of language, without which all words are dead. Sense is wrought out of experience, the knowledge of human life and actions, or of the liberal arts, which the Greeks called Ἐγκυκλοπαι-δείαν. Words are the people's, yet there is a choice of them to be made; for *verborum delectus origo est eloquentiæ.* They are to be chose according to the persons we make speak, or the things we speak of. Some are of the camp, some of the council-board, some of the shop, some of the sheepcot, some of the pulpit, some of the bar, etc. And herein is seen their elegance and propriety, when we use them fitly and draw them forth to their just strength and nature by way of translation or metaphor. But in this translation we must only serve necessity (*nam temere nihil transfertur a prudenti*) or commodity, which is a kind of necessity: that is, when we either absolutely want a word to express by, and that is necessity; or when we have not so fit a word, and that is commodity; as when we avoid loss by it, and escape obsceneness, and gain in the grace and property which helps significance. Metaphors far-fet hinder to be understood; and affected, lose their grace. Or when the person fetcheth his translations from a wrong place: as if a privy councillor should at the table take his metaphor from a dicing-house, or ordinary, or a vintner's vault; or a justice of peace draw his similitudes from the mathematics; or a divine from a bawdy-house, or taverns; or a gentleman of Northamptonshire, Warwickshire, or the Midland, should fetch all the illustrations to his country neighbors from shipping, and tell them of the mainsheet and the bowline. Metaphors are thus many times deformed, as in him that said, *Castratam morte Africani rempublicam;* and another, *Stercus curiæ Glauciam,* and *Cana nive conspuit Alpes.* All attempts that are new in this kind, are dangerous, and somewhat hard, before they be softened with use. A man coins not a new word without some peril and less fruit; for if it happen to be received, the praise is but moderate; if refused, the scorn is assured. Yet we must adventure; for things at first hard and rough are by use made tender and gentle. It is an honest error that is committed, following great chiefs.

CONSUETUDO

(cum seq.)

Custom is the most certain mistress of language, as the public stamp makes the current money. But we must not be too frequent with the mint, every day coining, nor fetch words from the extreme and utmost ages; since the chief virtue of a style is perspicuity, and nothing so vicious in it as to need an interpreter. Words borrowed of antiquity do lend a kind of majesty to style, and are not without their delight sometimes; for they have the authority of years, and out of their intermission do win themselves a kind of gracelike newness. But the eldest of the present, and newest of the past language, is the best. For what was the ancient language, which some men so dote upon, but the ancient custom? Yet when I name custom, I understand not the vulgar custom; for that were a precept no less dangerous to language than life, if we should speak or live after the manners of the vulgar: but that I call custom of speech, which is the consent of the learned; as custom of life, which is the consent of the good. Virgil was most loving of antiquity; yet how rarely doth he insert *aquai* and *pictai!* Lucretius is scabrous and rough in these; he seeks them: as some do Chaucerisms with us, which were better expunged and banished. Some words are to be culled out for ornament and colour, as we gather flowers to straw houses or make garlands; but they are better when they grow to our style as in a meadow, where, though the mere grass and greenness delights, yet the variety of flowers doth heighten and beautify. Marry, we must not play or riot too much with them, as in paronomasies; nor use too swelling or ill-sounding words, *quæ per salebras, altaque saxa cadunt.* It is true, there is no sound but shall find some lovers, as the bitterest confections are grateful to some palates. Our composition must be more accurate in the beginning and end than in the midst, and in the end more than in the beginning; for through the midst the stream bears us. And this is attained by custom, more than care or diligence. We must express readily and fully, not profusely There is difference between a liberal and prodigal hand. As it is

a great point of art, when our matter requires it, to enlarge and
veer out all sail, so to take it in and contract it, is of no less praise,
when the argument doth ask it.   Either of them hath their fitness
in the place.   A good man always profits by his endeavour, by his
help, yea, when he is absent; nay, when he is dead, by his example
and memory : so good authors in their style.   A strict and succinct
style is that where you can take away nothing without loss, and
that loss to be manifest.

DE STILO

Tacitus, The Laconic, Suetonius, Seneca, and Fabianus. — The
brief style is that which expresseth much in little; the concise
style, which expresseth not enough but leaves somewhat to be
understood; the abrupt style, which hath many breaches, and doth
not seem to end but fall.   The congruent and harmonious fitting
of parts in a sentence hath almost the fastening and force of knitting and connection; as in stones well squared, which will rise
strong a great way without mortar.

Periods are beautiful when they are not too long; for so they
have their strength too, as in a pike or javelin.   As we must take
the care that our words and sense be clear, so if the obscurity
happen through the hearer's or reader's want of understanding, I am
not to answer for them, no more than for their not listening or
marking ; I must neither find them ears nor mind.   But a man
cannot put a word so in sense but something about it will illustrate
it, if the writer understand himself; for order helps much to perspicuity, as confusion hurts.   *Rectitudo lucem adfert; obliquitas et
circumductio offuscat.*   We should therefore speak what we can the
nearest way, so as we keep our gait, not leap ; for too short may as
well be not let into the memory, as too long not kept in.   *Obscuri-
tas offundit tenebras.*   Whatsoever loseth the grace and clearness,
converts into a riddle ; the obscurity is marked, but not the value.
That perisheth, and is passed by, like the pearl in the fable.   Our
style should be like a skein of silk, to be carried and found by the
right thread, not ravelled and perplexed : then all is a knot, a heap.
There are words that do as much raise a style as others can depress
it.   Superlation and overmuchness amplifies; it may be above

faith, but never above a mean. It was ridiculous in Cestius, when he said of Alexander:

Fremit oceanus, quasi indignetur, quod terras relinquas.

But propitiously from Virgil:

Credas innare revulsas
Cycladas.

He doth not say it was so, but seemed to be so. Although it be somewhat incredible, that is excused before it be spoken. But there are hyperboles which will become one language, that will by no means admit another. As *Eos esse P[opuli] R[omani] exercitus, qui cœlum possint perrumpere*, who would say with us, but a madman? Therefore we must consider in every tongue what is used, what received. Quintilian warns us, that in no kind of translation, or metaphor, or allegory, we make a turn from what we began; as if we fetch the original of our metaphor from sea and billows, we end not in flames and ashes: it is a most foul inconsequence. Neither must we draw out our allegory too long, lest either we make ourselves obscure, or fall into affectation, which is childish. But why do men depart at all from the right and natural ways of speaking? Sometimes for necessity, when we are driven, or think it fitter, to speak that in obscure words, or by circumstance, which uttered plainly would offend the hearers; or to avoid obsceneness, or sometimes for pleasure, and variety, as travellers turn out of the highway, drawn either by the commodity of a footpath, or the delicacy or freshness of the fields. And all this is called ἐσχηματισμένη, or figured language.

Oratio imago animi. — Language most shows a man: Speak, that I may see thee. It springs out of the most retired and inmost parts of us, and is the image of the parent of it, the mind. No glass renders a man's form or likeness so true as his speech. Nay, it is likened to a man; and as we consider feature and composition in a man, so words in language; in the greatness, aptness, sound structure, and harmony of it.

Structura et statura. — Some men are tall and big, so some language is high and great: *sublimis*. Then the words are chosen, their sound ample, the composition full, the absolution plenteous,

and poured out, all grave, sinewy, and strong. Some are little and
dwarfs, *humilis, pumila;* so of speech, it is humble and low, the
words poor and flat, the members and periods thin and weak, without knitting or number. *Mediocris plana et placida.* — The middle
are of a just stature. There the language is plain and pleasing;
even without stopping, round without swelling: all well-turned,
composed, elegant, and accurate. *Vitiosa oratio, vasta, tumens,
enormis, affectata, abjecta.* — The vicious language is vast and gaping, swelling and irregular: when it contends to be high, full of
rock, mountain, and pointedness; as it affects to be low, it is abject,
and creeps, full of bogs and holes. And according to their subject
these styles vary, and lose their names: for that which is high and
lofty, declaring excellent matter, becomes vast and tumorous,
speaking of petty and inferior things; so that which was even and
apt in a mean and plain subject, will appear most poor and humble
in a high argument. Would you not laugh to meet a great councillor of State in a flat cap, with his trunk hose, and a hobby-horse
cloak, his gloves under his girdle, and yond haberdasher in a velvet
gown, furred with sables? There is a certain latitude in these
things, by which we find the degrees.

The next thing to the stature is the figure, *figura,* and feature in
language, that is, whether it be round and straight, which consists
of short and succinct periods, numerous and polished; or square
and firm, which is to have equal and strong parts everywhere
answerable, and weighed.

The third is the skin and coat, *cutis sive cortex,* which rests in the
well-joining, cementing, and coagmentation of words, *compositio;*
whenas it is smooth, gentle, and sweet, like a table upon which you
may run your finger without rubs, and your nail cannot find a joint;
not horrid, rough, wrinkled, gaping, or chapped.

After these, the flesh, blood, and bones come in question. We
say it is a fleshy style, *carnosa,* when there is much periphrasis,
and circuit of words; and when with more than enough, it grows
fat and corpulent, *adipata, redundans: arvina orationis,* full of suet
and tallow. It hath blood and juice when the words are proper
and apt, their sound sweet, and the phrase neat and picked — *oratio
uncta, et bene pasta.* But where there is redundancy, both the blood

and juice are faulty and vicious : — *Redundat sanguine, qua multo plus dicit, quam necesse est.* Juice in language is somewhat less than blood; for if the words be but becoming and signifying, and the sense gentle, there is juice; but where that wanteth, the language is thin, flagging, poor, starved, scarce covering the bone, *jejuna, macilenta, strigosa,* and shews like stones in a sack. Some men, to avoid redundancy, run into that; and while they strive to have no ill blood or juice, they lose their good. There be some styles, again, that have not less blood, but less flesh and corpulence. These are bony and sinewy, *ossea et nervosa ; Ossa habent, et nervos.*

De poetica. — We have spoken sufficiently of oratory, let us now make a diversion to poetry. Poetry, in the primogeniture, had many peccant humours, and is made to have more now, through the levity and inconstancy of men's judgments. Whereas, indeed, it is the most prevailing eloquence, and of the most exalted charact. Now the discredits and disgraces are many it hath received through men's study of depravation or calumny; their practice being to give it diminution of credit, by lessening the professors' estimation, and making the age afraid of their liberty; and the age is grown so tender of her fame, as she calls all writings "aspersions." That is the state word, the phrase of court, Placentia College, which some call Parasites' Place, the Inn of Ignorance.

. . . .

POETA, ETC.

What is a poet? — A poet, *poeta,* is that which by the Greeks is called κατ᾿ ἐξοχήν, ὁ ποιητής, a maker, or a feigner : his art, an art of imitation or feigning; expressing the life of man in fit measure, numbers, and harmony ; according to Aristotle from the word ποιεῖν, which signifies to make or feign. Hence he is called a poet, not he which writeth in measure only, but that feigneth and formeth a fable, and writes things like the truth. For the fable and fiction is, as it were, the form and soul of any poetical work or poem.

What mean you by a poem? — A poem, *poema,* is not alone any work or composition of the poet's in many or few verses; but even one alone verse sometimes makes a perfect poem. As when Æneas hangs up and consecrates the arms of Abas with this inscription:

Æneas hæc de Danais victoribus arma,

and calls it a poem or *carmen*. Such are those in Martial:

Omnia, Castor, emis: sic fiet, ut omnia vendas,

and —

Pauper videri Cinna vult, et est pauper.

So were Horace his odes called *Carmina*, his lyric songs. And Lucretius designs a whole book in his sixth —

Quod in primo quoque carmine claret.

And anciently all the oracles were called *Carmina;* or whatever sentence was expressed, were it much or little, it was called an Epic, Dramatic, Lyric, Elegiac, or Epigrammatic poem.

But how differs a Poem from what we call a Poesy? — A poem, as I have told you, is the work of the poet; the end and fruit of his labour and study. Poesy, *poesis*, is his skill or craft of making; the very fiction itself, the reason or form of the work. And these three voices differ, as the thing done, the doing, and the doer; the thing feigned, the feigning, and the feigner; so the poem, the poesy, and the poet. Now the poesy is the habit or the art; nay, rather the queen of arts, *artium regina*, which had her original from heaven, received thence from the Hebrews, and had in prime estimation with the Greeks, transmitted to the Latins and all nations that professed civility. The study of it, if we will trust Aristotle, offers to mankind a certain rule and pattern of living well and happily, disposing us to all civil offices of society. If we will believe Tully, it nourisheth and instructeth our youth, delights our age, adorns our prosperity, comforts our adversity, entertains us at home, keeps us company abroad, travels with us, watches, divides the times of our earnest and sports, shares in our country recesses and recreations; insomuch as the wisest and best learned have thought her the absolute mistress of manners and nearest of kin to virtue. And whereas they entitle philosophy to be a rigid and austere poesy, they have, on the contrary, styled poesy a dulcet and gentle philosophy, which leads on and guides us by the hand to action with a ravishing delight and incredible sweetness. But before we handle the kinds of poems, with their special differences, or make court to the art itself as a mistress, I would lead you to the knowledge of our poet by a perfect information what he is or should be by nature, by exercise, by imitation, by study, and so bring him down through the disciplines of grammar, logic, rhetoric, and the ethics, adding somewhat out of all, peculiar to himself, and worthy of your admittance or reception.

First, we require in our poet or maker (for that title our language affords him elegantly with the Greek) a goodness of natural wit, *ingenium*. For whereas all other arts consist of doctrine and precepts, the poet must be able by nature and instinct to pour out the treasure of his mind, and as Seneca saith, *Aliquando secundum Anacreontem insanire jucundum esse;* by which he understands the poetical rapture. And according to that of Plato, *Frustra poeticas fores sui compos pulsavit.* And of Aristotle, *Nullum magnum ingenium sine mixtura dementiæ fuit. Nec potest grande aliquid, et supra cæteros loqui, nisi mota mens.* Then it riseth higher, as by a divine instinct, when it contemns common and known conceptions. It utters somewhat above a mortal mouth. Then it gets aloft and flies away with his rider, whither before it was doubtful to ascend. This the poets understood by their Helicon, Pegasus, or Parnassus; and this made Ovid to boast,

> Est deus in nobis, agitante calescimus illo:
> Sedibus æthereis spiritus ille venit.

And Lipsius to affirm, " *Scio poetam neminem præstantem fuisse, sine parte quadam uberiore divinæ auræ.*" And hence it is that the coming up of good poets (for I mind not *mediocres* or *imos*) is so thin and rare among us. Every beggarly corporation affords the State a mayor or two bailiffs yearly; but *solus rex, aut poeta, non quotannis nascitur.*

To this perfection of nature in our poet we require exercise of those parts, *exercitatio*, and frequent. If his wit will not arrive suddenly at the dignity of the ancients, let him not yet fall out with it, quarrel, or be over hastily angry, offer to turn it away from study in a humour; but come to it again upon better cogitation, try another time with labour. If then it succeed not, cast not away the quills yet, nor scratch the wainscot, beat not the poor desk, but bring all to the forge and file again; torn it anew. There is no statute law of the kingdom bids you be a poet against your will or the first quarter; if it comes in a year or two, it is well. The common rimers pour forth verses, such as they are, *ex tempore;* but there never come[s] from them one sense worth the life of a day. A rimer and a poet are two things. It is said of the incomparable Virgil that he brought forth his verses like a bear, and after formed them with licking. Scaliger the father writes it of him, that he made a quantity of verses in the morning, which afore night he reduced to a less number. But that which Valerius Maximus hath left recorded of Euripides, the tragic poet, his answer to Alcestis, another poet, is as memorable as modest; who, when it was told to Alcestis that Euripides had in three days brought forth but three verses, and those with some difficulty and throes, Alcestis, glorying he could with ease have sent forth a hundred in the space, Euripides roundly replied, "Like enough; but here is the difference: thy verses will not last those three days, mine will to all time." Which was as much as to tell him he could not write a verse. I have met many of these rattles that made a noise and buzzed. They had their hum, and no more. Indeed, things wrote with labour deserve to be so read, and will last their age.

The third requisite in our poet or maker is imitation, *imitatio*, to be able to convert the substance or riches of another poet to his own use. To make choice of one excellent man above the rest, and so to follow him till he grow very he, or so like him as the copy may be mistaken for the principal. Not as a creature that swallows what it takes in, crude, raw, or undigested; but that feeds with an appetite, and hath a stomach to concoct, divide, and turn all into nourishment. Not to imitate servilely, as Horace saith, and catch at vices for virtue, but to draw forth out of the best and choicest flowers, with the bee, and turn all into honey, work it into one relish and savour; make our imitation sweet; observe how the best writers have imitated, and follow them: how Virgil and Statius have imitated Homer; how Horace, Archilochus; how Alcæus, and the other lyrics; and so of the rest.

But that which we especially require in him is an exactness of
study and multiplicity of reading, *lectio*, which maketh a full man,
not alone enabling him to know the history or argument of a poem
and to report it, but so to master the matter and style, as to show
he knows how to handle, place, or dispose of either with elegancy
when need shall be.   And not think he can leap forth suddenly a
poet by dreaming he hath been in Parnassus, or having washed his
lips, as they say, in Helicon.   There goes more to his making than
so ; for to nature, exercise, imitation, and study art must be added
to make all these perfect.   *Ars coron*[*at opus*].   And though these
challenge to themselves much in the making up of our maker, it is
art only can lead him to perfection, and leave him there in possession, as planted by her hand.   It is the assertion of Tully, if to an
excellent nature there happen an accession or conformation of
learning and discipline, there will then remain somewhat noble and
singular.   For, as Simylus [1] saith in Stobæus, Οὔτε φύσις ἱκανὴ γίνε-
ται τέχνης ἄτερ, οὔτε πᾶν τέχνη μὴ φύσιν κεκτημένη, without art nature
can never be perfect ; and without nature art can claim no being.
But our poet must beware that his study be not only to learn of
himself ; for he that shall affect to do that confesseth his ever
having a fool to his master.   He must read many, but ever the best
and choicest ; those that can teach him anything he must ever
account his masters, and reverence.   Among whom Horace and he
that taught him, Aristotle, deserved to be the first in estimation.
Aristotle was the first accurate critic and truest judge, nay, the
greatest philosopher the world ever had ; for he noted the vices of
all knowledges in all creatures, and out of many men's perfections
in a science he formed still one art.   So he taught us two offices
together, how we ought to judge rightly of others, and what we
ought to imitate specially in ourselves : but all this in vain without
a natural wit and a poetical nature in chief.   For no man, so soon
as he knows this or reads it, shall be able to write the better ; but
as he is adapted to it by nature, he shall grow the perfecter writer.
He must have civil prudence and eloquence, and that whole, not
taken up by snatches or pieces in sentences or remnants when he
will handle business or carry counsels, as if he came then out of

[1] *v. sup.*, p. 32.

the declaimer's gallery, or shadow furnished but out of the body of the State, which commonly is the school of men : *Virorum schola respub*[*lica*]. The poet is the nearest borderer upon the orator, and expresseth all his virtues, though he be tied more to numbers, is his equal in ornament, and above him in his strengths. And of the kind the comic comes nearest; because in moving the minds of men, and stirring of affections, in which oratory shows, and especially approves her eminence, he chiefly excels. What figure of a body was Lysippus ever able to form with his graver, or Apelles to paint with his pencil, as the comedy to life expresseth so many and various affections of the mind? There shall the spectator see some insulting with joy, others fretting with melancholy, raging with anger, mad with love, boiling with avarice, undone with riot, tortured with expectation, consumed with fear : no perturbation in common life but the orator finds an example of it in the scene. And then for the elegancy of language, read but this inscription on the grave of a comic poet :

> Immortales mortales si fas esset flere,
> Flerent divæ Camœnæ Nævium poetam ;
> Itaque postquam est Orcino traditus thesauro,
> Obliti sunt Romæ lingua loqui Latina.

Or that modester testimony given by Lucius Ælius Stilo upon Plautus, who affirmed, "*Musas, si Latine loqui voluissent, Plautino sermone fuisse locuturas.*" And that illustrious judgment by the most learned M[arcus] Varro of him, who pronounced him the prince of letters and elegancy in the Roman language.

I am not of that opinion to conclude a poet's liberty within the narrow limits of laws which either the grammarians or philosophers prescribe. For before they found out those laws there were many excellent poets that fulfilled them, amongst whom none more perfect than Sophocles, who lived a little before Aristotle. Which of the Greeklings durst ever give precepts to Demosthenes? or to Pericles, whom the age surnamed Heavenly, because he seemed to thunder and lighten with his language? or to Alcibiades, who had rather Nature for his guide than Art for his master? But whatsoever nature at any time dictated to the most happy, or long exercise to the most laborious, that the wisdom and learning of Aristotle hath brought into an art, because he understood the causes of things; and what other men did by chance or custom he doth by reason; and not only found out the way not to err, but the short way we should take not to err.

Many things in Euripides hath Aristophanes wittily reprehended, not out of art, but out of truth. For Euripides is sometimes peccant, as he is most times perfect. But judgment when it is greatest, if reason doth not accompany it, is not ever absolute.

To judge of poets is only the faculty of poets; and not of all poets, but the best. *Nemo infelicius de poetis judicavit, quam qui de poetis scripsit.* But some will say critics are a kind of tinkers, that make more faults than they mend ordinarily. See their diseases and those of grammarians. It is true, many bodies are the worse for the meddling with; and the multitude of physicians hath destroyed many sound patients with their wrong practice. But the office of a true critic or censor is, not to throw by a letter anywhere, or damn an innocent syllable, but lay the words together, and amend them; judge sincerely of the author and his matter, which is the sign of solid and perfect learning in a man. Such was Horace, an author of much civility, and, if any one among the heathen can be, the best master both of virtue and wisdom; an excellent and true judge upon cause and reason, not because he thought so, but because he knew so out of use and experience.

Cato, the grammarian, a defender of Lucilius.

> Cato Grammaticus, Latina Siren,
> Qui solus legit, et facit poetas.

Quintilian of the same heresy, but rejected. Horace his judgment of Chœrilus defended against Joseph Scaliger, and of Laberius against Julius. But chiefly his opinion of Plautus vindicated against many that are offended, and say it is a hard censure upon the parent of all conceit and sharpness. And they wish it had not fallen from so great a master and censor in the art, whose bondmen knew better how to judge of Plautus than any that dare patronize the family of learning in this age; who could not be ignorant of the judgment of the times in which he lived, when poetry and the Latin language were at the height; especially being a man so conversant and inwardly familiar with the censures of great men that did discourse of these things daily amongst themselves. Again, a man so gracious and in high favour with the Emperor, as Augustus often called him his witty manling, for the littleness of his stature; and, if we may trust antiquity, had designed him for a secretary of estate, and invited him to the palace, which he modestly prayed off and refused. Horace did so highly esteem Terence his comedies, as he ascribes the art in comedy to him alone among the Latins, and joins him with Menander.

Now, let us see what may be said for either, to defend Horace his judgment to posterity, and not wholly to condemn Plautus.

. . . .

COMEDY AND TRAGEDY

The parts of a comedy and tragedy. — The parts of a comedy are the same with a tragedy, and the end is partly the same, for they both delight, and teach; the comics are called διδάσκαλοι of the Greeks no less than the tragics. Nor is the moving of laughter always the end of comedy; that is rather a fowling for the people's delight, or their fooling. For, as Aristotle says rightly, the moving of laughter is a fault in comedy, a kind of turpitude that depraves some part of a man's nature without a disease. As a wry face without pain moves laughter, or a deformed vizard, or a rude clown dressed in a lady's habit and using her actions; we dislike and scorn such representations which made the ancient philosophers ever think laughter unfitting in a wise man. And this induced Plato to esteem of Homer as a sacrilegious person, because he presented the gods sometimes laughing. As also it is divinely said of Aristotle, that to seem ridiculous is a part of dishonesty, and foolish. So that what either in the words or sense of an author, or in the language or actions of men, is awry or depraved doth strangely stir mean affections, and provoke for the most part to laughter. And therefore it was clear that all insolent and obscene speeches, jests upon the best men, injuries to particular persons, perverse and sinister sayings and the rather unexpected in the old comedy did move laughter, especially where it did imitate any dishonesty; and scurrility came forth in the place of wit, which, who understands the nature and genius of laughter cannot but perfectly know.

Of which Aristophanes affords an ample harvest, having not only outgone Plautus or any other in that kind, but expressed all the moods and figures of what is ridiculous oddly. In short, as vinegar is not accounted good until the wine be corrupted, so jests that are true and natural seldom raise laughter with the beast, the multitude. They love nothing that is right and proper. The farther it runs from reason or possibility with them the better it is. What could have made them laugh, like to see Socrates presented, that example of all good life, honesty, and virtue, to have him hoisted up with a pulley, and there play the philosopher in a basket; measure how many foot a flea could skip geometrically, by a just scale, and edify the people from the engine? This was theatrical wit, right stage jesting, and relishing a playhouse, invented for scorn and laughter; whereas, if it had savoured of equity, truth, perspicuity, and candour, to have tasten a wise or a learned palate, — spit it out presently! this is bitter and profitable : this instructs and would inform us! what need we know anything, that are nobly born, more than a horse-race, or a hunting-match, our day to break with citizens, and such innate mysteries? This is truly leaping from the stage to the tumbril again, reducing all wit to the original dung-cart.

THE FABLE

OF THE MAGNITUDE AND COMPASS OF ANY FABLE, EPIC OR DRAMATIC

What the measure of a fable is. — The fable or plot of a poem defined. — The epic fable, differing from the dramatic. — To the resolving of this question we must first agree in the definition of the fable. The fable is called the imitation of one entire and perfect action, whose parts are so joined and knit together, as nothing in the structure can be changed, or taken away, without impairing or troubling the whole, of which there is a proportionable magnitude in the members. As for example : if a man would build a house, he would first appoint a place to build it in, which he would define within certain bounds. So in the constitution of a poem, the action is aimed at by the poet, which answers place in a building, and that action hath his largeness, compass, and proportion. But as a court or king's palace requires other dimensions than a private house, so the epic asks a magnitude from other poems, since what is place in the one is action in the other; the difference is in space. So that by this definition we conclude the fable to be the imitation of one perfect and entire action, as one perfect and entire place is required to a building. By perfect, we understand that to which nothing is wanting, as place to the building that is raised, and action to the fable that is formed. It is perfect, perhaps not for a court or king's palace, which requires a greater ground, but for the structure we would raise; so the space of the action may not prove large enough for the epic fable, yet be perfect for the dramatic, and whole.

What we understand by whole. — Whole we call that, and perfect, which hath a beginning, a midst, and an end. So the place of any building may be whole and entire for that work, though too little for a palace. As to a tragedy or a comedy, the action may be convenient and perfect that would not fit an epic poem in magnitude. So a lion is a perfect creature in himself, though it be less than that of a buffalo or a rhinocerote. They differ but *in specie:* either in the kind is absolute; both have their parts, and either the whole. Therefore, as in every body so in every action, which is the subject of a just work, there is required a certain proportionable greatness, neither too vast nor too minute. For that which happens to the eyes when we behold a body, the same happens to the memory when we contemplate an action. I look upon a monstrous giant, as Tityus, whose body covered nine acres of land, and mine eye sticks upon every part; the whole that consists of those parts will never be taken in at one entire view. So in a fable, if the action be too great, we can never comprehend the whole together in our imagination. Again, if it be too little, there ariseth no pleasure out of the object; it affords the view no stay; it is beheld, and vanisheth at once. As if we should look upon an ant or pismire, the parts fly the sight, and the whole considered is almost nothing.

The same happens in action, which is the object of memory, as the body is of sight. Too vast oppresseth the eyes, and exceeds the memory; too little scarce admits either.

What [is] the utmost bound of a fable. — Now in every action it behoves the poet to know which is his utmost bound, how far with fitness and a necessary proportion he may produce and determine it; that is, till either good fortune change into the worse, or the worse into the better. For as a body without proportion cannot be goodly, no more can the action, either in comedy or tragedy, without his fit bounds. And every bound, for the nature of the subject, is esteemed the best that is largest, till it can increase no more; so it behoves the action in tragedy or comedy to be let grow till the necessity ask a conclusion; wherein two things are to be considered: first, that it exceed not the compass of one day; next, that there be place left for digression and art. For the episodes and digressions in a fable are the same that household stuff and other furniture are in a house. And so far form the measure and extent of a fable dramatic.

What [we understand] by one and entire. — Now that it should be one and entire. One is considerable two ways; either as it is only separate, and by itself, or as being composed of many parts, it begins to be one as those parts grow or are wrought together. That it should be one the first way alone, and by itself, no man that hath tasted letters ever would say, especially having required before a just magnitude and equal proportion of the parts in themselves. Neither of which can possibly be, if the action be single and separate, not composed of parts, which laid together in themselves, with an equal and fitting proportion, tend to the same end; which thing out of antiquity itself hath deceived many, and more this day it doth deceive.

So many there be of old that have thought the action of one man to be one, as of Hercules, Theseus, Achilles, Ulysses, and other heroes; which is both foolish and false, since by one and the same person many things may be severally done which cannot fitly be referred or joined to the same end: which not only the excellent tragic poets, but the best masters of the epic, Homer and Virgil,

saw.   For though the argument of an epic poem be far more diffused
and poured out than that of tragedy, yet Virgil, writing of Æneas,
hath pretermitted many things.   He neither tells how he was born,
how brought up, how he fought with Achilles, how he was snatched
out of the battle by Venus; but that one thing, how he came into
Italy, he prosecutes in twelve books.   The rest of his journey, his
error by sea, the sack of Troy, are put not as the argument of
the work, but episodes of the argument.   So Homer laid by many
things of Ulysses, and handled no more than he saw tended to one
and the same end.

Contrary to which, and foolishly, those poets did, whom the
philosopher taxeth, of whom one gathered all the actions of Theseus,
another put all the labours of Hercules in one work.   So did he
whom Juvenal mentions in the beginning, "hoarse Codrus," that
recited a volume compiled, which he called his *Theseid*, not yet
finished, to the great trouble both of his hearers and himself;
amongst which there were many parts had no coherence nor kindred one with other, so far they were from being one action, one
fable.   For as a house, consisting of divers materials, becomes one
structure and one dwelling, so an action, composed of divers parts,
may become one fable, epic or dramatic.   For example, in a tragedy,
look upon Sophocles his *Ajax*: Ajax, deprived of Achilles's armour,
which he hoped from the suffrage of the Greeks, disdains, and,
growing impatient of the injury, rageth, and turns mad.   In that
humour he doth many senseless things, and at last falls upon the
Grecian flock and kills a great ram for Ulysses: returning to his
sense, he grows ashamed of the scorn, and kills himself; and is by
the chiefs of the Greeks forbidden burial   These things agree and
hang together, not as they were done, but as seeming to be done,
which made the action whole, entire, and absolute.

*The conclusion concerning the whole, and the parts. — Which are
episodes.* — For the whole, as it consisteth of parts, so without all
the parts it is not the whole; and to make it absolute is required
not only the parts, but such parts as are true.   For a part of the
whole was true, which, if you take away, you either change the
whole or it is not the whole.   For if it be such a part, as, being

present or absent, nothing concerns the whole, it cannot be called
a part of the whole; and such are the episodes, of which hereafter.
For the present here is one example: the single combat of Ajax
with Hector, as it is at large described in Homer, nothing belongs
to this Ajax of Sophocles.

. . . .

You admire no poems but such as run like a brewer's cart upon
the stones, hobbling:

> Et, quæ per salebras, altaque saxa cadunt,
> Actius et quidquid Pacuviusque vomunt.
> Attonitusque legis terraï, frugiferaï.

XVII

SELECTIONS FROM THE SPANISH CRITICS OF THE SEVENTEENTH CENTURY

(The importance of the Spanish critics of this period is, that they, alone of Europeans out of England, had a living and vigorous "Romantic" literature in their drama. They met the discrepancies of this from the neo-classic norm — which they, like others, accepted from the Italians — in a rather illogical and half-hearted manner, but they did try to meet them. If we could accept Bolingbroke's assertion, reported by Spence, that Dryden confessed his indebtedness to Spanish critics, they would have a fresh interest for us; but I have been unable to find any sufficient corroboration of this in Dryden himself. The books here quoted, especially the *Cigarrales* of Tirso de Molina, are mostly very rare. Only Lope and Pinciano exist in modern reprints; the other passages may be found in Señor Menéndez y Pelayo's invaluable *Historia de las Ideas Estéticas en España*, ed. 2, Madrid, in progress.)

A. TIRSO DE MOLINA (1624). THE LIBERTY OF DRAMA

After arguing that the enforced inclusion in a single day of all circumstances necessary (to comedy more particularly) involves a greater, not a lesser loss of verisimilitude than the breach of the unities,[1] *and (even more powerfully) from the unquestioned diversity of natural, to the just allowable diversity of artificial, kinds, Tirso concludes by asking why comedy may not* vary the laws of those who have gone before, and industriously graft the tragic upon the comic, extracting a pleasant mixture from those two opposite forms of poetry, and, by taking part of both, introduce personages as grave as those of the one and as jocose and laughable as those of the

---

[1] The creator of Don Juan, without knowing it, throws all Sir Philip Sidney's argument (*v. sup.*, p. 97) into hopeless rout by asking quietly "whether it is reasonable that a character who begins to pay his court in the morning should set up housekeeping with the lady at night"?

other?   *He ends with an ingenious and (since they were craftsfellows)
very generous defence of Lope de Vega, who, in the teeth of his own
practice, had in his* Arte Nuevo de Hacer Comedias *stigmatized the
national drama as barbarous and popular; and represents him as
speaking in natural modesty and self-depreciation.*

> *Cigarrales de Toledo* (Madrid 1624); quoted at length by
> Menéndez y Pelayo, *op. cit. sup.*, iii. 457–460.

Even before Tirso the national liberty of unity-breaking, and of the
practice of tragicomedy, had been defended, with similar apologies for
Lope, as by the following:

B. ALFONSO SANCHEZ? (1618). THE REAL "RULE"

We *have* an "art"; we *have* "precepts" which are binding on
us. — And the principal precept is — To Imitate Nature: for which
reason the works of poets express the nature, the customs, and the
spirit of the age in which they are written. . . .   If the Spanish
Drama were to adjust itself to the rules and laws of the ancients,
it would proceed *against* nature, and *against* the fundamentals of
poetry.

> Quoted in M. y P. iii. 448–450, where quotations in the same sense from
> a still earlier writer, Ricardo de Turia (1616), will be found.

The formal critics of Spain, however, had kept closer to the Italians,
and to Aristotle the master of the Italians; and it was doubtless in a sort
of fear of them that Lope had admitted the "barbarousness" of the
national theatre.   Yet there were jets of independence even in these
preceptistas until late in the 17th century.   In one of the earliest and
best of them we read as follows:

C. PINCIANO (1596). UNIVERSALITY OF POETRY

Poetry has no *particular* object, but rather the entire body of all
arts and sciences; which it embraces, and indeed overpasses, inasmuch as it extends to things and thoughts that never were, but
might have been.

> M. y P. iii. 332.   *Filosofía Antigua Poética* p. 133, ed. Peña
> (Valladolid 1894).

But Pinciano thought the Fable the " soul " and the diction merely the " body " of poetry — in the orthodox Classic-Italian way; and though he does not deny diversity of action, it must be only as different members make one body.   Again consider the following :

D.   GONZALES DE SALAS (1633).   ON THE LIBERTY OF POETRY

It is not to be thought that we are necessarily bound to the strict ancient precepts.   A man's wits are free to alter the rules of art — always taking his stand on the laws of Nature.   (*The Spaniards say better* Naturaleza, " naturalness," *which word would have saved French and English critics from many slips.*) . . .   Art may be altered and improved according to the mutation of ages and the difference of tastes . . . etc., etc.   M. y P. iii. 366.

XVIII

SELECTIONS FROM THE FRENCH CRITICS OF THE SEVENTEENTH CENTURY

(The whole of this volume — and much more — might easily be filled with extracts from this source. The following, however, from Boileau, Rapin, and Le Bossu, will show sufficiently the tenets which had most power in France itself and over the rest of Europe.)

A. BOILEAU. PASSAGES FROM L'ART POÉTIQUE (1669-1674). "GOOD SENSE."

Whatsoever subject we treat, be it pleasant or sublime, let Good Sense always keep company with our rhymes.[1] Any apparent discord between them is an absurdity : rhyme is but a slave and must obey. When you once set yourself to seek it wisely, the understanding easily gets in the habit of finding it; it submits without difficulty to the yoke of Reason, and, far from hampering her, does service and brings wealth. But when it is left uncontrolled, it rebels, and sense has to run after to catch it up. Love Reason, then : let your writings always borrow from her at once their brilliancy and their value. Too many, carried away by insensate excitement, fetch their thoughts far from plain sense : they would think themselves degraded if, in their monstrous [2] verses, they gave a thought which another had given before them. Let *us* avoid these excesses ; let us leave to Italy the glittering folly of these sham diamonds. Everything must tend towards Good Sense.

i. 27–45.

---

[1] It is perhaps well to keep "rhymes" : but it is clear that Boileau was also thinking of "verse" in general.

[2] This became a catchword with the school down to La Harpe. Beauty *must* be "regularly" beautiful.

In good verses let the sense invariably divide the words so as to make a break at the hemistich, and mark the pause there.

i. 105–106.

Never offer the spectator anything incredible : even the truth may sometimes seem to lack the appearance of truth.   An unreasonable marvel is without attraction for me : the mind is not moved by what it does not believe.

ii. 47–50.

Ah ! how absurd is the design of an ignorant poet who, out of so many heroes, chooses " Childebrand " !   The harsh or eccentric sound of a single name will often make an entire poem seem burlesque or barbarous.

iii. 241–244.

Authors ! lend an ear to my instructions.   Would you have your abundant invention please ?   Then let your Muse, fertile in learned teachings, everywhere join the solid and useful with the agreeable. A sensible reader shuns vain amusement, and wishes to make his very recreations profitable.

iv. 85–90.

Let Nature, then, be your only study.

iii. 359.

We must never separate ourselves from Nature.

iii. 414.

B. RAPIN (1672). RÉFLEXIONS SUR LA POÉTIQUE

It is by no means true that, as most people think, some madness ought to enter into the character of Poetry.[1]

§ v.

It is only for the purpose of being useful that Poetry ought to be agreeable : pleasure is only a means which she uses for the end of profit.

§ x.

I make no pretence of justifying the necessity, justice, and truth of these rules [*of Aristotle*] in long discourse. . . .   I take all that for granted.   I only say that, if you consider them well, you will find that they are merely made to methodize Nature, to follow her

---

[1] This is of great importance, because the doctrine of *Furor Poeticus* had been largely admitted by the critics of the 16th century, and of the earlier 17th, as a sort of escapement, or easement, to the rigid " rule " system. Rapin, as an unflinching " Good Sense " man, bars it at once.

step by step. . . .   If there is not unity of place, time, and action, in poems, there is no verisimilitude. . . .   The *Poetic* of Horace, which is merely an interpretation of that of Aristotle, sufficiently shows the necessity of subjecting oneself to rules.   § xii.

C. LE BOSSU (d. 1680). TRAITÉ DU POËME ÉPIQUE

Although it is possible that Reason might have prescribed the rules of Poetic beforehand, it is undeniable that the invention of poets, and the choice which it has pleased them to make, have given Poetry its actual matter and form.   It is, therefore, in the excellent works of the Ancients that we must seek the foundations of this art, and we must limit ourselves to those to whom all others have given the glory, either of having most happily practised it, or of having most judiciously collected and laid down its rules.   The Greeks and the Latins have given us examples of both kinds. Aristotle and Horace have left Rules, which have made all the learned hold them for the Masters of the Art Poetic : and the poems of Homer and Virgil are, by the consent of all ages, the completest models that have ever appeared in this style of writing. So that, if ever just and great authority has been able to give laws and rules to any art, these four persons have certainly possessed that authority in its entirety as regards Epic, which is the only kind of Poetry of which we shall here speak.

It is true that the men of our time may have wit, even as the Ancients had it, and that in matters which depend on choice and invention, they also may have just and happy imaginations.   But it would be unjust to maintain that the new Rules destroy those of our earlier masters, or that they ought to put to condemnation the work of those who could not foresee our caprices, nor suit ourselves to the genius of persons who were to be born in other ages, in other communities, under a religion quite different from theirs, and with manners, customs, and languages quite unconnected. As therefore I have not undertaken this work to educate poets in the manner of to-day, with which I am not sufficiently acquainted, but only as a foundation for my design of commenting on Virgil's *Æneid,* I need not dwell on what has been invented in these late times. I shall not easily be persuaded that the ideas of some modern writers furnish a universal reason, and a common notion, which Nature ought to have put in Virgil's head. But, leaving posterity to decide whether these novelties have been well or ill imagined, I shall only dwell on what I think to find in Homer, in Aristotle, and in Horace. I shall interpret these each by the others, and Virgil by all three, as having had one single genius and one single idea of Epic Poesy.[1]

Bk. I ch. i.

[1] Le Bossu has the reputation of a mere hide-bound pedant. It is *possible* that the latter part of this passage is merely ironic. But it is fair to him to point out that, *with its inevitable counterpart*, it furnishes a really complete critical standpoint. If the moderns are not to prescribe to Virgil, Virgil must not prescribe to the moderns. But the age looked only at the earlier part ; and a famous passage of Pope (*v. inf.*) is much more inspired by Le Bossu than by anything to be found *totidem verbis* in Boileau or Rapin.

XIX

DRYDEN

I. RHYME AND BLANK VERSE

(The following, Dryden's earliest critical deliverance, in the Epistle Dedicatory of the *Rival Ladies*, 1664, already contains the three main notes of his criticism : (1) the occasional slips of fact, such as " *Queen* Gorboduc " and the statement that the play is in rhyme ; (2) the ingenious and almost passionate, but temporary, *engouement* for particular theses, views, sides of criticism — as here for rhymed drama ; (3) the wide, synoptic, appreciative, really historic and really literary, *savouring* of literature, in which no earlier critic had approached and in which few later have surpassed him.[1])

I here present you, my lord, with that in print, which you had the goodness not to dislike upon the stage ; and account it happy to have met you here in England ; it being, at best, like small wines, to be drunk out upon the place, and has not body enough to endure the sea. I know not whether I have been so careful of the plot and language as I ought ; but, for the latter, I have endeavoured to write English, as near as I could distinguish it from the tongue of pedants, and that of affected travellers. Only I am sorry, that (speaking so noble a language as we do) we have not a more certain measure of it, as they have in France, where they have an Academy erected for that purpose, and endowed with large privileges by the present king. I wish we might at length leave to borrow words from other nations, which is now a wantonness in us, not a necessity ; but so long as some affect to speak them, there will not want others, who will have the boldness to write them.

[1] Nearly the whole of Dryden's criticism will be found admirably edited by Professor W. P. Ker in 2 vols., *Essays of John Dryden*, Oxford 1900 ; the whole is in the present editor's revision of Scott's *Dryden*, 18 vols., Edinburgh 1881–1893. Some half dozen reprints of the *Dramatic Poesy* (separate or with additions) have appeared lately.

But I fear, lest, defending the received words, I shall be accused for following the new way, I mean, of writing scenes in verse. Though, to speak properly, it is not so much a new way amongst us, as an old way new revived ; for, many years before Shakespeare's plays, was the tragedy of *Queen Gorboduc*, in English verse, written by that famous Lord Buckhurst, afterwards Earl of Dorset, and progenitor to that excellent person, who (as he inherits his soul and title) I wish may inherit his good fortune. But, supposing our countrymen had not received this writing till of late; shall we oppose ourselves to the most polished and civilized nations of Europe ? Shall we, with the same singularity, oppose the world in this, as most of us do in pronouncing Latin ? Or do we desire that the brand, which Barclay has (I hope unjustly) laid upon the English, should still continue ? *Angli suos ac sua omnia impense miran-tur ; cæteras nationes despectui habent.* All the Spanish and Italian tragedies I have yet seen are writ in rhyme. For the French, I do not name them, because it is the fate of our countrymen to admit little of theirs among us, but the basest of their men, the extravagancies of their fashions, and the frippery of their merchandise. Shakespeare (who, with some errors not to be avoided in that age, had undoubtedly a larger soul of poesy than ever any of our nation) was the first who, to shun the pains of continual rhyming, invented that kind of writing which we call blank verse, but the French, more properly, *prose mesuré ;* into which the English tongue so naturally slides, that, in writing prose, it is hardly to be avoided. And therefore, I admire some men should perpetually stumble in a way so easy, and inverting the order of their words, constantly close their lines with verbs, which though commended sometimes in writing Latin, yet we were whipt at Westminster if we used it twice together. I knew some, who, if they were to write in blank verse, *Sir, I ask your pardon*, would think it sounded more heroically to write, *Sir, I your pardon ask*. I should judge him to have little command of English, whom the necessity of a rhyme should force often upon this rock ; though sometimes it cannot easily be avoided ; and indeed this is the only inconvenience with which rhyme can be charged. This is that which makes them say, rhyme is not natural, it being only so, when the poet either makes a vicious choice of words, or places them, for rhyme sake, so unnaturally as no man would in ordinary speaking; but when it is so judiciously ordered, that the first word in the verse seems to beget the second, and that the next, till that becomes the last word in the line, which, in the negligence of prose, would be so; it must then be granted, rhyme has all the advantages of prose, besides its own. But the excellence and dignity of it were never fully known till Mr. Waller taught it; he first made writing easily an art; first showed us to conclude the sense, most commonly in distichs, which, in the verse of those before him, runs on for so many lines together, that the reader is out of breath to overtake it. This sweetness of Mr. Waller's lyric poesy was afterwards followed in the epic by Sir John Denham, in his *Cooper's Hill*, a poem which, your lordship knows, for the majesty of the style, is, and ever will be, the exact standard of good writing. But if we owe the invention of it to Mr. Waller, we are acknowledging for the noblest use of it to Sir William Davenant, who at once brought it upon the stage, and made it perfect, in the *Siege of Rhodes*.

The advantages which rhyme has over blank verse are so many, that it were lost time to name them. Sir Philip Sidney, in his *Defence of Poesy*, gives us one, which, in my opinion, is not the least considerable; I mean the help it brings to memory, which rhyme so knits up, by the affinity of sounds, that, by remembering the last word in one line, we often call to mind both the verses. Then, in the quickness of repartees (which in discoursive scenes fall very often), it has so particular a grace, and is so aptly suited to them, that the sudden smartness of the answer, and the sweetness of the rhyme, set off the beauty of each other. But that benefit which I consider most in it, because I have not seldom found it, is, that it bounds and circumscribes the fancy. For imagination in a poet is a faculty so wild and lawless, that, like an high-ranging spaniel, it must have clogs tied to it, lest it outrun the judgment. The great easiness of blank verse renders the poet too luxuriant; he is tempted to say many things, which might better be omitted, or at least shut up in fewer words; but when the difficulty of artful rhyming is interposed, where the poet commonly confines his sense to his couplet, and must contrive that sense into such words, that the rhyme shall naturally follow them, not they the rhyme; the fancy then gives leisure to the judgment to come in, which, seeing so heavy a tax imposed, is ready to cut off all unnecessary expenses. This last consideration has already answered an objection which some have made, that rhyme is only an embroidery of sense, to make that, which is ordinary in itself, pass for excellent with less examination. But certainly, that, which most regulates the fancy, and gives the judgment its busiest employment, is like to bring forth the richest and clearest thoughts. The poet examines that most, which he produceth with the greatest leisure, and which he knows, must pass the severest test of the audience, because they are aptest to have it ever in their memory; as the stomach makes the best concoction, when it strictly embraces the nourishment, and takes account of every little particle as it passes through. But, as the best medicines may lose their virtue, by being ill applied, so is it with verse, if a fit subject be not chosen for it. Neither must the argument alone, but the characters and persons be great and noble; otherwise (as Scaliger says of Claudian) the poet will be *ignobiliore materia depressus.* The scenes, which, in my opinion, most commend it, are those of argumentation and discourse, on the result of which the doing or not doing some considerable action should depend.

II. FROM THE ESSAY OF DRAMATIC POESY

Strictly speaking, almost the whole of this famous essay should — at least might — find place here. But it is now far more readily accessible than it was even a few years ago — indeed, more so than many much later documents; and it will therefore be easy, for those who wish, to connect these following *apices* of its criticism with their lower slopes.

A. Two Bad Poets [1]

"I could wish with all my heart," replied Crites, "that many whom we know were as bountifully thanked upon the same condition, that they would never trouble us again. For amongst others,

---

[1] These two unfortunates were, the first apparently Wild of the *Iter Boreale,* the second *possibly* Flecknoe.

I have a mortal apprehension of two poets, whom this victory, with the help of both her wings, will never be able to escape." "'T is easy to guess whom you intend," said Lisideius; "and without naming them, I ask you, if one of them does not perpetually pay us with clenches upon words, and a certain clownish kind of raillery? if now and then he does not offer at a catachresis or Clevelandism, wresting and torturing a word into another meaning: in fine, if he be not one of those whom the French would call *un mauvais buffon;* one who is so much a well-willer to the satire, that he intends at least to spare no man; and though he cannot strike a blow to hurt any, yet he ought to be punished for the malice of the action, as our witches are justly hanged, because they think themselves to be such; and suffer deservedly for believing they did mischief, because they meant it." "You have described him," said Crites, "so exactly, that I am afraid to come after you with my other extremity of poetry: he is one of those who, having had some advantage of education and converse, knows better than the other what a poet should be, but puts it into practice more unluckily than any man; his style and matter are everywhere alike; he is the most calm, peaceable writer you ever read: he never disquiets your passions with the least concernment, but still leaves you in as even a temper as he found you; he is a very leveller in poetry: he creeps along with ten little words in every line, and helps out his numbers with *For to,* and *Unto,* and all the pretty expletives he can find, till he drags them to the end of another line, while the sense is left tired half way behind it: he doubly starves all his verses, first for want of thought, and then of expression; his poetry neither has wit in it, nor seems to have it; like him in Martial.

Pauper videri Cinna vult, et est pauper.

" He affects plainness, to cover his want of imagination: when he writes the serious way, the highest flight of his fancy is some miserable antithesis, or seeming contradiction; and in the comic he is still reaching at some thin conceit, the ghost of a jest, and that too flies before him, never to be caught; these swallows which we see before us on the Thames are the just resemblance of

his wit: you may observe how near the water they stoop, how
many proffers they make to dip, and yet how seldom they touch it;
and when they do, it is but the surface: they skim over it but
to catch a gnat, and then mount into the air and leave it." "Well,
gentlemen," said Eugenius, "you may speak your pleasure of these
authors; but though I and some few more about the town may
give you a peaceable hearing, yet assure yourselves, there are
multitudes who would think you malicious and them injured;
especially him whom you first described; he is the very Withers [1]
of the city: they have bought more editions of his works than
would serve to lay under all their pies at the Lord Mayor's
Christmas."

B. The Advantages of Tragicomedy or Mingled Plot [2]

"I grant the French have performed what was possible on
the ground-work of the Spanish plays; what was pleasant before,
they have made regular; but there is not above one good play
to be writ on all those plots; they are too much alike to please
often; which we need not the experience of our own stage to
justify. As for their new way of mingling mirth with serious
plot, I do not, with Lisideius, condemn the thing, though I cannot
approve their manner of doing it: he tells us, we cannot so speedily
recollect ourselves after a scene of great passion and concernment,
as to pass to another of mirth and humour, and to enjoy it with
any relish: but why should he imagine the soul of man more
heavy than his senses? Does not the eye pass from an unpleasant
object to a pleasant in a much shorter time than is required to
this? and does not the unpleasantness of the first commend

---

[1] It must be remembered that George Wither had for many years been
pouring out the most absolute rubbish, possessing no resemblance whatever to
his charming early work.

[2] Dryden's argument for what we may almost call the English Drama, is all
the more cogent because he cannot here be accused of mere advocacy of his
own cause. He has mixed tragedy and comedy often enough, and perhaps not
always well; but he showed, in the *Conquest of Granada* during his "heroic"
fit, and in *All for Love* when he had shaken this off, that he could do wonders
without any intentional comedy at all.

the beauty of the latter? The old rule of logic might have convinced him, that contraries, when placed near, set off each other. A continued gravity keeps the spirit too much bent; we must refresh it sometimes, as we bait in a journey, that we may go on with greater ease. A scene of mirth, mixed with tragedy, has the same effect upon us which our music has betwixt the acts; which we find a relief to us from the best plots and language of the stage, if the discourses have been long. I must therefore have stronger arguments, ere I am convinced that compassion and mirth in the same subject destroy each other; and in the mean time cannot but conclude, to the honour of our nation, that we have invented, increased, and perfected a more pleasant way of writing for the stage, than was ever known to the ancients or moderns of any nation, which is tragicomedy.

"And this leads me to wonder why Lisideius and many others should cry up the barrenness of the French plots, above the variety and copiousness of the English. Their plots are single; they carry on one design, which is pushed forward by all the actors, every scene in the play contributing and moving towards it. Our plays, besides the main design, have under-plots or by-concernments, of less considerable persons and intrigues, which are carried on with the motion of the main plot: as they say the orb of the fixed stars, and those of the planets, though they have motions of their own, are whirled about by the motion of the *primum mobile*, in which they are continued: that similitude expresses much of the English stage; for if contrary motions may be found in nature to agree; if a planet can go east and west at the same time: one way by virtue of his own motion, the other by the force of the first mover: it will not be difficult to imagine how the under-plot, which is only different, not contrary to the great design, may naturally be conducted along with it."

C. The Absurdity of the Strict Unities of Time and Place

"By their servile observations of the unities of time and place, and the integrity of scenes, they have brought on themselves that dearth of plot, and narrowness of imagination, which may be observed in all their plays. How many beautiful accidents might naturally happen in two or three days, which cannot arrive with any probability in the compass of twenty-four hours? There is time to be allowed also for maturity of design, which, amongst great and prudent persons, such as are often represented in tragedy, cannot, with any likelihood of truth, be brought to pass at so short a warning. Farther, by tying themselves strictly to the unity of place, and unbroken scenes, they are forced many times to omit some beauties which cannot be shown where the act began; but might, if the scene were interrupted, and the stage cleared for the persons to enter in another place; and therefore the French poets are often forced upon absurdities; for if the act begins in a chamber, all the persons in the play must have some business or other to come thither, or else they are not to be shewn that act; and sometimes their characters are very unfitting to appear there: as, suppose it were the king's bed-chamber; yet the meanest man in the tragedy must come and dispatch his business there, rather than in the lobby or courtyard (which is fitter for him), for fear the stage should be cleared, and the scenes broken. Many times they fall by it in a greater inconvenience; for they keep their scenes unbroken, and yet change the place; as in one of their newest plays, where the act begins in the street. There a gentleman is to meet his friend; he sees him with his man, coming out from his father's house; they talk together, and the first goes out: the second, who is a lover, has made an appointment with his mistress; she appears at the window, and then we are to imagine the scene lies under it. This gentleman is called away, and leaves his servant with his mistress; presently her father is heard from within; the young lady is afraid the serving-man should be discovered, and thrusts him into a place of safety, which is supposed to be her closet. After this, the father enters to the daughter, and now the scene is in a house; for he is seeking from one room to another for this poor Philipin, or French Diego, who is heard from within, drolling and breaking many a miserable conceit on the subject of his sad condition. In this ridiculous manner the play goes forward, the stage being never empty all the while: so that the street, the window, the houses, and the closet, are made to walk about, and the persons to stand still. Now what, I beseech you, is more easy than to write a regular French play, or more difficult than to write an irregular English one, like those of Fletcher, or of Shakespeare?"

D. THE CHARACTERS OF SHAKESPEARE, FLETCHER, AND JONSON

"To begin, then, with Shakespeare: he was the man who of all modern, and perhaps ancient poets, had the largest and most comprehensive soul. All the images of nature were still present to him, and he drew them, not laboriously, but luckily; when he describes any thing, you more than see it, you feel it too. Those who accuse him to have wanted learning, give him the greater commendation: he was naturally learned; he needed not the spectacles of books to read nature; he looked inwards, and found her there. I cannot say he is everywhere alike; were he so, I should do him injury to compare him with the greatest of mankind. He is many times flat, insipid; his comic wit degenerating into clenches, his serious swelling into bombast. But he is always great, when some great occasion is presented to him; no man can say he ever had a fit subject for his wit, and did not then raise himself as high above the rest of poets,

Quantum lenta solent inter viburna cupressi.

"The consideration of this made Mr. Hales of Eton say, that there was no subject of which any poet ever writ, but he would produce it much better done in Shakespeare; and however others are now generally preferred before him, yet the age wherein he lived, which had contemporaries with him Fletcher and Jonson, never equalled them to him in their esteem: and in the last king's court, when Ben's reputation was at highest, Sir John Suckling, and with him the greater part of the courtiers, set our Shakespeare far above him.

"Beaumont and Fletcher, of whom I am next to speak, had, with the advantage of Shakespeare's wit, which was their precedent, great natural gifts, improved by study. Beaumont especially being so accurate a judge of plays, that Ben Jonson, while he lived, submitted all his writings to his censure, and, 'tis thought, used his judgment in correcting, if not contriving, all his plots. What value he had for him, appears by the verses he writ to him; and therefore I need speak no farther of it. The first play that brought Fletcher and him in esteem was their *Philaster:* for before that, they had written two or three very unsuccessfully, as the like is reported of Ben Jonson, before he writ *Every Man in his Humour.* Their plots were generally more regular than Shakespeare's, especially those which were made before Beaumont's death; and they understood and imitated the conversation of gentlemen much better; whose wild debaucheries, and quickness of wit in repartees, no poet before them could paint as they have done. Humour, which Ben Jonson derived from particular persons, they made it not their business to describe: they represented all the passions very lively, but above all, love. I am apt to believe the English language in them arrived to its highest perfection: what words have since been taken in, are rather superfluous than ornamental. Their plays are now the most pleasant and frequent entertainments of the stage; two of theirs being acted through the year for one of Shakespeare's or Jonson's: the reason is, because there is a certain gaiety in their comedies, and pathos in their more serious plays, which suits generally with all men's humours. Shakespeare's language is likewise a little obsolete, and Ben Jonson's wit comes short of theirs.

" As for Jonson, to whose character I am now arrived, if we look upon him while he was himself (for his last plays were but his dotages), I think him the most learned and judicious writer which any theatre ever had. He was a most severe judge of himself, as well as others. One cannot say he wanted wit, but rather that he was frugal of it. In his works you find little to retrench or alter. Wit, and language, and humour also in some measure, we had before him; but something of art was wanting to the drama, till he came. He managed his strength to more advantage than any who preceded him. You seldom find him making love in any of his scenes, or endeavouring to move the passions; his genius was too sullen and saturnine to do it gracefully, especially when he knew he came after those who had performed both to such an height. Humour was his proper sphere; and in that he delighted most to represent mechanic people. He was deeply conversant in the ancients, both Greek and Latin, and he borrowed boldly from them : there is scarce a poet or historian among the Roman authors of those times whom he has not translated in *Sejanus* and *Catiline.* But he has done his robberies so openly, that one may see he fears not to be taxed by any law. He invades authors like a monarch ; and what would be theft in other poets, is only victory in him. With the spoils of these writers he so represents old Rome to us, in its rites, ceremonies, and customs, that if one of their poets had written either of his tragedies, we had seen less of it than in him. If there was any fault in his language, 't was that he weaved it too closely and laboriously, in his comedies especially : perhaps too, he did a little too much Romanize our tongue, leaving the words which he translated almost as much Latin as he found them : wherein, though he learnedly followed their language, he did not enough comply with the idiom of ours. If I would compare him with Shakespeare, I must acknowledge him the more correct poet, but Shakespeare the greater wit. Shakespeare was the Homer, or father of our dramatic poets ; Jonson was the Virgil, the pattern of elaborate writing ; I admire him, but I love Shakespeare. To conclude of him ; as he has given us the most correct plays, so in the precepts which he has laid down in his *Discoveries,* we have as many and profitable rules for perfecting the stage, as any wherewith the French can furnish us."

III. DEFENCE OF THE ESSAY

REVISED DEFENCE OF RHYME AGAINST SIR ROBERT HOWARD[1]

But to return to verse : whether it be natural or not in plays, is a problem which is not demonstrable of either side : 't is enough for me that he acknowledges he had rather read good verse than prose : for if all the enemies of verse will confess as much, I shall not need to prove that it is natural. I am satisfied, if it cause delight : for delight is the chief, if not the only, end of poesy :

---

[1] Who, having been introduced as " Crites " in the *Essay,* opposing rhymed drama, had replied tartly in the Preface to his *Duke of Lerma.*

instruction can be admitted but in the second place ; for poesy only instructs as it delights.   'T is true, that to imitate well is a poet's work ; but to affect the soul, and excite the passions, and above all to move admiration (which is the delight of serious plays) a bare imitation will not serve.   The converse, therefore, which a poet is to imitate, must be heightened with all the arts and ornaments of poesy ; and must be such, as, strictly considered, could never be supposed spoken by any without premeditation.

As for what he urges, that "a play will still be supposed to be a composition of several persons speaking *ex tempore ;* and that good verses are the hardest things which can be imagined to be so spoken," I must crave leave to dissent from his opinion, as to the former part of it : for, if I am not deceived, a play is supposed to be the work of the poet, imitating or representing the conversation of several persons ; and this I think to be as clear, as he thinks the contrary.

But I will be bolder, and do not doubt to make it good, though a paradox, that one great reason why prose is not to be used in serious plays, is, because it is too near the nature of converse : there may be too great a likeness ; as the most skilful painters affirm, that there may be too near a resemblance in a picture : to take every lineament and feature, is not to make an excellent piece ; but to take so much only as will make a beautiful resemblance of the whole ; and, with an ingenious flattery of nature, to heighten the beauties of some part, and hide the deformities of the rest.   For so says Horace :

> Ut pictura poesis erit. . . .
> Hæc amat obscurum, vult hæc sub luce videri,
> Judicis argutum quæ non formidat acumen.
> . . . et quæ
> Desperat tractata nitescere posse, relinquit.

In *Bartholomew Fair*, or the lowest kind of comedy, that degree of heightening is used, which is proper to set off that subject.   'T is true the author was not there to go out of prose, as he does in his higher arguments of comedy, *The Fox*, and *Alchemist ;* yet he does so raise his matter in that prose, as to render it delightful ; which he could never have performed, had he only said or done those very things that are daily spoken or practised in the Fair; for then the Fair itself would be as full of pleasure to an ingenious person as the play; which we manifestly see it is not. But he hath made an excellent lazar of it: the copy is of price, though the original be vile. You see in *Catiline* and *Sejanus*, where the argument is great, he sometimes ascends to verse, which shows he thought it not unnatural in serious plays: and had his genius been as proper for rhyme, as it was for humour, or had the age in which he lived attained to as much knowledge in verse as ours, it is probable he would have adorned those subjects with that kind of writing.

Thus prose, though the rightful prince, yet is by common consent deposed, as too weak for the government of serious plays; and he failing, there now start up two competitors; one the nearer in blood, which is blank verse; the other more fit for the ends of government, which is rhyme. Blank verse is, indeed, the nearer prose, but he is blemished with the weakness of his predecessor. Rhyme (for I will deal clearly) has somewhat of the usurper in him; but he is brave• and generous, and his dominion pleasing. For this reason of delight, the ancients (whom I will still believe as wise as those who so confidently correct them) wrote all their tragedies in verse, though they knew it most remote from conversation.

But I perceive I am falling into the danger of another rebuke from my opponent; for when I plead that "the ancients used verse," I prove not that they would have admitted rhyme, had it then been written: all I can say is only this; that it seems to have succeeded verse by the general consent of poets in all modern languages: for almost all their serious plays are written in it: which, though it be no demonstration that therefore they ought to be so, yet at least the practice first, and then the continuation of it, shows that it attained the end, which was to please; and if that cannot be compassed here, I will be the first who shall lay it down. For I confess my chief endeavours are to delight the age in which I live. If the humour of this be for low comedy, small accidents, and raillery, I will force my genius to obey it, though with more reputation I could write in verse. I know I am not so fitted by nature to write comedy: I want that gaiety of humour which is required to it. My conversation is slow and dull, my humour

saturnine and reserved : in short, I am none of those who endeavour
to break jests in company, or make repartees. So that those who
decry my comedies do me no injury, except it be in point of profit :
reputation in them is the last thing to which I shall pretend.

IV. "THE STORY IS THE LEAST PART"[1]

But these little critics do not well consider what is the work of
a poet, and what the graces of a poem : the story is the least part
of either : I mean the foundation of it, before it is modelled by the
art of him who writes it; who forms it with more care, by exposing
only the beautiful parts of it to view, than a skilful lapidary sets a
jewel. On this foundation of the story, the characters are raised:
and, since no story can afford characters enough for the variety of
the English stage, it follows, that it is to be altered and enlarged
with new persons, accidents, and designs, which will almost make
it new. When this is done, the forming it into acts and scenes,
disposing of actions and passions into their proper places, and
beautifying both with descriptions, similitudes, and propriety of
language, is the principal employment of the poet; as being the
largest field of fancy, which is the principal quality required in
him : for so much the word ποιητής implies. Judgment, indeed, is
necessary in him; but it is fancy that gives the life-touches, and
the secret graces to it; especially in serious plays, which depend
not much on observation. For, to write humour in comedy (which
is the theft of poets from mankind), little of fancy is required;
the poet observes only what is ridiculous and pleasant folly, and
by judging exactly what is so, he pleases in the representation of it.

But, in general, the employment of a poet is like that of a curious
gunsmith, or watchmaker : the iron or silver is not his own; but
they are the least part of that which gives the value : the price
lies wholly in the workmanship. And he who works dully on a
story, without moving laughter in a comedy, or raising concernment

---

[1] In this, as in so many casual and *ad hoc* observations of his, Dryden
launches a veritable critical battle-ship (or fire-ship, perhaps, rather). First
fable, then characters, then diction, etc., had been, in a steep slope of descent,
the hierarchical arrangement of the ancients : it is here exactly reversed.

in a serious play, is no more to be accounted a good poet, than a gunsmith of the Minories is to be compared with the best workman of the town.

Preface to An Evening's Love, sub fin.

V. SHAKESPEARE AND FLETCHER

For what remains, the excellency of that poet was, as I have said, in the more manly passions; Fletcher's in the softer. Shakespeare writ better betwixt man and man; Fletcher betwixt man and woman. Consequently the one described friendship better, the other love; yet Shakespeare taught Fletcher to write love, and Juliet and Desdemona are originals. It is true the scholar had the softer soul; but the master had the kinder. Friendship is both a virtue and a passion essentially; Love is a passion only in its nature, and is not a virtue but by accident. Good nature makes friendship; but effeminacy love. Shakespeare had an universal mind which comprehended all characters and passions; Fletcher a more confined and limited — for though he treated love in perfection, yet honour, ambition, revenge, and generally all the stronger passions, he touched not, or not masterly. To conclude all, he was a limb of Shakespeare.

Preface to Troilus and Cressida.

VI. REMARKS ON RYMER

These remarks were never published by Dryden, but there is no reasonable doubt of their genuineness. For their history, see Scott's *Dryden* (with the present editor's comments), xv. 379 *sq.* Thomas Rymer, who has been described by Macaulay, in superlative for once at least scarcely hyperbolic, as "the worst critic who ever lived," published in 1678 a little volume on *The Tragedies of the Last Age*, and gave a copy of it to Dryden, with whom he was both then and at periods afterwards, though not always, on good terms. On the fly-leaves of this Dryden seems to have written some Heads of an Answer which he never worked up. The general drift is rather to outflank, than directly to oppose, Rymer's exaltation of Greek above English drama.

The answerer ought to prove two things : First that the fable is not the greatest masterpiece of a tragedy, though it be the foundation of it. Secondly that other ends, as suitable to the nature of tragedy, may be found in the English, which were not in the Greek.

. . . .

And one reason of that success, is, in my opinion, this, that Shakespeare and Fletcher have written to the genius of the age and nation in which they lived : for though nature, as he objects, is the same in all places, and reason too the same, yet the climate, the age, the disposition of the people, to which a poet writes, may be so different, that what pleased the Greeks would not satisfy an English audience.

. . . .

It is not enough that Aristotle has said so, for Aristotle drew his models of tragedy from Sophocles and Euripides : AND, IF HE HAD SEEN OURS, MIGHT HAVE CHANGED HIS MIND.

VII. THE VIA MEDIA OF TRANSLATION [1]

The consideration of these difficulties, in a servile, literal translation, not long since made two of our famous wits, Sir John Denham and Mr. Cowley, to contrive another way of turning authors into our tongue, called, by the latter of them, imitation. As they were friends, I suppose they communicated their thoughts on this subject to each other ; and therefore their reasons for it are little different, though the practice of one is much more moderate. I take imitation of an author, in their sense, to be an endeavour of a later poet to write like one who has written before him, on the same subject ; that is, not to translate his words, or to be confined to his sense, but only to set him as a pattern, and to write, as he supposes that author would have done, had he lived in our age, and in our country.   Yet I dare not say, that either of them have carried this libertine way of rendering authors (as Mr. Cowley calls it) so far as my definition reaches ; for, in the Pindaric odes, the customs and ceremonies of ancient Greece are still preserved.   But I know

---

[1] From the Preface to the *Translation of Ovid's Epistles.*

not what mischief may arise hereafter from the example of such an innovation, when writers of unequal parts to him shall imitate so bold an undertaking. To add and to diminish what we please, which is the way avowed by him, ought only to be granted to Mr. Cowley, and that too only in his translation of Pindar; because he alone was able to make him amends, by giving him better of his own, whenever he refused his author's thoughts. Pindar is generally known to be a dark writer, to want connection, (I mean as to our understanding,) to soar out of sight, and leave his reader at a gaze. So wild and ungovernable a poet cannot be translated literally; his genius is too strong to bear a chain, and, Samson-like, he shakes it off. A genius so elevated and unconfined as Mr. Cowley's, was but necessary to make Pindar speak English, and that was to be performed by no other way than imitation. But if Virgil, or Ovid, or any regular intelligible authors, be thus used, it is no longer to be called their work, when neither the thoughts nor words are drawn from the original; but instead of them there is something new produced, which is almost the creation of another hand. By this way, it is true, somewhat that is excellent may be invented, perhaps more excellent than the first design; though Virgil must be still excepted, when that perhaps takes place. Yet he who is inquisitive to know an author's thoughts, will be disappointed in his expectation; and it is not always that a man will be contented to have a present made him, when he expects the payment of a debt. To state it fairly; imitation of an author is the most advantageous way for a translator to show himself, but the greatest wrong which can be done to the memory and reputation of the dead. Sir John Denham (who advised more liberty than he took himself) gives his reason for his innovation, in his admirable preface before the translation of the second *Æneid*: "Poetry is of so subtile a spirit, that, in pouring out of one language into another, it will all evaporate; and, if a new spirit be not added in the transfusion, there will remain nothing but a *caput mortuum*." I confess this argument holds good against a literal translation; but who defends it? Imitation and verbal version are, in my opinion, the two extremes which ought to be avoided; and therefore, when I have proposed the mean betwixt them, it will be seen how far his argument will reach.

No man is capable of translating poetry, who, besides a genius to that art, is not a master both of his author's language, and of his own; nor must we understand the language only of the poet, but his particular turn of thoughts and expression, which are the characters that distinguish, and as it were individuate him from all other writers. When we are come thus far, it is time to look into ourselves, to conform our genius to his, to give his thought either the same turn, if our tongue will bear it, or, if not, to vary but the dress, not to alter or destroy the substance. The like care must be taken of the more outward ornaments, the words. When they appear (which is but seldom) literally graceful, it were an injury to the author that they should be changed. But, since every language is so full of its own proprieties, that what is beautiful in one, is often barbarous, nay sometimes nonsense, in another, it would be unreasonable to limit a translator to the narrow compass of his author's words: it is enough if he choose out some expression which does not vitiate the sense. I suppose he may stretch his chain to such a latitude; but, by innovation of thoughts, methinks, he breaks it. By this means the spirit of an author may be transfused, and yet not lost: and thus it is plain, that the reason alleged by Sir John Denham has no further force than to expression; for thought, if it be translated truly, cannot be lost in another language; but the words that convey it to our apprehension (which are the image and ornament of that thought,) may be so ill chosen, as to make it appear in an unhandsome dress, and rob it of its native lustre. There is, therefore, a liberty to be allowed for the expression; neither is it necessary that words and lines should be confined to the measure of their original. The sense of an author, generally speaking, is to be sacred and inviolable. If the fancy of Ovid be luxuriant, it is his character to be so; and if I retrench it, he is no longer Ovid. It will be replied, that he receives advantage by this lopping of his superfluous branches; but I rejoin, that a translator has no such right. When a painter copies from the life, I suppose he has no privilege to alter features, and lineaments, under pretence that his picture will look better: perhaps the face, which he has drawn, would be more exact, if the eyes or nose were altered; but it is his business to make it resemble the original. In two cases

only there may a seeming difficulty arise ; that is, if the thought
be notoriously trivial, or dishonest ; but the same answer will serve
for both, that then they ought not to be translated : —

—— Et quæ
Desperes tractata nitescere posse, relinquas.

Thus I have ventured to give my opinion on this subject against
the authority of two great men, but I hope without offence to either
of their memories ; for I both loved them living, and reverence
them now they are dead. But if, after what I have urged, it be
thought by better judges, that the praise of a translation consists in
adding new beauties to the piece, thereby to recompense the loss
which it sustains by change of language, I shall be willing to
be taught better, and to recant. In the meantime, it seems to me
that the true reason why we have so few versions which are tolerable, is not from the too close pursuing of the author's sense, but
because there are so few who have all the talents which are
requisite for translation, and that there is so little praise, and so
small encouragement, for so considerable a part of learning.

VIII. GOOD–BYE TO RANT [1]

In a play-house, everything contributes to impose upon the judgment ; the lights, the scenes, the habits, and, above all, the grace
of action, which is commonly the best where there is the most
need of it, surprise the audience, and cast a mist upon their understandings ; not unlike the cunning of a juggler, who is always
staring us in the face, and overwhelming us with gibberish, only
that he may gain the opportunity of making the cleaner conveyance of his trick. But these false beauties of the stage are no

---

[1] This interesting apology " for his own house " — bombast — is from the Dedication of the *Spanish Friar* (1681). Dryden makes up for his justice on himself by being rather *un*just to Chapman ; but though never actually shipwrecked
on the loadstone rock of " Good Sense," he sometimes drifted towards it. The
" famous modern poet " was Naugerius, or Navagero; and while the victim was
actually Martial, not Statius, it seems very probable that the idol was Catullus,
not Virgil.

more lasting than a rainbow; when the actor ceases to shine upon them, when he gilds them no longer with his reflection, they vanish in a twinkling. I have sometimes wondered, in the reading, what was become of those glaring colours which amazed me in *Bussy d'Ambois* upon the theatre; but when I had taken up what I supposed a fallen star, I found I had been cozened with a jelly; nothing but a cold, dull mass, which glittered no longer than it was shooting; a dwarfish thought, dressed up in gigantic words, repetition in abundance, looseness of expression, and gross hyperboles; the sense of one line expanded prodigiously into ten; and, to sum up all, uncorrect English, and a hideous mingle of false poetry, and true nonsense; or, at best, a scantling of wit, which lay gasping for life, and groaning beneath a heap of rubbish. A famous modern poet used to sacrifice every year a Statius to Virgil's manes; and I have indignation enough to burn a D'AMBOIS annually, to the memory of Jonson. But now, my lord, I am sensible, perhaps too late, that I have gone too far: for, I remember some verses of my own *Maximin* and *Almanzor*, which cry vengeance upon me for their extravagance, and which I wish heartily in the same fire with Statius and Chapman. All I can say for those passages, which are, I hope, not many, is, that I knew they were bad enough to please, even when I writ them; but I repent of them amongst my sins; and, if any of their fellows intrude by chance into my present writings, I draw a stroke over all those Delilahs of the theatre; and am resolved I will settle myself no reputation by the applause of fools. It is not that I am mortified to all ambition, but I scorn as much to take it from half-witted judges, as I should to raise an estate by cheating of bubbles. Neither do I discommend the lofty style in tragedy, which is naturally pompous and magnificent; but nothing is truly sublime that is not just and proper. If the ancients had judged by the same measure, which a common reader takes, they had concluded Statius to have written higher than Virgil, for,

Quæ superimposito moles geminata Colosso

carries a more thundering kind of sound than

Tityre, tu patulæ recubans sub tegmine fagi:

yet Virgil had all the majesty of a lawful prince, and Statius only the blustering of a tyrant. But when men affect a virtue which they cannot easily reach, they fall into a vice, which bears the nearest resemblance to it. Thus, an injudicious poet, who aims at loftiness, runs easily into the swelling puffy style, because it looks like greatness. I remember, when I was a boy, I thought inimitable Spenser a mean poet, in comparison of Sylvester's *Dubartas*, and was rapt into an ecstasy when I read these lines —

> Now, when the winter's keener breath began
> To crystallize the Baltic ocean ;
> To glaze the lakes, to bridle up the floods,
> And periwig with snow the bald-pate woods : — *

I am much deceived if this be not abominable fustian, that is, thoughts and words ill-sorted, and without the least relation to each other; yet I dare not answer for an audience, that they would not clap it on the stage : so little value there is to be given to the common cry, that nothing but madness can please madmen, and the poet must be of a piece with the spectators, to gain a reputation with them. But, as in a room, contrived for state, the height of the roof should bear a proportion to the area; so, in the heightenings of poetry, the strength and vehemence of figures should be suited to the occasion, the subject, and the persons. All beyond this is monstrous: it is out of nature, it is an excrescence, and not a living part of poetry.

IX. CRITICASTRY [1]

There are a sort of blundering half-witted people who make a great noise about a verbal slip; though Horace would instruct them better in true criticism ;

> non ego paucis, etc.

True judgment in Poetry, like that in Painting, takes a view of the whole together, whether it be good or not; and where the beauties

---

* Dryden has elsewhere ridiculed this absurd passage. The original has "periwig with *wool*." — SCOTT.

[1] From the Preface to the Second Miscellany (1685).

are more than the faults, concludes for the poet against the little
judge. 'T is a sign that malice is hard driven when 't is forced to
lay hold on a word or a syllable : to arraign a man is one thing,
and to cavil at him is another.

Preface to the Second Part of Poetical Miscellanies.

Ill writers are commonly the sharpest censors; for they, as the
best poet and the best patron [1] said —

> When in the full perfection of decay
> Turn vinegar, and come again in play.

Thus the corruption of a poet is the generation of a critic.

Dedication of the Third Part of Miscellany Poems.

There are a middle sort of readers (as we hold there is a middle
state of souls) such as have a further insight than the former yet
have not the capacity of judging right. For I speak not of those
who are bribed by a party, and know better, if they were not corrupted ; but I mean a company of warm young men, who are not
arrived so far as to discern the difference between fustian or osten-
tatious sentences, and the true sublime.

Dedication of the Æneis.

X. DRYDEN'S OUTFIT IN CRITICISM [2]

When I was myself in the rudiments of my poetry, without
name or reputation in the world, having rather the ambition of
a writer than the skill; when I was drawing the outlines of
an art, without any living master to instruct me in it ; — an art
which had been better praised than studied here in England,
wherein Shakespeare, who created the stage among us, had rather
written happily than knowingly and justly, and Jonson who by
studying Horace, had been acquainted with the rules, yet seemed
to envy to posterity that knowledge, and, like an inventor of some
useful art, to make a monopoly of his learning — when thus, as
I may say, before the use of the loadstone, or knowledge of

---

[1] Dorset.

[2] Note that Dryden here (writing in 1693) says nothing about any indebtedness, earlier or later than the *Essay*, to *Spanish* critics (*cf.* p. 136).

the compass, I was sailing in a vast ocean, without other help than the polestar of the Ancients, and the rules of the French stage amongst the Moderns, which are extremely different from ours, by reason of their opposite taste : — yet even then I had the presumption to dedicate to your Lordship a very unfinished piece I confess, and which can only be excused by the little experience of the author and the modesty of the title *An Essay*.[1]

Discourse concerning Satire.

XI. HIS MASTERS IN PROSODY

I hope I have translated closely enough, and given them [2] the same turn of verse which they had in the original; and this I may say, without vanity, is not the talent of every poet. He who has arrived the nearest to it, is the ingenious and learned Sandys, the best versifier of the former age; if I may properly call it by that name, which was the former part of this concluding century. For Spenser and Fairfax both flourished in the reign of Queen Elizabeth; great masters in our language, and who saw much further into the beauties of our numbers, than those who immediately followed them. Milton was the poetical son of Spenser, and Mr. Waller of Fairfax; for we have our lineal descents and clans as well as other families. Spenser more than once insinuates, that the soul of Chaucer was transfused into his body; * and that he was begotten by him two hundred years after his decease. Milton has acknowledged to me, that Spenser was his original; and many besides myself have heard our famous Waller own, that he derived the harmony of his numbers from *Godfrey of Bulloigne*, which was turned into English by Mr. Fairfax.

Preface to Fables.

XII. CHAUCER

It remains that I say somewhat of Chaucer in particular.

In the first place, as he is the father of English poetry, so I hold him in the same degree of veneration as the Grecians held Homer,

---

[1] *I.e., of Dramatic Poesy.*   [2] The *Ovidian* passages.

* I cannot find any such passages in Spenser as are here alluded to. — SCOTT. Dryden often writes loosely : he thought no doubt of *F. Q.*, IV. 2. xxxiv. 7.

or the Romans Virgil. He is a perpetual fountain of good sense; learned in all sciences; and, therefore, speaks properly on all subjects. As he knew what to say, so he knows also when to leave off; a continence which is practised by few writers, and scarcely by any of the ancients, excepting Virgil and Horace. One of our late great poets [1] is sunk in his reputation, because he could never forgive any conceit which came in his way; but swept, like a drag-net, great and small. There was plenty enough, but the dishes were ill sorted; whole pyramids of sweetmeats for boys and women, but little of solid meat for men. All this proceeded not from any want of knowledge, but of judgment. Neither did he want that in discerning the beauties and faults of other poets, but only indulged himself in the luxury of writing; and perhaps knew it was a fault, but hoped the reader would not find it. For this reason, though he must always be thought a great poet, he is no longer esteemed a good writer; and for ten impressions, which his works have had in so many successive years, yet at present a hundred books are scarcely purchased once a twelvemonth; for, as my last Lord Rochester said, though somewhat profanely, "Not being of God, he could not stand."

Chaucer followed nature everywhere, but was never so bold to go beyond her; and there is a great difference of being *poeta* and *nimis poeta*, if we may believe Catullus,[2] as much as betwixt a modest behaviour and affectation. The verse of Chaucer, I confess, is not harmonious to us; but it is like the eloquence of one whom Tacitus commends, it was *auribus istius temporis accommodata*. They who lived with him, and some time after him, thought it musical; and it continues so, even in our judgment, if compared with the numbers of Lydgate and Gower, his contemporaries: — there is the rude sweetness of a Scotch tune in it, which is natural and pleasing, though not perfect. It is true, I cannot go so far as he who published the last edition of him; for he would make us believe the fault is in our ears, and that there were really ten syllables in a verse where we find but nine: but this opinion is not worth confuting; it is so gross and obvious an error, that common sense (which is a rule in everything but

---

[1] Cowley.   [2] Not Catullus, but Martial, iii. 44.

matters of faith and revelation) must convince the reader, that
equality of numbers, in every verse which we call heroic, was
either not known, or not always practised, in Chaucer's age.
It were an easy matter to produce some thousands of his verses,
which are lame for want of half a foot, and sometimes a whole one,
and which no pronunciation can make otherwise. We can only say,
that he lived in the infancy of our poetry, and that nothing is
brought to perfection at the first. We must be children before we
grow men. There was an Ennius, and in process of time a
Lucilius, and a Lucretius, before Virgil and Horace; even after
Chaucer there was a Spenser, a Harrington, a Fairfax, before
Waller and Denham were in being; and our numbers were in their
nonage till these last appeared.

. . . .

He must have been a man of a most wonderful comprehensive
nature, because, as it has been truly observed of him, he has taken
into the compass of his *Canterbury Tales* the various manners
and humours (as we now call them) of the whole English nation,
in his age. Not a single character has escaped him. All his
pilgrims are severally distinguished from each other; and not only
in their inclinations, but in their very physiognomies and persons.
Baptista Porta [1] could not have described their natures better, than
by the marks which the poet gives them. The matter and manner
of their tales, and of their telling, are so suited to their different
educations, humours, and callings, that each of them would be
improper in any other mouth. Even the grave and serious characters are distinguished by their several sorts of gravity: their
discourses are such as belong to their age, their calling, and their
breeding; such as are becoming of them, and of them only. Some
of his persons are vicious, and some virtuous; some are unlearned,
or (as Chaucer calls them) lewd, and some are learned. Even the
ribaldry of the low characters is different: the Reeve, the Miller,
and the Cook, are several men, and distinguished from each other
as much as the mincing Lady-Prioress and the broad-speaking, gap-
toothed Wife of Bath. But enough of this; there is such a variety
of game springing up before me, that I am distracted in my choice,

----

[1] The famous Italian physiognomist.

and know not which to follow. It is sufficient to say, according to the proverb, that here is God's plenty. We have our forefathers and great-grand-dames all before us, as they were in Chaucer's days: their general characters are still remaining in mankind, and even in England, though they are called by other names than those of monks, and friars, and canons, and lady-abbesses, and nuns; for mankind is ever the same, and nothing lost out of nature, though everything is altered. May I have leave to do myself the justice, (since my enemies will do me none, and are so far from granting me to be a good poet, that they will not allow me so much as to be a Christian, or a moral man), may I have leave, I say, to inform my reader, that I have confined my choice to such tales of Chaucer as savour nothing of immodesty. If I had desired more to please than to instruct, the Reeve, the Miller, the Shipman, the Merchant, the Sumner, and, above all, the Wife of Bath, in the prologue to her tale, would have procured me as many friends and readers, as there are beaux and ladies of pleasure in the town. But I will no more offend against good manners. I am sensible, as I ought to be, of the scandal I have given by my loose writings; and make what reparation I am able, by this public acknowledgment. If anything of this nature, or of profaneness, be crept into these poems, I am so far from defending it, that I disown it, *totum hoc indictum volo*. Chaucer makes another manner of apology for his broad speaking, and Boccace makes the like; but I will follow neither of them. Our countryman, in the end of his characters, before the *Canterbury Tales*, thus excuses the ribaldry, which is very gross in many of his novels —

> But firste, I praie you of your curtesie,
> That ye ne arette it not my vilanie
> Though that I plainly speke in this matere,
> To tellen you hir wordes, and hir chere:
> Ne though I speke hir wordes proprely,
> For this ye knowen al so well as I,
> Who so shall telle a tale after a man,
> He moste reherse as neighe as ever he can:
> Everich word, if it be in his charge,
> All speke he, never so rudely and so large:
> Or elles he moste tellen his tale untrewe,

> Or feinen thinges, or finden wordes newe:
> He may not spare, although he were his brother,
> He moste as wel sayn o word as an other.
> Crist spake himself ful brode in holy writ,
> And wel ye wote no vilanie is it,
> Eke Plato sayeth, who so can him rede,
> The wordes moste ben cosin to the dede.

Yet if a man should have enquired of Boccace or of Chaucer, what need they had of introducing such characters, where obscene words were proper in their mouths, but very indecent to be heard? I know not what answer they could have made; for that reason, such tales shall be left untold by me. You have here a specimen of Chaucer's language, which is so obsolete, that his sense is scarce to be understood; and you have likewise more than one example of his unequal numbers, which were mentioned before. Yet many of his verses consist of ten syllables, and the words not much behind our present English: as for example, these two lines, in the description of the carpenter's young wife —

> Winsing she was, as is a jolly colt,
> Long as a mast, and upright as a bolt.

I have almost done with Chaucer, when I have answered some objections relating to my present work. I find some people are offended that I have turned these tales into modern English; because they think them unworthy of my pains, and look on Chaucer as a dry, old-fashioned wit, not worthy reviving. I have often heard the late Earl of Leicester say, that Mr. Cowley himself was of that opinion; who, having read him over at my lord's request, declared he had no taste of him. I dare not advance my opinion against the judgment of so great an author; but I think it fair, however, to leave the decision to the public. Mr. Cowley was too modest to set up for a dictator; and being shocked perhaps with his old style, never examined into the depth of his good sense. Chaucer, I confess, is a rough diamond, and must first be polished, ere he shines. I deny not likewise, that, living in our early days of poetry, he writes not always of a piece; but sometimes mingles trivial things with those of greater moment. Sometimes also, though not often, he runs riot, like Ovid, and knows not

when he has said enough.   But there are more great wits besides
Chaucer, whose fault is their excess of conceits, and those ill sorted.
An author is not to write all he can, but only all he ought.   Having observed this redundancy in Chaucer, (as it is an easy matter
for a man of ordinary parts to find a fault in one of greater,) I have
not tied myself to a literal translation ; but have often omitted what
I judged unnecessary, or not of dignity enough to appear in the
company of better thoughts.   I have presumed further, in some
places, and added somewhat of my own where I thought my author
was deficient, and had not given his thoughts their true lustre, for
want of words in the beginning of our language.   And to this I was
the more emboldened, because (if I may be permitted to say it of
myself) I found I had a soul congenial to his, and that I had been
conversant in the same studies.   Another poet, in another age, may
take the same liberty with my writings ; if at least they live long
enough to deserve correction.   It was also necessary sometimes to
restore the sense of Chaucer, which was lost or mangled in the
errors of the press.   Let this example suffice at present : in the
story of Palamon and Arcite, where the temple of Diana is described,
you find these verses, in all the editions of our author —

> Ther saw I Dane yturned til a tree,
> I mene not hire the goddesse Diane,
> But Venus daughter, which that hight Dane

which, after a little consideration, I knew was to be reformed into
this sense, — that Daphne, the daughter of Peneus, was turned
into a tree.   I durst not make thus bold with Ovid, lest some
future Milbourne should arise, and say, I varied from my author,
because I understood him not.

But there are other judges, who think I ought not to have
translated Chaucer into English, out of a quite contrary notion :
they suppose there is a certain veneration due to his old language ;
and that it is little less than profanation and sacrilege to alter it.
They are further of opinion, that somewhat of his good sense will
suffer in this transfusion, and much of the beauty of his thoughts
will infallibly be lost, which appear with more grace in their
old habit.   Of this opinion was that excellent person, whom I

mentioned, the late Earl of Leicester, who valued Chaucer as much
as Mr. Cowley despised him. My lord dissuaded me from this
attempt, (for I was thinking of it some years before his death,)
and his authority prevailed so far with me, as to defer my undertaking while he lived, in deference to him: yet my reason was not
convinced with what he urged against it. If the first end of a
writer be to be understood, then, as his language grows obsolete
his thoughts must grow obscure —

> Multa renascentur, quæ nunc cecidere ; cadentque
> Quæ nunc sunt in honore vocabula, si volet usus,
> Quem penes arbitrium est et jus et norma loquendi.

When an ancient word, for its sound and significancy, deserves
to be revived, I have that reasonable veneration for antiquity
to restore it. All beyond this is superstition. Words are not like
landmarks, so sacred as never to be removed; customs are changed,
and even statutes are silently repealed, when the reason ceases for
which they were enacted. As for the other part of the argument,
— that his thoughts will lose of their original beauty by the
innovation of words, — in the first place, not only their beauty,
but their being is lost, where they are no longer understood, which
is the present case. I grant that something must be lost in all
transfusion, that is, in all translations ; but the sense will remain,
which would otherwise be lost, or at least be maimed, when it
is scarce intelligible, and that but to a few. How few are there,
who can read Chaucer, so as to understand him perfectly? And if
imperfectly, then with less profit, and no pleasure. It is not for
the use of some old Saxon friends, that I have taken these pains
with him: let them neglect my version, because they have no need
of it. I made it for their sakes, who understand sense and poetry
as well as they, when that poetry and sense is put into words which
they understand. I will go further, and dare to add, that what
beauties I lose in some places, I give to others which had them not
originally : but in this I may be partial to myself; let the reader
judge, and I submit to his decision. Yet I think I have just
occasion to complain of them, who, because they understand
Chaucer, would deprive the greater part of their countrymen of

the same advantage, and hoard him up, as misers do their grandam gold, only to look on it themselves, and hinder others from making use of it. In sum, I seriously protest, that no man ever had, or can have, a greater veneration for Chaucer than myself. I have translated some part of his works, only that I might perpetuate his memory, or at least refresh it, amongst my countrymen. If I have altered him anywhere for the better, I must at the same time acknowledge, that I could have done nothing without him. *Facile est inventis addere* is no great commendation; and I am not so vain to think I have deserved a greater.

Preface to *Fables*.

XX

BYSSHE'S "ART OF POETRY"

The *Art of Poetry* (with a Dictionary of Rhymes and a methodical anthology of passages for imitation) of Edward Bysshe, first published in the year of Dryden's death (or in 1702 ?), is not a work of literature. But it was constantly reprinted; in spite of the sneers of Gildon (who came a little later with a more elaborate and pretentious work on the same subject) it enjoyed popularity, and exercised influence, throughout the 18th century; and the metrical laws to be here quoted were accepted, in their peremptory and almost Athanasian rigour, with docility by the orthodox, from Johnson to the least poetaster, during that time. They clearly influenced even such a man as Guest, who died but a couple of decades from the beginning of the 20th, and it would be rash to say that suspicions of their orthodoxy after all do not lurk here and there at the present moment. The editions of the book, I believe, vary somewhat. The following quotations are taken from the *Third* "with large improvements" (London 1708).

I have inserted not only similes, allusions, characters and descriptions; but also the most natural and sublime thoughts of our modern poets on all subjects whatever. I say, of our *modern*, for though some of the ancient, as Chaucer, Spenser and others, have not been excelled, perhaps not equalled, by any that have succeeded them, either in justness of description, or in propriety and greatness of thought: yet their language is now become so antiquated and obsolete that most readers of our age have no ear for them. And this is the reason that the good Shakespeare himself is not so frequently cited in this collection as he would otherwise deserve to be.

Preface.

The structure of our verses, whether blank or in rhyme, consists in a certain number of syllables; not in feet composed of long and short syllables, as the verses of the Greeks and Romans.

Chap. i, opening.

Verses of double rhyme require a syllable more than those of single rhyme. . . .   This must also be observed in blank verse. . . . And this verse of Milton,

<blockquote>Void of all succour and needful comfort,</blockquote>

wants a syllable, for, being accented on the last save one, it ought to have 11.   *Ibid.*

Our poetry admits, for the most part, but of three sorts of verses : that is to say of verses of 10, 8, or 7 syllables.   Chap. i § 1.

In these [*heroic*] verses two things are chiefly to be considered :
1. The seat of the accent.
2. The pause.   *Ibid.*

In a verse of 10 syllables this [*strongest*] accent must be either at the 2d, 4th, or 6th : which produces 5 several pauses, that is to say at the 3d, 4th, 5th, 6th, or 7th syllable.   *Ibid.*

The Construction or Sense should never end at a syllable where the pause ought not to be made ; as at the 8th and 9th. . . .   So unequal a division can produce no true harmony ; and for this reason, too, the pauses at the 3d and 7th syllables, though not wholly to be condemned, ought to be but sparingly practised.   *Ibid.*

The foregoing rules [of *accent on the even places,* and *pause* MAINLY *at the 4th, 5th, or 6th syllable*] ought indispensably to be followed in all our verses of 10 syllables ; and the observation of them will produce Harmony, the neglect of them harshness and discord.

Ibid.

The verses of 9 and of 11 syllables are of two sorts ; one is those that are accented on the last save one, which are only the verses of double rhyme that belong to those of 8 and 10 syllables. . . . The other is those that are accented on the last syllable,[1] which are employed only in compositions for music, and in the lowest sort of burlesque poetry, the disagreeableness of their measure having wholly excluded them from grave and serious subjects.

Chap. i § 2.

[1] *I.e.,* anapæstic lines with anacrusis, or with dissyllabic substitution.

Our poetry being very much polished and refined since the days of Chaucer, Spenser, and the other ancient poets, some rules which they neglected . . . have been practised by the best of the moderns.

The first is to avoid, as much as possible, the concourse of vowels. . . . The *e* of the particle *the* ought always to be cut off before words that begin with a vowel.

.   .   .   .

The second [is] to contract the two last syllables of the Preter-perfect tenses of all the verbs that will admit of it. . . . It is a fault to make *amazèd* of three syllables and *lovèd* of two. . . . The second person of the Present and Preterperfect tenses of all verbs ought to be contracted in like manner, as *thou lov'st*, for *thou lovest*. . . .

The third Rule is, not to make use of several words in a verse that begin by the same letter.

.   .   .   .

The fourth is to avoid ending a verse by an adjective, when a substantive begins the following. . . .

.   .   .   .

The fifth is to avoid the frequent use of words of many syllables.

Chap. i § 3.

Beauteous is but two syllables, *victorious* but three ; and it is a fault in Dryden to make it four.

Chap. i § 4.

But if the accent be upon the first syllable . . . it is a fault to make *riot* one syllable, as Milton has done in this verse,

Their riot ascends above their lofty towers.

Ibid.

Bysshe, as might be expected, is very copious on what he calls "Elision," by which he, like other writers of his period, means not merely elision proper, but the omission of a middle syllable, or the cutting off of an initial. He fully approves the hideous things — *am'rous, endeav'ring, t' amuse, she 's, you 've,* — which disfigure orthodox 18th century poetry as results of the frantic endeavour to stifle trisyllabic feet.

Our ancient poets frequently made use of intermixed rhyme in their heroic poems, which they disposed into stanzas and cantos. . . . But this is now wholly laid aside.

Chap. iii § 2.

Except in the contemptuous reference to catalectic or otherwise incom
plete anapæstic verse cited above, it is to be noticed that Bysshe *never*
mentions "triple time" measures at all. The beautiful lyrics in Dryden's
plays, the charming *vers de société* which Prior and others had already
begun to write, all apparently — and beyond reasonable doubt really —
underlay in his mind the charge of " disagreeableness of measure."

XXI

ADDISON

I. TRUE AND FALSE WIT [1]

Spectator, No. 62. Friday, May 11, 1711.

Scribendi recte sapere est et principium et fons. — Horace.

Mr. Locke has an admirable reflexion upon the difference of Wit and Judgment, whereby he endeavours to shew the reason why they are not always the talents of the same person. His words are as follows : *And hence, perhaps, may be given some reason of that common observation, That men who have a great deal of wit and prompt memories, have not always the clearest judgment, or deepest reason. For Wit lying most in the assemblage of ideas, and putting those together with quickness and variety, wherein can be found any resemblance or congruity, thereby to make up pleasant pictures and agreeable visions in the fancy ; Judgment, on the contrary, lies quite on the other side, in separating carefully one from another, ideas wherein can be found the least difference, thereby to avoid being misled by similitude, and by affinity to take one thing for another. This is a way of proceeding quite contrary to Metaphor and Allusion ; wherein, for the most part, lies that entertainment and pleasantry of wit which strikes so lively on the fancy, and is therefore so acceptable to all people.*

This is, I think, the best and most philosophical account that I have ever met with of Wit, which generally, though not always, consists in such a resemblance and congruity of ideas as this author mentions. I shall only add to it, by way of explanation, that every

---

[1] This paper is preceded by several others attacking fantastically shaped verses, *bouts-rimés*, acrostics, anagrams, puns, etc., and followed by a Vision of Falsehood embodying the lesson in Addison's favourite manner.

resemblance of ideas is not that which we call Wit, unless it be
such an one that gives *delight* and *surprise* to the reader : these two
properties seem essential to Wit, more particularly the last of them.
In order therefore that the resemblance in the ideas be Wit, it is
necessary that the ideas should not lie too near one another in the
nature of things; for where the likeness is obvious, it gives no
surprise.   To compare one man's singing to that of another, or to
represent the whiteness of any object by that of milk and snow, or
the variety of its colours by those of the rainbow, cannot be called
Wit, unless besides this obvious resemblance, there be some further
congruity discovered in the two ideas that is capable of giving the
reader some surprise.   Thus when a poet tells us, the bosom of his
mistress is as white as snow, there is no Wit in the comparison;
but when he adds, with a sigh, that it is as cold too, it then grows
into Wit.   Every reader's memory may supply him with innumerable instances of the same nature.   For this reason, the similitudes
in heroic poets, who endeavour rather to fill the mind with great
conceptions, than to divert it with such as are new and surprising,
have seldom any thing in them that can be called Wit.   Mr. Locke's
account of Wit, with this short explanation, comprehends most of
the species of Wit, as metaphors, similitudes, allegories, enigmas,
mottos, parables, fables, dreams, visions, dramatic writings, burlesque, and all the methods of allusion : as there are many other
pieces of Wit (how remote soever they may appear at first sight,
from the foregoing description) which upon examination will be
found to agree with it.

As *true Wit* generally consists in this resemblance and congruity of
ideas, *false Wit* chiefly consists in the resemblance and congruity
sometimes of single letters, as in anagrams, chronograms, lipograms,
and acrostics : sometimes of syllables, as in echoes and doggerel
rhymes : sometimes of words, as in puns and quibbles ; and sometimes of whole sentences or poems, cast into the figures of *eggs*, *axes*,
or *altars :* nay, some carry the notion of Wit so far, as to ascribe it
even to external mimicry ; and to look upon a man as an ingenious
person, that can resemble the tone, posture, or face of another.

As *true Wit* consists in the resemblance of ideas, and *false Wit*
in the resemblance of words, according to the foregoing instances ;

there is another kind of Wit which consists partly in the resemblance of ideas, and partly in the resemblance of words; which for
distinction sake I shall call *mixt Wit*. This kind of Wit is that
which abounds in Cowley, more than in any author that ever wrote.
Mr. Waller has likewise a great deal of it. Mr. Dryden is very
sparing in it. Milton had a genius much above it. Spenser is
in the same class with Milton. The Italians, even in their Epic
poetry, are full of it. Monsieur Boileau, who formed himself upon
the ancient poets, has every where rejected it with scorn. If we
look after mixt Wit among the Greek writers, we shall find it
no where but in the Epigrammatists. There are indeed some
strokes of it in the little poem ascribed to Musæus, which by that,
as well as many other marks, betrays itself to be a modern composition. If we look into the Latin writers, we find none of this
mixt Wit in Virgil, Lucretius, or Catullus; very little in Horace,
but a great deal of it in Ovid, and scarce any thing else in Martial.

Out of the innumerable branches of *mixt Wit*, I shall choose
one instance which may be met with in all the writers of this class.
The passion of love in its nature has been thought to resemble fire;
for which reason the words fire and flame are made use of to signify
love. The witty poets therefore have taken an advantage from
the doubtful meaning of the word fire, to make an infinite number
of witticisms. Cowley observing the cold regard of his mistress's
eyes, and at the same time their power of producing love in him,
considers them as burning-glasses made of ice; and finding himself
able to live in the greatest extremities of love, concludes the Torrid
Zone to be habitable. When his mistress has read his letter written
in juice of lemon by holding it to the fire, he desires her to read it
over a second time by love's flames. When she weeps, he wishes
it were inward heat that distilled those drops from the limbeck.
When she is absent he is beyond eighty, that is, thirty degrees
nearer the Pole than when she is with him. His ambitious love is
a fire that naturally mounts upwards; his happy love is the beams
of Heaven, and his unhappy love flames of Hell. When it does
not let him sleep, it is a flame that sends up no smoke; when it is
opposed by counsel and advice, it is a fire that rages the more by
the wind's blowing upon it. Upon the dying of a tree in which he

had cut his loves, he observes that his written flames had burnt up and withered the tree. When he resolves to give over his passion, he tells us that one burnt like him for ever dreads the fire. His heart is an Etna, that instead of Vulcan's shop encloses Cupid's forge in it. His endeavouring to drown his love in wine, is throwing oil upon the fire. He would insinuate to his mistress, that the fire of love, like that of the sun (which produces so many living creatures) should not only warm but beget. Love in another place cooks Pleasure at his fire. Sometimes the poet's heart is frozen in every breast, and sometimes scorched in every eye. Sometimes he is drowned in tears, and burnt in love, like a ship set on fire in the middle of the sea.

The reader may observe in every one of these instances, that the poet mixes the qualities of fire with those of love; and in the same sentence speaking of it both as a passion and as real fire, surprises the reader with those seeming resemblances or contradictions that make up all the wit in this kind of writing. Mixt Wit therefore is a composition of pun and true Wit, and is more or less perfect as the resemblance lies in the ideas or in the words : its foundations are laid partly in falsehood and partly in truth : Reason puts in her claim for one half of it, and Extravagance for the other. The only province therefore for this kind of Wit, is epigram, or those little occasional poems that in their own nature are nothing else but a tissue of epigrams. I cannot conclude this head of mixt Wit, without owning that the admirable poet out of whom I have taken the examples of it, had as much true Wit as any author that ever writ; and indeed all other talents of an extraordinary genius.

It may be expected, since I am upon this subject, that I should take notice of Mr. Dryden's definition of Wit; which, with all the deference that is due to the judgment of so great a man, is not so properly a definition of Wit, as of good writing in general. Wit, as he defines it, is " a propriety of words and thoughts adapted to the subject." * If this be a true definition of Wit, I am apt to think

---

* " If Wit has truly been defined as a propriety of thoughts and words, then that definition will extend to all sorts of poetry. . . . Propriety of thought is that fancy which arises naturally from the subject, or which the poet adapts to it. Propriety of words is the clothing of these thoughts with such expressions as are naturally proper to them." — Dryden's Preface to *Albion and Albanius.*

that Euclid was the greatest wit that ever set pen to paper: it is certain that never was a greater propriety of words and thoughts adapted to the subject, than what that author has made use of in his *Elements*. I shall only appeal to my reader, if this definition agrees with any notion he has of Wit: if it be a true one I am sure Mr. Dryden was not only a better poet, but a greater wit than Mr. Cowley; and Virgil a much more facetious man than either Ovid or Martial.

Bouhours, whom I look upon to be the most penetrating of all the French critics, has taken pains to shew, that it is impossible for any thought to be beautiful which is not just, and has not its foundation in the nature of things: that the basis of all Wit is truth; and that no thought can be valuable, of which good sense is not the ground-work. Boileau has endeavoured to inculcate the same notions in several parts of his writings, both in prose and verse. This is that natural way of writing, that beautiful simplicity, which we so much admire in the compositions of the Ancients; and which no body deviates from, but those who want strength of genius to make a thought shine in its own natural beauties. Poets who want this strength of genius to give that majestic simplicity to Nature, which we so much admire in the works of the Ancients, are forced to hunt after foreign ornaments, and not to let any piece of Wit of what kind soever escape them. I look upon these writers as Goths in Poetry, who, like those in Architecture, not being able to come up to the beautiful simplicity of the old Greeks and Romans, have endeavoured to supply its place with all the extravagancies of an irregular fancy. Mr. Dryden makes a very handsome observation, on Ovid's writing a letter from Dido to Æneas, in the following words. "Ovid," says he (speaking of Virgil's fiction of Dido and Æneas), "takes it up after him, even in the same age, and makes an ancient heroine of Virgil's new-created Dido; dictates a letter for her just before her death to the ungrateful fugitive; and, very unluckily for himself, is for measuring a sword with a man so much superior in force to him on the same subject. I think I may be judge of this, because I have translated both. The famous author of the *Art of Love* has nothing of his own; he borrows all from a greater master in his own profession, and, which is worse,

improves nothing which he finds: Nature fails him, and being
forced to his old shift, he has recourse to Witticism. This passes
indeed with his soft admirers, and gives him the preference to
Virgil in their esteem."

Were not I supported by so great an authority as that of Mr.
Dryden, I should not venture to observe, that the taste of most of
our English poets, as well as readers, is extremely Gothic. He
quotes Monsieur Segrais for a threefold distinction of the readers
of poetry : in the first of which he comprehends the rabble of
readers, whom he does not treat as such with regard to their
quality, but to their numbers and coarseness of their tastes. His
words are as follow : " Segrais has distinguished the readers of
poetry, according to their capacity of judging, into three classes.
(He might have said the same of writers too, if he had pleased.)
In the lowest form he places those whom he calls *Les Petits Esprits*,
such things as are our upper-gallery audience in a play-house ; who
like nothing but the husk and rind of Wit, prefer a quibble, a conceit, an epigram, before solid sense and elegant expression : these
are mob readers. If Virgil and Martial stood for Parliament-men,
we know already who would carry it. But though they make the
greatest appearance in the field, and cry the loudest, the best on 't
is they are but a sort of French Huguenots, or Dutch Boors, brought
over in herds, but not naturalized ; who have not lands of two
pounds per annum in Parnassus, and therefore are not privileged to
poll. Their authors are of the same level, fit to represent them on
a mountebank's stage, or to be masters of the ceremonies in a bear-
garden : yet these are they who have the most admirers. But it
often happens, to their mortification, that as their readers improve
their stock of sense (as they may by reading better books, and by
conversation with men of judgment), they soon forsake them."

I must not dismiss this subject without observing that as Mr.
Locke in the passage above-mentioned has discovered the most fruitful source of Wit, so there is another of a quite contrary nature to it,
which does likewise branch itself out into several kinds. For not only
the *resemblance*, but the *opposition* of ideas, does very often produce
Wit ; as I could shew in several little points, turns, and antitheses,
that I may possibly enlarge upon in some future speculation.

II. REMARKS ON MILTON

(Addison's famous *Spectator* essays on *Paradise Lost* are almost wholly
occupied with a now merely curious demonstration that the *same* beauties
which the rigidly classical critics had found in Homer and Virgil are also
to be found in Milton, and with a continuous commentary on "Beauties,"
etc. A few more general observations, here and there, show that the
critic was not beyond his age, but help to give a clear view of Criticism
in that age.)

His Diction

SPECTATOR, *No.* 285. *Saturday, January* 26, 1712.

Ne, quicunque Deus, quicunque adhibebitur heros,
Regali conspectus in auro nuper et ostro,
Migret in obscuras humili sermone tabernas :
Aut, dum vitat humum, nubes et inania captet. — HORACE.

Having already treated of the fable, the characters, and sentiments in the *Paradise Lost,* we are in the last place to consider the
language ; and as the learned world is very much divided upon
Milton as to this point, I hope they will excuse me if I appear particular in any of my opinions, and incline to those who judge the
most advantageously of the author.

It is requisite that the language of an heroic poem should be both
perspicuous and sublime. In proportion as either of these two
qualities are wanting, the language is imperfect. Perspicuity is
the first and most necessary qualification; insomuch that a good-
natured reader sometimes overlooks a little slip even in the
grammar or syntax, where it is impossible for him to mistake the
poet's sense. Of this kind is that passage in Milton, wherein he
speaks of Satan.

> —— God and his Son except,
> Created thing nought valu'd he nor shunn'd.

And that in which he describes Adam and Eve.

> Adam the goodliest man of men since born
> His sons, the fairest of her daughters Eve.

It is plain, that in the former of these passages according to the
natural syntax, the Divine Persons mentioned in the first line are

represented as created beings; and that, in the other, Adam and
Eve are confounded with their sons and daughters.   Such little
blemishes as these, when the thought is great and natural, we
should, with Horace, impute to a pardonable inadvertency, or to
the weakness of human nature, which cannot attend to each minute
particular, and give the last finishing to every circumstance in so
long a work.   The ancient critics therefore, who were acted by a
spirit of candour, rather than that of cavilling, invented certain
figures of speech, on purpose to palliate little errors of this nature
in the writings of those authors who had so many greater beauties
to atone for them.

If clearness and perspicuity were only to be consulted, the poet
would have nothing else to do but to clothe his thoughts in the
most plain and natural expressions.   But since it often happens
that the most obvious phrases, and those which are used in ordinary conversation, become too familiar to the ear, and contract a
kind of meanness by passing through the mouths of the vulgar, a
poet should take particular care to guard himself against idiomatic
ways of speaking.   Ovid and Lucan have many poornesses of
expression upon this account, as taking up with the first phrases
that offered, without putting themselves to the trouble of looking
after such as would not only have been natural, but also elevated
and sublime.   Milton has but few failings in this kind, of which,
however, you may meet with some instances, as in the following
passages.

> Embryos and idiots, eremites and friars,
> *White*, *black*, and *grey*, with all their *trumpery*,
> Here pilgrims roam ——
> —— A while discourse they hold,
> *No fear lest dinner cool;* when thus began
> Our author ——
> Who of all ages to succeed, but feeling
> The evil on him brought by me, will curse
> My head, ill fare our ancestor impure,
> *For this we may thank* Adam ——

The great masters in Composition, knew very well that many an
elegant phrase becomes improper for a poet or an orator, when it
has been debased by common use.   For this reason the works of

ancient authors, which are written in dead languages, have a great advantage over those which are written in languages that are now spoken. Were there any mean phrases or idioms in Virgil and Homer, they would not shock the ear of the most delicate modern reader, so much as they would have done that of an old Greek or Roman, because we never hear them pronounced in our streets, or in ordinary conversation.

It is not therefore sufficient, that the language of an epic poem be perspicuous, unless it be also sublime. To this end it ought to deviate from the common forms and ordinary phrases of speech. The judgment of a poet very much discovers itself in shunning the common roads of expression, without falling into such ways of speech as may seem stiff and unnatural; he must not swell into a false sublime, by endeavouring to avoid the other extreme. Among the Greeks, Æschylus, and sometimes Sophocles, were guilty of this fault; among the Latins, Claudian and Statius; and among our own countrymen, Shakespeare and Lee. In these authors the affectation of greatness often hurts the perspicuity of the style, as in many others the endeavour after perspicuity prejudices its greatness.

Aristotle has observed, that the idiomatic style may be avoided, and the sublime formed, by the following methods. First, by the use of metaphors: such are those of Milton.

> *Imparadised* in one another's arms.
> —— And in his hand a reed
> Stood waving *tipt* with fire. ——
> The grassy clods now *calv'd*, ——
> *Spangled* with eyes ——

In these and innumerable other instances, the metaphors are very bold but just; I must however observe that the metaphors are not so thick sown in Milton, which always savours too much of wit; that they never clash with one another, which, as Aristotle observes, turns a sentence into a kind of an enigma or riddle; and that he seldom has recourse to them where the proper and natural words will do as well.

Another way of raising the language, and giving it a poetical turn, is to make use of the idioms of other tongues. Virgil is full

of the Greek forms of speech, which the critics call *Hellenisms*, as
Horace in his *Odes* abounds with them much more than Virgil. I
need not mention the several dialects which Homer has made use
of for this end. Milton, in conformity with the practice of the
ancient poets, and with Aristotle's rule, has infused a great many
Latinisms, as well as Græcisms, and sometimes Hebraisms, into the
language of his poem ; as towards the beginning of it.

> *Nor* did they *not* perceive the evil plight
> In which they were, *or* the fierce pains not feel.
> Yet to their Gen'ral's voice they soon obey'd. ——
> —— Who shall tempt with wand'ring feet
> The dark unbottom'd infinite abyss,
> And through the *palpable obscure* find out
> His uncouth way, or spread his airy flight
> Upborn with indefatigable wings
> Over the *vast abrupt!* ——
> —— So both ascend
> In the visions of God ——

Under this head may be reckoned the placing the adjective after
the substantive, the transposition of words, the turning the adjective into a substantive, with several other foreign modes of speech
which this poet has naturalized to give his verse the greater sound,
and throw it out of prose.

The third method mentioned by Aristotle is what agrees with the
genius of the Greek language more than with that of any other
tongue, and is therefore more used by Homer than by any other
poet. I mean the lengthening of a phrase by the addition of words,
which may either be inserted or omitted, as also by the extending
or contracting of particular words by the insertion or omission of
certain syllables. Milton has put in practice this method of raising
his language, as far as the nature of our tongue will permit, as
in the passage above-mentioned, *eremite*, for what is hermit, in
common discourse. If you observe the measure of his verse, he
has with great judgment suppressed a syllable in several words, and
shortened those of two syllables into one, by which method, besides
the above-mentioned advantage, he has given a greater variety to
his numbers. But this practice is more particularly remarkable in

the names of persons and of countries, as *Beëlzebub, Hessebon*, and in many other particulars, wherein he has either changed the name, or made use of that which is not the most commonly known, that he might the better depart from the language of the vulgar.

The same reason recommended to him several old words, which also makes his poem appear the more venerable, and gives it a greater air of antiquity.

I must likewise take notice, that there are in Milton several words of his own coining, as *Cerberean, miscreated, Hell-doom'd, embryon* atoms, and many others. If the reader is offended at this liberty in our English poet, I would recommend him to a discourse in Plutarch, which shows us how frequently Homer has made use of the same liberty.

Milton, by the above-mentioned helps, and by the choice of the noblest words and phrases which our tongue would afford him, has carried our language to a greater height than any of the English poets have ever done before or after him, and made the sublimity of his style equal to that of his sentiments.

I have been the more particular in these observations on Milton's style, because it is that part of him in which he appears the most singular. The remarks I have here made upon the practice of other poets, with my observations out of Aristotle, will perhaps alleviate the prejudice which some have taken to his poem upon this account; though after all, I must confess that I think his style, though admirable in general, is in some places too much stiffened and obscured by the frequent use of those methods, which Aristotle has prescribed for the raising of it.

This redundancy of those several ways of speech, which Aristotle calls *foreign language*, and with which Milton has so very much enriched, and in some places darkened the language of his poem, was the more proper for his use, because his poem is written in blank verse. Rhyme, without any other assistance, throws the language off from prose, and very often makes an indifferent phrase pass unregarded; but where the verse is not built upon rhymes, there pomp of sound, and energy of expression, are indispensably necessary to support the style, and keep it from falling into the flatness of prose.

Those who have not a taste for this elevation of style, and are apt to ridicule a poet when he departs from the common forms of expression, would do well to see how Aristotle has treated an ancient author called Euclid, for his insipid mirth upon this occasion. Mr. Dryden used to call these sort of men his prose-critics.

I should, under this head of the language, consider Milton's numbers, in which he has made use of several elisions, which are not customary among other English poets, as may be particularly observed in his cutting off the letter *y*, when it precedes a vowel. This, and some other innovations in the measure of his verse, has varied his numbers in such a manner, as makes them incapable of satiating the ear, and cloying the reader, which the same uniform measure would certainly have done, and which the perpetual returns of rhyme never fail to do in long narrative poems. I shall close these reflections upon the language of *Paradise Lost*, with observing that Milton has copied after Homer rather than Virgil in the length of his periods, the copiousness of his phrases, and the running of his verses into one another.

His Fable, etc., and Language again

Spectator, *No.* 297. *Saturday, February 9*, 1712.

—— *velut si*
Egregio inspersos reprendas corpore nævos. — Horace.

After what I have said in my last Saturday's paper, I shall enter on the subject of this without further preface, and remark the several defects which appear in the fable, the characters, the sentiments, and the language of Milton's *Paradise Lost;* not doubting but the reader will pardon me, if I allege at the same time whatever may be said for the extenuation of such defects. The first imperfection which I shall observe in the fable is that the event of it is unhappy.

The fable of every poem is, according to Aristotle's division, either *simple* or *implex*. It is called simple when there is no change of fortune in it : implex, when the fortune of the chief actor changes from bad to good, or from good to bad. The implex fable is thought the most perfect; I suppose, because it is more proper to stir up the passions of the reader, and to surprise him with a greater variety of accidents.

The implex fable is therefore of two kinds : in the first the chief actor makes his way through a long series of dangers and difficulties, till he arrives at honour and prosperity, as we see in the story of Ulysses. In the second, the chief actor in the poem falls from some eminent pitch of honour and prosperity, into misery and disgrace. Thus we see Adam and Eve sinking from a state of innocence and happiness, into the most abject condition of sin and sorrow.

The most taking tragedies among the Ancients were built on this last sort of implex fable, particularly the tragedy of Œdipus, which proceeds upon a story, if we may believe Aristotle, the most proper for tragedy that could be invented by the wit of man. I have taken some pains in a former paper to shew, that this kind of implex fable, wherein the event is unhappy, is more apt to affect an audience than that of the first kind; notwithstanding many excellent pieces among the Ancients, as well as most of those which have been written of late years in our own country, are raised upon contrary plans. I must however own, that I think this kind of fable, which is the most perfect in tragedy, is not so proper for an heroic poem.

Milton seems to have been sensible of this imperfection in his fable, and has therefore endeavoured to cure it by several expedients; particularly by the mortification which the great Adversary of Mankind meets with upon his return to the assembly of infernal spirits, as it is described in a beautiful passage of the tenth book ; and likewise by the vision wherein Adam at the close of the poem sees his offspring triumphing over his great enemy, and himself restored to a happier Paradise than that from which he fell.

There is another objection against Milton's fable, which is indeed almost the same with the former, though placed in a different light, namely, that the hero in the *Paradise Lost* is unsuccessful, and by no means a match for his enemies. This gave occasion to Mr. Dryden's reflection, that the Devil was in reality Milton's hero. I think I have obviated this objection in my first paper. The *Paradise Lost* is an epic or a narrative poem, and he that looks for an hero in it, searches for that which Milton never intended; but if he will needs fix the name of an hero upon any person in it, 't is certainly the Messiah who is the hero, both in the principal action, and in the chief episodes. Paganism could not furnish out a real action for a fable greater than that of the *Iliad* or *Æneid,* and therefore an heathen could not form a higher notion of a poem than one of that kind, which they call an heroic. Whether Milton's is not of a sublimer nature I will not presume to determine: it is sufficient that I shew there is in the *Paradise Lost* all the greatness of plan, regularity of design, and masterly beauties which we discover in Homer and Virgil.

I must in the next place observe, that Milton has interwoven in the texture of his fable some particulars which do not seem to have probability enough for an epic poem, particularly in the actions which he ascribes to Sin and Death, and the picture which he draws of the Limbo of Vanity, with other passages in the second book. Such allegories rather savour of the spirit of Spenser and Ariosto, than of Homer and Virgil.

In the structure of his poem he has likewise admitted of too many digressions. It is finely observed by Aristotle, that the author of an heroic poem should seldom speak himself, but throw as much of his work as he can into the mouths of those who are his principal actors. Aristotle has given no reason for this precept; but I presume it is because the mind of the reader is more awed and elevated when he hears Æneas or Achilles speak, than when Virgil or Homer talk in their own persons. Besides that assuming the character of an eminent man is apt to fire the imagination, and raise the ideas of the author. Tully tells us, mentioning his *Dialogue of Old Age,* in which Cato is the chief speaker, that upon a review of it he was agreeably imposed upon, and fancied that it was Cato, and not he himself, who uttered his thoughts on that subject.

If the reader would be at the pains to see how the story of the *Iliad* and the *Æneid* is delivered by those persons who act in it, he will be surprised to find how little in either of these poems proceeds from the authors. Milton has, in the general disposition of his fable, very finely observed this great rule; insomuch that there is scarce a third part of it which comes from the poet; the rest is spoken either by Adam and Eve, or by some good or evil spirit who is engaged either in their destruction or defence.

From what has been here observed it appears, that digressions are by no means to be allowed of in an epic poem. If the poet, even in the ordinary course of his narration, should speak as little as possible, he should certainly never let his narration sleep for the sake of any reflections of his own. I have often observed, with a secret admiration, that the longest reflection in the *Æneid* is in that passage of the tenth book, where Turnus is represented as dressing himself in the spoils of Pallas, whom he had slain. Virgil here lets his fable stand still for the sake of the following remark. "How is the mind of man ignorant of futurity, and unable to bear prosperous fortune with moderation? The time will come when Turnus shall wish that he had left the body of Pallas untouched, and curse the day on which he dressed himself in these spoils." As the great event of the *Æneid*, and the death of Turnus, whom Æneas slew because he saw him adorned with the spoils of Pallas, turns upon this incident, Virgil went out of his way to make this reflection upon it, without which so small a circumstance might possibly have slipped out of his reader's memory. Lucan, who was an injudicious poet, lets drop his story very frequently for the sake of his unnecessary digressions, or his *diverticula*, as Scaliger calls them.[1] If he gives us an account of the prodigies which preceded the Civil War, he declaims upon the occasion, and shews how much happier it would be for man, if he did not feel his evil fortune before it comes to pass; and suffer not only by its real weight, but by the apprehension of it. Milton's complaint for his blindness, his panegyric on marriage, his reflections on Adam and Eve's going naked, of the angels eating, and several other passages in his poem, are liable to the same exception, though I must confess there is so great a beauty in these very digressions, that I would not wish them out of his poem.

I have, in a former paper, spoken of the *characters* of Milton's *Paradise Lost*, and declared my opinion, as to the allegorical persons who are introduced in it.

[1] *Poetices* Lib. iii cap. 25.

If we look into the *sentiments*, I think they are sometimes defective under the following heads: first, as there are several of them too much pointed, and some that degenerate even into puns. Of this last kind I am afraid is that in the first book, where speaking of the Pigmies, he calls them,

> —— The small *infantry*
> Warr'd on by cranes ——

Another blemish that appears in some of his thoughts, is his frequent allusion to heathen fables, which are not certainly of a piece with the divine subject, of which he treats. I do not find fault with these allusions, where the poet himself represents them as fabulous, as he does in some places, but where he mentions them as truths and matters of fact. The limits of my paper will not give me leave to be particular in instances of this kind; the reader will easily remark them in his perusal of the poem.

A third fault in his sentiments, is an unnecessary ostentation of learning, which likewise occurs very frequently. It is certain that both Homer and Virgil were masters of all the learning of their times, but it shews itself in their works after an indirect and concealed manner. Milton seems ambitious of letting us know, by his excursions on free-will and predestination, and his many glances upon history, astronomy, geography, and the like, as well as by the terms and phrases he sometimes makes use of, that he was acquainted with the whole circle of arts and sciences.

If, in the last place, we consider the *language* of this great poet, we must allow what I have hinted in a former paper, that it is often too much laboured, and sometimes obscured by old words, transpositions, and foreign idioms. Seneca's objection to the style of a great author, *Riget ejus oratio, nihil in ea placidum nihil lene,* is what many critics make to Milton: as I cannot wholly refuse it, so I have already apologized for it in another paper; to which I may further add, that Milton's sentiments and ideas were so wonderfully sublime, that it would have been impossible for him to have represented them in their full strength and beauty, without having recourse to these foreign assistances. Our language sunk under him, and was unequal to that greatness of soul, which furnished him with such glorious conceptions.

A second fault in his language is, that he often affects a kind of jingle in his words, as in the following passages, and many others:

> And brought into the *world* a *world* of woe.
>
> —— Begirt th' Almighty throne
> *Beseeching* or *besieging* ——
>
> This *tempted* our *attempt* ——
>
> At one slight *bound* high overleapt all *bound.*

I know there are figures for this kind of speech, that some of the greatest ancients have been guilty of it, and that Aristotle himself has given it a place in his *Rhetoric* among the beauties of that art. But as it is in itself poor and trifling, it is I think at present universally exploded by all the masters of polite writing.

The last fault which I shall take notice of in Milton's style, is the frequent use of what the learned call *technical words,* or terms of art. It is one of the great beauties of poetry, to make hard things intelligible, and to deliver what is abstruse of itself in such easy language as may be understood by ordinary readers: besides, that the knowledge of a poet should rather seem born with him, or inspired, than drawn from books and systems. I have often wondered how Mr. Dryden could translate a passage out of Virgil after the following manner.

> Tack to the larboard, and stand off to sea.
> Veer starboard sea and land. ——

Milton makes use of *larboard* in the same manner. When he is upon building he mentions *Doric pillars, pilasters, cornice, frieze, architrave.* When he talks of heavenly bodies, you meet with *ecliptic* and *eccentric,* the *trepidation, stars dropping from the zenith, rays culminating from the equator.* To which might be added many instances of the like kind in several other arts and sciences.

I shall in my next papers give an account of the many particular beauties in Milton, which would have been too long to insert under those general heads I have already treated of, and with which I intend to conclude this piece of criticism.

Summary

I have now finished my observations on a work which does an
honour to the English nation. I have taken a general view of it
under these four heads, the fable, the characters, the sentiments,
and the language, and made each of them the subject of a particular paper. I have in the next place spoken of the censures which
our author may incur under each of these heads, which I have confined to two papers, though I might have enlarged the number, if I had
been disposed to dwell on so ungrateful a subject. I believe, however, that the severest reader will not find any little fault in heroic
poetry, which this author has fallen into, that does not come under
one of those heads among which I have distributed his several
blemishes. After having thus treated at large of *Paradise Lost*,
I could not think it sufficient to have celebrated this poem in
the whole, without descending to particulars. I have therefore
bestowed a paper upon each book, and endeavoured not only to prove
that the poem is beautiful in general, but to point out its particular
beauties, and to determine wherein they consist. I have endeavoured to shew how some passages are beautiful by being sublime,
others by being soft, others by being natural; which of them are
recommended by the passion, which by the moral, which by the
sentiment, and which by the expression. I have likewise endeavoured to shew how the genius of the poet shines by a happy invention, a distant allusion, or a judicious imitation; how he has copied
or improved Homer or Virgil, and raised his own imaginations by
the use which he has made of several poetical passages in Scripture.
I might have inserted also several passages of Tasso, which our
author has imitated; but as I do not look upon Tasso to be a sufficient voucher, I would not perplex my reader with such quotations,
as might do more honour to the Italian than the English poet. In
short, I have endeavoured to particularize those innumerable kinds
of beauty, which it would be tedious to recapitulate, but which are
essential to poetry, and which may be met with in the works of this
great author. Had I thought, at my first engaging in this design,
that it would have led me to so great a length, I believe I should
never have entered upon it; but the kind reception which it has

met with among those whose judgments I have a value for, as well as the uncommon demands which my bookseller tells me have been made for these particular discourses, give me no reason to repent of the pains I have been at in composing them.

III. THE PLEASURES OF THE IMAGINATION

(It will be observed that Addison carefully guards against the confusion of *his* Imagination with the Shakespearean-Coleridgean variety.)

DEFINITION

SPECTATOR, *No.* 411. *Saturday, June* 21, 1712.

Avia Pieridum peragro loca, nullius ante
Trita solo; juvat integros accedere fonteis;
Atque haurire. — LUCRETIUS.

Our sight is the most perfect and most delightful of all our senses. It fills the mind with the largest variety of ideas, converses with its objects at the greatest distance, and continues the longest in action without being tired or satiated with its proper enjoyments.   The sense of feeling can indeed give us a notion of extension, shape, and all other ideas that enter at the eye, except colours ; but at the same time it is very much straitened and confined in its operations, to the number, bulk, and distance of its particular objects. Our sight seems designed to supply all these defects, and may be considered as a more delicate and diffusive kind of touch, that spreads itself over an infinite multitude of bodies, comprehends the largest figures, and brings into our reach some of the most remote parts of the universe.

It is this sense which furnishes the Imagination with its ideas ; so that by the pleasures of the Imagination or Fancy (which I shall use promiscuously) I here mean such as arise from visible objects, either when we have them actually in our view, or when we call up their ideas in our minds by paintings, statues, descriptions, or any the like occasion.   We cannot indeed have a single image in the Fancy that did not make its first entrance through the sight ; but we have the power of retaining, altering, and compounding those images, which we have once received, into all the varieties of picture and vision that are most agreeable to the Imagination; for by this faculty a man in a dungeon is capable of entertaining himself with scenes and landscapes more beautiful than any that can be found in the whole compass of nature.

There are few words in the English language which are employed in a more loose and uncircumscribed sense than those of the Fancy and the Imagination. I therefore thought it necessary to fix and determine the notion of these two words, as I intend to make use of them in the thread of my following speculations, that the reader may conceive rightly what is the subject which I proceed upon. I must therefore desire him to remember, that by the pleasures of the Imagination, I mean only such pleasures as arise originally from sight, and that I divide these pleasures into two kinds: my design being first of all to discourse of those primary pleasures of the imagination, which entirely proceed from such objects as are before our eyes; and in the next place to speak of those secondary pleasures of the Imagination which flow from the ideas of visible objects, when the objects are not actually before the eye, but are called up into our memories, or formed into agreeable visions of things that are either absent or fictitious.

The pleasures of the Imagination, taken in the full extent, are not so gross as those of sense, nor so refined as those of the understanding. The last are, indeed, more preferable, because they are founded on some new knowledge or improvement in the mind of man; yet it must be confest, that those of the Imagination are as great and as transporting as the other. A beautiful prospect delights the soul, as much as a demonstration; and a description in Homer has charmed more readers than a chapter in Aristotle. Besides, the pleasures of the Imagination have this advantage, above those of the understanding, that they are more obvious, and more easy to be acquired. It is but opening the eye, and the scene enters. The colours paint themselves on the Fancy, with very little attention of thought or application of mind in the beholder. We are struck, we know not how, with the symmetry of any thing we see, and immediately assent to the beauty of an object, without enquiring into the particular causes and occasions of it.

A man of a polite imagination is let into a great many pleasures, that the vulgar are not capable of receiving. He can converse with a picture, and find an agreeable companion in a statue. He meets with a secret refreshment in a description, and often feels a greater satisfaction in the prospect of fields and meadows, than another does in the possession. It gives him, indeed, a kind of property in everything he sees, and makes the most rude uncultivated parts of nature administer to his pleasures : so that he looks upon the world, as it were in another light, and discovers in it a multitude of charms, that conceal themselves from the generality of mankind.

There are, indeed, but very few who know how to be idle and innocent, or have a relish of any pleasures that are not criminal ; every diversion they take is at the expense of some one virtue or another, and their very first step out of business is into vice or folly. A man should endeavour, therefore, to make the sphere of his innocent pleasures as wide as possible, that he may retire into them with safety, and find in them such a satisfaction as a wise man would not blush to take. Of this nature are those of the Imagination, which do not require such a bent of thought as is necessary to our more serious employments, nor, at the same time, suffer the mind to sink into that negligence and remissness, which are apt to accompany our more sensual delights, but, like a gentle exercise to the faculties, awaken them from sloth and idleness, without putting them upon any labour or difficulty.

We might here add, that the pleasures of the Fancy are more conducive to health, than those of the understanding, which are worked out by dint of thinking, and attended with too violent a labour of the brain. Delightful scenes, whether in nature, painting, or poetry, have a kindly influence on the body, as well as the mind, and not only serve to clear and brighten the Imagination, but are able to disperse grief and melancholy, and to set the animal spirits in pleasing and agreeable motions. For this reason Sir Francis Bacon, in his essay upon Health, has not thought it improper to prescribe to his reader a poem or a prospect, where he particularly dissuades him from knotty and subtle disquisitions, and advises him to pursue studies that fill the mind with splendid and illustrious objects, as histories, fables, and contemplations of nature.

I have in this paper, by way of introduction, settled the notion of those pleasures of the Imagination which are the subject of my present undertaking, and endeavoured, by several considerations, to recommend to my reader the pursuit of those pleasures. I shall, in my next paper, examine the several sources from whence these pleasures are derived.[1]

The Fairy Way of Writing [2]

Spectator, No. 419.   Tuesday, July 1, 1712.

—— mentis gratissimus error. — Horace.

There is a kind of writing, wherein the poet quite loses sight of Nature, and entertains his reader's imagination with the characters and actions of such persons as have many of them no existence, but what he bestows on them.   Such are fairies, witches, magicians, demons, and departed spirits.   This Mr. Dryden calls *the Fairy Way of Writing*, which is, indeed, more difficult than any other that depends on the poet's fancy, because he has no pattern to follow in it, and must work altogether out of his own invention.

There is a very odd turn of thought required for this sort of writing, and it is impossible for a poet to succeed in it, who has not a particular cast of fancy, and an imagination naturally fruitful and superstitious.   Besides this he ought to be very well versed in legends and fables, antiquated romances, and the traditions of nurses and old women, that he may fall in with our natural prejudices, and humour those notions which we have imbibed in our infancy.   For otherwise he will be apt to make his fairies talk like people of his own species, and not like other sets of beings, who

---

[1] Addison does, in fact, proceed in a most interesting series of papers on Taste in the Arts generally, and more particularly in Literature, always on the basis of ideals furnished by sight at first or second hand.

[2] I have seen this phrase attributed, and by no unlettered person, to Charles Lamb. It is actually derived from Dryden's Preface to *King Arthur*, his "fairy" opera; but no doubt Addison gave it much wider currency, and Lamb may have taken it from him.

converse with different objects, and think in a different manner from that of mankind;

Sylvis deducti caveant, me judice, Fauni
Ne velut innati triviis ac pæne forenses
Aut nimium teneris juvenentur versibus. — HORACE.

I do not say with Mr. Bayes in the *Rehearsal*, that spirits must not be confined to speak sense, but it is certain their sense ought to be a little discoloured, that it may seem particular, and proper to the person and the condition of the speaker.

These descriptions raise a pleasing kind of horror in the mind of the reader, and amuse his imagination with the strangeness and novelty of the persons who are represented in them. They bring up into our memory the stories we have heard in our childhood, and favour those secret terrors and apprehensions to which the mind of man is naturally subject. We are pleased with surveying the different habits and behaviours of foreign countries, how much more must we be delighted and surprised when we are led, as it were, into a new creation, and see the persons and manners of another species? Men of cold fancies, and philosophical dispositions, object to this kind of poetry, that it has not probability enough to affect the Imagination. But to this it may be answered, that we are sure, in general, there are many intellectual beings in the world besides ourselves, and several species of spirits, who are subject to different laws and economies from those of mankind; when we see, therefore, any of these represented naturally, we cannot look upon the representation as altogether impossible; nay, many are prepossest with such false opinions, as dispose them to believe these particular delusions; at least, we have all heard so many pleasing relations in favour of them, that we do not care for seeing through the falsehood, and willingly give ourselves up to so agreeable an imposture.

The Ancients have not much of this poetry among them, for, indeed, almost the whole substance of it owes its original to the darkness and superstition of later ages, when pious frauds were made use of to amuse mankind, and frighten them into a sense of their duty. Our forefathers looked upon Nature with more reverence and horror, before the world was enlightened by learning and philosophy, and loved to astonish themselves with the apprehensions

of witchcraft, prodigies, charms, and enchantments.   There was not
a village in England, that had not a ghost in it, the church-yards
were all haunted, every large common had a circle of fairies belonging to it, and there was scarce a shepherd to be met with who had
not seen a spirit.

Among all the poets of this kind our English are much the best,
by what I have yet seen; whether it be that we abound with more
stories of this nature, or that the genius of our country is fitter for
this sort of poetry.   For the English are naturally fanciful, and
very often disposed by that gloominess and melancholy of temper,
which is so frequent in our nation, to many wild notions and visions,
to which others are not so liable.

Among the English, Shakespeare has incomparably excelled all
others.   That noble extravagance of fancy which he had in so great
perfection, thoroughly qualified him to touch this weak superstitious part of his reader's imagination; and made him capable of
succeeding, where he had nothing to support him besides the
strength of his own genius.   There is something so wild and yet
so solemn in the speeches of his ghosts, fairies, witches, and the
like imaginary persons, that we cannot forbear thinking them
natural, though we have no rule by which to judge of them, and
must confess, if there are such beings in the world, it looks highly
probable that they should talk and act as he has represented them.

There is another sort of imaginary beings, that we sometimes
meet with among the poets, when the author represents any passion,
appetite, virtue, or vice, under a visible shape, and makes it a person or an actor in his poem.   Of this nature are the descriptions
of Hunger and Envy in Ovid, of Fame in Virgil, and of Sin and
Death in Milton.   We find a whole creation of the like shadowy
persons in Spenser, who had an admirable talent in representations
of this kind.   I have discoursed of these emblematical persons in
former papers, and shall therefore only mention them in this place.
Thus we see how many ways Poetry addresses itself to the Imagination, as it has not only the whole circle of Nature for its province,
but makes new worlds of its own, shews us persons who are not to
be found in being, and represents even the faculties of the Soul,
with her several virtues and vices, in a sensible shape and character.

XXII

POPE

I. SELECTIONS FROM THE ESSAY ON CRITICISM[1]

'T is hard to say, if greater want of skill
Appear in writing or in judging ill;
But, of the two, less dang'rous is th' offence
To tire our patience, than mislead our sense.
Some few in that, but numbers err in this,
Ten censure wrong for one who writes amiss;
A fool might once himself alone expose,
Now one in verse makes many more in prose.

'T is with our judgments as our watches, none
Go just alike, yet each believes his own.
In poets as true genius is but rare,
True taste as seldom is the critic's share;
Both must alike from Heav'n derive their light,
These born to judge, as well as those to write.
Let such teach others who themselves excel,
And censure freely who have written well.
Authors are partial to their wit, 't is true,
But are not critics to their judgment too?

Yet if we look more closely, we shall find
Most have the seeds of judgment in their mind:
Nature affords at least a glimm'ring light;
The lines, tho' touch'd but faintly, are drawn right.
But as the slightest sketch, if justly trac'd,

---

[1] The only passages of this famous verse-summary of "neo-classic" ideas
not given are 30–45 (an unimportant flirt at the *stupidity* of certain critics);
and the long and not uninteresting, but again to us less important digression
(452–611) on the *morals* of Criticism and partly of Poetry.

Is by ill-colouring but the more disgrac'd,
So by false learning is good sense defac'd:
Some are bewilder'd in the maze of schools,
And some made coxcombs Nature meant but fools.
In search of wit these lose their common sense,
And then turn critics in their own defence.
.   .   .   .

But you who seek to give and merit fame,
And justly bear a Critic's noble name,
Be sure yourself and your own reach to know,
How far your genius, taste, and learning go;
Launch not beyond your depth, but be discreet,
And mark that point where sense and dullness meet.
Nature to all things fix'd the limits fit,
And wisely curb'd proud man's pretending wit.
As on the land while here the ocean gains,
In other parts it leaves wide sandy plains;
Thus in the soul while memory prevails,
The solid pow'r of understanding fails;
Where beams of warm imagination play,
The memory's soft figures melt away.
One science only will one genius fit;
So vast is art, so narrow human wit:
Not only bounded to peculiar arts,
But oft in those confin'd to single parts.
Like kings we lose the conquests gain'd before,
By vain ambition still to make them more;
Each might his sev'ral province well command,
Would all but stoop to what they understand.
First follow Nature, and your judgment frame
By her just standard, which is still the same:
Unerring NATURE, still divinely bright,
One clear, unchang'd, and universal light,
Life, force, and beauty, must to all impart,
At once the source, and end, and test of Art.
Art from that fund each just supply provides,
Works without show, and without pomp presides:

In some fair body thus th' informing soul
With spirits feeds, with vigour fills the whole,
Each motion guides, and ev'ry nerve sustains;
Itself unseen, but in th' effects, remains.
Some, to whom Heav'n in wit has been profuse,
Want as much more, to turn it to its use;
For wit and judgment often are at strife,
Tho' meant each other's aid, like man and wife.
'T is more to guide, than spur the Muse's steed;
Restrain his fury, than provoke his speed;
The winged courser, like a gen'rous horse,
Shows most true mettle when you check his course.
  Those RULES of old discovered, not devis'd,
Are Nature still, but Nature methodiz'd;
Nature, like liberty, is but restrain'd
By the same laws which first herself ordain'd.
  Hear how learn'd Greece her useful rules indites,
When to repress, and when indulge our flights:
High on Parnassus' top her sons she show'd,
And pointed out those arduous paths they trod;
Held from afar, aloft, th' immortal prize,
And urg'd the rest by equal steps to rise.
Just precepts thus from great examples giv'n,
She drew from them what they deriv'd from Heav'n.
The gen'rous Critic fann'd the Poet's fire,
And taught the world with reason to admire.
Then Criticism the Muse's handmaid prov'd,
To dress her charms, and make her more belov'd:
But following wits from that intention stray'd,
Who could not win the mistress, woo'd the maid;
Against the Poets their own arms they turn'd,
Sure to hate most the men from whom they learn'd.
So modern 'pothecaries, taught the art
By doctor's bills to play the doctor's part,
Bold in the practice of mistaken rules,
Prescribe, apply, and call their masters fools.
Some on the leaves of ancient authors prey,

Nor time nor moths e'er spoil'd so much as they.
Some drily plain, without invention's aid,
Write dull receipts how poems may be made.
These leave the sense, their learning to display,
And those explain the meaning quite away.

You then whose judgment the right course would steer,
Know well each ANCIENT's proper character;
His fable, subject, scope in ev'ry page;
Religion, country, genius of his age:
Without all these at once before your eyes,
Cavil you may, but never criticize.
Be Homer's works your study and delight,
Read them by day, and meditate by night;
Thence form your judgment, thence your maxims bring,
And trace the Muses upward to their spring.
Still with itself compar'd, his text peruse;
And let your comment be the Mantuan Muse.

When first young Maro in his boundless mind
A work t' outlast immortal Rome design'd,
Perhaps he seem'd above the critic's law,
And but from Nature's fountains scorn'd to draw:
But when t' examine ev'ry part he came,
Nature and Homer were, he found, the same.
Convinc'd, amaz'd, he checks the bold design;
And rules as strict his labour'd work confine,
As if the Stagirite o'erlook'd each line,
Learn hence for ancient rules a just esteem;
To copy nature is to copy them.

Some beauties yet no precepts can declare,
For there's a happiness as well as care.
Music resembles poetry, in each
Are nameless graces which no methods teach,
And which a master-hand alone can reach.
If, where the rules not far enough extend,
(Since rules were made but to promote their end)
Some lucky licence answer to the full
Th' intent propos'd, that licence is a rule.

Thus Pegasus, a nearer way to take,
May boldly deviate from the common track;
From vulgar bounds with brave disorder part,
And snatch a grace beyond the reach of art,
Which without passing thro' the judgment, gains
The heart, and all its end at once attains.
In prospects thus, some objects please our eyes,
Which out of nature's common order rise,
The shapeless rock, or hanging precipice.
Great wits sometimes may gloriously offend,
And rise to faults true critics dare not mend.
But tho' the Ancients thus their rules invade,
(As Kings dispense with laws themselves have made)
Moderns, beware! or if you must offend
Against the precept, ne'er transgress its end;
Let it be seldom, and compell'd by need;
And have, at least, their precedent to plead.
The critic else proceeds without remorse,
Seizes your fame, and puts his laws in force.
   I know there are, to whose presumptuous thoughts
Those freer beauties, ev'n in them, seem faults.
Some figures monstrous and mis-shap'd appear,
Consider'd singly, or beheld too near,
Which, but proportion'd to their light, or place,
Due distance reconciles to form and grace.
A prudent chief not always must display
His pow'rs in equal ranks, and fair array,
But with th' occasion and the place comply,
Conceal his force, nay seem sometimes to fly.
Those oft are stratagems which error seem,
Nor is it Homer nods, but we that dream.
   Still green with bays each ancient altar stands,
Above the reach of sacrilegious hands;
Secure from flames, from envy's fiercer rage,
Destructive war, and all-involving age.
See, from each clime the learn'd their incense bring!
Hear, in all tongues consenting pæans ring!

In praise so just let ev'ry voice be join'd,
And fill the gen'ral chorus of mankind.
Hail, Bards triumphant! born in happier days;
Immortal heirs of universal praise!
Whose honours with increase of ages grow,
As streams roll down, enlarging as they flow;
Nations unborn your mighty names shall sound,
And worlds applaud that must not yet be found!
Oh may some spark of your celestial fire
The last, the meanest of your sons inspire,
(That on weak wings, from far, pursues your flights;
Glows while he reads, but trembles as he writes)
To teach vain wits a science little known,
T' admire superior sense, and doubt their own!

   Of all the causes which conspire to blind
Man's erring judgment, and misguide the mind,
What the weak head with strongest bias rules,
Is *Pride*, the never-failing vice of fools.
Whatever nature has in worth denied,
She gives in large recruits of needful pride;
For as in bodies, thus in souls, we find
What wants in blood and spirits, swell'd with wind:
Pride, where wit fails, steps in to our defence,
And fills up all the mighty void of sense.
If once right reason drives that cloud away,
Truth breaks upon us with resistless day.
Trust not yourself; but your defects to know,
Make use of ev'ry friend — and ev'ry foe.

   A *little learning* is a dang'rous thing;
Drink deep, or taste not the Pierian spring:
There shallow draughts intoxicate the brain,
And drinking largely sobers us again.
Fir'd at first sight with what the Muse imparts,
In fearless youth we tempt the heights of Arts,
While from the bounded level of our mind
Short views we take, nor see the lengths behind;
But more advanc'd, behold with strange surprise

New distant scenes of endless science rise!
So pleas'd at first the tow'ring Alps we try,
Mount o'er the vales, and seem to tread the sky,
Th' eternal snows appear already past,
And the first clouds and mountains seem the last;
But, those attain'd, we tremble to survey
The growing labours of the lengthen'd way,
Th' increasing prospect tires our wand'ring eyes,
Hills peep o'er hills, and Alps on Alps arise!

A perfect judge will read each work of wit
With the same spirit that its author writ:
Survey the WHOLE, nor seek slight faults to find
Where nature moves, and rapture warms the mind;
Nor lose, for that malignant dull delight,
The gen'rous pleasure to be charm'd with wit.
But in such lays as neither ebb, nor flow,
Correctly cold, and regularly low,
That shunning faults, one quiet tenour keep;
We cannot blame indeed — but we may sleep.
In wit, as nature, what affects our hearts
Is not th' exactness of peculiar parts;
'T is not a lip, or eye, we beauty call,
But the joint force and full result of all.
Thus when we view some well-proportion'd dome,
(The world's just wonder, and ev'n thine, O Rome!)
No single parts unequally surprise,
All comes united to th' admiring eyes;
No monstrous height, or breadth, or length appear;
The Whole at once is bold, and regular.

Whoever thinks a faultless piece to see,
Thinks what ne'er was, nor is, nor e'er shall be.
In every work regard the writer's end,
Since none can compass more than they intend;
And if the means be just, the conduct true,
Applause, in spite of trivial faults, is due;
As men of breeding, sometimes men of wit,
T' avoid great errors, must the less commit:

Neglect the rules each verbal critic lays,
For not to know some trifles, is a praise.
Most critics, fond of some subservient art,
Still make the whole depend upon a part:
They talk of principles, but notions prize,
And all to one lov'd folly sacrifice.

Once on a time, La Mancha's knight, they say,
A certain bard encount'ring on the way,
Discours'd in terms as just, with looks as sage,
As e'er could Dennis of the Grecian stage;
Concluding all were desp'rate sots and fools,
Who durst depart from Aristotle's rules.
Our author, happy in a judge so nice,
Produc'd his play, and begg'd the knight's advice;
Made him observe the subject, and the plot,
The manners, passions, unities; what not?
All which, exact to rule, were brought about,
Were but a combat in the lists left out.
"What! leave the combat out?" exclaims the knight;
Yes, or we must renounce the Stagirite.
"Not so by Heav'n" (he answers in a rage),
"Knights, squires, and steeds, must enter on the stage."
So vast a throng the stage can ne'er contain.
"Then build a new, or act it in a plain."

Thus critics, of less judgment than caprice,
Curious not knowing, not exact but nice,
Form short ideas; and offend in art
(As most in manners) by a love to parts.

Some to *Conceit* alone their taste confine,
And glitt'ring thoughts struck out at ev'ry line;
Pleas'd with a work where nothing's just or fit;
One glaring chaos and wild heap of wit.
Poets like painters, thus, unskill'd to trace
The naked nature and the living grace,
With gold and jewels cover ev'ry part,
And hide with ornaments their want of art.
True wit is nature to advantage dress'd,

What oft was thought, but ne'er so well express'd;
Something, whose truth convinc'd at sight we find,
That gives us back the image of our mind.
As shades more sweetly recommend the light,
So modest plainness sets off sprightly wit.
For works may have more wit than does 'em good,
As bodies perish thro' excess of blood.

   Others for *Language* all their care express,
And value books, as women men, for dress:
Their praise is still, — the Style is excellent:
The Sense, they humbly take upon content.
Words are like leaves; and where they most abound,
Much fruit of sense beneath is rarely found,
False eloquence, like the prismatic glass,
Its gaudy colours spreads on ev'ry place;
The face of nature we no 'more survey,
All glares alike, without distinction gay:
But true expression, like th' unchanging sun,
Clears and improves whate'er it shines upon,
It gilds all objects, but it alters none.
Expression is the dress of thought, and still
Appears more decent, as more suitable;
A vile conceit in pompous words express'd,
Is like a clown in regal purple dress'd:
For diff'rent styles with diff'rent subjects sort,
As several garbs with country, town, and court.
Some by old words to fame have made pretence,
Ancients in phrase, mere moderns in their sense;
Such labour'd nothings, in so strange a style,
Amaze th' unlearn'd, and make the learned smile.
Unlucky, as Fungoso in the play,
These sparks with awkward vanity display
What the fine gentleman wore yesterday;
And but so mimic ancient wits at best,
As apes our grandsires, in their doublets drest.
In words, as fashions, the same rule will hold;
Alike fantastic, if too new, or old:

Be not the first by whom the new are tried,
Nor yet the last to lay the old aside.
  But most by Numbers judge a poet's song;
And smooth or rough, with them is right or wrong:
In the bright Muse though thousand charms conspire,
Her voice is all these tuneful fools admire;
Who haunt Parnassus but to please their ear,
Not mend their minds; as some to church repair,
Not for the doctrine, but the music there.
These equal syllables alone require,
Tho' oft the ear the open vowels tire;
While expletives their feeble aid do join;
And ten low words oft creep in one dull line:
While they ring round the same unvaried chimes,
With sure returns of still expected rhymes;
Where-e'er you find "the cooling western breeze,"
In the next line, it "whispers through the trees:"
If crystal streams "with pleasing murmurs creep,"
The reader's threaten'd (not in vain) with "sleep:"
Then, at the last and only couplet fraught
With some unmeaning thing they call a thought,
A needless Alexandrine ends the song,
That, like a wounded snake, drags its slow length along.
Leave such to tune their own dull rhymes, and know
What's roundly smooth or languishingly slow;
And praise the easy vigour of a line,
Where Denham's strength, and Waller's sweetness join.
True ease in writing comes from art, not chance,
As those move easiest who have learn'd to dance.
'T is not enough no harshness gives offence,
The sound must seem an echo to the sense:
Soft is the strain when Zephyr gently blows,
And the smooth stream in smoother numbers flows;
But when loud surges lash the sounding shore,
The hoarse, rough verse should like the torrent roar:
When Ajax strives some rock's vast weight to throw.
The line too labours, and the words move slow;

Not so, when swift Camilla scours the plain,
Flies o'er th' unbending corn, and skims along the main
Hear how Timotheus' varied lays surprise,
And bid alternate passions fall and rise!
While, at each change, the son of Libyan Jove
Now burns with glory, and then melts with love,
Now his fierce eyes with sparkling fury glow,
Now sighs steal out, and tears begin to flow:
Persians and Greeks like turns of nature found,
And the world's victor stood subdu'd by Sound!
The pow'r of music all our hearts allow,
And what Timotheus was, is DRYDEN now.

Avoid extremes; and shun the fault of such,
Who still are pleas'd too little or too much.
At ev'ry trifle scorn to take offence,
That always shows great pride, or little sense;
Those heads, as stomachs, are not sure the best,
Which nauseate all, and nothing can disgest.
Yet let not each gay turn thy rapture move;
For fools admire, but men of sense approve:
As things seem large which we thro' mists descry,
Dullness is ever apt to magnify.

Some foreign writers, some our own despise;
The Ancients only, or the Moderns prize.
Thus Wit, like Faith, by each man is applied
To one small sect, and all are damn'd beside.
Meanly they seek the blessing to confine,
And force that sun but on a part to shine,
Which not alone the southern wit sublimes,
But ripens spirits in cold northern climes;
Which from the first has shone on ages past,
Enlights the present, and shall warm the last;
Tho' each may feel increases and decays,
And see now clearer and now darker days.
Regard not then if wit be old or new,
But blame the false, and value 'till the true.

Some ne'er advance a judgment of their own,
But catch the spreading notion of the town;
They reason and conclude by precedent,
And own stale nonsense which they ne'er invent.
Some judge of authors' names, not works, and then
Nor praise nor blame the writings, but the men.
Of all this servile herd the worst is he
That in proud dullness joins with Quality,
A constant critic at the great man's board,
To fetch and carry nonsense for my lord.
What woful stuff this madrigal would be,
In some starv'd hackney sonneteer, or me?
But let a lord once own the happy lines,
How the wit brightens! how the style refines!
Before his sacred name flies ev'ry fault,
And each exalted stanza teems with thought!

The vulgar thus through imitation err;
As oft the learn'd by being singular;
So much they scorn the crowd, that if the throng
By chance go right, they purposely go wrong;
So schismatics the plain believers quit,
And are but damn'd for having too much wit.
Some praise at morning what they blame at night;
But always think the last opinion right.
A Muse by these is like a mistress us'd,
This hour she's idoliz'd, the next abus'd;
While their weak heads, like towns unfortified,
'Twixt sense and nonsense daily change their side.
Ask them the cause; they're wiser still, they say;
And still to-morrow's wiser than to-day.
We think our fathers fools, so wise we grow,
Our wiser sons, no doubt, will think us so.
Once School-divines this zealous isle o'er-spread;
Who knew most Sentences, was deepest read;
Faith, Gospel, all, seem'd made to be disputed,
And none had sense enough to be confuted:
Scotists and Thomists, now, in peace remain,

Amidst their kindred cobwebs in Duck-lane.
If Faith itself has diff'rent dresses worn,
What wonder modes in Wit should take their turn?
Oft', leaving what is natural and fit,
The current folly proves the ready wit;
And authors think their reputation safe,
Which lives as long as fools are pleas'd to laugh.

. . . .

The bookful blockhead, ignorantly read,
With loads of learned lumber in his head,
With his own tongue still edifies his ears,
And always list'ning to himself appears.
All books he reads, and all he reads assails,
From Dryden's Fables down to Durfey's Tales.
With him, most authors steal their works, or buy;
Garth did not write his own *Dispensary.*
Name a new play, and he's the poet's friend,
Nay show'd his faults — but when would poets mend?
No place so sacred from such fops is barr'd,
Nor is Paul's church more safe than Paul's churchyard:
Nay, fly to altars; there they'll talk you dead:
For fools rush in where angels fear to tread.
Distrustful sense with modest caution speaks,
It still looks home, and short excursions makes;
But rattling nonsense in full volleys breaks,
And never shock'd, and never turn'd aside,
Bursts out, resistless, with a thund'ring tide.
But where's the man, who counsel can bestow,
Still pleas'd to teach, and yet not proud to know?
Unbiass'd, or by favour, or by spite;
Not dully prepossess'd, nor blindly right;
Tho' learn'd, well-bred ; and tho' well-bred, sincere,
Modestly bold, and humanly severe:
Who to a friend his faults can freely show,
And gladly praise the merit of a foe?
Blest with a taste exact, yet unconfin'd;
A knowledge both of books and human kind:

Gen'rous converse; a soul exempt from pride;
And love to praise, with reason on his side?
  Such once were Critics; such the happy few,
Athens and Rome in better ages knew.
The mighty Stagirite first left the shore,
Spread all his sails, and durst the deeps explore:
He steer'd securely, and discover'd far,
Led by the light of the Mæonian Star.
Poets, a race long unconfin'd, and free,
Still fond and proud of savage liberty,
Receiv'd his laws; and stood convinc'd 't was fit,
Who conquer'd Nature, should preside o'er Wit.
  Horace still charms with graceful negligence,
And without method talks us into sense,
Will, like a friend, familiarly convey
The truest notions in the easiest way.
He, who supreme in judgment, as in wit,
Might boldly censure, as he boldly writ,
Yet judg'd with coolness, tho' he sung with fire;
His precepts teach but what his works inspire.
Our critics take a contrary extreme,
They judge with fury, but they write with fle'me:
Nor suffers Horace more in wrong translations
By wits, than critics in as wrong quotations.
  See Dionysius Homer's thoughts refine,
And call new beauties forth from ev'ry line!
  Fancy and art in gay Petronius please,
The scholar's learning, with the courtier's ease.
  In grave Quintilian's copious work, we find
The justest rules, and clearest method join'd:
Thus useful arms in magazines we place,
All rang'd in order, and dispos'd with grace,
But less to please the eye, than arm the hand,
Still fit for use, and ready at command.
  Thee, bold Longinus! all the Nine inspire,
And bless their Critic with a Poet's fire.
An ardent judge, who zealous in his trust,

With warmth gives sentence, yet is always just;
Whose own example strengthens all his laws;
And is himself that great Sublime he draws.

Thus long succeeding critics justly reign'd,
Licence repress'd, and useful laws ordain'd.
Learning and Rome alike in empire grew;
And arts still follow'd where her eagles flew;
From the same foes, at last, both felt their doom,
And the same age saw learning fall, and Rome.
With tyranny, then superstition join'd,
As that the body, this enslav'd the mind;
Much was believ'd, but little understood,
And to be dull was constru'd to be good;
A second deluge learning thus o'er-run,
And the monks finish'd what the Goths begun.

At length Erasmus, that great injur'd name,
(The glory of the priesthood, and the shame!)
Stemm'd the wild torrent of a barb'rous age,
And drove those holy Vandals off the stage.

But see! each Muse, in LEO's golden days,
Starts from her trance, and trims her wither'd bays,
Rome's ancient Genius, o'er its ruins spread,
Shakes off the dust, and rears his rev'rend head.
Then Sculpture and her sister-arts revive;
Stones leap'd to form, and rocks began to live;
With sweeter notes each rising temple rung;
A Raphael painted, and a Vida sung.
Immortal Vida: on whose honour'd brow
The Poet's bays and Critic's ivy grow:
Cremona now shall ever boast thy name,
As next in place to Mantua, next in fame!

But soon by impious arms from Latium chas'd,
Their ancient bounds the banish'd Muses pass'd;
Thence arts o'er all the northern world advance,
But Critic-learning flourish'd most in France:
The rules a nation, born to serve, obeys;
And Boileau still in right of Horace sways.

But we, brave Britons, foreign laws despis'd,
And kept unconquer'd, and unciviliz'd;
Fierce for the liberties of wit, and bold,
We still defied the Romans, as of old.
Yet some there were, among the sounder few
Of those who less presum'd, and better knew,
Who durst assert the juster ancient cause,
And here restor'd Wit's fundamental laws.
Such was the Muse, whose rules and practice tell,
"Nature's chief master-piece is writing well."
Such was Roscommon, not more learn'd than good,
With manners gen'rous as his noble blood;
To him the wit of Greece and Rome was known,
And ev'ry author's merit, but his own.
Such late was Walsh — the Muse's judge and friend,
Who justly knew to blame or to commend;
To failings mild, but zealous for desert;
The clearest head, and the sincerest heart.
This humble praise, lamented shade! receive,
This praise at least a grateful Muse may give:
The Muse, whose early voice you taught to sing,
Prescrib'd her heights, and prun'd her tender wing,
(Her guide now lost) no more attempts to rise,
But in low numbers short excursions tries:
Content, if hence th' unlearn'd their wants may view,
The learn'd reflect on what before they knew:
Careless of censure, nor too fond of fame;
Still pleas'd to praise, yet not afraid to blame,
Averse alike to flatter, or offend;
Not free from faults, nor yet too vain to mend.

II. FROM THE EPISTLE TO AUGUSTUS[1]

Authors, like coins, grow dear as they grow old;
It is the rust we value, not the gold.
Chaucer's worst ribaldry is learn'd by rote,
And beastly Skelton heads of houses quote :
One likes no language but the *Faery Queen ;*
A Scot will fight for *Christ's Kirk o' the Green ;*
And each true Briton is to Ben so civil,
He swears the Muses met him at the Devil.

Tho' justly Greece her eldest sons admires,
Why should not we be wiser than our sires?
In ev'ry public virtue we excel ;
We build, we paint, we sing, we dance as well,
And learned Athens to our art must stoop,
Could she behold us tumbling thro' a hoop.

If time improve our wit as well as wine,
Say at what age a poet grows divine ?
Shall we, or shall we not, account him so,
Who died, perhaps, an hundred years ago?
End all dispute ; and fix the year precise
When British bards begin t' immortalize ?

" Who lasts a century can have no flaw,
" I hold that wit a Classic, good in law."

Suppose he wants a year, will you compound?
And shall we deem him Ancient, right and sound,
Or damn to all eternity at once,
At ninety-nine, a Modern and a dunce ?

" We shall not quarrel for a year or two ;
" By courtesy of England, he may do."

[1] This might of course, as is always the case with Pope, be very extensively
annotated. But here it is enough to observe that *every* expression addressed or
referring to George II is ironical, and that the interesting and famous passage
" We conquered France," etc., refers to some period of English history which
has entirely escaped English historians. We begin at l. 35. The actual opening, 1–34, merely contains an address to the King of the politely impertinent
kind just glanced at. The other omitted passages are either of the same drift,
or concerned with morals and manners rather than literature.

Then by the rule that made the Horse-tail bare,
I pluck out year by year, as hair by hair,
And melt down Ancients like a heap of snow:
While you to measure merits, look in Stowe,
And estimating authors by the year,
Bestow a garland only on a bier.

Shakespeare (whom you and ev'ry play-house bill
Style the divine, the matchless, what you will)
For gain, not glory, wing'd his roving flight,
And grew immortal in his own despite.
Ben, old and poor, as little seem'd to heed
The life to come, in ev'ry poet's creed.
Who now reads Cowley? if he pleases yet,
His moral pleases, not his pointed wit:
Forget his epic, nay Pindaric art;
But still I love the language of his heart.

"Yet surely, surely, these were famous men!
"What boy but hears the sayings of old Ben?
"In all debates where critics bear a part,
"Not one but nods, and talks of Jonson's Art,
"Of Shakespeare's Nature, and of Cowley's Wit;
"How Beaumont's judgment check'd what Fletcher writ;
"How Shadwell hasty, Wycherley was slow;
"But for the passions, Southern sure and Rowe.
"These, only these, support the crowded stage,
"From eldest Heywood down to Cibber's age."

All this may be; the People's voice is odd,
It is, and it is not, the voice of God.
To *Gammer Gurton* if it give the bays,
And yet deny the *Careless Husband* praise,
Or say our fathers never broke a rule;
Why then, I say, the public is a fool.
But let them own, that greater faults than we
They had, and greater virtues, I'll agree.
Spenser himself affects the obsolete,
And Sidney's verse halts ill on Roman feet:
Milton's strong pinion now not Heav'n can bound,

Now serpent-like, in prose he sweeps the ground,
In quibbles angel and archangel join,
And God the Father turns a School-divine.
Not that I 'd lop the beauties from his book,
Like slashing Bentley with his desp'rate hook,
Or damn all Shakespeare, like th' affected fool
At court, who hates whate'er he read at school.

But for the wits of either Charles's days,
The mob of gentlemen who wrote with ease;
Sprat, Carew, Sedley, and a hundred more,
(Like twinkling stars the Miscellanies o'er)
One simile, that solitary shines
In the dry desert of a thousand lines,
Or lengthen'd thought that gleams through many a page,
Has sanctified whole poems for an age.
I lose my patience, and I own it too,
When works are censur'd, not as bad but new;
While if our elders break all reason's laws,
These fools demand not pardon, but applause.

On Avon's bank, where flow'rs eternal blow,
If I but ask, if any weed can grow;
One tragic sentence if I dare deride
Which Betterton's grave action dignified,
Or well-mouth'd Booth with emphasis proclaims,
(Tho' but, perhaps, a muster-roll of names)
How will our fathers rise up in a rage,
And swear, all shame is lost in George's age!
You 'd think no fools disgrac'd the former reign,
Did not some grave examples yet remain,
Who scorn a lad should teach his father skill,
And, having once been wrong, will be so still.
He, who to seem more deep than you or I,
Extols old bards, or Merlin's prophecy,
Mistake him not; he envies, not admires,
And to debase the sons, exalts the sires.
Had ancient times conspir'd to disallow
What then was new, what had been ancient now?

Or what remain'd, so worthy to be read
By learned critics, of the mighty dead ?
    In days of ease, when now the weary sword
Was sheath'd, and *Luxury* with *Charles* restor'd;
In ev'ry taste of foreign Courts improv'd,
" All, by the King's example, liv'd and lov'd."
Then peers grew proud in horsemanship t' excel,
Newmarket's glory rose, as Britain's fell;
The soldier breath'd the gallantries of France,
And ev'ry flow'ry courtier writ romance.
Then marble, soften'd into life, grew warm:
And yielding metal flow'd to human form:
Lely on animated canvas stole
The sleepy eye, that spoke the melting soul.
No wonder then, when all was love and sport,
The willing Muses were debauch'd at court:
On each enervate string they taught the note
To pant, or tremble thro' an eunuch's throat.
    .   .   .   .

    Unhappy Dryden ! — In all Charles's days,
Roscommon only boasts unspotted bays;
And in our own (excuse some courtly stains)
No whiter page than Addison remains.
He, from the taste obscene reclaims our youth,
And sets the passions on the side of Truth,
Forms the soft bosom with the gentlest art,
And pours each human virtue in the heart.
Let Ireland tell, how wit upheld her cause,
Her trade supported, and supplied her laws;
And leave on SWIFT this grateful verse engrav'd:
' The rights a Court attack'd, a Poet sav'd.'
Behold a hand that wrought a nation's cure,
Stretch'd to relieve the idiot and the poor,
Proud vice to brand, or injur'd worth adorn,
And stretch the ray to ages yet unborn.
Not but there are, who merit other palms;
Hopkins and Sternhold glad the heart with psalms;

The boys and girls whom charity maintains,
Implore your help in these pathetic strains:
How could devotion touch the country pews,
Unless the gods bestow'd a proper Muse?
Verse cheers their leisure, verse assists their work,
Verse prays for peace, or sings down Pope and Turk.
The silenc'd preacher yields to potent strain,
And feels that grace his pray'r besought in vain;
The blessing thrills thro' all the lab'ring throng,
And Heav'n is won by violence of song.

.   .   .   .

    We conquer'd France, but felt our captive's charms;
Her arts victorious triumph'd o'er our arms;
Britain to soft refinements less a foe,
Wit grew polite, and numbers learn'd to flow.
Waller was smooth; but Dryden taught to join
The varying verse, the full-resounding line,
The long majestic march, and energy divine,
Tho' still some traces of our rustic vein
And splay-foot verse, remain'd, and will remain.
Late, very late, correctness grew our care,
When the tir'd nation breath'd from civil war.
Exact Racine, and Corneille's noble fire,
Show'd us that France had something to admire.
Not but the tragic spirit was our own,
And full in Shakespeare, fair in Otway shone:
But Otway fail'd to polish or refine,
And fluent Shakespeare scarce effac'd a line.
Ev'n copious Dryden wanted, or forgot,
The last and greatest art, the art to blot.
Some doubt, if equal pains, or equal fire
The humbler Muse of Comedy require.
But in known images of life, I guess
The labour greater, as th' indulgence less.
Observe how seldom ev'n the best succeed:
Tell me if Congreve's fools are fools indeed?
What pert, low dialogue has Farquhar writ!

How Van wants grace, who never wanted wit!
The stage how loosely does Astræa tread,
Who fairly puts all characters to bed!
And idle Cibber, how he breaks the laws,
To make poor Pinky eat with vast applause!
But fill their purse, our poets' work is done,
Alike to them, by pathos or by pun.

O you! whom Vanity's light bark conveys
On Fame's mad voyage by the wind of praise,
With what a shifting gale your course you ply,
For ever sunk too low, or borne too high!
Who pants for glory finds but short repose,
A breath revives him, or a breath o'erthrows.
Farewell the stage! if just as thrives the play,
The silly bard grows fat, or falls away.

There still remains, to mortify a wit,
The many-headed monster of the pit:
A senseless, worthless, and unhonour'd crowd;
Who, to disturb their betters mighty proud,
Clatt'ring their sticks before ten lines are spoke,
Call for the farce, the bear, or the black-joke.
What dear delight to Britons farce affords!
Ever the taste of mobs, but now of lords;
(Taste, that eternal wanderer, which flies
From heads to ears, and now from ears to eyes.)
The play stands still; damn action and discourse,
Back fly the scenes, and enter foot and horse;
Pageants on pageants, in long order drawn,
Peers, heralds, bishops, ermine, gold and lawn;
The champion too! and, to complete the jest,
Old Edward's armour beams on Cibber's breast.
With laughter sure Democritus had died,
Had he beheld an audience gape so wide.
Let bear or elephant be e'er so white,
The people, sure, the people are the sight!
Ah luckless poet! stretch thy lungs and roar,
That bear or elephant shall heed thee more;

While all its throats the gallery extends,
And all the thunder of the pit ascends!
Loud as the wolves, on Orcas' stormy steep,
Howl to the roarings of the northern deep,
Such is the shout, the long-applauding note,
At Quin's high plume, or Oldfield's petticoat;
Or when from court a birth-day suit bestow'd,
Sinks the lost actor in the tawdry load.
Booth enters — hark! the universal peal!
"But has he spoken?" Not a syllable.
What shook the stage, and made the people stare?
Cato's long wig, flow'r'd gown, and lacquer'd chair.

Yet lest you think I rally more than teach,
Or praise malignly arts I cannot reach,
Let me for once presume t' instruct the times,
To know the poet from the man of rhymes:
'T is he, who gives my breast a thousand pains,
Can make me feel each passion that he feigns;
Enrage, compose, with more than magic art,
With pity, and with terror, tear my heart;
And snatch me, o'er the earth, or thro' the air,
To Thebes, to Athens, when he will, and where.

But not this part of the poetic state
Alone, deserves the favour of the great;
Think of those authors, sir, who would rely
More on a reader's sense, than gazer's eye.
Or who shall wander where the Muses sing?
Who climb their mountain, or who taste their spring?
How shall we fill a library with wit,
When Merlin's cave is half unfurnish'd yet?

My Liege! why writers little claim your thought,
I guess; and, with their leave, will tell the fault:
We poets are (upon a poet's word)
Of all mankind, the creatures most absurd:
The season, when to come, and when to go,
To sing, or cease to sing, we never know;
And if we will recite nine hours in ten,

You lose your patience, just like other men.
Then too we hurt ourselves, when to defend
A single verse, we quarrel with a friend;
Repeat unask'd; lament, the wit's too fine
For vulgar eyes, and point out ev'ry line.
But most, when straining with too weak a wing,
We needs will write Epistles to the King;
And from the moment we oblige the town,
Expect a place, or pension from the crown;
Or dubb'd Historians, by express command,
T' enroll your triumphs o'er the seas and land,
Be call'd to court to plan some work divine,
As once for LOUIS, Boileau and Racine.

    Yet think, great sir! (so many virtues shown)
Ah think, what poet best may make them known?
Or choose at least some minister of grace,
Fit to bestow the Laureate's weighty place.

    Charles, to late times to be transmitted fair,
Assign'd his figure to Bernini's care;
And great Nassau to Kneller's hand decreed
To fix him graceful on the bounding steed;
So well in paint and stone they judg'd of merit:
But kings in wit may want discerning spirit.
The hero William, and the martyr Charles,
One knighted Blackmore, and one pension'd Quarles;
Which made old Ben, and surly Dennis swear,
"No lord's anointed, but a Russian bear."
  Not with such majesty, such bold relief,
The forms august, of king, or conqu'ring chief,
E'er swell'd on marble; as in verse have shin'd
(In polish'd verse) the manners and the mind.
Oh! could I mount on the Mæonian wing,
Your arms, your actions, your repose to sing!
What seas you travers'd, and what fields you fought!
Your country's peace, how oft, how dearly bought!
How barb'rous rage subsided at your word,
And nations wonder'd while they dropp'd the sword!

How, when you nodded, o'er the land and deep,
Peace stole her wing, and wrapt the world in sleep;
Till earth's extremes your mediation own,
And Asia's tyrants tremble at your throne —
But verse, alas! your majesty disdains;
And I'm not us'd to panegyric strains:
The zeal of fools offends at any time,
But most of all, the zeal of fools in rhyme.
Besides, a fate attends on all I write,
That when I aim at praise, they say I bite.
A vile encomium doubly ridicules:
There's nothing blackens like the ink of fools.
If true, a woeful likeness; and if lies,
" Praise undeserv'd is scandal in disguise:"
Well may he blush, who gives it, or receives;
And when I flatter, let my dirty leaves
(Like journals, odes, and such forgotten things
As Eusden, Philips, Settle, writ of kings)
Clothe spice, line trunks, or, flutt'ring in a row,
Befringe the rails of Bedlam and Soho.

XXIII

JOHNSON

1. FROM THE RAMBLER

A. THE SEAMY SIDE OF CRITICISM [1]

But, though it should happen that an author is capable of excelling, yet his merit may pass without notice, huddled in the variety of things, and thrown into the general miscellany of life. He that endeavours after fame by writing, solicits the regard of a multitude fluctuating in pleasures, or immersed in business, without time for intellectual amusements; he appeals to judges, prepossessed by passions, or corrupted by prejudices, which preclude their approbation of any new performance. Some are too indolent to read any thing, till its reputation is established; others too envious to promote that fame which gives them pain by its increase. What is new is opposed, because most are unwilling to be taught; and what is known is rejected, because it is not sufficiently considered, that men more frequently require to be reminded than informed. The learned are afraid to declare their opinion early, lest they should put their reputation in hazard; the ignorant always imagine themselves giving some proof of delicacy, when they refuse to be pleased: and he that finds his way to reputation through all these obstructions, must acknowledge that he is indebted to other causes besides his industry, his learning, or his wit.

[1] The opening numbers of *The Rambler* are occupied with reflections on literature, and the chances of the man of letters, which are full of Johnson's melancholy wisdom. This paragraph (No. 2) contains the root and essence of the more florid Allegory of Criticism which fills No. 3.

B. SELECTIONS FROM CRITICISMS ON MILTON

I. HEROIC VERSE [1]

The heroic measure of the English language may be properly considered as pure or mixed. It is pure when the accent rests upon every second syllable through the whole line.

> Courage uncertain dangers may abate,
> But whó can beár th' appróach of cértain fáte? — DRYDEN.

> Here Love his golden shafts employs, here lights
> His cónstant lámp, and wáves his púrple wíngs,
> Reigns here, and revels; not in the bought smile
> Of hárlots, lóveless, jóyless, únendéared. — MILTON.

The accent may be observed, in the second line of Dryden, and the second and fourth of Milton, to repose upon every second syllable.

The repetition of this sound or percussion at equal times, is the most complete harmony of which a single verse is capable, and should therefore be exactly kept in distichs, and generally in the last line of a paragraph, that the ear may rest without any sense of imperfection.

But, to preserve the series of sounds untransposed in a long composition, is not only very difficult, but tiresome and disgusting; for we are soon wearied with the perpetual recurrence of the same cadence. Necessity has therefore enforced the mixed measure, in which some variation of the accents is allowed: this, though it always injures the harmony of the line, considered by itself, yet compensates the loss by relieving us from the continual tyranny of the same sound, and makes us more sensible of the harmony of the pure measure.

Of these mixed numbers every poet affords us innumerable instances, and Milton seldom has two pure lines together, as will appear if any of his paragraphs be read with attention merely to the music.

---

[1] This (No. 86) has been inserted to show the effect of the rigid ten-syllable alternate-accent view of English verse, on the criticism, by a very great critic, of all but the greatest artist in that verse.

> Thus at their shady lodge arrived, both stood,
> Both turn'd, and under open sky adored
> The God that made both sky, air, earth, and heaven,
> Which they beheld; the moon's resplendent globe,
> *And starry pole: thou also mad'st the night,*
> Maker omnipotent! and thou the day,
> Which we in our appointed work employ'd
> Have finish'd, happy in our mutual help,
> *And mutual love, the crown of all our bliss*
> Ordain'd by thee; and this delicious place,
> For us too large; where thy abundance wants
> Partakers, and uncropp'd falls to the ground;
> But thou hast promised from us two a race
> To fill the earth, who shall with us extol
> Thy goodness infinite, both when we wake,
> And when we seek, as now, thy gift of sleep.

In this passage it will be at first observed that all the lines are not equally harmonious, and upon a nearer examination it will be found that only the fifth and ninth lines are regular, and the rest are more or less licentious with respect to the accent. In some the accent is equally upon two syllables together, and in both strong. As

> Thus at their shady lodge arrived, *both stood,*
> *Both turn'd,* and under open sky adored
> The God that made both sky, *air, earth,* and heaven.

In others the accent is equally upon two syllables, but upon both weak.

> —— A race
> To fill the earth, who shall with us extol
> Thy goodness in*finite,* both when we wake,
> *And when* we seek, as now, thy gift of sleep.

In the first pair of syllables the accent may deviate from the rigour of exactness, without any unpleasing diminution of harmony, as may be observed in the lines already cited, and more remarkably in this,

> —— Thou also mad'st the night,
> *Maker* omnipotent! and thou the day.

But, excepting in the first pair of syllables, which may be considered as arbitrary, a poet who, not having the invention or knowledge of Milton, has more need to allure his audience by musical cadences, should seldom suffer more than one aberration from the rule in any single verse.

There are two lines in this passage more remarkably unharmonious:

> ——— This delicious place,
> For us too large; *where thy* abundance wants
> Partakers, and uncropp'd *falls to* the ground.

Here the third pair of syllables in the first, and fourth pair in the second verse, have their accents retrograde or inverted; the first syllable being strong or acute, and the second weak. The detriment which the measure suffers by this inversion of the accents is sometimes less perceptible, when the verses are carried one into another, but is remarkably striking in this place, where the vicious verse concludes a period, and is yet more offensive in rhyme, when we regularly attend to the flow of every single line. This will appear by reading a couplet in which Cowley, an author not sufficiently studious of harmony, has committed the same fault.

> ——— His harmless life
> Does with substantial blessedness abound,
> And the soft wings of peace *cover* him round.

In these the law of metre is very grossly violated by mingling combinations of sounds directly opposite to each other, as Milton expresses in his sonnet, by *committing short and long,* and setting one part of the measure at variance with the rest. The ancients, who had a language more capable of variety than ours, had two kinds of verse, the *Iambic,* consisting of short and long syllables alternately, from which our heroic measure is derived, and the *Trochaic,* consisting in a like alternation of long and short. These were considered as opposites, and conveyed the contrary images of speed and slowness; to confound them, therefore, as in these lines, is to deviate from the established practice. But where the senses are to judge, authority is not necessary, the ear is sufficient to detect dissonance, nor should I have sought auxiliaries on such an occasion against any name but that of Milton.

II. "Elisions" [1]

The great peculiarity of Milton's versification, compared with that of later poets, is the elision of one vowel before another, or the suppression of the last syllable of a word ending with a vowel, when a vowel begins the following word.   As

> —— Knowledge
> Oppresses else with surfeit, and soon turns
> Wisdom to fol*ly*, as nourishment to wind.

This licence, though now disused in English poetry, was practised by our old writers, and is allowed in many other languages ancient and modern, and therefore the critics on *Paradise Lost* have, without much deliberation, commended Milton for continuing it.   But one language cannot communicate its rules to another. We have already tried and rejected the hexameter of the ancients, the double close of the Italians, and the Alexandrine of the French ; and the elision of vowels, however graceful it may seem to other nations, may be very unsuitable to the genius of the English tongue.

There is reason to believe that we have negligently lost part of our vowels, and that the silent *e*, which our ancestors added to the most of our monosyllables, was once vocal.   By this detruncation of our syllables, our language is overstocked with consonants, and it is more necessary to add vowels to the beginning of words, than to cut them off from the end.

Milton therefore seems to have somewhat mistaken the nature of our language, of which the chief defect is ruggedness and asperity, and has left our harsh cadences yet harsher.   But his elisions are not all equally to be censured ; in some syllables they may be allowed, and perhaps in a few may be safely imitated.   The abscission of a vowel is undoubtedly vicious when it is strongly sounded, and makes, with its associate consonant, a full and audible syllable.

> —— What he gives,
> Spiritual, may to purest spirits be found,
> *No* ingrateful food, and food alike these pure
> Intelligential substances require.

[1] Another (No. 88) to show the result of ignoring or refusing trisyllabic feet.

—— Fruits, — Hesperian fables true,
If true, here on*ly*, and of delicious taste.

—— Evening now approach'd,
For we have al*so* our evening and our morn.

—— Of guests he makes them slaves,
Inhospita*bly*, and kills their infant males.

And vital vir*tue* infused, and vital warmth
Throughout the fluid mass. ——

God made *thee* of choice his own, and of his own
To serve him.

I believe every reader will agree, that in all those passages,
though not equally in all, the music is injured, and in some the
meaning obscured.   There are other lines in which the vowel is cut
off, but it is so faintly pronounced in common speech, that the loss
of it in poetry is scarcely perceived ; and therefore such compliance
with the measure may be allowed.

—— Nature breeds
Perverse, all monstrous, all prodigious things,
Abomina*ble*, inuttera*ble* ; and worse
Than fables yet have feign'd ——

—— From the shore
They view'd the vast immensura*ble* abyss,
Impenetra*ble*, impal'd with circling fire.

To none communica*ble* in earth or heaven.

Yet even these contractions increase the roughness of a language
too rough already ; and though in long poems they may be sometimes suffered, it never can be faulty to forbear them.
    Milton frequently uses in his poems the hypermetrical or redund-
ant line of eleven syllables.

—— Thus it shall befal
Him who to worth in woman over-trust*ing*
Lets her will rule. ——

I also err'd in over-much admir*ing*.

Verses of this kind occur almost in every page ; but, though they
are not unpleasing or dissonant, they ought not to be admitted into

heroic poetry, since the narrow limits of our language allow us no other distinction of epic and tragic measures, than is afforded by the liberty of changing at will the terminations of the dramatic lines, and bringing them by that relaxation of metrical rigour nearer to prose.

III. MILTON'S PAUSES [1]

It is very difficult to write on the minuter parts of literature without failing either to please or instruct.   Too much nicety of detail disgusts the greatest part of readers, and to throw a multitude of particulars under general heads, and lay down rules of extensive comprehension, is to common understandings of little use.   They who undertake these subjects are therefore always in danger, as one or other inconvenience arises to their imagination, of frighting us with rugged science, or amusing us with empty sound.

In criticising the work of Milton, there is, indeed, opportunity to intersperse passages that can hardly fail to relieve the languors of attention ; and since, in examining the variety and choice of the pauses with which he has diversified his numbers, it will be necessary to exhibit the lines in which they are to be found, perhaps the remarks may be well compensated by the examples, and the irksomeness of grammatical disquisitions somewhat alleviated.   Milton formed his scheme of versification by the poets of Greece and Rome, whom he proposed to himself for his models, so far as the difference of his language from theirs would permit the imitation. There are indeed many inconveniences inseparable from our heroic measure compared with that of Homer and Virgil ; inconveniences, which it is no reproach to Milton not to have overcome, because they are in their own nature insuperable ; but against which he has struggled with so much art and diligence, that he may at least be said to have deserved success.

The hexameter of the ancients may be considered as consisting of fifteen syllables, so melodiously disposed, that, as every one knows who has examined the poetical authors, very pleasing and

---

[1] There is of course nothing for it save *De Gustibus* here (No. 90).   To *us* " Pure ; " and " Her son." are resplendent beauties.   But it can be at least urged that Johnson's theory *made* them defects.

sonorous lyric measures are formed from the fragments of the heroic. It is, indeed, scarce possible to break them in such a manner, but that *invenias etiam disjecta membra poetæ*, some harmony will still remain, and the due proportions of sound will always be discovered. This measure therefore allowed great variety of pauses, and great liberties of connecting one verse with another, because wherever the line was interrupted, either part singly was musical. But the ancients seemed to have confined this privilege to hexameters; for in their other measures, though longer than the English heroic, those who wrote after the refinements of versification, venture so seldom to change their pauses, that every variation may be supposed rather a compliance with necessity than the choice of judgment.

Milton was constrained within the narrow limits of a measure not very harmonious in the utmost perfection; the single parts, therefore, into which it was to be sometimes broken by pauses, were in danger of losing the very form of verse. This has, perhaps, notwithstanding all his care, sometimes happened.

As harmony is the end of poetical measures, no part of a verse ought to be so separated from the rest as not to remain still more harmonious than prose, or to show, by the disposition of the tones, that it is part of a verse. This rule in the old hexameter might be easily observed, but in English will very frequently be in danger of violation; for the order and regularity of accents cannot well be perceived in a succession of fewer than three syllables, which will confine the English poet to only five pauses; it being supposed, that when he connects one line with another, he should never make a full pause at less distance than that of three syllables from the beginning or end of a verse.

That this rule should be universally and indispensably established, perhaps cannot be granted; something may be allowed to variety, and something to the adaptation of the numbers to the subject; but it will be found generally necessary, and the ear will seldom fail to suffer by its neglect.

Thus when a single syllable is cut off from the rest, it must either be united to the line with which the sense connects it, or be sounded alone. If it be united to the other line, it corrupts its harmony; if disjoined, it must stand alone, and with regard to music be superfluous; for there is no harmony in a single sound, because it has no proportion to another.

> —— Hypocrites austerely talk,
> Defaming as impure what God declares
> *Pure;* and commands to some, leaves free to all.

When two syllables likewise are abscinded from the rest, they evidently want some associate sounds to make them harmonious.

> —— Eyes ——
> —— more wakeful than to drowse,
> Charm'd with Arcadian pipe, the past'ral reed
> Of Hermes, or his opiate rod.   *Meanwhile*
> To re-salute the world with sacred light
> Leucothea waked.

> He ended, and the Son gave signal high
> To the bright minister that watch'd: *he blew*
> His trumpet.

> First in the east his glorious lamp was seen,
> Regent of day; and all th' horizon round
> Invested with bright rays, jocund to run
> His longitude through heaven's high road; *the grey*
> Dawn, and the Pleiades, before him danced,
> Shedding sweet influence.

The same defect is perceived in the following line, where the pause is at the second syllable from the beginning.

> —— The race
> Of that wild rout that tore the Thracian bard
> In Rhodope where woods and rocks had ears
> To rapture, till the savage clamour drown'd
> Both harp and voice; nor could the Muse defend
> *Her son.*   So fail not thou, who thee implores.

When the pause falls upon the third syllable or the seventh, the harmony is better preserved; but as the third and seventh are weak syllables, the period leaves the ear unsatisfied, and in expectation of the remaining part of the verse.

> —— He, with his horrid crew,
> Lay vanquish'd, rolling in the fiery gulf,

Confounded though immor*tal*. But his doom
Reserved him to more wrath ; for now the thought
Both of lost happiness and lasting pain
Torments *him*.

   God, — with frequent intercourse,
Thither will send his winged messengers
On errands of supernal grace. So sung
The glorious train ascend*ing*.

It may be, I think, established as a rule, that a pause which
concludes a period should be made for the most part upon a strong
syllable, as the fourth and sixth ; but those pauses which only sus-
pend the sense may be placed upon the weaker. Thus the rest in
the third line of the first passage satisfies the ear better than in the
fourth, and the close of the second quotation better than that of
the third.

      —— The evil soon
Drawn back, redounded (as a flood) on those
From whom it *sprung ;* impossible to mix
With *blessedness*.

      —— What we by day
   Lop overgrown, or prune, or prop, or bind,
One night or two with wanton growth derides,
Tending to *wild*.

The paths and bowers doubt not but our joint hands
Will keep from wilderness with ease as wide
As we need walk, till younger hands ere long
Assist *us*.

The rest in the fifth place has the same inconvenience as in the
seventh and third, that the syllable is weak.

Beast now with beast 'gan war, and fowl with fowl,
And fish with fish, to graze the herb all leaving,
Devour'd each *other ;* Nor stood much in awe
Of man, but fled *him*, or with countenance grim,
Glared on him pass*ing*.

The noblest and most majestic pauses which our versification
admits, are upon the fourth and sixth syllables, which are both

strongly sounded in a pure and regular verse, and at either of which the line is so divided, that both members participate of harmony.

> But now at last the sacred influence
> Of light *appears*, and from the walls of heaven
> Shoots far into the bosom of dim night
> A glimmering *dawn:* here Nature first begins
> Her farthest verge, and chaos to retire.

But far above all others, if I can give any credit to my own ear, is the rest upon the sixth syllable, which, taking in a complete compass of sound, such as is sufficient to constitute one of our lyric measures, makes a full and solemn close. Some passages which conclude at this stop, I could never read without some strong emotions of delight or admiration.

> Before the hills appear'd, or fountain flow'd,
> Thou with the eternal wisdom didst converse,
> Wisdom thy sister, and with her didst play
> In presence of the almighty Father, pleased
> With thy celestial *song.*

> Or other worlds they seem'd, or happy isles,
> Like those Hesperian gardens famed of old,
> Fortunate fields, and groves, and flowery vales,
> Thrice happy isles! But who dwelt happy there,
>   He stay'd not to in*quire.*

> —— He blew
> His trumpet, heard in Oreb since, perhaps,
> When God descended; and, perhaps, once more
> To sound at general *doom.*

If the poetry of Milton be examined, with regard to the pauses and flow of his verses into each other, it will appear that he has performed all that our language would admit; and the comparison of his numbers with those who have cultivated the same manner of writing, will show that he excelled as much in the lower as the higher parts of his art, and that his skill in harmony was not less than his invention or his learning.

IV. The Responsibilities of the Critic [1]

There are few books on which more time is spent by young students, than on treatises which deliver the characters of authors; nor any which oftener deceive the expectation of the reader, or fill his mind with more opinions which the progress of his studies and the increase of his knowledge oblige him to resign.

Baillet has introduced his collection of the decisions of the learned, by an enumeration of the prejudices which mislead the critic, and raise the passions in rebellion against the judgment. His catalogue, though large, is imperfect; and who can hope to complete it? The beauties of writing have been observed to be often such as cannot in the present state of human knowledge be evinced by evidence, or drawn out into demonstrations; they are therefore wholly subject to the imagination, and do not force their effects upon a mind preoccupied by unfavourable sentiments, nor overcome the counteraction of a false principle or of stubborn partiality.

To convince any man against his will is hard, but to please him against his will is justly pronounced by Dryden to be above the reach of human abilities. Interest and passion will hold out long against the closest siege of diagrams and syllogisms, but they are absolutely impregnable to imagery and sentiment; and will for ever bid defiance to the most powerful strains of Virgil or Homer, though they may give way in time to the batteries of Euclid or Archimedes.

In trusting therefore to the sentence of a critic, we are in danger not only from that vanity which exalts writers too often to the dignity of teaching what they are yet to learn, from that negligence which sometimes steals upon the most vigilant caution, and that fallibility to which the condition of nature has subjected every human understanding; but from a thousand extrinsic and accidental

---

[1] This admirable essay (No. 93), which is a sort of extension and commentary of the paragraph given above (as A), is not openly connected with the Miltonic strictures. But it immediately precedes the last of them,. and is apparently a sort of indirect apologia therefor. The concluding paper itself is an excellently sensible one — on the then fashionable doctrine of suiting the sound to the sense, as illustrated (or thought to be illustrated) in *Paradise Lost*.

causes, from every thing which can excite kindness or malevolence, veneration or contempt.

Many of those who have determined with great boldness upon the various degrees of literary merit, may be justly suspected of having passed sentence, as Seneca remarks of Claudius,

> Una tantum parte audita,
> Sæpe et nulla,

without much knowledge of the cause before them: for it will not easily be imagined of Langbaine, Borrichius, or Rapin, that they had very accurately perused all the books which they praise or censure; or that, even if nature and learning had qualified them for judges, they could read for ever with the attention necessary to just criticism. Such performances, however, are not wholly without their use; for they are commonly just echoes to the voice of fame, and transmit the general suffrage of mankind when they have no particular motives to suppress it.

Critics, like the rest of mankind, are very frequently misled by interest. The bigotry with which editors regard the authors whom they illustrate or correct, has been generally remarked. Dryden was known to have written most of his critical dissertations only to recommend the work upon which he then happened to be employed: and Addison is suspected to have denied the expediency of poetical justice, because his own Cato was condemned to perish in a good cause.

There are prejudices which authors, not otherwise weak or corrupt, have indulged without scruple; and perhaps some of them are so complicated with our natural affections, that they cannot easily be disentangled from the heart. Scarce any can hear with impartiality a comparison between the writers of his own and another country: and though it cannot, I think, be charged equally on all nations, that they are blinded with this literary patriotism, yet there are none that do not look upon their authors with the fondness of affinity, and esteem them as well for the place of their birth, as for their knowledge or their wit. There is, therefore, seldom much respect due to comparative criticism, when the competitors are of different countries, unless the judge is of a nation equally indifferent to both. The Italians could not for a long time believe, that there was any learning beyond the mountains; and the French seem generally persuaded, that there are no wits or reasoners equal to their own. I can scarcely conceive that if Scaliger had not considered himself as allied to Virgil, by being born in the same country, he would have found his works so much superior to those of Homer, or have thought the controversy worthy of so much zeal, vehemence, and acrimony.

There is, indeed, one prejudice, and only one, by which it may be doubted whether it is any dishonour to be sometimes misguided. Criticism has so often given occasion to the envious and ill-natured, of gratifying their malignity, that some have thought it necessary to recommend the virtue of candour without restriction, and to preclude all future liberty of censure. Writers possessed with this opinion are continually enforcing civility and decency, recommending to critics the proper diffidence of themselves, and inculcating the veneration due to celebrated names.

I am not of opinion that these professed enemies of arrogance and severity have much more benevolence or modesty than the rest of mankind; or that they feel in their own hearts, any other intention than to distinguish themselves by their softness and delicacy. Some are modest because they are timorous, and some are lavish of praise because they hope to be repaid.

There is, indeed, some tenderness due to living writers, when they attack none of those truths which are of importance to the happiness of mankind, and have committed no other offence than that of betraying their own ignorance or dulness. I should think it cruelty to crush an insect who had provoked me only by buzzing in my ear; and would not willingly interrupt the dream of harmless stupidity, or destroy the jest which makes its author laugh. Yet I am far from thinking this tenderness universally necessary, for he that writes may be considered as a kind of general challenger, whom every one has a right to attack; since he quits the common rank of life, steps forward beyond the lists, and offers his merit to the public judgment. To commence author is to claim praise, and no man can justly aspire to honour, but at the hazard of disgrace.

But, whatever be decided concerning contemporaries, whom he that knows the treachery of the human heart, and considers how often we gratify our own pride or envy, under the appearance of contending for elegance and propriety, will find himself not much inclined to disturb; there can surely be no exemptions pleaded to secure them from criticism, who can no longer suffer by reproach, and of whom nothing now remains but their writings and their names. Upon these authors the critic is undoubtedly at full liberty to exercise the strictest severity, since he endangers only his own fame; and, like Æneas, when he drew his sword in the infernal regions, encounters phantoms which cannot be wounded. He may, indeed, pay some regard to established reputation; but he can by that show of reverence consult only his own security, for all other motives are now at an end.

The faults of a writer of acknowledged excellence are more dangerous, because the influence of his example is more extensive; and the interest of learning requires that they should be discovered and stigmatized, before they have the sanction of antiquity conferred upon them, and become precedents of indisputable authority.

It has, indeed, been advanced by Addison, as one of the characteristics of a true critic, that he points out beauties rather than faults. But it is rather natural to a man of learning and genius to apply himself chiefly to the study of writers who have more beauties than faults to be displayed: for the duty of criticism is neither to depreciate, nor dignify by partial representations, but to hold out the light of reason, whatever it may discover; and to promulgate the determinations of truth, whatever she shall dictate.

C. CRITICISM OF SPENSER [1]

To imitate the fictions and sentiments of Spenser can incur no reproach, for allegory is perhaps one of the most pleasing vehicles of instruction. But I am very far from extending the same respect to his diction and his stanza. His style was in his own time allowed to be vicious, so darkened with old words and peculiarities of phrase,

---

[1] Johnson was no doubt thinking chiefly of Shenstone, Thomson, and West in the reference to "some men of learning and genius" which introduces this criticism (No. 121). It is, of course, a very unfortunate one — very much below the censures of Milton, which have preceded it, and more like those in the later " Life " of that poet. But its very misfortunes are documents.

and so remote from common use, that Jonson boldly pronounces
him to have written no language. His stanza is at once difficult
and unpleasing; tiresome to the ear by its uniformity, and to the
attention by its length. It was at first formed in imitation of the
Italian poets, without due regard to the genius of our language.
The Italians have little variety of termination, and were forced to
contrive such a stanza as might admit the greatest number of
similar rhymes; but our words end with so much diversity, that it
is seldom convenient for us to bring more than two of the same
sound together. If it be justly observed by Milton, that rhyme
obliges poets to express their thoughts in improper terms, these
improprieties must always be multiplied, as the difficulty of rhyme
is increased by long concatenations.

The imitators of Spenser are indeed not very rigid censors of
themselves, for they seem to conclude that, when they have dis-
figured their lines with a few obsolete syllables, they have accomplished their design, without considering that they ought not only
to admit old words, but to avoid new. The laws of imitation are
broken by every word introduced since the time of Spenser, as the
character of Hector is violated by quoting Aristotle in the play.
It would indeed be difficult to exclude from a long poem all modern
phrase, though it is easy to sprinkle it with gleanings of antiquity.
Perhaps, however, the style of Spenser might by long labour be
justly copied; but life is surely given us for higher purposes than
to gather what our ancestors have wisely thrown away, and to learn
what is of no value, but because it has been forgotten.

D. OF TRAGICOMEDY AND "JUDGING BY THE EVENT"[1]

Criticism has sometimes permitted fancy to dictate the laws by
which fancy ought to be restrained, and fallacy to perplex the

---

[1] No passage, perhaps, in Johnson serves to show his critical greatness better
than this (No. 156); nor does any, in him or another, better show that association of contradictories which often does (and perhaps should) mark great criticism. In the first few paragraphs, and partly in the last, he is very nearly
Samson to the temple of the Classical Philistia: in the others he puts the pillars
back again, and Gaza escapes—for the time.

principles by which fallacy is to be detected; her superintendence of others has betrayed her to negligence of herself; and, like the ancient Scythians, by extending her conquests over distant regions, she has left her throne vacant to her slaves.

Among the laws of which the desire of extending authority, or ardour of promoting knowledge, has prompted the prescription, all which writers have received, had not the same original right to our regard. Some are to be considered as fundamental and indispensable, others only as useful and convenient; some as dictated by reason and necessity, others as enacted by despotic antiquity; some as invincibly supported by their conformity to the order of nature and operations of the intellect; others as formed by accident, or instituted by example, and therefore always liable to dispute and alteration.

That many rules have been advanced without consulting nature or reason, we cannot but suspect, when we find it peremptorily decreed by the ancient masters, that *only three speaking personages should appear at once upon the stage;* a law which, as the variety and intricacy of modern plays has made it impossible to be observed, we now violate without scruple, and, as experience proves, without inconvenience.

The original of this precept was merely accidental. Tragedy was a monody, or solitary song in honour of Bacchus, improved afterwards into a dialogue by the addition of another speaker: but the ancients, remembering that the tragedy was at first pronounced only by one, durst not for some time venture beyond two: at last, when custom and impunity had made them daring, they extended their liberty to the admission of three, but restrained themselves by a critical edict from further exorbitance.

By what accident the number of acts was limited to five, I know not that any author has informed us; but certainly it is not determined by any necessity arising either from the nature of action or propriety of exhibition. An act is only the representation of such a part of the business of a play as proceeds in an unbroken tenor, or without any intermediate pause. Nothing is more evident than that of every real, and by consequence of every dramatic action, the intervals may be more or fewer than five; and indeed the rule is upon the English stage every day broken in effect, without any other mischief than that which arises from an absurd endeavour to observe it in appearance. Whenever the scene is shifted the act ceases, since some time is necessarily supposed to elapse while the personages of the drama change their place.

With no greater right to our obedience have the critics confined the dramatic action to a certain number of hours. Probability requires that the time of action should approach somewhat nearly to that of exhibition, and those plays will always be thought most happily conducted which crowd the greatest variety into the least space. But since it will frequently happen that some delusion must be admitted, I know not where the limits of imagination can be fixed. It is rarely observed that minds, not prepossessed by mechanical criticism, feel any offence from the extension of the intervals between the acts; nor can I conceive it absurd or impossible, that he who can multiply three hours into twelve or twenty-four, might image with equal ease a greater number.

I know not whether he that professes to regard no other laws than those of nature, will not be inclined to receive tragicomedy to his protection, whom, however generally condemned, her own laurels have hitherto shaded from the fulminations of criticism. For what is there in the mingled drama which impartial reason can condemn? The connection of important with trivial incidents, since it is not only common but perpetual in the world, may surely be allowed upon the stage, which pretends only to be the mirror of life. The impropriety of suppressing passions before we have raised them to the intended agitation, and of diverting the expectation from an event which we keep suspended only to raise it, may be speciously urged. But will not experience show this objection to be rather subtile than just? Is it not certain that the tragic and comic affections have been moved alternately with equal force; and that no plays have oftener filled the eye with tears, and the breast with palpitation, than those which are variegated with interludes of mirth?

I do not however think it safe to judge of works of genius merely by the event. The resistless vicissitudes of the heart, this alternate prevalence of merriment and solemnity, may sometimes be more properly ascribed to the vigour of the writer than the justness of the design : and, instead of vindicating tragicomedy by the success of Shakespeare, we ought, perhaps, to pay new honours to that transcendent and unbounded genius that could preside over the passions in sport; who, to actuate the affections, needed not the slow gradation of common means, but could fill the heart with instantaneous jollity or sorrow, and vary our disposition as he changed his scenes. Perhaps the effects even of Shakespeare's poetry might have been yet greater, had he not counteracted himself; and we might have been more interested in the distresses of his heroes, had we not been so frequently diverted by the jokes of his buffoons.

There are other rules more fixed and obligatory. It is necessary that of every play the chief action should be single; for, since a play represents some transaction through its regular maturation to its final event, two actions equally important must evidently constitute two plays.

As the design of tragedy is to instruct by moving the passions, it must always have a hero, a personage apparently and incontestably superior to the rest, upon whom the attention may be fixed, and the anxiety suspended. For though, of two persons opposing each other with equal abilities and equal virtue, the auditor will inevitably, in time, choose his favourite; yet, as that choice must be without any cogency of conviction, the hopes or fears which it raises will be faint and languid. Of two heroes acting in confederacy against a common enemy, the virtues or dangers will give little emotion, because each claims our concern with the same right, and the heart lies at rest between equal motives.

It ought to be the first endeavour of a writer to distinguish nature from custom; or that which is established because it is right, from that which is right only because it is established; that he may neither violate essential principles by a desire of novelty, nor debar himself from the attainment of beauties within his view, by a needless fear of breaking rules which no literary dictator had authority to enact.

E. "MEANNESS" IN SHAKESPEARE [1]

Words become low by the occasions to which they are applied, or the general character of them who use them; and the disgust which they produce arises from the revival of those images with which they are commonly united. Thus, if, in the most solemn discourse, a phrase happens to occur which has been successfully employed in some ludicrous narrative, the gravest auditor finds it difficult to refrain from laughter, when they who are not prepossessed by the same accidental association, are utterly unable to guess the reason of his merriment. Words which convey ideas of dignity in one age, are banished from elegant writing or conversation in another, because they are in time debased by vulgar mouths, and can be no longer heard without the involuntary recollection of unpleasing images.

When Macbeth is confirming himself in the horrid purpose of stabbing his king, he breaks out amidst his emotions into a wish natural for a murderer:

> ——— Come, thick night!
> And pall thee in the dunnest smoke of hell,
> That my keen knife see not the wound it makes;
> Nor Heaven peep through the blanket of the dark,
> To cry, Hold, hold!

In this passage is exerted all the force of poetry; that force which calls new powers into being, which embodies sentiment, and animates matter; yet, perhaps, scarce any man now peruses it without some disturbance of his attention from the counteraction of the words to the ideas. What can be more dreadful than to implore the presence of night, invested, not in common obscurity, but in the smoke of hell? Yet the efficacy of this invocation is destroyed by the insertion of an epithet now seldom heard but in the stable,

---

[1] This memorable passage (No. 168) is cited not to cast contempt upon Johnson (did not even Coleridge boggle at " blanket " ?), but because it is at once bane and antidote. " Dun " is now never heard in stables; " knife " has no special " connection with sordid offices " ; some of us, even in and from early childhood, have never felt the least inclination to laugh, but much to shudder, at " the blanket of the dark." " This is this to me, and that to thee ! "

and *dun* night may come or go without any other notice than contempt.

If we start into raptures when some hero of the *Iliad* tells us that δόρυ μαίνεται, his lance rages with eagerness to destroy; if we are alarmed at the terror of the soldiers commanded by Cæsar to hew down the sacred grove, who dreaded, says Lucan, lest the axe aimed at the oak should fly back upon the striker :

> *Si robora sacra ferirent,*
> *In sua credebant redituras membra secures,*
>
> None dares with impious steel the grove to rend
> Lest on himself the destined stroke descend ;

we cannot surely but sympathize with the horrors of a wretch about to murder his master, his friend, his benefactor, who suspects that the weapon will refuse its office, and start back from the breast which he is preparing to violate. Yet this sentiment is weakened by the name of an instrument used by butchers and cooks in the meanest employments ; we do not immediately conceive that any crime of importance is to be committed with a *knife ;* or who does not, at last, from the long habit of connecting a knife with sordid offices, feel aversion rather than terror ?

Macbeth proceeds to wish, in the madness of guilt, that the inspection of Heaven may be intercepted, and that he may, in the involutions of infernal darkness, escape the eye of Providence. This is the utmost extravagance of determined wickedness : yet this is so debased by two unfortunate words, that while I endeavour to impress on my reader the energy of the sentiment, I can scarcely check my risibility, when the expression forces itself upon my mind ; for who, without some relaxation of his gravity, can hear of the avengers of guilt *peeping through a blanket ?*

2. FROM THE PREFACE TO SHAKESPEARE

Shakespeare is, above all writers, at least above all modern writers, the poet of nature; the poet that holds up to his readers a faithful mirror of manners and of life. His characters are not modified by the customs of particular places, unpractised by the rest of the world; by the peculiarities of studies or professions, which can operate but upon small numbers; or by the accidents of transient fashions or temporary opinions: they are the genuine progeny of common humanity, such as the world will always supply, and observation will always find.   His persons act and speak by the influence of those general passions and principles by which all minds are agitated, and the whole system of life is continued in motion.   In the writings of other poets a character is too often an individual: in those of Shakespeare it is commonly a species.

It is from this wide extension of design that so much instruction is derived.   It is this which fills the plays of Shakespeare with practical axioms and domestic wisdom.   It was said of Euripides, that every verse was a precept; and it may be said of Shakespeare, that from his works may be collected a system of civil and economical prudence.   Yet his real power is not shewn in the splendour of particular passages, but by the progress of his fable, and the tenor of his dialogue: and he that tries to recommend him by select quotations, will succeed like the pedant in Hierocles, who, when he offered his house to sale, carried a brick in his pocket as a specimen.

It will not easily be imagined how much Shakespeare excels in accommodating his sentiments to real life, but by comparing him with other authors.   It was observed of the ancient schools of declamation that the more diligently they were frequented, the more was the student disqualified for the world, because he found nothing there which he should ever meet in any other place.   The same remark may be applied to every stage but that of Shakespeare. The theatre, when it is under any other direction, is peopled by such characters as were never seen, conversing in a language which was never heard, upon topics which will never arise in the commerce of mankind.   But the dialogue of this author is often so evidently determined by the incident which produces it, and is pursued with so much ease and simplicity, that it seems scarcely to claim the merit of fiction, but to have been gleaned by diligent selection out of common conversation, and common occurrences.

Upon every other stage the universal agent is love, by whose power all good and evil is distributed, and every action quickened or retarded. To bring a lover, a lady, and a rival into the fable; to entangle them in contradictory obligations, perplex them with oppositions of interest, and harass them with violence of desires inconsistent with each other; to make them meet in rapture, and part in agony; to fill their mouths with hyperbolical joy and outrageous sorrow; to distress them as nothing human ever was distressed; to deliver them as nothing human ever was delivered; is the business of a modern dramatist. For this, probability is violated, life is misrepresented, and language is depraved. But love is only one of many passions; and as it has no great influence upon the sum of life, it has little operation in the dramas of a poet, who caught his ideas from the living world, and exhibited only what he saw before him. He knew that any other passion, as it was regular or exorbitant, was a cause of happiness or calamity.

Characters thus ample and general were not easily discriminated and preserved, yet perhaps no poet ever kept his personages more distinct from each other. I will not say with Pope, that every speech may be assigned to the proper speaker, because many speeches there are which have nothing characteristical; but, perhaps, though some may be equally adapted to every person, it will be difficult to find that any can be properly transferred from the present possessor to another claimant. The choice is right, when there is reason for choice.

Other dramatists can only gain attention by hyperbolical or aggravated characters, by fabulous and unexampled excellence or depravity, as the writers of barbarous romances invigorated the reader by a giant and a dwarf; and he that should form his expectation of human affairs from the play, or from the tale, would be equally deceived. Shakespeare has no heroes; his scenes are occupied only by men, who act and speak as the reader thinks that he should himself have spoken or acted on the same occasion: even where the agency is supernatural, the dialogue is level with life. Other writers disguise the most natural passions and most frequent incidents, so that he who contemplates them in the book will not know them in the world: Shakespeare approximates the remote, and familiarizes the wonderful; the event which he represents will not happen, but, if it were possible, its effects would probably be such as he has assigned; * and it may be said, that he has not only shewn human nature as it acts in real exigencies, but as it would be found in trials, to which it cannot be exposed.

This therefore is the praise of Shakespeare, that his drama is the mirror of life; that he who has mazed his imagination, in following the phantoms which other writers raise up before him, may here be cured of his delirious ecstasies, by reading human sentiments in human language, by scenes from which a hermit may estimate the transactions of the world, and a confessor predict the progress of the passions.

His adherence to general nature has exposed him to the censure of critics, who form their judgments upon narrower principles. Dennis and Rymer think his Romans not sufficiently Roman; and Voltaire censures his kings as not completely royal. Dennis is offended that Menenius, a senator of Rome, should play the buffoon; and Voltaire perhaps thinks decency violated when the Danish usurper is represented as a drunkard. But Shakespeare always makes nature predominate over accident; and, if he preserves the essential character, is not very careful of distinctions superinduced and adventitious. His story requires Romans or kings, but he thinks only on men. He knew that Rome, like every other city, had men of all dispositions; and wanting a buffoon, he went into the senate-house for that which the senate-house would certainly have afforded him. He was inclined to shew an usurper and a murderer not only odious, but despicable; he therefore added drunkenness to his other qualities, knowing that kings love wine like other men, and that wine exerts its natural power upon kings. These are the petty cavils of petty minds; a poet overlooks the casual distinction of country and condition, as a painter, satisfied with the figure, neglects the drapery.

The censure which he has incurred by mixing comic and tragic scenes, as it extends to all his works, deserves more consideration. Let the fact be first stated, and then examined.

* Quærit quod nusquam est gentium, reperit tamen,
Facit illud verisimile quod mendacium est.
Plauti Pseudolus Act I Sc. iv. — Steevens.

Shakespeare's plays are not in the rigorous and critical sense either tragedies or comedies, but compositions of a distinct kind; exhibiting the real state of sublunary nature, which partakes of good and evil, joy and sorrow, mingled with endless variety of proportion and innumerable modes of combination; and expressing the course of the world, in which the loss of one is the gain of another; in which, at the same time, the reveller is hasting to his wine, and the mourner burying his friend; in which the malignity of one is sometimes defeated by the frolic of another; and many mischiefs and many benefits are done and hindered without design.

Out of this chaos of mingled purposes and casualties the ancient poets, according to the laws which custom had prescribed, selected some the crimes of men, and some their absurdities; some the momentous vicissitudes of life, and some the lighter occurrences; some the terrors of distress, and some the gaieties of prosperity. Thus rose the two modes of imitation, known by the names of *tragedy* and *comedy*, compositions intended to promote different ends by contrary means, and considered as so little allied, that I do not recollect among the Greeks or Romans a single writer who attempted both.

Shakespeare has united the powers of exciting laughter and sorrow not only in one mind, but in one composition. Almost all his plays are divided between serious and ludicrous characters, and, in the successive evolutions of the design, sometimes produce seriousness and sorrow, and sometimes levity and laughter.

That this is a practice contrary to the rules of criticism will be readily allowed; but there is always an appeal open from criticism to nature. The end of writing is to instruct; the end of poetry is to instruct by pleasing. That the mingled drama may convey all the instruction of tragedy or comedy cannot be denied, because it includes both in its alternations of exhibition, and approaches nearer than either to the appearance of life, by showing how great machinations and slender designs may promote or obviate one another, and the high and the low coöperate in the general system by unavoidable concatenation.

It is objected that by this change of scenes the passions are interrupted in their progression, and that the principal event, being not advanced by a due gradation of preparatory incidents, wants at last the power to move, which constitutes the perfection of dramatic poetry. This reasoning is so specious that it is received as true even by those who in daily experience feel it to be false. The interchanges of mingled scenes seldom fail to produce the intended vicissitudes of passion. Fiction cannot move so much but that the attention may be easily transferred; and though it must be allowed that pleasing melancholy be sometimes interrupted by unwelcome levity, yet let it be considered likewise that melancholy is often not pleasing, and that the disturbance of one man may be the relief of another; and that different auditors have different habitudes; and that, upon the whole, all pleasure consists in variety.

The players, who in their edition divided our author's works into comedies, histories, and tragedies, seem not to have distinguished the three kinds by any very exact or definite ideas.

An action which ended happily to the principal persons, however serious or distressful through its immediate incidents, in their opinion constituted a comedy. This idea of comedy continued long amongst us; and plays were written, which, by changing the catastrophe, were tragedies to-day, and comedies to-morrow.

Tragedy was not in those times a poem of more general dignity or elevation than comedy; it required only a calamitous conclusion, with which the common criticism of that age was satisfied, whatever light pleasure it afforded in its progress.

History was a series of actions, with no other than chronological succession, independent of each other, and without any tendency to introduce or regulate the conclusion. It is not always very nicely distinguished from tragedy. There is not much nearer approach to unity of action in the tragedy of *Antony and Cleopatra*, than in the history of *Richard the Second*. But a history might be continued through many plays; as it had no plan, it had no limits.

Through all these denominations of the drama Shakespeare's mode of composition is the same; an interchange of seriousness and merriment, by which the mind is softened at one time and exhilarated at another. But whatever be his purpose, whether to gladden or depress, or to conduct the story, without vehemence or emotion,

through tracts of easy and familiar dialogue, he never fails to attain
his purpose; as he commands us to laugh or mourn, or sit silent
with quiet expectation, in tranquillity without indifference.

When Shakespeare's plan is understood most of the criticisms of
Rymer and Voltaire vanish away. The play of *Hamlet* is opened,
without impropriety, by two sentinels; Iago bellows at Brabantio's
window, without injury to the scheme of the play, though in terms
which a modern audience would not easily endure; the character
of Polonius is seasonable and useful; and the grave-diggers themselves may be heard with applause.

Shakespeare engaged in dramatic poetry with the world open
before him; the rules of the ancients were yet known to few; the
public judgment was unformed: he had no example of such fame
as might force him upon imitation, nor critics of such authority as
might restrain his extravagance; he therefore indulged his natural
disposition; and his disposition, as Rymer has remarked, led him
to comedy. In tragedy he often writes, with great appearance of
toil and study, what is written at last with little felicity; but, in his
comic scenes, he seems to produce, without labour, what no labour
can improve. In tragedy he is always struggling after some occasion
to be comic; but in comedy he seems to repose, or to luxuriate, as
in a mode of thinking congenial to his nature. In his tragic scenes
there is always something wanting, but his comedy often surpasses
expectation or desire. His comedy pleases by the thoughts and
the language, and his tragedy for the greater part by incident and
action. His tragedy seems to be skill, his comedy to be instinct.

The force of his comic scenes has suffered little diminution from
the changes made by a century and a half, in manners or in words.
As his personages act upon principles arising from genuine passion,
very little modified by particular forms, their pleasures and vexations are communicable to all times and to all places; they are
natural and therefore durable: the adventitious peculiarities of personal habits are only superficial dyes, bright and pleasing for a
little while, yet soon fading to a dim tinct, without any remains of
their former lustre; but the discriminations of true passion are the
colours of nature: they pervade the whole mass and can only perish
with the body that exhibits them. The accidental compositions of

heterogeneous modes are dissolved by the chance which combines them ; but the uniform simplicity of primitive qualities neither admits increase nor suffers decay. The sand heaped by one flood is scattered by another, but the rock always continues in its place. The stream of time, which is continually washing the dissoluble fabrics of other poets, passes without injury by the adamant of Shakespeare.

3. THE CHARACTER OF POLONIUS

(The admiration justly and universally expressed for this note warrants, and in fact demands, its insertion.)

This account [Warburton's] of the character of Polonius, though it sufficiently reconciles the seeming inconsistency of so much wisdom with so much folly, does not perhaps correspond exactly to the ideas of our author. The commentator makes the character of Polonius a character only of manners, discriminated by properties, superficial, accidental, and acquired. The poet intended a nobler delineation of a mixed character of manners and of nature. Polonius is a man bred in courts, exercised in business, stored with observation, confident in his knowledge, proud of his eloquence, and declining into dotage. His mode of oratory is truly represented as designed to ridicule the practice of those times, of prefaces that made no introduction, and of method that embarrassed rather than explained. This part of his character is accidental, the rest is natural. Such a man is positive and confident, because he knows that his mind was once strong, and knows not that it is become weak. Such a man excels in general principles, but fails in the particular application. He is knowing in retrospect, and ignorant in foresight. While he depends upon his memory, and can draw from his repositories of knowledge, he utters weighty sentences, and gives useful counsel; but as the mind in its enfeebled state cannot be kept long busy and intent, the old man is subject to sudden dereliction of his faculties, he loses the order of his ideas, and entangles himself in his own thoughts, till he recovers the leading principle, and falls again into his former train. This idea of dotage encroaching upon wisdom will solve all the phenomena of the character of Polonius.

4. "THE STREAKS OF THE TULIP."[1] FROM RASSELAS

"The business of a poet," said Imlac, "is to examine, not the individual but the species; to remark general properties and large appearances. He does not number the streaks of the tulip, or describe the different shades in the verdure of the forest; he is to exhibit in his portraits of nature, such prominent and striking features, as recall the original to every mind; and must neglect the minuter discriminations, which one may have remarked, and another have neglected, for those characteristics which are alike obvious to vigilance and to carelessness."[2]

(The *Lives of the Poets* are, with rare exceptions, *all* of importance; and those of Milton, Cowley, Dryden, Pope, and Gray, at least, are indispensable to the English-reading student of criticism. It has therefore seemed unnecessary to give excerpts which could not be really representative, especially as the original, as a whole or in greater or lesser parts, is easily and cheaply accessible and hardly in a page superfluous.)

[1] This passage is perhaps the most philosophical and authoritative exposition of the conventionalizing and generalizing tendency in the neo-Classic idea of poetry.

[2] *Rasselas*, chap. x, *sub fin.* In the two remaining paragraphs of the chapter the poet is (as it may seem to different minds) compensated or injured afresh by being enjoined to cultivate the largest and at the same time the minutest familiarity with the "modes of life," entrusted with philosophical and legislatorial prerogatives, and bidden to acquire almost universal knowledge and command of style.

XXIV

SELECTIONS FROM THE PRECURSORS OF ROMANTICISM IN ENGLAND

SHENSTONE (d. 1763)

FROM ESSAYS ON MEN AND MANNERS

Rhymes, in elegant poetry, should consist of syllables that are long in pronunciation : such as " are," " ear," " ire," " ore," " your " ; in which a nice ear will find more agreeableness than in these — " gnat," " net," " knit," " knot," " nut." [1]

. . . .

There is a vast beauty (to me) in using a word of a particular nature in the 8th and 9th syllables of an English verse.   I mean what is virtually a dactyl.   For instance,

> And pikes, the tyrants of the watry plains.

Let any person of an ear substitute " liquid " instead of " watry," and he will find the disadvantage. [2]

. . . .

The words " no more " have a singular pathos, reminding us at once of past pleasure and the future exclusion of it.

. . . .

[1] This is not at all a trivial observation, but shows the dawn of distaste for the sharp snapping couplet.   As soon as the ear yearns for a " long-drawn sweetness," it is ready for *enjambement*, for those postponed rhymes which Johnson thought " uncertain," and for many other happy far-off things.

[2] That is to say, Shenstone pines — partially and unknowing, it may be — for *trisyllabic substitution*.   He *spells* " watry " (or more probably " wat'ry," for these Essays were not published by himself), in accordance with the Bysshian heresy-tyranny ; but he pronounces wa|te|ry, as nature and poetic beauty demand.   (See also below on " the absurdity of contraction.")

Every good poet includes a critic : the reverse will not hold.

.   .   .   .

As there are evidently words in English poetry that have the
force of a dactyl, and, if properly inserted, have no small beauty
on that account, it seems absurd to contract or print them otherwise than at length —

>   The loose wall tottering o'er the trembling shade.[1]

.   .   .   .

I have sometimes thought Virgil so remarkably musical, that
were his lines read to a musician wholly ignorant of the language,
by a person of capacity to give each word its proper accent, he
would not fail to distinguish in it all the graces of harmony.[2]

GRAY (cir. 1760)

Verses of eight syllables are so far from being obliged to have
their cæsura on the fourth, that Milton, the best example of an
exquisite ear that I can produce, varies it continually.

.   .   .   .

The measure [*Spenser's in* Shep. Kal. *February, etc., and practically
that of* Christabel], like our usual verse of eight syllables, is Dimeter
Iambic : but admits of a Trochee, Spondee, Amphibrachys, Anapæst,
etc., in almost every place.

.   .   .   .

[*From an Apology for Lydgate.*]   It is folly to judge of the
understanding and of the patience of those times by our own.
They loved, I will not say tediousness, but length, and a kind of
incumbrance in narration.   The vulgar do so still. . . .   But we
need not confine ourselves to the vulgar, and to understandings
beneath our own.   *Circumstance* ever was, and ever will be, the life
and the essence both of oratory and of poetry.   It has, in some
sort, the same effect upon every mind that it has upon that of the
populace : and I fear the quickness and delicate impatience of

---

[1] Here he takes more courage.   In a little he would have seen that
" tot|tĕrĭng ŏer " is an anapæst, though " tottering " may be a dactyl : and all
would have been well.

[2] The wonderful pregnancy of these few remarks can only be indicated, not
commented on, here.

ᴛhese polished times in which we live, are but the forerunners
of the decline of all those beautiful arts which depend upon the
imagination.[1]

HURD (1762)

FROM LETTERS ON CHIVALRY AND ROMANCE

(The contempt with which Hurd *as a critic* has been spoken of is not
intelligible. Like many other men of his time, he had by no means come
to a catholic point of clear view; and his annotations on Addison, written
later and when, like most men who have lived long in a transition period,
he was disgusted at the younger generation outrunning him, are sometimes
ridiculous. But it is practically enough to point to the date above, and the
texts below, to show that he had more than " glimmerings.")

May there not be something in the Gothic Romance peculiarly
suited to the views of a genius and to the ends of poetry? And
may not the philosophic moderns have gone too far in their perpetual ridicule and contempt of it?

.   .   .   .

Under [the] idea, then, of a Gothic, not classical poem, the *Fairy
Queen* is to be read and criticised. And on these principles it
would not be difficult to unfold its merit, in another way than has
been hitherto attempted.

.   .   .   .

When an architect examines a *Gothic* structure by *Grecian* rules,
he finds nothing but deformity. But the Gothic architecture has
its own rules, by which when it comes to be examined, it is seen to
have its merit as well as the Grecian. The question is not, which
of the two is conducted in the simplest or finest taste : but whether
there be not sense and design in both, when scrutinized by the laws
on which each is projected. The same observation holds of the
two sorts of poetry.

.   .   .   .

So that, if you will say anything against the poet's method, you
must say that he should not have chosen this subject. But this

[1] From the scanty wreckage of notes for the *History of English Poetry*, which
Gray never wrote.

objection arises from your classic ideas of Unity, which have no place here : and are in every view foreign to the purpose. . . . If you ask, then, what *is* this Unity of Spenser's Poem ? I say, It consists in the relation of its several adventures to one common *original*, the appointment of the Fairy Queen — and to one common *end*, the completion of the Fairy Queen's injunctions. . . . This it is true is not the Classic Unity, which consists in the representation of one entire action : but it is an Unity of another sort, an Unity resulting from the respect which a number of related actions have to one common purpose.   In other words, it is an unity of *Design*, and not of *Action*.

.   .   .   .

But the source of bad criticism, as universally of bad philosophy, is the abuse of terms.   A poet they say must follow *nature :* and by nature, we are to suppose, can only be meant the known and experienced course of affairs in this world.   Whereas the poet has a world of his own, where experience has less to do than consistent imagination. . . .   [In this] all is marvellous and extraordinary ; yet not *unnatural* in one sense. . . .   This trite maxim of *following Nature* is farther mistaken in applying it indiscriminately to *all* sorts of Poetry etc.

XXV

SELECTIONS FROM THE GERMAN CRITICS OF THE EIGHTEENTH CENTURY

(Here again, and here most of all, the warning has to be repeated that there is no pretence or intention of "ladling out the ocean in pailfuls," or rather teaspoonfuls. The three extracts from Gottsched, Gellert (a title only), and Lessing will mark the three 18th-century stages of that German critical thought which had a considerable — though a mainly indirect, and often much exaggerated — influence on English. The first illustrates that unhesitating neo-classicism which, in the earlier 18th century, was represented by Muratori (who, however, had in some ways much wider views) in Italy, by Luzán in Spain, and by Voltaire in France; but which in England was chequered, and rendered to some extent inconsistent, by the national Shakespeare-worship and the very general respect for Milton. The second illustrates the period of compromise and "looking over the shoulder"; the third that of the Romantic Revolt. I have not thought it necessary to quote anything from Goethe, who was rather a very powerful *diffuser* than an original in criticism, or from the Schlegels, whose best results, like Goethe's, are better represented by Coleridge.)

A. GOTTSCHED (1742). THE OUTER AND NARROWER RULE

It is absolutely true that the Fable is the capital point (*Hauptwerk*) of Poetry.

If this [*Milton's Pandemonium*] is not the ridiculous pushed to its furthest point, I do not know what poetical devices can be thought to have verisimilitude and what not.

Whether so foul and really horrible an allegory [*as Milton's Sin and Death*] has sufficient verisimilitude I shall express no fresh opinion of my own, but leave every one to his own thoughts of it.

The Paradise of Fools is no better.

Versuch einer kritischen Dichtkunst ch. **vi.**

Etc. etc. The warm championship of Milton, in opposition to Gottsched, by the Swiss critics Bodmer and Breitinger (who were also devoted to *mediæval* German literature) brought about, by no very slow degrees, a complete revolution in German taste.

B. GELLERT. COMPROMISE AS TO THE RULE

The very title of a dissertation-lecture by this amiable opportunist, *How far the Use of Rules in Eloquence and Poetry Extends* (to be found in his *Works*, v. 153), shows the turn of the tide sufficiently. Its gist is that rules are good and useful, but only *in general*, and with a pretty absolute licence of exemption for genius.

C. LESSING. THE INNER AND LARGER RULE

(It may sometimes have happened that readers, accustomed to see Lessing extolled as the Deliverer of Criticism, were disappointed and puzzled in coming to his actual work. Such puzzlement and disappointment may be obviated by the simple caution that in neither of his famous critical books was Lessing aiming at *general* criticism of literature, or even of poetry. In the *Laocoon* he is discussing certain æsthetic relationships or contrasts between poetry and the other arts : in the *Hamburg Dramaturgy*, not merely the theatre alone, but still more strictly the *acting* theatre. And in this latter he is conditioned, not always beneficially, by a violent Antigallicanism, and by an Anglomania, creditable but a very little indiscriminate. But the few short passages which follow will show the real benefit — and it was immense — that he conferred by emancipating without anarchy; by inculcating not anarchy at all, but the Inner and Larger Rule; and above all by the little caution quoted last that what he says is "for thoughts." The neo-classic method had almost excluded *thinking* in regard to particular points and works. You bought your stop-watch at the orthodox shop, looked at it, and that was enough. Lessing gave the Germans Goethe, and us Coleridge.)

I. THE ANARCHISTS AND THE TRUE "RULE"

We have now, God be thanked, a generation of critics whose highest exercise in their art is to throw suspicion on the whole of Criticism. "Genius," they cry, "genius sets itself over all rules. The work of genius *is* the rule." . . . So do they flatter genius —

I suppose that we may take them too for geniuses.   But they betray too much that they have not a spark of it themselves, when in one and the same breath they add, "Rules oppress genius."   As if genius would let itself be oppressed by anything whatsoever ! especially by what, as they confess, is derived from itself.   Not every critic of art is a genius : but every genius is born a critic of art.   He has within himself the evidence of all rules : but he seizes, remembers, and follows only those that express his own feelings for him in words.   And can *these* expressions of his own feelings restrain his action ?   Argue with him as you like, he takes you only so far as your generalities strike him as recognizable in the particular case of the moment.   This alone he remembers ; and it affects him, as he works, just as the memory of a happy example or an individual experience might do.   To assert, therefore, that rules and criticism can oppress genius, is in other words to assert that practice and example are oppressive — it is to limit genius not merely to itself, but to its own first attempts.[1]

H. D. 96.

II.   "FOR THOUGHTS"

I remind my readers here that these papers attempt anything rather than to contain a complete dramatic system.   I am therefore not obliged to solve all the difficulties that I raise.   My thoughts may seem to have very little consistency — yea, even to contradict themselves — provided that they are at least matter for thoughts in others.   I would here but strew "germs of cognition" (*fermenta cognitionis*).[2]

Ibid. 95 *sub fin.*

---

[1] We may see in this passage how far the "turn of the see-saw" had gone. Lessing has actually forgotten that genius *had* been limited to certain "happy examples " ; had been ordered to regard them *not* in this light, but as prohibiting and exclusive restrictions.

[2] At the end of the *Dramaturgy* (No. 104) Lessing avows absolute faith in Aristotle, absolute *un*faith in the French travesties of him, and infinite indebtedness to the English theatre for helping Germans to break the French bonds. But his *eirenicon* of Aristotle and Shakespeare themselves remains unwritten — only "strewed germinally."

XXVI

WORDSWORTH ON POETRY AND POETIC DICTION

1. PREFACE TO SECOND EDITION OF LYRICAL BALLADS, 1800

The first volume of these Poems has already been submitted to general perusal. It was published as an experiment, which, I hoped, might be of some use to ascertain how far, by fitting to metrical arrangement a selection of the real language of men in a state of vivid sensation, that sort of pleasure and that quantity of pleasure may be imparted, which a Poet may rationally endeavour to impart.

I had formed no very inaccurate estimate of the probable effect of those Poems : I flattered myself that they who should be pleased with them would read them with more than common pleasure : and, on the other hand, I was well aware, that by those who should dislike them they would be read with more than common dislike. The result has differed from my expectation in this only, that a greater number have been pleased than I ventured to hope I should please.

.   .   .   .

Several of my friends are anxious for the success of these Poems, from a belief, that, if the views with which they were composed were indeed realised, a class of poetry would be produced, well adapted to interest mankind permanently, and not unimportant in the quality and in the multiplicity of its moral relations : and on this account they have advised me to prefix a systematic defence of the theory upon which the Poems were written. But I was unwilling to undertake the task, knowing that on this occasion the reader would look coldly upon my arguments, since I might be suspected of having been principally influenced by the selfish and foolish hope of *reasoning* him into an approbation of these particular Poems: and I was still more unwilling to undertake the task, because adequately to display the opinions, and fully to enforce the arguments, would require a space wholly disproportionate to a preface. For, to treat the subject with the clearness and coherence of which it is susceptible, it would be necessary to give a full account of the present state of the public taste in this country, and to determine how far this taste is healthy or depraved; which, again, could not be determined without pointing out in what manner language and the human mind act and re-act on each other, and without retracing the revolutions, not of literature alone, but likewise of society itself. I have therefore altogether declined to enter regularly upon this defence; yet I am sensible that there would be something like impropriety in abruptly obtruding upon the public, without a few words of introduction, poems so materially different from those upon which general approbation is at present bestowed.

It is supposed, that by the act of writing in verse an author makes a formal engagement that he will gratify certain known habits of association; that he not only thus apprises the reader that certain classes of ideas and expressions will be found in his book, but that others will be carefully excluded. This exponent or symbol held forth by metrical language must in different eras of literature have excited very different expectations: for example, in the age of Catullus, Terence, and Lucretius, and that of Statius or Claudian; and in our own country, in the age of Shakespeare and Beaumont and Fletcher, and that of Donne and Cowley, or Dryden, or Pope. I will not take upon me to determine the exact import of the promise which, by the act of writing in verse, an author in the present day makes to his reader: but it will undoubtedly appear to many persons that I have not fulfilled the terms of an engagement thus voluntarily contracted. They who have been accustomed to the gaudiness and inane phraseology of many modern writers, if they persist in reading this book to its conclusion, will, no doubt, frequently have to struggle with feelings of strangeness and awkwardness: they will look round for poetry, and will be induced to

enquire by what species of courtesy these attempts can be permitted to assume that title. I hope therefore the reader will
not censure me for attempting to state what I have proposed to
myself to perform; and also (as far as the limits of a preface
will permit) to explain some of the chief reasons which have
determined me in the choice of my purpose : that at least he may
be spared any unpleasant feeling of disappointment, and that I
myself may be protected from one of the most dishonourable
accusations which can be brought against an author ; namely, that
of an indolence which prevents him from endeavouring to ascertain
what is his duty, or, when his duty is ascertained, prevents him
from performing it.

The principal object, then, proposed in these Poems was to
choose incidents and situations from common life, and to relate or
describe them, throughout, as far as was possible in a selection of
language really used by men, and, at the same time, to throw over
them a certain colouring of imagination, whereby ordinary things
should be presented to the mind in an unusual aspect; and, further,
and above all, to make these incidents and situations interesting by
tracing in them, truly though not ostentatiously, the primary laws
of our nature : chiefly, as far as regards the manner in which we
associate ideas in a state of excitement.   Humble and rustic life
was generally chosen, because in that condition the essential passions of the heart find a better soil in which they can attain their
maturity, are less under restraint, and speak a plainer and more
emphatic language ; because in that condition of life our elementary
feelings co-exist in a state of greater simplicity, and, consequently,
may be more accurately contemplated, and more forcibly communicated; because the manners of rural life germinate from those
elementary feelings, and, from the necessary character of rural
occupations, are more easily comprehended, and are more durable;
and lastly, because in that condition the passions of men are incorporated with the beautiful and permanent forms of nature.   The
language, too, of these men has been adopted (purified indeed from
what appear to be its real defects, from all lasting and rational
causes of dislike or disgust) because such men hourly communicate
with the best objects from which the best part of language is

originally derived; and because, from their rank in society and the sameness and narrow circle of their intercourse, being less under the influence of social vanity, they convey their feelings and notions in simple and unelaborated expressions. Accordingly, such a language, arising out of repeated experience and regular feelings, is a more permanent, and a far more philosophical language, than that which is frequently substituted for it by poets, who think that they are conferring honour upon themselves and their art, in proportion as they separate themselves from the sympathies of men, and indulge in arbitrary and capricious habits of expression, in order to furnish food for fickle tastes, and fickle appetites, of their own creation.*

I cannot, however, be insensible to the present outcry against the triviality and meanness, both of thought and language, which some of my contemporaries have occasionally introduced into their metrical compositions; and I acknowledge that this defect, where it exists, is more dishonourable to the writer's own character than false refinement or arbitrary innovation, though I should contend at the same time, that it is far less pernicious in the sum of its consequences. From such verses the poems in these volumes will be found distinguished at least by one mark of difference, that each of them has a worthy *purpose*. Not that I always began to write with a distinct purpose formally conceived; but habits of meditation have, I trust, so prompted and regulated my feelings, that my descriptions of such objects as strongly excite those feelings, will be found to carry along with them a *purpose*. If this opinion be erroneous, I can have little right to the name of a Poet. For all good poetry is the spontaneous overflow of powerful feelings : and though this be true, Poems to which any value can be attached were never produced on any variety of subjects but by a man who, being possessed of more than usual organic sensibility, had also thought long and deeply. For our continued influxes of feeling are modified and directed by our thoughts, which are indeed the representatives of all our past feelings; and as, by contemplating

---

* It is worth while here to observe, that the affecting parts of Chaucer are almost always expressed in language pure and universally intelligible even to this day.

the relation of these general representatives to each other, we discover what is really important to men, so, by the repetition and continuance of this act, our feelings will be connected with important subjects, till at length, if we be originally possessed of much sensibility, such habits of mind will be produced, that, by obeying blindly and mechanically the impulses of those habits, we shall describe objects, and utter sentiments, of such a nature, and in such connection with each other, that the understanding of the reader must necessarily be in some degree enlightened, and his affections strengthened and purified.

It has been said that each of these Poems has a purpose. Another circumstance must be mentioned which distinguishes these Poems from the popular poetry of the day; it is this, that the feeling therein developed gives importance to the action and situation, and not the action and situation to the feeling.

A sense of false modesty shall not prevent me from asserting, that the reader's attention is pointed to this mark of distinction, far less for the sake of these particular Poems than from the general importance of the subject. The subject is indeed important! For the human mind is capable of being excited without the application of gross and violent stimulants; and he must have a very faint perception of its beauty and dignity who does not know this, and who does not further know, that one being is elevated above another in proportion as he possesses this capability. It has therefore appeared to me, that to endeavour to produce or enlarge this capability is one of the best services in which, at any period, a writer can be engaged; but this service, excellent at all times, is especially so at the present day. For a multitude of causes, unknown to former times, are now acting with a combined force to blunt the discriminating powers of the mind, and, unfitting it for all voluntary exertion, to reduce it to a state of almost savage torpor. The most effective of these causes are the great national events which are daily taking place, and the increasing accumulation of men in cities, where the uniformity of their occupations produces a craving for extraordinary incident, which the rapid communication of intelligence hourly gratifies. To this tendency of life and manners the literature and theatrical exhibitions of the country have conformed themselves. The invaluable works of our elder writers, I had almost said the works of Shakespeare and Milton, are driven into neglect by frantic novels, sickly and stupid German tragedies, and deluges of idle and extravagant stories in verse. — When I think upon this degrading thirst after outrageous stimulation, I am almost ashamed to have spoken of the feeble endeavour made in these volumes to counteract it; and, reflecting upon the magnitude of the general evil, I should be oppressed with no dishonourable melancholy, had I not a deep impression of certain inherent and indestructible qualities of the human mind, and likewise of certain powers in the great and permanent objects that act upon it, which are equally inherent and indestructible; and were there not added to this impression a belief, that the time is approaching when the evil will be systematically opposed, by men of greater powers, and with far more distinguished success.

Having dwelt thus long on the subjects and aim of these Poems, I shall request the reader's permission to apprise him of a few circumstances relating to their *style*, in order, among other reasons, that he may not censure me for not having performed what I never attempted. The reader will find that personifications of abstract ideas rarely occur in these volumes; and are utterly rejected, as an ordinary device to elevate the style, and raise it above prose. My purpose was to imitate, and, as far as is possible, to adopt the very language of men; and assuredly such personifications do not make any natural or regular part of that language. They are, indeed, a figure of speech occasionally prompted by passion, and I have made use of them as such; but have endeavoured utterly to reject them as a mechanical device of style, or as a family language which writers in metre seem to lay claim to by prescription. I have wished to keep the reader in the company of flesh and blood, persuaded that by so doing I shall interest him. Others who pursue a different track will interest him likewise; I do not interfere with their claim, but wish to prefer a claim of my own. There will also be found in these volumes little of what is usually called poetic diction; as much pains has been taken to avoid it as is ordinarily taken to produce it; this has been done for the reason already alleged, to bring my language near to the language of men; and further, because the pleasure which I have proposed to myself to impart, is of a kind very different from that which is supposed by many persons to be the proper object of poetry. Without being culpably particular, I do not know how to give my reader a more exact notion of the style in which it was my wish and intention to write, than by informing him that I have at all times endeavoured to look steadily at my subject; consequently, there is I hope in these Poems little falsehood of description, and my ideas are expressed in language fitted to their respective importance. Something must have been gained by this practice, as it is friendly to one property of all good poetry, namely, good sense: but it has necessarily cut me off from a large portion of phrases and figures of speech which from father to son have long been regarded as the common inheritance of poets. I have also thought it expedient to restrict myself still further, having abstained from the use of many expressions, in themselves proper and beautiful, but which have been foolishly repeated by bad poets, till such feelings of disgust are connected with them as it is scarcely possible by any art of association to overpower.

If in a poem there should be found a series of lines, or even a single line, in which the language, though naturally arranged, and according to the strict laws of metre, does not differ from that of prose, there is a numerous class of critics, who, when they stumble upon these prosaisms, as they call them, imagine that they have made a notable discovery, and exult over the poet as over a man ignorant of his own profession. Now these men would establish a canon of criticism which the reader will conclude he must utterly reject, if he wishes to be pleased with these volumes. And it would be a most easy task to prove to him, that not only the language of a large portion of every good poem, even of the most elevated character, must necessarily, except with reference to the metre, in no respect differ from that of good prose, but likewise that some of the most interesting parts of the best poems will be found to be strictly the language of prose when prose is well written. The truth of this assertion might be demonstrated by innumerable passages from almost all the poetical writings, even of Milton himself. To illustrate the subject in a general manner, I will here adduce a short composition of Gray, who was at the head of those who, by their reasonings, have attempted to widen the space of separation betwixt prose and metrical composition, and was more than any other man curiously elaborate in the structure of his own poetic diction.

> In vain to me the smiling mornings shine,
> And reddening Phœbus lifts his golden fire;
> The birds in vain their amorous descant join,
> Or cheerful fields resume their green attire.
> These ears, alas! for other notes repine;
> *A different object do these eyes require;*
> *My lonely anguish melts no heart but mine;*
> *And in my breast the imperfect joys expire;*
> Yet morning smiles the busy race to cheer,
> And new-born pleasure brings to happier men;
> The fields to all their wonted tribute bear;
> To warm their little loves the birds complain.
> *I fruitless mourn to him that cannot hear,*
> *And weep the more because I weep in vain.*

It will easily be perceived, that the only part of this sonnet which is of any value is the lines printed in italics; it is equally obvious, that, except in the rhyme, and in the use of the single word "fruitless" for fruitlessly, which is so far a defect, the language of these lines does in no respect differ from that of prose.

By the foregoing quotation it has been shown that the language of prose may yet be well adapted to poetry; and it was previously asserted, that a large portion of the language of every good poem can in no respect differ from that of good prose. We will go further. It may be safely affirmed, that there neither is, nor can be, any *essential* difference between the language of prose and metrical composition. We are fond of tracing the resemblance between poetry and painting, and, accordingly, we call them sisters: but where shall we find bonds of connection sufficiently strict to typify the affinity betwixt metrical and prose composition? They both speak by and to the same organs; the bodies in which both of them are clothed may be said to be of the same substance, their affections are kindred, and almost identical, not necessarily differing even in degree; Poetry * sheds no tears " such as Angels weep," but natural and human tears; she can boast of no celestial ichor that distinguishes her vital juices from those of prose; the same human blood circulates through the veins of them both.

If it be affirmed that rhyme and metrical arrangement of themselves constitute a distinction which overturns what has just been said on the strict affinity of metrical language with that of prose, and paves the way for other artificial distinctions which the mind voluntarily admits, I answer that the language of such poetry as is here recommended is, as far as is possible, a selection of the language really spoken by men; that this selection, wherever it is made with true taste and feeling, will of itself form a distinction far greater than would at first be imagined, and will entirely separate the composition from the vulgarity and meanness of ordinary life; and, if metre be superadded thereto, I believe that a dissimilitude will be produced altogether sufficient for the gratification of a rational mind. What other distinction would we have? Whence is it to come? And where is it to exist? Not, surely, where the poet speaks through the mouths of his characters: it cannot be necessary here, either for elevation of style, or any of its supposed ornaments: for, if the poet's subject be judiciously chosen, it will naturally, and upon fit occasion, lead him to passions the language of which, if selected truly and judiciously, must necessarily be dignified and variegated, and alive with metaphors and figures. I forbear to speak of an incongruity which would shock the intelligent reader, should the poet interweave any foreign splendour of his own with that which the passion naturally suggests: it is sufficient to say that such addition is unnecessary. And, surely, it is more probable that those passages, which with propriety abound

* I here use the word "Poetry" (though against my own judgment) as opposed to the word Prose, and synonymous with metrical composition. But much confusion has been introduced into criticism by this contradistinction of Poetry and Prose, instead of the more philosophical one of Poetry and Matter of Fact, or Science. The only strict antithesis to Prose is Metre; nor is this, in truth, a *strict* antithesis, because lines and passages of metre so naturally occur in writing prose, that it would be scarcely possible to avoid them, even were it desirable.

with metaphors and figures, will have their due effect, if, upon other occasions where the passions are of a milder character, the style also be subdued and temperate.

But, as the pleasure which I hope to give by the Poems now presented to the reader must depend entirely on just notions upon this subject, and, as it is in itself of high importance to our taste and moral feelings, I cannot content myself with these detached remarks. And if, in what I am about to say, it shall appear to some that my labour is unnecessary, and that I am like a man fighting a battle without enemies, such persons may be reminded, that, whatever be the language outwardly holden by men, a practical faith in the opinions which I am wishing to establish is almost unknown. If my conclusions are admitted, and carried as far as they must be carried if admitted at all, our judgments concerning the works of the greatest poets both ancient and modern will be far different from what they are at present, both when we praise, and when we censure : and our moral feelings influencing and influenced by these judgments will, I believe, be corrected and purified.

Taking up the subject, then, upon general grounds, let me ask, what is meant by the word Poet? What is a Poet? To whom does he address himself? And what language is to be expected from him?—He is a man speaking to men: a man, it is true, endowed with more lively sensibility, more enthusiasm and tenderness, who has a greater knowledge of human nature, and a more comprehensive soul, than are supposed to be common among mankind; a man pleased with his own passions and volitions, and who rejoices more than other men in the spirit of life that is in him; delighting to contemplate similar volitions and passions as manifested in the goings-on of the Universe, and habitually impelled to create them where he does not find them. To these qualities he has added a disposition to be affected more than other men by absent things as if they were present; an ability of conjuring up in himself passions, which are indeed far from being the same as those produced by real events, yet (especially in those parts of the general sympathy which are pleasing and delightful) do more nearly resemble the passions produced by real events, than anything which, from the motions of their own minds merely, other men are accustomed to feel in themselves : — whence, and from practice, he has acquired a greater readiness and power in expressing what he thinks and feels, and especially those thoughts and feelings which, by his own choice, or from the structure of his own mind, arise in him without immediate external excitement.

But whatever portion of this faculty we may suppose even the greatest Poet to possess, there cannot be a doubt that the language which it will suggest to him, must often, in liveliness and truth, fall short of that which is uttered by men in real life, under the actual pressure of those passions, certain shadows of which the Poet thus produces, or feels to be produced, in himself.

However exalted a notion we would wish to cherish of the character of a Poet, it is obvious, that while he describes and imitates passions, his employment is in some degree mechanical, compared with the freedom and power of real and substantial action and suffering. So that it will be the wish of the Poet to bring his feelings near to those of the persons whose feelings he describes, nay, for short spaces of time, perhaps, to let himself slip into an entire delusion, and even confound and identify his own feelings with theirs; modifying only the language which is thus suggested to him by a consideration that he describes for a particular purpose, that of giving pleasure. Here, then, he will apply the principle of selection which has been already insisted upon. He will depend upon this for removing what would otherwise be painful or disgusting in the passion; he will feel that there is no necessity to trick out or to elevate nature : and, the more industriously he applies this principle, the deeper will be his faith that no words, which *his* fancy or imagination can suggest, will be to be compared with those which are the emanations of reality and truth.

But it may be said by those who do not object to the general spirit of these remarks, that, as it is impossible for the Poet to produce upon all occasions language as exquisitely fitted for the passion as that which the real passion itself suggests, it is proper that he should consider himself as in the situation of a translator, who does not scruple to substitute excellencies of another kind for those which are unattainable by him ; and endeavours occasionally to surpass his original, in order to make some amends for the general inferiority to which he feels that he must submit. But this would be to encourage idleness and unmanly despair. Further, it is the language of men who speak of what they do not understand; who talk of Poetry as of a matter of amusement and idle pleasure; who will converse with us as gravely about a *taste* for Poetry, as they express it, as if it were a thing as indifferent as a taste for rope-dancing, or Frontiniac or Sherry. Aristotle, I have been told, has said, that Poetry is the most philosophic of all writing: it is so : its object is truth, not individual and local, but general, and operative ; not standing upon external testimony, but carried alive into the heart by passion ; truth which is its own testimony, which gives competence and confidence to the tribunal to which it appeals, and receives them from the same tribunal. Poetry is the image of man and nature. The obstacles which stand in the way of the fidelity of the Biographer and Historian, and of their consequent utility, are incalculably greater than those which are to be encountered by the Poet who comprehends the dignity of his art. The Poet writes under one restriction only, namely, the necessity of giving immediate pleasure to a human being possessed of that information which may be expected from him, not as a lawyer, a physician, a mariner, an astronomer, or a natural philosopher, but as a Man. Except this one restriction, there is no object standing between the Poet and the image of things ; between this, and the Biographer and Historian, there are a thousand.

Nor let this necessity of producing immediate pleasure be considered as a degradation of the Poet's art. It is far otherwise. It is an acknowledgment of the beauty of the universe, an acknowledgment the more sincere, because not formal, but indirect ; it is a task light and easy to him who looks at the world in the spirit of love : further, it is a homage paid to the native and naked dignity of man, to the grand elementary principle of pleasure, by which he knows, and feels, and lives, and moves. We have no sympathy but what is propagated by pleasure : I would not be misunderstood ; but wherever we sympathize with pain, it will be found that the sympathy is produced and carried on by subtle combinations with pleasure. We have no knowledge, that is, no general principles drawn from the contemplation of particular facts, but what has been built up by pleasure, and exists in us by pleasure alone. The Man of Science, the Chemist and Mathematician, whatever difficulties and disgusts they may have had to struggle with, know and feel this. However painful may be the objects with which the Anatomist's knowledge is connected, he feels that his knowledge is pleasure; and where he has no pleasure he has no knowledge. What then does the Poet? He considers man and the objects that surround him as acting and reacting upon each other, so as to produce an infinite complexity of pain and pleasure; he considers man in his own nature and in his ordinary life as contemplating this with a certain quantity of immediate knowledge, with certain convictions, intuitions, and deductions, which from habit acquire the quality of intuitions; he considers him as looking upon this complex scene of ideas and sensations, and finding everywhere objects that immediately excite in him sympathies which, from the necessities of his nature, are accompanied by an overbalance of enjoyment.

To this knowledge which all men carry about with them, and to these sympathies in which, without any other discipline than that of our daily life, we are fitted to take delight, the Poet principally directs his attention. He considers man and nature as essentially adapted to each other, and the mind of man as naturally the mirror of the fairest and most interesting properties of nature. And thus the Poet, prompted by this feeling of pleasure, which accompanies him through the whole course of his studies, converses with general nature, with affections akin to those, which, through labour and length of time, the Man of Science has raised up in himself, by conversing with those particular parts of nature which are the objects of his studies. The knowledge both of the Poet and the Man of Science is pleasure; but the knowledge of the one cleaves to us as a necessary part of our existence, our natural and unalienable inheritance; the other is a personal and individual acquisition, slow to come to us, and by no habitual and direct sympathy connecting us with our fellow-beings. The Man of Science seeks truth as a remote and unknown benefactor; he cherishes and loves it in his solitude: the Poet, singing a song in which all human beings join with him, rejoices in the presence of truth as our visible friend and hourly companion. Poetry is the breath and finer spirit of all knowledge; it is the impassioned expression which is in the countenance of all science. Emphatically may it be said of the poet, as Shakespeare hath said of man, "that he looks before and after." He is the rock of defence for human nature; an upholder and preserver, carrying everywhere with him relationship and love. In spite of difference of soil and climate, of language and manners, of laws and customs: in spite of things silently gone out of mind, and things violently destroyed; the Poet binds together by passion and knowledge the vast empire of human society, as it is spread over the whole earth, and over all time. The objects of the Poet's thoughts are everywhere; though the eyes and senses of men are, it is true, his favourite guides, yet he will follow whersoever he can find an atmosphere of sensation in which to move his wings. Poetry is the first and last of all knowledge — it is as immortal as the heart of man. If the labours of Men of Science should ever create any material revolution, direct or indirect, in our condition, and in the impressions which we habitually receive, the Poet will sleep then no more than at present; he will be ready to follow the steps of the man of science, not only in those general indirect effects, but he will be at his side, carrying sensation into the midst of the objects of the science itself. The remotest discoveries of the Chemist, the Botanist, or Mineralogist, will be as proper objects of the Poet's art as any upon which it can be employed, if the time should ever come when these things shall be familiar to us, and the relations under which they are contemplated by the followers of these respective sciences shall be manifestly and palpably material to us as enjoying and suffering beings. If the time should ever come when what is now called science, thus familiarized to men, shall be ready to put on, as it were, a form of flesh and blood, the Poet will lend his divine spirit to aid the transfiguration, and will welcome the Being thus produced, as a dear and genuine inmate of the household of man. It is not, then, to be supposed that any one, who holds that sublime notion of Poetry which I have attempted to convey, will break in upon the sanctity and truth of his pictures by transitory and accidental ornaments, and endeavour to excite admiration of himself by arts, the necessity of which must manifestly depend upon the assumed meanness of his subject.

What has been thus far said applies to Poetry in general; but especially to those parts of composition where the Poet speaks through the mouths of his characters; and upon this point it appears to authorize the conclusion that there are few persons of good sense, who would not allow that the dramatic parts of composition are defective, in proportion as they deviate from the real language of nature, and are coloured by a diction of the Poet's own, either peculiar to him as an individual Poet or belonging simply to Poets in general; to a body of men who, from the circumstance of their composition being in metre, it is expected will employ a particular language.

It is not, then, in the dramatic parts of composition that we look for this distinction of language; but still it may be proper and necessary where the Poet speaks to us in his own person and character. To this I answer by referring the reader to the description before given of a Poet. Among the qualities there enumerated as principally conducing to form a Poet, is implied nothing differing in kind from other men, but only in degree. The sum of what was said is, that the Poet is chiefly distinguished from other men by a greater promptness to think and feel without immediate external excitement, and a greater power in expressing such thoughts and feelings as are produced in him in that manner. But these passions and thoughts and feelings are the general passions and thoughts and feelings of men. And with what are they connected? Undoubtedly with our moral sentiments and animal sensations, and with the causes which excite these; with the operations of the elements, and the appearances of the visible universe; with storm and sunshine, with the revolutions of the seasons, with cold and heat, with loss of friends and kindred, with injuries and resentments, gratitude and hope, with fear and sorrow. These, and the like, are the sensations and objects which the Poet describes, as they are the sensations of other men, and the objects which interest them. The Poet thinks and feels in the spirit of human passions. How, then, can his language differ in any material degree from that of all other men who feel vividly and see clearly?

It might be *proved* that it is impossible. But supposing that this were not the case, the Poet might then be allowed to use a peculiar language when expressing his feelings for his own gratification, or that of men like himself. But Poets do not write for Poets alone, but for men. Unless therefore we are advocates for that admiration which subsists upon ignorance, and that pleasure which arises from hearing what we do not understand, the Poet must descend from this supposed height; and, in order to excite rational sympathy, he must express himself as other men express themselves. To this it may be added, that while he is only selecting from the real language of men, or, which amounts to the same thing, composing accurately in the spirit of such selection, he is treading upon safe ground, and we know what we are to expect from him. Our feelings are the same with respect to metre; for, as it may be proper to remind the reader, the distinction of metre is regular and uniform, and not, like that which is produced by what is usually called POETIC DICTION, arbitrary, and subject to infinite caprices upon which no calculation whatever can be made. In the one case, the reader is utterly at the mercy of the poet, respecting what imagery or diction he may choose to connect with the passion; whereas, in the other, the metre obeys certain laws, to which the poet and reader both willingly submit because they are certain, and because no interference is made by them with the passion but such as the concurring testimony of ages has shown to heighten and improve the pleasure which coexists with it.

It will now be proper to answer an obvious question, namely, Why, professing these opinions, have I written in verse? To this, in addition to such answer as is included in what has been already said, I reply, in the first place, Because, however I may have restricted myself, there is still left open to me what confessedly constitutes the most valuable object of all writing, whether in prose or verse; the great and universal passions of men, the most general and interesting of their occupations, and the entire world of nature before me — to supply endless combinations of forms and imagery. Now, supposing for a moment that whatever is interesting in these objects may be as vividly described in prose, why should I be condemned for attempting to superadd to such description, the charm which, by the consent of all nations, is acknowledged to exist in metrical language? To this, by such as are yet unconvinced, it may be answered that a very small part of the pleasure given by poetry depends upon the metre, and that it is injudicious to write in metre, unless it be accompanied with the other artificial distinctions of style with which metre is usually accompanied, and that, by such deviation, more will be lost from the shock which will thereby be given to the reader's associations than will be counterbalanced by any pleasure which he can derive from the general power of numbers. In answer to those who still contend for the necessity of accompanying metre with certain appropriate colours of style in order to the accomplishment of its appropriate end, and who also, in my opinion, greatly underrate the power of metre in itself, it might, perhaps, as far as relates to these volumes, have been almost sufficient to observe, that poems are extant, written upon more humble subjects, and in a still more naked and simple style, which have continued to give pleasure from generation to generation. Now, if nakedness and simplicity be a defect, the fact here mentioned affords a strong presumption that poems somewhat less naked and simple are capable of affording pleasure at the present day; and, what I wished *chiefly* to attempt, at present, was to justify myself for having written under the impression of this belief.

But various causes might be pointed out why, when the style is manly, and the subject of some importance, words metrically arranged will long continue to impart such a pleasure to mankind as he who proves the extent of that pleasure will be desirous to impart. The end of Poetry is to produce excitement in coexistence with an overbalance of pleasure; but, by the supposition, excitement is an unusual and irregular state of the mind; ideas and feelings do not, in that state, succeed each other in accustomed order. If the words, however, by which this excitement is produced be in themselves powerful, or the images and feelings have an undue proportion of pain connected with them, there is some danger that the excitement may be carried beyond its proper bounds. Now the co-presence of something regular, something to which the mind has been accustomed in various moods and in a less excited state, cannot but have great efficacy in tempering and restraining the passion by an intertexture of ordinary feeling, and of feeling not strictly and necessarily connected with the passion. This is unquestionably true; and hence, though the opinion will at first appear paradoxical, from the tendency of metre to divest language, in a certain degree, of its reality, and thus to throw a sort of half-consciousness of unsubstantial existence over the whole composition, there can be little doubt but that more pathetic situations and sentiments, that is, those which have a greater proportion of pain connected with them, may be endured in metrical composition, especially in rhyme, than in prose. The metre of the old ballads is very artless; yet they contain many passages which would illustrate this opinion; and, I hope, if the following Poems be attentively perused, similar instances will be found in them. This opinion may be further illustrated by appealing to the reader's own experience of the reluctance with which he comes to the reperusal of the distressful parts of *Clarissa Harlowe*, or the *Gamester*; while Shakespeare's writings, in the most pathetic scenes, never act upon us, as pathetic, beyond the bounds of pleasure — an effect which, in a much greater degree than might at first be imagined, is to be ascribed to small, but continual and regular impulses of pleasurable surprise from the metrical arrangement.— On the other hand (what it must be allowed will much more frequently happen) if the poet's words should be incommensurate with the passion, and inadequate to raise the reader to a height of desirable excitement, then, (unless the poet's choice of his metre has been grossly injudicious) in the feelings of pleasure which the reader has been accustomed to connect with metre in general, and in the feeling, whether cheerful or melancholy, which he has been accustomed to connect with that particular movement of metre, there will be found something which will greatly contribute to impart passion to the words, and to effect the complex end which the poet proposes to himself.

If I had undertaken a SYSTEMATIC defence of the theory here maintained, it would have been my duty to develop the various causes upon which the pleasure received from metrical language depends. Among the chief of these causes is to be reckoned a

principle which must be well known to those who have made any
of the Arts the object of accurate reflection; namely, the pleasure
which the mind derives from the perception of similitude in dissimilitude. This principle is the great spring of the activity of
our minds, and their chief feeder. From this principle the direction of the sexual appetite, and all the passions connected with it,
take their origin: it is the life of our ordinary conversation; and
upon the accuracy with which similitude in dissimilitude, and dissimilitude in similitude, are perceived, depend our taste and our
moral feelings. It would not be a useless employment to apply
this principle to the consideration of metre, and to show that metre
is hence enabled to afford much pleasure, and to point out in what
manner that pleasure is produced. But my limits will not permit
me to enter upon this subject, and I must content myself with a
general summary.

I have said that poetry is the spontaneous overflow of powerful
feelings: it takes its origin from emotion recollected in tranquillity: the emotion is contemplated till, by a species of reaction, the
tranquillity gradually disappears, and an emotion, kindred to that
which was before the subject of contemplation, is gradually produced, and does itself actually exist in the mind. In this mood
successful composition generally begins, and in a mood similar to
this it is carried on; but the emotion, of whatever kind, and in
whatever degree, from various causes, is qualified by various
pleasures, so that in describing any passions whatsoever, which are
voluntarily described, the mind will, upon the whole, be in a state
of enjoyment. If Nature be thus cautious to preserve in a state of
enjoyment a being so employed, the Poet ought to profit by the
lesson held forth to him, and ought especially to take care, that,
whatever passions he communicates to his reader, those passions,
if his reader's mind be sound and vigorous, should always be
accompanied with an overbalance of pleasure. Now the music of
harmonious metrical language, the sense of difficulty overcome, and
the blind association of pleasure which has been previously received
from works of rhyme or metre of the same or similar construction,
an indistinct perception perpetually renewed of language closely
resembling that of real life, and yet, in the circumstance of metre,

differing from it so widely — all these imperceptibly make up a complex feeling of delight, which is of the most important use in tempering the painful feeling always found intermingled with powerful descriptions of the deeper passions. This effect is always produced in pathetic and impassioned poetry; while, in lighter compositions, the ease and gracefulness with which the poet manages his numbers are themselves confessedly a principal source of the gratification of the reader. All that it is *necessary* to say, however, upon this subject, may be effected by affirming, what few persons will deny, that, of two descriptions, either of passions, manners, or characters, each of them equally well executed, the one in prose and the other in verse, the verse will be read a hundred times where the prose is read once.

Having thus explained a few of my reasons for writing in verse, and why I have chosen subjects from common life, and endeavoured to bring my language near to the real language of men, if I have been too minute in pleading my own cause, I have at the same time been treating a subject of general interest; and for this reason a few words shall be added with reference solely to these particular poems, and to some defects which will probably be found in them. I am sensible that my associations must have sometimes been particular instead of general, and that, consequently, giving to things a false importance, I may have sometimes written upon unworthy subjects; but I am less apprehensive on this account, than that my language may frequently have suffered from those arbitrary connections of feelings and ideas with particular words and phrases, from which no man can altogether protect himself. Hence I have no doubt that, in some instances, feelings, even of the ludicrous, may be given to my readers by expressions which appeared to me tender and pathetic. Such faulty expressions, were I convinced they were faulty at present, and that they must necessarily continue to be so, I would willingly take all reasonable pains to correct. But it is dangerous to make these alterations on the simple authority of a few individuals, or even of certain classes of men; for where the understanding of an author is not convinced, or his feelings altered, this cannot be done without great injury to himself: for his own feelings are his stay and support; and, if he set them aside in one instance, he may be induced to repeat this act till his mind shall lose all confidence in itself, and become utterly debilitated. To this it may be added, that the critic ought never to forget that he is himself exposed to the same errors as the poet, and, perhaps, in a much greater degree : for there can be no presumption in saying of most readers, that it is not probable they will be so well acquainted with the various stages of meaning through which words have passed, or with the fickleness or stability of the relations of particular ideas to each other; and, above all, since they are so much less interested in the subject, they may decide lightly and carelessly.

Long as the reader has been detained, I hope he will permit me to caution him against a mode of false criticism which has been applied to poetry, in which the language closely resembles that of life and nature. Such verses have been triumphed over in parodies, of which Dr. Johnson's stanza is a fair specimen :

> I put my hat upon my head
> And walked into the Strand,
> And there I met another man
> Whose hat was in his hand.

Immediately under these lines let us place one of the most justly-admired stanzas of the *Babes in the Wood*.

> These pretty Babes with hand in hand
> Went wandering up and down ;
> But never more they saw the Man
> Approaching from the Town.

In both these stanzas the words, and the order of the words, in no respect differ from the most unimpassioned conversation. There are words in both, for example, "the Strand," and "the Town," connected with none but the most familiar ideas; yet the one stanza we admit as admirable, and the other as a fair example of the superlatively contemptible. Whence arises this difference ? Not from the metre, not from the language, not from the order of the words; but the *matter* expressed in Dr. Johnson's stanza is contemptible. The proper method of treating trivial and simple verses, to which Dr. Johnson's stanza would be a fair parallelism, is not to say, this is a bad kind of poetry, or, this is not poetry ; but, this wants sense ; it is neither interesting in itself, nor can *lead* to any thing interesting ; the images neither originate in that sane state of feeling which arises out of thought, nor can excite thought or feeling in the reader. This is the only sensible manner of dealing with such verses. Why trouble yourself about the species till you have previously decided upon the genus ? Why take pains to prove that an ape is not a Newton, when it is self-evident that he is not a man ?

One request I must make of my reader, which is, that in judging these Poems he would decide by his own feelings genuinely, and not by reflection upon what will probably be the judgment of others. How common is it to hear a person say, I myself do not object to this style of composition, or this or that expression, but, to such and such classes of people it will appear mean or ludicrous ! This mode of criticism, so destructive of all sound unadulterated judgment, is almost universal : let the reader then abide, independently, by his own feelings, and, if he finds himself affected, let him not suffer such conjectures to interfere with his pleasure.

If an author, by any single composition, has impressed us with respect for his talents, it is useful to consider this as affording a presumption, that on other occasions where we have been displeased, he, nevertheless, may not have written ill or absurdly; and further, to give him so much credit for this one composition as may induce us to review what has displeased us, with more care than we should otherwise have bestowed upon it. This is not only an act of justice, but, in our decisions upon poetry especially, may conduce, in a high degree, to the improvement of our own taste : for an *accurate* taste in poetry, and in all the other arts, as Sir Joshua Reynolds has observed, is an *acquired* talent, which can only be produced by thought and a long-continued intercourse with the best models of composition. This is mentioned, not with so ridiculous a purpose as to prevent the most inexperienced reader from judging for himself, (I have already said that I wish him to judge for himself ;) but merely to temper the rashness of decision, and to suggest that, if poetry be a subject on which much time has not been bestowed, the judgment may be erroneous ; and that, in many cases, it necessarily will be so.

Nothing would, I know, have so effectually contributed to further the end which I have in view, as to have shown of what kind the pleasure is, and how that pleasure is produced, which is confessedly produced by metrical composition essentially different from that which I have here endeavoured to recommend : for the reader will say that he has been pleased by such composition ; and what more can be done for him ? The power of any art is limited ; and he will suspect, that, if it be proposed to furnish him with new friends, that can be only upon condition of his abandoning his old friends. Besides, as I have said, the reader is himself conscious of the pleasure which he has received from such composition, composition to which he has peculiarly attached the endearing name of Poetry ; and all men feel an habitual gratitude, and something of an honourable bigotry, for the objects which have long continued to please them : we not only wish to be pleased, but to be pleased in that particular way in which we have been accustomed to be pleased. There is in these feelings enough to resist a host of arguments ; and I should be the less able to combat them successfully, as I am willing to allow, that, in order entirely to enjoy the poetry which I am recommending, it would be necessary to give up much of what is ordinarily enjoyed. But, would my limits have permitted me to point out how this pleasure is produced, many obstacles might have been removed, and the reader assisted in perceiving that the powers of language are not so limited as he may suppose ; and that it is possible for poetry to give other enjoyments, of a purer, more lasting, and more exquisite nature. This part of the subject has not been altogether neglected, but it has not been so much my present aim to prove, that the interest excited by some other kinds of poetry is less vivid, and less worthy of the nobler powers of the mind, as to offer reasons for presuming, that if my purpose were fulfilled, a species of poetry would be produced, which is genuine poetry ; in its nature well adapted to interest mankind permanently, and likewise important in the multiplicity and quality of its moral relations.

From what has been said, and from a perusal of the Poems, the reader will be able clearly to perceive the object which I had in view : he will determine how far it has been attained ; and, what is a much more important question, whether it be worth attaining: and upon the decision of these two questions will rest my claim to the approbation of the public.

2. APPENDIX TO PREFACE

See page 267 — "what is usually called POETIC DICTION."

Perhaps, as I have no right to expect that attentive perusal, without which, confined, as I have been, to the narrow limits of a preface, my meaning cannot be thoroughly understood, I am anxious to give an exact notion of the sense in which the phrase poetic diction has been used; and for this purpose, a few words shall here be added, concerning the origin and characteristics of the phraseology, which I have condemned under that name.

The earliest poets of all nations generally wrote from passion excited by real events; they wrote naturally, and as men: feeling powerfully as they did, their language was daring, and figurative. In succeeding times, poets, and men ambitious of the fame of poets, perceiving the influence of such language, and desirous of producing the same effect without being animated by the same passion, set themselves to a mechanical adoption of these figures of speech, and made use of them, sometimes with propriety, but much more frequently applied them to feelings and thoughts with which they had no natural connection whatsoever. A language was thus insensibly produced, differing materially from the real language of men in *any situation*. The reader or hearer of this distorted language found himself in a perturbed and unusual state of mind : when affected by the genuine language of passion he had been in a perturbed and unusual state of mind also : in both cases he was willing that his common judgment and understanding should be laid asleep, and he had no instinctive and infallible perception of the true to make him reject the false ; the one served as a passport for the other. The emotion was in both cases delightful, and no wonder if he confounded the one with the other, and believed them both to be produced by the same, or similar causes. Besides, the poet spake to him in the character of a man to be looked up to, a man of genius and authority. Thus, and from a variety of other causes, this distorted language was received with admiration ; and poets, it is probable, who had before contented themselves for the most part with misapplying only expressions which at first had been dictated by real passion, carried the abuse still further, and introduced phrases composed apparently in the spirit of the original figurative language of passion, yet altogether of their own invention, and characterized by various degrees of wanton deviation from good sense and nature.

It is indeed true, that the language of the earliest poets was felt to differ materially from ordinary language, because it was the language of extraordinary occasions; but it was really spoken by men, language which the poet himself had uttered when he had been affected by the events which he described, or which he had heard uttered by those around him. To this language it is probable that metre of some sort or other was early superadded. This separated the genuine language of Poetry still further from common life, so that whoever read or heard the poems of these earliest poets felt himself moved in a way in which he had not been accustomed to be moved in real life, and by causes manifestly different from those which acted upon him in real life. This was the great temptation to all the corruptions which have followed : under the protection of this feeling succeeding poets constructed a phraseology which had one thing, it is true, in common with the genuine language of poetry, namely, that it was not heard in ordinary conversation ; that it was unusual. But the first poets, as I have said, spake a language which, though unusual, was still the language of men. This circumstance, however, was disregarded by their successors ; they found that they could please by easier means : they became proud of modes of expression which they themselves had invented, and which were uttered only by themselves. In process of time metre became a symbol or promise of this unusual language, and whoever took upon him to write in metre, according as he possessed more or less of true poetic genius, introduced less or more of this adulterated phraseology into his compositions, and the true and the false were inseparably interwoven until, the taste of men becoming gradually perverted, this language was received as a natural language : and at length, by the influence of books upon men, did to a certain degree really become so.

Abuses of this kind were imported from one nation to another, and with the progress of refinement this diction became daily more and more corrupt, thrusting out of sight the plain humanities of nature by a motley masquerade of tricks, quaintnesses, hieroglyphics, and enigmas.

It would not be uninteresting to point out the causes of the pleasure given by this extravagant and absurd diction. It depends upon a great variety of causes, but upon none, perhaps, more than its influence in impressing a notion of the peculiarity and exaltation of the poet's character, and in flattering the reader's self-love by bringing him nearer to a sympathy with that character ; an effect which is accomplished by unsettling ordinary habits of thinking, and thus assisting the reader to approach to that perturbed and dizzy state of mind in which if he does not find himself, he imagines that he is *balked* of a peculiar enjoyment which poetry can and ought to bestow.

The sonnet quoted from Gray, in the Preface, except the lines printed in italics, consists of little else but this diction, though not of the worst kind ; and indeed, if one may be permitted to say so, it is far too common in the best writers both ancient and modern. Perhaps in no way, by positive example, could more easily be given a notion of what I mean by the phrase *poetic diction* than by refer- ring to a comparision between the metrical paraphrase which we have of passages in the Old and New Testament, and those pass- ages as they exist in our common Translation. See Pope's *Messiah* throughout ; Prior's "Did sweeter sounds adorn my flowing tongue," etc., etc.; "Though I speak with the tongues of men and of angels," etc., etc., *1st Corinthians*, chap. xiii. By way of immediate example, take the following of Dr. Johnson :

> Turn on the prudent Ant thy heedless eyes,
> Observe her labours, Sluggard, and be wise ;
> No stern command, no monitory voice,
> Prescribes her duties, or directs her choice ;
> Yet, timely provident, she hastes away
> To snatch the blessings of a plenteous day ;
> When fruitful Summer loads the teeming plain,
> She crops the harvest, and she stores the grain.
> How long shall sloth usurp thy useless hours,

Unnerve thy vigour, and enchain thy powers?
While artful shades thy downy couch enclose,
And soft solicitation courts repose,
Amidst the drowsy charms of dull delight,
Year chases year with unremitted flight,
Till Want now following, fraudulent and slow,
Shall spring to seize thee, like an ambush'd foe.

From this hubbub of words pass to the original. "Go to the Ant, thou Sluggard, consider her ways, and be wise: which having no guide, overseer, or ruler, provideth her meat in the summer, and gathereth her food in the harvest. How long wilt thou sleep, O Sluggard? When wilt thou arise out of thy sleep? Yet a little sleep, a little slumber, a little folding of the hands to sleep. So shall thy poverty come as one that travelleth, and thy want as an armed man." *Proverbs*, chap. vi.

One more quotation, and I have done. It is from Cowper's *Verses supposed to be written by Alexander Selkirk:*

Religion! what treasure untold
    Resides in that heavenly word!
More precious than silver and gold,
    Or all that this earth can afford.
But the sound of the church-going bell
    These valleys and rocks never heard,
Ne'er sigh'd at the sound of a knell,
    Or smiled when a Sabbath appeared.

Ye winds, that have made me your sport,
    Convey to this desolate shore
Some cordial endearing report
    Of a land I must visit no more.
My Friends, do they now and then send
    A wish or a thought after me?
O tell me I yet have a friend,
    Though a friend I am never to see.

This passage is quoted as an instance of three different styles of composition. The first four lines are poorly expressed; some critics would call the language prosaic; the fact is, it would be bad prose, so bad, that it is scarcely worse in metre. The epithet "church-going" applied to a bell, and that by so chaste a writer as

Cowper, is an instance of the strange abuses which poets have introduced into their language, till they and their readers take them as matters of course, if they do not single them out expressly as objects of admiration. The two lines "Ne'er sighed at the sound," etc., are, in my opinion, an instance of the language of passion wrested from its proper use, and, from the mere circumstance of the composition being in metre, applied upon an occasion that does not justify such violent expressions; and I should condemn the passage, though perhaps few readers will agree with me, as vicious poetic diction. The last stanza is throughout admirably expressed: it would be equally good whether in prose or verse, except that the reader has an exquisite pleasure in seeing such natural language so naturally connected with metre. The beauty of this stanza tempts me to conclude with a principle which ought never to be lost sight of, and which has been my chief guide in all I have said, — namely, that in works *of imagination and sentiment*, for of these only have I been treating, in proportion as ideas and feelings are valuable, whether the composition be in prose or in verse, they require and exact one and the same language. Metre is but adventitious to composition, and the phraseology for which that passport is necessary, even where it may be graceful at all, will be little valued by the judicious.

3. FROM ESSAY SUPPLEMENTARY TO PREFACE (1815)

POETIC CRITICISM

With the young of both sexes, poetry is, like love, a passion; but, for much the greater part of those who have been proud of its power over their minds, a necessity soon arises of breaking the pleasing bondage; or it relaxes of itself; — the thoughts being occupied in domestic cares, or the time engrossed by business. Poetry then becomes only an occasional recreation; while to those whose existence passes away in a course of fashionable pleasure, it is a species of luxurious amusement. In middle and declining age, a scattered number of serious persons resort to poetry, as to religion, for a protection against the pressure of trivial employments, and as a consolation for the afflictions of life. And, lastly, there are many, who, having been enamoured of this art in their youth, have found leisure, after youth was spent, to cultivate general literature ; in which poetry has continued to be comprehended *as a study.*

Into the above classes the readers of poetry may be divided; critics abound in them all; but from the last only can opinions be collected of absolute value, and worthy to be depended upon, as prophetic of the destiny of a new work. The young, who in nothing can escape delusion, are especially subject to it in their intercourse with poetry. The cause, not so obvious as the fact is unquestionable, is the same as that from which erroneous judgments in this art, in the minds of men of all ages, chiefly proceed; but upon youth it operates with peculiar force. The appropriate business of poetry, (which, nevertheless, if genuine, is as permanent as pure science,) her appropriate employment, her privilege and her *duty*, is to treat of things not as they *are*, but as they *appear;* not as they exist in themselves, but as they *seem* to exist to the *senses*, and to the *passions.* What a world of delusion does this acknowledged obligation prepare for the inexperienced ! what temptations to go astray are here held forth for them whose thoughts have been little disciplined by the understanding, and whose feelings revolt from the sway of reason ! — When a juvenile reader is in the height of his rapture with some vicious passage, should experience throw in doubts, or common-sense suggest suspicions, a lurking consciousness that the realities of the Muse are but shows, and that her liveliest excitements are raised by transient shocks of conflicting feeling and successive assemblages of contradictory thoughts — is ever at hand to justify extravagance, and to sanction absurdity. But, it may be asked, as these illusions are unavoidable, and, no doubt, eminently useful to the mind as a process, what good can be gained by making observations, the tendency of which is to diminish the confidence of youth in its feelings, and thus to abridge its innocent and even profitable pleasures ? The reproach implied in the question could not be warded off, if youth were incapable of being delighted with what is truly excellent ; or, if these errors always terminated of themselves in due season. But, with the majority, though their force be abated, they continue through life. Moreover, the fire of youth is too vivacious an element to be extinguished or damped by a philosophical remark; and, while there is no danger that what has been said will be injurious or painful to the ardent and the confident, it may prove beneficial to those who, being enthusiastic, are, at the same time, modest and ingenuous. The intimation may unite with their own misgivings to regulate their sensibility, and to bring in, sooner than it would otherwise have arrived, a more discreet and sound judgment.

If it should excite wonder that men of ability, in later life, whose understandings have been rendered acute by practice in affairs, should be so easily and so far imposed upon when they happen to take up a new work in verse, this appears to be the cause ; — that, having discontinued their attention to poetry, whatever progress may have been made in other departments of knowledge, they have not, as to this art, advanced in true discernment beyond the age of youth. If, then, a new poem fall in their way, whose attractions are of that kind which would have enraptured them during the heat of youth, the judgment not being improved to a degree that they shall be disgusted, they are dazzled ; and prize and cherish the faults for having had power to make the present time vanish before them, and to throw the mind back, as by enchantment, into the happiest season of life. As they read, powers seem to be revived, passions are regenerated, and pleasures restored. The book was probably taken up after an escape from the burden of business, and with a wish to forget the world, and all its vexations and anxieties. Having obtained this wish, and so much more, it is natural that they should make report as they have felt.

If men of mature age, through want of practice, be thus easily beguiled into admiration of absurdities, extravagances, and mis-placed ornaments, thinking it proper that their understandings should enjoy a holiday, while they are unbending their minds with verse, it may be expected that such readers will resemble their former selves also in strength of prejudice, and an inaptitude to be moved by the unostentatious beauties of a pure style. In the higher poetry, an enlightened critic chiefly looks for a reflection of the wisdom of the heart and the grandeur of the imagination. Wherever these appear, simplicity accompanies them ; Magnificence herself, when legitimate, depending upon a simplicity of her own, to regulate her ornaments. But it is a well-known property of human nature, that our estimates are ever governed by comparisons, of which we are conscious with various degrees of distinctness. Is it not, then, inevitable (confining these observations to the effects of style merely) that an eye, accustomed to the glaring hues of diction by which such readers are caught and excited, will for the most part be rather repelled than attracted by an original work, the colouring of which is disposed according to a pure and refined scheme of harmony ? It is in the fine arts as in the affairs of life, no man can *serve* (*i.e.*, obey with zeal and fidelity) two Masters.

As poetry is most just to its own divine origin when it administers the comforts and breathes the spirit of religion, they who have learned to perceive this truth, and who betake themselves to reading verse for sacred purposes, must be preserved from numerous illusions to which the two classes of readers, whom we have been considering, are liable. But, as the mind grows serious from the weight of life, the range of its passions is contracted accordingly ; and its sympathies become so exclusive, that many species of high excellence wholly escape, or but languidly excite its notice. Besides, men who read from religious or moral inclinations, even when the subject is of that kind which they approve, are beset with misconceptions and mistakes peculiar to themselves. Attaching so much inportance to the truths which interest them, they are prone to overrate the authors by whom those truths are expressed and enforced. They come prepared to impart so much passion to the poet's language, that they remain unconscious how little, in fact, they receive from it. And, on the other hand, religious faith is to him who holds it so momentous a thing, and error appears to be attended with such tremendous consequences, that, if opinions touching upon religion occur which the reader condemns, he not only cannot sympathize with them, however animated the expression, but there is, for the most part, an end put to all satisfaction and enjoyment. Love, if it before existed, is converted into dislike ; and the heart of the reader is set against the author and his book. — To these excesses, they, who from their professions ought to be the most guarded against them, are perhaps the most liable ; I mean those

sects whose religion, being from the calculating understanding, is
cold and formal. For when Christianity, the religion of humility,
is founded upon the proudest faculty of our nature, what can be
expected but contradictions ? Accordingly, believers of this cast
are at one time contemptuous ; at another, being troubled, as they
are and must be, with inward misgivings, they are jealous and
suspicious ; — and at all seasons, they are under temptation to
supply, by the heat with which they defend their tenets, the anima-
tion which is wanting to the constitution of the religion itself.

Faith was given to man that his affections, detached from the
treasures of time, might be inclined to settle upon those of eternity :
— the elevation of his nature, which this habit produces on earth,
being to him a presumptive evidence of a future state of existence ;
and giving him a title to partake of its holiness. The religious man
values what he sees chiefly as an "imperfect shadowing forth" of
what he is incapable of seeing. The concerns of religion refer to
indefinite objects, and are too weighty for the mind to support them
without relieving itself by resting a great part of the burthen upon
words and symbols. The commerce between man and his Maker
cannot be carried on but by a process where much is represented in
little, and the Infinite Being accommodates himself to a finite
capacity. In all this may be perceived the affinity between religion and poetry ; between religion — making up the deficiencies of
reason by faith ; and poetry — passionate for the instruction of
reason ; between religion — whose element is infinitude, and whose
ultimate trust is the supreme of things, submitting herself to circum-
scription, and reconciled to substitutions ; and poetry — ethereal
and transcendent, yet incapable to sustain her existence without
sensuous incarnation. In this community of nature may be perceived also the lurking incitements of kindred error ; — so that we
shall find that no poetry has been more subject to distortion, than
that species, the argument and scope of which is religious ; and no
lovers of the art have gone farther astray than the pious and the
devout.

Whither then shall we turn for that union of qualifications which
must necessarily exist before the decisions of a critic can be of
absolute value ? For a mind at once poetical and philosophical ;

for a critic whose affections are as free and kindly as the spirit of society, and whose understanding is severe as that of dispassionate government? Where are we to look for that initiatory composure of mind which no selfishness can disturb? For a natural sensibility that has been tutored into correctness without losing anything of its quickness; and for active faculties, capable of answering the demands which an author of original imagination shall make upon them, associated with a judgment that cannot be duped into admiration by aught that is unworthy of it? — among those and those only, who, never having suffered their youthful love of poetry to remit much of its force, have applied to the consideration of the laws of this art the best power of their understandings. At the same time it must be observed — that, as this class comprehends the only judgments which are trustworthy, so does it include the most erroneous and perverse. For to be mistaught is worse than to be untaught; and no perverseness equals that which is supported by system, no errors are so difficult to root out as those which the understanding has pledged its credit to uphold. In this class are contained censors, who, if they be pleased with what is good, are pleased with it only by imperfect glimpses, and upon false principles; who, should they generalize rightly, to a certain point, are sure to suffer for it in the end; who, if they stumble upon a sound rule, are fettered by misapplying it, or by straining it too far; being incapable of perceiving when it ought to yield to one of higher order. In it are found critics too petulant to be passive to a genuine poet, and too feeble to grapple with him; men, who take upon them to report of the course which *he* holds whom they are utterly unable to accompany, — confounded if he turn quick upon the wing, dismayed if he soar steadily "into the region"; — men of palsied imaginations and indurated hearts; in whose minds all healthy action is languid, who therefore feed as the many direct them, or, with the many, are greedy after vicious provocatives; — judges, whose censure is auspicious, and whose praise ominous! In this class meet together the two extremes of best and worst.

The observations presented in the foregoing series are of too ungracious a nature to have been made without reluctance; and, were it only on this account, I would invite the reader to try them by the test of comprehensive experience. If the number of judges who can be confidently relied upon be in reality so small, it ought to follow that partial notice only, or neglect, perhaps long continued, or attention wholly inadequate to their merits, must have been the fate of most works in the higher departments of poetry; and that, on the other hand, numerous productions have blazed into popularity, and have passed away, leaving scarcely a trace behind them : it will be further found, that when authors shall have at length raised themselves into general admiration and maintained their ground, errors and prejudices have prevailed concerning their genius and their works, which the few who are conscious of those errors and prejudices would deplore ; if they were not recompensed by perceiving that there are select spirits for whom it is ordained that their fame shall be in the world an existence like that of virtue, which owes its being to the struggles it makes, and its vigour to the enemies whom it provokes ; — a vivacious quality, ever doomed to meet with opposition, and still triumphing over it ; and, from the nature of its dominion, incapable of being brought to the sad con-clusion of Alexander, when he wept that there were no more worlds for him to conquer.

This passage is followed by a survey — long, interesting, but very strongly prejudiced in view, and not always quite impeccably accurate in fact — of English poetry, and its reception ; which leads to a finale on

POPULAR JUDGMENT

If there be one conclusion more forcibly pressed upon us than another by the review which has been given of the fortunes and fate of poetical works, it is this, — that every author, so far as he is great and at the same time *original*, has had the task of *creating* the taste by which he is to be enjoyed : so has it been, so will it continue to be. This remark was long since made to me by the philosophical friend for the separation of whose poems from my own I have previously expressed my regret. The predecessors of an original genius of a high order will have smoothed the way for all that he has in common with them ; — and much he will have in common; but, for what is peculiarly his own, he will be called upon to clear and often to shape his own road: — he will be in the condition of Hannibal among the Alps.

And where lies the real difficulty of creating that taste by which a truly original poet is to be relished? Is it in breaking the bonds of custom, in overcoming the prejudices of false refinement, and displacing the aversions of inexperience? Or, if he labour for an object which here and elsewhere I have proposed to myself, does it consist in divesting the reader of the pride that induces him to dwell upon those points wherein men differ from each other, to the exclusion of those in which all men are alike, or the same; and in making him ashamed of the vanity that renders him insensible of the appropriate excellence which civil arrangements, less unjust than might appear, and Nature illimitable in her bounty, have conferred on men who may stand below him in the scale of society? Finally, does it lie in establishing that dominion over the spirits of readers by which they are to be humbled and humanized, in order that they may be purified and exalted?

If these ends are to be attained by the mere communication of *knowledge*, it does *not* lie here. — TASTE, I would remind the reader, like IMAGINATION, is a word which has been forced to extend its services far beyond the point to which philosophy would have confined them. It is a metaphor, taken from a *passive* sense of the human body, and transferred to things which are in their essence *not* passive, — to intellectual *acts* and *operations*. The word, Imagination, has been overstrained, from impulses honourable to mankind, to meet the demands of the faculty which is perhaps the noblest of our nature. In the instance of Taste, the process has been reversed; and from the prevalence of dispositions at once injurious and discreditable, being no other than that selfishness which is the child of apathy, — which, as nations decline in productive and creative power, makes them value themselves upon a presumed refinement of judging. Poverty of language is the primary cause of the use which we make of the word, Imagination; but the word, Taste, has been stretched to the sense which it bears in modern Europe by habits of self-conceit, inducing that inversion in the order of things whereby a passive faculty is made paramount among the faculties conversant with the fine arts.   Proportion and congruity, the requisite knowledge being supposed, are subjects upon which taste may be trusted; it is competent to this office; — for in its intercourse with these the mind is *passive*, and is affected painfully or pleasurably as by an instinct.   But the profound and the exquisite in feeling, the lofty and universal in thought and imagination; or, in ordinary language, the pathetic and the sublime; — are neither of them, accurately speaking, objects of a faculty which could ever without a sinking in the spirit of nations have been designated by the metaphor — *Taste*.   And why?   Because without the exertion of a coöperating *power* in the mind of the reader, there can be no adequate sympathy with either of these emotions : without this auxiliary impulse, elevated or profound passion cannot exist.

Passion, it must be observed, is derived from a word which signifies *suffering;* but the connection which suffering has with effort, with exertion, and *action*, is immediate and inseparable. How strikingly is this property of human nature exhibited by the fact, that, in popular language, to be in a passion, is to be angry ! — But,

> Anger in hasty *words* or *blows*
> Itself discharges on its foes.

To be moved, then, by a passion, is to be excited, often to external, and always to internal, effort; whether for the continuance and strengthening of the passion, or for its suppression, accordingly as the course which it takes may be painful or pleasurable.   If the latter, the soul must contribute to its support, or it never becomes vivid, — and soon languishes, and dies.   And this brings us to the point.   If every great poet with whose writings men are familiar, in the highest exercise of his genius, before he can be thoroughly enjoyed, has to call forth and to communicate *power*, this service, in a still greater degree, falls upon an original writer, at his first appearance in the world. — Of genius the only proof is, the act of doing well what is worthy to be done, and what was never done before : Of genius, in the fine arts, the only infallible sign is the widening the sphere of human sensibility, for the delight, honour, and benefit of human nature.   Genius is the introduction of a new element into the intellectual universe : or, if that be not allowed, it is the application of powers to objects on which they had not before been exercised, or the employment of them in such a manner as to produce effects hitherto unknown. What is all this but an advance, or a conquest, made by the soul of the poet? Is it to be supposed that the reader can make progress of this kind, like an Indian prince or general — stretched on his palanquin, and borne by his slaves? No; he is invigorated and inspirited by his leader, in order that he may exert himself; for he cannot proceed in quiescence, he cannot be carried like a dead weight. Therefore to create taste is to call forth and bestow power, of which knowledge is the effect; and *there* lies the true difficulty.

As the pathetic participates of an *animal* sensation, it might seem — that, if the springs of this emotion were genuine, all men, possessed of competent knowledge of the facts and circumstances, would be instantaneously affected. And, doubtless, in the works of every true poet will be found passages of that species of excellence, which is proved by effects immediate and universal. But there are emotions of the pathetic that are simple and direct, and others — that are complex and revolutionary; some — to which the heart yields with gentleness; others — against which it struggles with pride; these varieties are infinite as the combinations of circumstance and the constitutions of character. Remember, also, that the medium through which, in poetry, the heart is to be affected — is language; a thing subject to endless fluctuations and arbitrary associations. The genius of the poet melts these down for his purpose; but they retain their shape and quality to him who is not capable of exerting, within his own mind, a corresponding energy. There is also a meditative, as well as a human, pathos; an enthusiastic, as well as an ordinary, sorrow; a sadness that has its seat in the depths of reason, to which the mind cannot sink gently of itself — but to which it must descend by treading the steps of thought. And for the sublime, — if we consider what are the cares that occupy the passing day, and how remote is the practice and the course of life from the sources of sublimity in the soul of man, can it be wondered that there is little existing preparation for a poet charged with a new mission to extend its kingdom, and to augment and spread its enjoyments?

Away, then, with the senseless iteration of the word *popular*, applied to new works in poetry, as if there were no test of excellence in this first of the fine arts but that all men should run after its productions, as if urged by an appetite, or constrained by a spell! — The qualities of writing best fitted for eager reception are either such as startle the world into attention by their audacity and extravagance; or they are chiefly of a superficial kind lying upon the surfaces of manners; or arising out of a selection and arrangement of incidents, by which the mind is kept upon the stretch of curiosity and the fancy amused without the trouble of thought. But in every thing which is to send the soul into herself, to be admonished of her weakness, or to be made conscious of her power: — wherever life and nature are described as operated upon by the creative or abstracting virtue of the imagination; wherever the instinctive wisdom of antiquity and her heroic passions uniting, in the heart of the poet, with the meditative wisdom of later ages, have produced that accord of sublimated humanity, which is at once a history of the remote past and a prophetic enunciation of the remotest future, *there*, the poet must reconcile himself for a season to few and scattered hearers. — Grand thoughts (and Shakespeare must often have sighed over this truth), as they are most naturally and most fitly conceived in solitude, so can they not be brought forth in the midst of plaudits, without some violation of their sanctity. Go to a silent exhibition of the productions of the sister art, and be convinced that the qualities which dazzle at first sight, and kindle the admiration of the multitude, are essentially different from those by which permanent influence is secured. Let us not shrink from following up these principles as far as they will carry us, and conclude with observing — that there never has been a period, and perhaps never will be, in which vicious poetry, of some kind or other, has not excited more zealous admiration, and been far more generally read, than good; but this advantage attends the good, that the *individual*, as well as the species, survives from age to age; whereas, of the depraved, though the species be immortal, the individual quickly *perishes ;* the object of present admiration vanishes, being supplanted by some other as easily produced; which, though no better, brings with it at

least the irritation of novelty, — with adaptation, more or less
skilful, to the changing humours of the majority of those who are
most at leisure to regard poetical works when they first solicit
their attention.

Is it the result of the whole, that, in the opinion of the writer,
the judgment of the people is not to be respected ?   The thought is
most injurious ; and, could the charge be brought against him, he
would repel it with indignation.   The people have already been
justified, and their eulogium pronounced by implication, when it
was said, above — that, of *good* poetry, the *individual*, as well as
the species, *survives*.   And how does it survive but through the
people ?   What preserves it but their intellect and their wisdom ?

> —— Past and future, are the wings
> On whose support, harmoniously conjoined,
> Moves the great Spirit of human knowledge ——   *MS.*

The voice that issues from this Spirit, is that Vox Populi which
the Deity inspires.   Foolish must he be who can mistake for this a
local acclamation, or a transitory outcry — transitory though it be
for years, local though from a nation.   Still more lamentable is his
error who can believe that there is any thing of divine infallibility
in the clamour of that small though loud portion of the community,
ever governed by factitious influence, which, under the name of
the PUBLIC, passes itself, upon the unthinking, for the PEOPLE.
Towards the Public, the writer hopes that he feels as much deference
as it is entitled to ; but to the People, philosophically characterized,
and to the embodied spirit of their knowledge, so far as it exists
and moves, at the present, faithfully supported by its two wings,
the past and the future, his devout respect, his reverence, is due.
He offers it willingly and readily ; and, this done, takes leave of
his readers, by assuring them — that, if he were not persuaded that
the contents of these volumes, and the work to which they are
subsidiary, evince something of the " Vision and the Faculty
divine ; " and that, both in words and things, they will operate in
their degree, to extend the domain of sensibility for the delight, the
honour, and the benefit of human nature, notwithstanding the many
happy hours which he has employed in their composition, and the

manifold comforts and enjoyments they have procured to him, he would not, if a wish could do it, save them from immediate destruction; — from becoming at this moment, to the world, as a thing that had never been.

4. FROM PREFACE TO EDITION OF 1815

THE REQUIREMENTS OF THE POET [1]

The powers requisite for the production of poetry are : first, those of Observation and Description, — *i.e.*, the ability to observe with accuracy things as they are in themselves, and with fidelity to describe them, unmodified by any passion or feeling existing in the mind of the describer : whether the things depicted be actually present to the senses, or have a place only in the memory. This power, though indispensable to a poet, is one which he employs only in submission to necessity, and never for a continuance of time : as its exercise supposes all the higher qualities of the mind to be passive, and in a state of subjection to external objects, much in the same way as a translator or engraver ought to be to his original. Secondly, Sensibility, — which, the more exquisite it is, the wider will be the range of a poet's perceptions ; and the more will he be incited to observe objects, both as they exist in themselves and as reacted upon by his own mind. (The distinction between poetic and human sensibility has been marked in the character of the Poet delineated in the original preface.) Thirdly, Reflection, — which makes the poet acquainted with the value of actions, images, thoughts, and feelings ; and assists the sensibility in perceiving their connection with each other. Fourthly, Imagination and Fancy, — to modify, to create, and to associate. Fifthly, Invention, — by which characters are composed out of materials supplied by observation ; whether of the poet's own heart and mind, or of external life and nature ; and such incidents and situations produced as are most impressive to the imagination, and most fitted to do

[1] It would not suit the plan of this work to comment on, but it is permissible to call attention to, the astounding *petitio principii* in Wordsworth's own note, given *infra*, to this passage.

justice to the characters, sentiments, and passions, which the poet undertakes to illustrate. And, lastly, Judgment, — to decide how and where, and in what degree, each of these faculties ought to be exerted; so that the less shall not be sacrificed to the greater; nor the greater, slighting the less, arrogate, to its own injury, more than its due. By judgment, also, is determined what are the laws and appropriate graces of every species of composition.*

* As sensibility to harmony of numbers, and the power of producing it, are invariably attendants upon the faculties above specified, nothing has been said upon those requisites.

XXVII

COLERIDGE ON WORDSWORTH AND POETRY

FROM BIOGRAPHIA LITERARIA (1817), CHAPS. XIV-XXII

(The excesses and the paralogisms of Wordsworth's Apologia could not escape Coleridge; but it would have been awkward for him, seeing that he had been a partner in the *Lyrical Ballads*, to take up the cudgels at once. Even in this examination, which appeared seventeen years later in the *Biographia Literaria*, he seems almost nervously anxious to avoid meeting his old comrade " manful under shield," and in some points (such as the relations of verse and poetry) obviously " hedges " and " transacts." Yet the whole examination is one of the very *apices* of English criticism; and for once it is free from the scrappiness, though not (as a whole and in the original) from some of the digression and desultoriness, which are apt to beset Coleridge's work. I have endeavoured here to strip it of these super-fluities, as far as is possible without spoiling its sequence and texture.)

THE LYRICAL BALLADS — PHILOSOPHIC DEFINITIONS OF A POEM AND POETRY

During the first year that Mr. Wordsworth and I were neighbours, our conversations turned frequently on the two cardinal points of poetry, the power of exciting the sympathy of the reader by a faithful adherence to the truth of nature, and the power of giving the interest of novelty by the modifying colours of imagination. The sudden charm, which accidents of light and shade, which moonlight or sunset, diffused over a known and familiar landscape, appeared to represent the practicability of combining both. These are the poetry of nature. The thought suggested itself (to which of us I do not recollect) that a series of poems might be composed of two sorts. In the one, the incidents and agents were to be, in part at least, supernatural; and the excellence aimed at was to consist in the interesting of the affections by the dramatic truth of such emotions, as would naturally accompany such situations, supposing them real.   And real in this sense they have been to every human being who, from whatever source of delusion, has at any time believed himself under supernatural agency.   For the second class, subjects were to be chosen from ordinary life; the characters and incidents were to be such as will be found in every village and its vicinity where there is a meditative and feeling mind to seek after them, or to notice them when they present themselves.

In this idea originated the plan of the *Lyrical Ballads;* in which it was agreed that my endeavours should be directed to persons and characters supernatural, or at least romantic; yet so as to transfer from our inward nature a human interest and a semblance of truth sufficient to procure for these shadows of imagination that willing suspension of disbelief for the moment, which constitutes poetic faith.   Mr. Wordsworth, on the other hand, was to propose to himself as his object, to give the charm of novelty to things of every day, and to excite a feeling analogous to the supernatural, by awakening the mind's attention from the lethargy of custom, and directing it to the loneliness and the wonders of the world before us; an inexhaustible treasure, but for which, in consequence of the film of familiarity and selfish solicitude, we have eyes, yet see not, ears that hear not, and hearts that neither feel nor understand.

With this view I wrote the *Ancient Mariner,* and was preparing, among other poems, the *Dark Ladie* and the *Christabel,* in which I should have more nearly realized my ideal than I had done in my first attempt.   But Mr. Wordsworth's industry had proved so much more successful, and the number of his poems so much greater, that my compositions, instead of forming a balance, appeared rather an interpolation of heterogeneous matter.   Mr. Wordsworth added two or three poems written in his own character, in the impassioned, lofty, and sustained diction which is characteristic of his genius.   In this form the *Lyrical Ballads* were published; and were presented by him, as an experiment, whether subjects, which from their nature rejected the usual ornaments and extra-colloquial style of poems in general, might not be so managed in the language of ordinary life as to produce the pleasurable interest which it is the peculiar business of poetry to impart. To the second edition he added a preface of considerable length; in which, notwithstanding some passages of apparently a contrary import, he was understood to contend for the extension of this style to poetry of all kinds, and to reject as vicious and indefensible all phrases and forms of style that were not included in what he (unfortunately, I think, adopting an equivocal expression) called the language of real life. From this preface, prefixed to poems in which it was impossible to deny the presence of original genius, however mistaken its direction might be deemed, arose the whole long-continued controversy. For from the conjunction of perceived power with supposed heresy I explain the inveteracy, and in some instances, I grieve to say, the acrimonious passions, with which the controversy has been conducted by the assailants.

Had Mr. Wordsworth's poems been the silly, the childish things which they were for a long time described as being; had they been really distinguished from the compositions of other poets merely by meanness of language and inanity of thought; had they indeed contained nothing more than what is found in the parodies and pretended imitations of them; they must have sunk at once, a dead weight, into the slough of oblivion, and have dragged the preface along with them. But year after year increased the number of Mr. Wordsworth's admirers. They were found, too, not in the lower classes of the reading public, but chiefly among young men of strong sensibility and meditative minds; and their admiration (inflamed perhaps in some degree by opposition) was distinguished by its intensity, I might almost say, by its religious fervour. These facts, and the intellectual energy of the author, which was more or less consciously felt, where it was outwardly and even boisterously denied, meeting with sentiments of aversion to his opinions, and of alarm at their consequences, produced an eddy of criticism, which would of itself have borne up the poems by the violence with which it whirled them round and round. With many parts of this preface, in the sense attributed to them, and which the words undoubtedly seem to authorize, I never concurred; but, on the contrary, objected to them as erroneous in principle, and as contradictory (in appearance at least) both to other parts of the same preface and to the author's own practice in the greater number of the poems themselves.   Mr. Wordsworth, in his recent collection, has, I find, degraded this prefatory disquisition to the end of his second volume, to be read or not at the reader's choice. But he has not, as far as I can discover, announced any change in his poetic creed.   At all events, considering it as the source of a controversy, in which I have been honoured more than I deserve by the frequent conjunction of my name with his, I think it expedient to declare, once for all, in what points I coincide with his opinions, and in what points I altogether differ.   But in order to render myself intelligible, I must previously, in as few words as possible, explain my ideas, first, of a poem; and secondly, of poetry itself, in kind and in essence.

The office of philosophical disquisition consists in just distinction; while it is the privilege of the philosopher to preserve himself constantly aware that distinction is not division.   In order to obtain adequate notions of any truth, we must intellectually separate its distinguishable parts; and this is the technical process of philosophy.   But having so done, we must then restore them in our conceptions to the unity in which they actually coexist; and this is the result of philosophy.   A poem contains the same elements as a prose composition; the difference, therefore, must consist in a different combination of them, in consequence of a different object proposed.   According to the difference of the object will be the difference of the combination.   It is possible that the object may be merely to facilitate the recollection of any given facts or observations by artificial arrangement; and the composition will be a poem, merely because it is distinguished from prose by metre, or by rhyme, or by both conjointly.   In this, the lowest sense, a man might attribute the name of a poem to the well-known enumeration of the days in the several months:

> Thirty days hath September,
> April, June, and November, etc.

and others of the same class and purpose.   And as a particular pleasure is found in anticipating the recurrence of sounds and quantities, all compositions that have this charm superadded, whatever be their contents, *may* be entitled poems.

So much for the superficial form. A difference of object and contents supplies an additional ground of distinction. The immediate purpose may be the communication of truths; either of truth absolute and demonstrable, as in works of science; or of facts experienced and recorded, as in history. Pleasure, and that of the highest and most permanent kind, may result from the attainment of the end; but it is not itself the immediate end. In other works the communication of pleasure may be the immediate purpose; and though truth, either moral or intellectual, ought to be the ultimate end, yet this will distinguish the character of the author, not the class to which the work belongs. Blest indeed is that state of society, in which the immediate purpose would be baffled by the perversion of the proper ultimate end; in which no charm of diction or imagery could exempt the *Bathyllus* even of an Anacreon, or the *Alexis* of Virgil, from disgust and aversion!

But the communication of pleasure may be the immediate object of a work not metrically composed; and that object may have been in a high degree attained, as in novels and romances. Would then the mere superaddition of metre, with or without rhyme, entitle these to the name of poems? The answer is, that nothing can permanently please, which does not contain in itself the reason why it is so, and not otherwise. If metre be superadded, all other parts must be made consonant with it. They must be such as to justify the perpetual and distinct attention to each part, which an exact correspondent recurrence of accent and sound are calculated to excite. The final definition then, so deduced, may be thus worded. A poem is that species of composition, which is opposed to works of science, by proposing for its immediate object pleasure, not truth; and from all other species (having this object in common with it) it is discriminated by proposing to itself such delight from the whole, as is compatible with a distinct gratification from each component part.

Controversy is not seldom excited in consequence of the disputants attaching each a different meaning to the same word; and in few instances has this been more striking than in disputes concerning

the present subject.   If a man chooses to call every composition
a poem, which is rhyme, or measure, or both, I must leave his
opinion uncontroverted.   The distinction is at least competent to
characterize the writer's intention.   If it were subjoined, that the
whole is likewise entertaining or affecting, as a tale, or as a series
of interesting reflections, I of course admit this as another fit
ingredient of a poem, and an additional merit.   But if the definition
sought for be that of a legitimate poem, I answer, it must be one
the parts of which mutually support and explain each other; all in
their proportion harmonizing with, and supporting the purpose and
known influences of metrical arrangement.   The philosophic critics
of all ages coincide with the ultimate judgment of all countries, in
equally denying the praises of a just poem, on the one hand to a
series of striking lines or distichs, each of which absorbing the
whole attention of the reader to itself, disjoins it from its context,
and makes it a separate whole, instead of a harmonizing part ; and
on the other hand, to an unsustained composition, from which the
reader collects rapidly the general result unattracted by the component parts.   The reader should be carried forward, not merely or
chiefly by the mechanical impulse of curiosity, or by a restless
desire to arrive at the final solution ; but by the pleasurable
activity of mind excited by the attractions of the journey itself.
Like the motion of a serpent, which the Egyptians made the emblem
of intellectual power ; or like the path of sound through the air,
at every step he pauses and half recedes, and from the retrogres-
sive movement collects the force which again carries him onward.
Præcipitandus est liber spiritus, says Petronius Arbiter most happily.
The epithet, *liber,* here balances the preceding verb : and it is not
easy to conceive more meaning condensed in fewer words.

But if this should be admitted as a satisfactory character of a
poem, we have still to seek for a definition of poetry.   The writings
of Plato, and Bishop Taylor, and the *Theoria Sacra* of Burnet,
furnish undeniable proofs that poetry of the highest kind may exist
without metre, and even without the contradistinguishing objects of
a poem.   The first chapter of *Isaiah* (indeed a very large proportion
of the whole book) is poetry in the most emphatic sense ; yet it
would be not less irrational than strange to assert, that pleasure,

and not truth, was the immediate object of the prophet. In short, whatever specific import we attach to the word poetry, there will be found involved in it, as a necessary consequence, that a poem of any length neither can be, nor ought to be, all poetry. Yet if a harmonious whole is to be produced, the remaining parts must be preserved in keeping with the poetry; and this can be no otherwise effected than by such a studied selection and artificial arrangement as will partake of one, though not a peculiar, property of poetry. And this again can be no other than the property of exciting a more continuous and equal attention than the language of prose aims at, whether colloquial or written.

My own conclusions on the nature of poetry, in the strictest use of the word, have been in part anticipated in the preceding disquisition on the fancy and imagination. What is poetry? is so nearly the same question with, what is a poet? that the answer to the one is involved in the solution of the other. For it is a distinction resulting from the poetic genius itself, which sustains and modifies the images, thoughts, and emotions of the poet's own mind. The poet, described in ideal perfection, brings the whole soul of man into activity, with the subordination of its faculties to each other, according to their relative worth and dignity. He diffuses a tone and spirit of unity, that blends, and (as it were) fuses, each into each, by that synthetic and magical power to which we have exclusively appropriated the name of imagination. This power, first put in action by the will and understanding, and retained under their irremissive, though gentle and unnoticed, control (*laxis effertur habenis*) reveals itself in the balance or reconciliation of opposite or discordant qualities: of sameness, with differences; of the general, with the concrete; the idea, with the image; the individual, with the representative; the sense of novelty and freshness, with old and familiar objects; a more than usual state of emotion, with more than usual order; judgment ever awake and steady self-possession, with enthusiasm and feeling profound or vehement; and while it blends and harmonizes the natural and the artificial, still subordinates art to nature; the manner to the matter; and our admiration of the poet to our sympathy with the poetry. "Doubtless," as Sir John Davies observes of the soul (and his words may with slight alteration be applied, and even more appropriately, to the poetic imagination), —

> Doubtless this could not be, but that she turns
> Bodies to spirit by sublimation strange,
> As fire converts to fire the things it burns,
> As we our food into our nature change.

> From their gross matter she abstracts their forms,
> And draws a kind of quintessence from things;
> Which to her proper nature she transforms
> To bear them light on her celestial wings.

> Thus does she, when from individual states
> She doth abstract the universal kinds;
> Which then reclothed in divers names and fates
> Steal access through our senses to our minds.

Finally, good sense is the body of poetic genius, fancy its drapery, motion its life, and imagination the soul that is everywhere, and in each; and forms all into one graceful and intelligent whole.

Here follows in Chap. XV an analysis of Shakespeare's *Venus and Adonis* and *Rape of Lucrece;* and in XVI some characteristic divagation on Italian poetry chiefly.

CHAPTER XVII. — "REAL" AND "RUSTIC" LIFE — THEORIES OF DICTION

As far, then, as Mr. Wordsworth in his preface contended, and most ably contended, for a reformation in our poetic diction; as far as he has evinced the truth of passion, and the dramatic propriety of those figures and metaphors in the original poets, which, stripped of their justifying reasons and converted into mere artifices of connection or ornament, constitute the characteristic falsity in the poetic style of the moderns; and as far as he has, with equal acuteness and clearness, pointed out the process by which this change was effected, and the resemblances between that state into which the reader's mind is thrown by the pleasurable confusion of thought from an unaccustomed train of words and images, and that state which is induced by the natural language of impassioned feeling; he undertook a useful task, and deserves all praise, both for the attempt and for the execution. The provocations to this remonstrance in behalf of truth and nature were still of perpetual recurrence before and after the publication of this preface.[1]

. . . .

My own differences from certain supposed parts of Mr. Wordsworth's theory ground themselves on the assumption that his words had been rightly interpreted, as purporting that the proper diction for poetry in general consists altogether in a language taken, with due exceptions, from the mouths of men in real life, a language which actually constitutes the natural conversation of men under the influence of natural feelings. My objection is, first, that in any sense this rule is applicable only to certain classes of poetry; secondly, that even to these classes it is not applicable, except in such a sense as hath never by any one (as far as I know or have read) been denied or doubted; and, lastly, that as far as, and in that degree in which, it is practicable, it is yet, as a rule, useless, if not injurious, and, therefore, either need not or ought not to be practised. The poet informs his reader that he had generally chosen low and rustic life, but not *as* low and rustic, or in order to repeat that pleasure of doubtful moral effect which persons of elevated rank and of superior refinement oftentimes derive from a happy imitation of the rude unpolished manners and discourse of their inferiors. For the pleasure so derived may be traced to three exciting causes. The first is the naturalness, in fact, of the things represented. The second is the apparent naturalness of the representation, as raised and qualified by an imperceptible infusion of the author's own knowledge and talent, which infusion does indeed constitute it an imitation, as distinguished from a mere copy. The third cause may be found in the reader's conscious feeling of his superiority, awakened by the contrast presented to him; even as for the same purpose the kings and great barons of yore retained sometimes actual clowns and fools but more frequently shrewd and witty fellows in that character. These, however, were not Mr. Wordsworth's objects. He chose low and

---

[1] The omitted passage has reference to Wordsworth's silent but steady extension of influence. It is interesting; but a digression.

rustic life, "because in that condition the essential passions of the heart find a better soil in which they can attain their maturity, are less under restraint, and speak a plainer and more emphatic language; because in that condition of life our elementary feelings coexist in a state of greater simplicity, and consequently may be more accurately contemplated and more forcibly communicated; because the manners of rural life germinate from those elementary feelings, and from the necessary character of rural occupations are more easily comprehended and are more durable; and, lastly, because in that condition the passions of men are incorporated with the beautiful and permanent forms of nature."

Now it is clear to me that in the most interesting of the poems, in which the author is more or less dramatic, as *The Brothers*, *Michael*, *Ruth*, *The Mad Mother*, etc., the persons introduced are by no means taken from low or rustic life in the common acceptation of those words; and it is not less clear, that the sentiments and language, as far as they can be conceived to have been really transferred from the minds and conversation of such persons, are attributable to causes and circumstances not necessarily connected with "their occupations and abode." The thoughts, feelings, language, and manners of the shepherd-farmers in the vales of Cumberland and Westmoreland, as far as they are actually adopted in those poems, may be accounted for from causes which will and do produce the same results in every state of life, whether in town or country. As the two principal, I rank that independence which raises a man above servitude or daily toil for the profit of others, yet not above the necessity of industry and a frugal simplicity of domestic life, and the accompanying unambitious, but solid and religious, education which has rendered few books familiar but the Bible and the liturgy or hymn-book. To this latter cause indeed, which is so far accidental that it is the blessing of particular countries and a particular age, not the product of particular places or employments, the poet owes the show of probability that his personages might really feel, think, and talk with any tolerable resemblance to his representation. It is an excellent remark of Dr. Henry More's,* that "a man of confined education, but of good

* *Enthusiasmus Triumphatus*, Sec. xxxv.

parts, by constant reading of the Bible, will naturally form a more winning and commanding rhetoric than those that are learned, the intermixture of tongues and of artificial phrases debasing their style."

It is, moreover, to be considered, that to the formation of healthy feelings, and a reflecting mind, negations involve impediments not less formidable than sophistication and vicious intermixture. I am convinced that for the human soul to prosper in rustic life a certain vantage-ground is prerequisite. It is not every man that is likely to be improved by a country life or by country labours. Education, or original sensibility, or both, must preëxist, if the changes, forms, and incidents of nature are to prove a sufficient stimulant. And where these are not sufficient, the mind contracts and hardens by want of stimulants, and the man becomes selfish, sensual, gross, and hard-hearted. Let the management of the Poor Laws in Liverpool, Manchester, or Bristol, be compared with the ordinary dispensation of the poor rates in agricultural villages, where the farmers are the overseers and guardians of the poor. If my own experience has not been particularly unfortunate, as well as that of the many respectable country clergymen with whom I have conversed on the subject, the result would engender more than scepticism concerning the desirable influences of low and rustic life in and for itself. Whatever may be concluded on the other side, from the stronger local attachments and enterprising spirit of the Swiss, and other mountaineers, applies to a particular mode of pastoral life, under forms of property that permit and beget manners truly republican, not to rustic life in general, or to the absence of artificial cultivation. On the contrary the mountaineers, whose manners have been so often eulogized, are in general better educated and greater readers than men of equal rank elsewhere. But where this is not the case, as among the peasantry of North Wales, the ancient mountains, with all their terrors and all their glories, are pictures to the blind and music to the deaf.

I should not have entered so much into detail upon this passage, but here seems to be the point to which all the lines of difference converge as to their source and centre. (I mean, as far as, and in whatever respect, my poetic creed *does* differ from the doctrines

promulged in this preface.)   I adopt with full faith the principle
of Aristotle, that poetry as poetry is essentially ideal,* that it
avoids and excludes all accidents ; that its apparent individualities
of rank, character, or occupation must be representative of a class ;
and that the persons of poetry must be clothed with generic attributes, with the common attributes of the class ; not with such as
one gifted individual might possibly possess, but such as from his
situation it is most probable before-hand that he would possess.   If
my premises are right, and my deductions legitimate, it follows that
there can be no poetic medium between the swains of Theocritus
and those of an imaginary golden age.

The characters of the vicar and the shepherd-mariner in the
poem of *The Brothers,* of the Shepherd of Green-head Gill in
the *Michael,* have all the verisimilitude and representative quality that the purposes of poetry can require.   They are persons

---

* Say not that I am recommending abstractions, for these class-characteristics
which constitute the instructiveness of a character are so modified and particul-
arized in each person of the Shakespearean drama, that life itself does not
excite more distinctly that sense of individuality which belongs to real existence.
Paradoxical as it may sound, one of the essential properties of geometry is not
less essential to dramatic excellence ; and Aristotle has accordingly required of
the poet an involution of the universal in the individual.   The chief differences
are, that in geometry it is the universal truth which is uppermost in the consciousness ; in poetry the individual form in which truth is clothed.   With the
ancients, and not less with the elder dramatists of England and France, both
comedy and tragedy were considered as kinds of poetry.   They neither sought
in comedy to make us laugh merely ; much less to make us laugh by wry faces,
accidents of jargon, slang phrases for the day, or the clothing of common-place
morals in metaphors drawn from the shops or mechanic occupations of their
characters.   Nor did they condescend in tragedy to wheedle away the applause
of the spectators, by representing before them facsimiles of their own mean
selves in all their existing meanness, or to work on their sluggish sympathies by
a pathos not a whit more respectable than the maudlin tears of drunkenness.
Their tragic scenes were meant to affect us indeed ; but yet within the bounds
of pleasure, and in union with the activity both of our understanding and
imagination.   They wished to transport the mind to a sense of its possible greatness, and to implant the germs of that greatness, during the temporary oblivion
of the worthless "thing we are," and of the peculiar state in which each man
happens to be, suspending our individual recollections and lulling them to sleep
amid the music of nobler thoughts.   *The Friend.*

of a known and abiding class, and their manners and sentiments
the natural product of circumstances common to the class.   Take
Michael for instance :

> An old man stout of heart and strong of limb :
> [*Quotation of some 40 lines.*]

On the other hand, in the poems which are pitched at a lower
note, as the *Harry Gill*, the *Idiot Boy*, etc., the feelings are those
of human nature in general; though the poet has judiciously laid
the scene in the country, in order to place himself in the vicinity
of interesting images, without the necessity of ascribing a senti-
mental perception of their beauty to the persons of his drama.   In
the *Idiot Boy*, indeed, the mother's character is not so much a real
and native product of a " situation where the essential passions of
the heart find a better soil, in which they can attain their maturity
and speak a plainer and more emphatic language," as it is an
impersonation of an instinct abandoned by judgment.   Hence the
two following charges seem to me not wholly groundless ; at least,
they are the only plausible objections which I have heard to that
fine poem.   The one is, that the author has not, in the poem itself,
taken sufficient care to preclude from the reader's fancy the disgusting images of ordinary, morbid idiocy, which yet it was by no
means his intention to represent.   He has even by the " burr, burr,
burr," uncounteracted by any preceding description of the boy's
beauty, assisted in recalling them.   The other is, that the idiocy
of the boy is so evenly balanced by the folly of the mother, as to
present to the general reader rather a laughable burlesque on the
blindness of anile dotage, than an analytic display of maternal
affection in its ordinary workings.

In *The Thorn*, the poet himself acknowledges in a note the
necessity of an introductory poem, in which he should have pour-
trayed the character of the person from whom the words of the
poem are supposed to proceed : a superstitious man moderately
imaginative, of slow faculties and deep feelings, " a captain of a
small trading vessel, for example, who, being past the middle age
of life, had retired upon an annuity, or small independent income,
to some village or country town of which he was not a native, or

in which he had not been accustomed to live. Such men, having nothing to do, become credulous and talkative from indolence." But in a poem, still more in a lyric poem (and the Nurse in Shakespeare's *Romeo and Juliet* alone prevents me from extending the remark even to dramatic poetry, if indeed the Nurse itself can be deemed altogether a case in point), it is not possible to imitate truly a dull and garrulous discourser without repeating the effects of dulness and garrulity. However this may be, I dare assert, that the parts (and these form the far larger portion of the whole) which might as well or still better have proceeded from the poet's own imagination, and have been spoken in his own character, are those which have given, and which will continue to give, universal delight; and that the passages exclusively appropriate to the supposed narrator, such as the last couplet of the third stanza,* the seven last lines of the tenth,† and the five following stanzas, with the exception of the four admirable lines at the commencement of the fourteenth, are felt by many unprejudiced and unsophisticated hearts, as sudden and unpleasant sinkings from the height to which the poet had previously lifted them, and to which he again reëlevates both himself and his reader.

If then I am compelled to doubt the theory, by which the choice of characters was to be directed, not only *a priori*, from grounds of reason, but both from the few instances in which the poet himself *need* be supposed to have been governed by it, and from the comparative inferiority of those instances; still more must I hesitate in my assent to the sentence which immediately follows the former citation, and which I can neither admit as particular fact, or as general rule. "The language too of these men is adopted (purified indeed from what appear to be its real defects, from all lasting and rational causes of dislike or disgust) because such men hourly communicate with the best objects from which the best part of language is originally derived; and because, from

---

* I 've measured it from side to side;
  'T is three feet long, and two feet wide.

† Nay, rack your brain — 't is all in vain,
  I 'll tell you every thing I know;
    [*Quotation of some 50 lines.*]

their rank in society, and the sameness and narrow circle of their intercourse, being less under the action of social vanity, they convey their feelings and notions in simple and unelaborated expressions." To this I reply, that a rustic's language, purified from all provincialism and grossness, and so far reconstructed as to be made consistent with the rules of grammar (which are in essence no other than the laws of universal logic, applied to psychological materials), will not differ from the language of any other man of common sense, however learned or refined he may be, except as far as the notions which the rustic has to convey are fewer and more indiscriminate. This will become still clearer, if we add the consideration (equally important though less obvious) that the rustic, from the more imperfect development of his faculties, and from the lower state of their cultivation, aims almost solely to convey insulated facts, either those of his scanty experience or his traditional belief; while the educated man chiefly seeks to discover and express those connections of things, or those relative bearings of fact to fact, from which some more or less general law is deducible. For facts are valuable to a wise man, chiefly as they lead to the discovery of the indwelling law, which is the true being of things, the sole solution of their modes of existence, and in the knowledge of which consists our dignity and our power.

As little can I agree with the assertion, that from the objects with which the rustic hourly communicates the best part of language is formed. For, first, if to communicate with an object implies such an acquaintance with it as renders it capable of being discriminately reflected on, the distinct knowledge of an uneducated rustic would furnish a very scanty vocabulary. The few things, and modes of action, requisite for his bodily conveniences would alone be individualized; while all the rest of nature would be expressed by a small number of confused general terms. Secondly, I deny that the words and combinations of words derived from the objects with which the rustic is familiar, whether with distinct or confused knowledge, can be justly said to form the best part of language. It is more than probable, that many classes of the brute creation possess discriminating sounds, by which they can convey to each other notices of such objects as concern their food, shelter, or safety. Yet we hesitate to call the aggregate of such sounds a language otherwise than metaphorically. The best part of human language, properly so called, is derived from reflection on the acts of the mind itself. It is formed by a voluntary appropriation of fixed symbols to internal acts, to processes and results of imagination, the greater part of which have no place in the consciousness of uneducated man; though in civilized society, by imitation and passive remembrance of what they hear from their religious instructors and other superiors, the most uneducated share in the harvest which they neither sowed or reaped. If the history of the phrases in hourly currency among our peasants were traced, a person not previously aware of the fact would be surprised at finding so large a number, which three or four centuries ago were the exclusive property of the universities and the schools, and at the commencement of the Reformation had been transferred from the school to the pulpit, and thus gradually passed into common life. The extreme difficulty, and often the impossibility, of finding words for the simplest moral and intellectual processes in the languages of uncivilized tribes has proved perhaps the weightiest obstacle to the progress of our most zealous and adroit missionaries. Yet these tribes are surrounded by the same nature as our peasants are; but in still more impressive forms; and they are, moreover, obliged to particularize many more of them. When therefore Mr. Wordsworth adds, "accordingly such a language" (meaning, as before, the language of rustic life purified from provincialism), "arising out of repeated experience and regular feelings, is a more permanent, and a far more philosophical, language than that which is frequently substituted for it by poets, who think they are conferring honour upon themselves and their art in proportion as they indulge in arbitrary and capricious habits of expression"; it may be answered, that the language which he has in view can be attributed to rustics with no greater right than the style of Hooker or Bacon to Tom Brown or Sir Roger L'Estrange. Doubtless, if what is peculiar to each were omitted in each, the result must needs be the same. Further, that the poet who uses an illogical diction, or a style fitted to excite only the low and changeable pleasure of wonder by means of groundless novelty, substitutes a language of folly and vanity, not for that of the rustic, but for that of good sense and natural feeling.

Here let me be permitted to remind the reader, that the positions which I controvert are contained in the sentences — " a selection of the real language of men " ; — "the language of these men [*i.e.*, men in low and rustic life] I propose to myself to imitate, and as far as possible to adopt the very language of men." " Between the language of prose and that of metrical composition there neither is, nor can be, any essential difference." It is against these exclusively that my opposition is directed.

I object, in the very first instance, to an equivocation in the use of the word "real." Every man's language varies, according to the extent of his knowledge, the activity of his faculties, and the depth or quickness of his feelings. Every man's language has, first, its individualities ; secondly, the common properties of the class to which he belongs ; and thirdly, words and phrases of universal use. The language of Hooker, Bacon, Bishop Taylor, and Burke differs from the common language of the learned class only by the superior number and novelty of the thoughts and relations which they had to convey. The language of Algernon Sidney differs not at all from that which every well-educated gentleman would wish to write, and (with due allowances for the undeliberateness and less connected train of thinking natural and proper to conversation) such as he would wish to talk. Neither one or the other differ[s] half as much from the general language of cultivated society as the language of Mr. Wordsworth's homeliest composition differs from that of a common peasant. For "real," therefore, we must substitute ordinary, or *lingua communis*. And this, we have proved, is no more to be found in the phraseology of low and rustic life than in that of any other class. Omit the peculiarities of each, and the result of course must be common to all. And assuredly the omissions and changes to be made in the language of rustics, before it could be transferred to any species of poem, except the drama or other professed imitation, are at least as numerous and weighty as would be required in adapting to the same purpose the ordinary language of tradesmen and manufacturers. Not to mention that the language so highly extolled by Mr. Wordsworth varies in every county, nay, in every village, according to the accidental character of the clergyman, the existence or non-existence of schools; or even, perhaps, as the exciseman, publican, or barber happen to be, or not to be, zealous politicians, and readers of the weekly newspaper *pro bono publico*. Anterior to cultivation the *lingua communis* of every country, as Dante has well observed, exists everywhere in parts, and nowhere as a whole.

Neither is the case rendered at all more tenable by the addition of the words, "in a state of excitement." For the nature of a man's words, when he is strongly affected by joy, grief, or anger, must necessarily depend on the number and quality of the general truths, conceptions, and images, and of the words expressing them, with which his mind had been previously stored. For the property of passion is not to create, but to set in increased activity. At least, whatever new connections of thoughts or images, or (which is equally, if not more than equally, the appropriate effect of strong excitement) whatever generalizations of truth or experience the heat of passion may produce, yet the terms of their conveyance must have preëxisted in his former conversations, and are only collected and crowded together by the unusual stimulation. It is indeed very possible to adopt in a poem the unmeaning repetitions, habitual phrases, and other blank counters which an unfurnished or confused understanding interposes at short intervals in order to keep hold of his subject, which is still slipping from him, and to give him time for recollection; or in mere aid of vacancy, as in the scanty companies of a country stage the same player pops backwards and forwards, in order to prevent the appearance of empty spaces, in the processions of *Macbeth* or *Henry VIII*. But what assistance to the poet, or ornament to the poem, these can supply, I am at a loss to conjecture. Nothing assuredly can differ either in origin or in mode more widely from the apparent tautologies of intense and turbulent feeling, in which the passion is greater and of longer endurance than to be exhausted or satisfied by a single representation of the image or incident exciting it. Such repetitions I admit to be a beauty of the highest kind; as illustrated by Mr. Wordsworth himself from the song of Deborah. "At her feet he bowed, he fell, he lay down: at her feet he bowed, he fell: where he bowed, there he fell down dead." — *Judges* v. 27.

CHAPTER XVIII. — METRICAL COMPOSITION ESSENTIALLY DIFFERENT FROM THAT OF PROSE

I conclude, therefore, that the attempt is impracticable; and that, were it not impracticable, it would still be useless. For the very power of making the selection implies the previous possession of the language selected. Or where can the poet have lived? And by what rules could he direct his choice, which would not have enabled him to select and arrange his words by the light of his own judgment? We do not adopt the language of a class by the mere adoption of such words exclusively as that class would use, or at least understand; but likewise by following the order in which the words of such men are wont to succeed each other. Now this order, in the intercourse of uneducated men, is distinguished from the diction of their superiors in knowledge and power by the greater disjunction and *separation* in the component parts of that, whatever it be, which they wish to communicate. There is a want of that prospectiveness of mind, that *surview*, which enables a man to foresee the whole of what he is to convey, appertaining to any one point; and by this means so to subordinate and arrange the different parts according to their relative importance, as to convey it at once, and as an organized whole.

Now I will take the first stanza, on which I have chanced to open, in the *Lyrical Ballads*. It is one of the most simple and the least peculiar in its language:

> In distant countries I have been,
> And yet I have not often seen
> A healthy man, a man full grown,
> Weep in the public roads, alone.
> But such a one, on English ground,
> And in the broad highway, I met;
> Along the broad highway he came,
> His cheeks with tears were wet.
> Sturdy he seemed, though he was sad,
> And in his arms a lamb he had.

The words here are doubtless such as are current in all ranks of life : and of course not less so in the hamlet and cottage, than in

the shop, manufactory, college, or palace.   But is this the order in
which the rustic would have placed the words?   I am grievously
deceived, if the following less compact mode of commencing the
same tale be not a far more faithful copy.   " I have been in a many
parts far and near, and I don't know that I ever saw before a man
crying by himself in the public road; a grown man I mean, that
was neither sick nor hurt," etc., etc.   But when I turn to the
following stanza in *The Thorn:*

> At all times of the day and night
> This wretched woman thither goes,
> And she is known to every star
> And every wind that blows:
> And there beside the thorn she sits,
> When the blue day-light's in the skies:
> And when the whirlwind's on the hill,
> Or frosty air is keen and still;
> And to herself she cries,
> Oh misery! Oh misery!
> Oh woe is me! Oh misery!

and compare this with the language of ordinary men, or with that
which I can conceive at all likely to proceed, in real life, from such
a narrator as is supposed in the note to the poem — compare it
either in the succession of the images or of the sentences — I am
reminded of the sublime prayer and hymn of praise which Milton,
in opposition to an established liturgy, presents as a fair specimen
of common extemporary devotion, and such as we might expect to
hear from every self-inspired minister of a conventicle!   And I
reflect with delight, how little a mere theory, though of his own
workmanship, interferes with the processes of genuine imagination
in a man of true poetic genius, who possesses, as Mr. Wordsworth,
if ever man did, most assuredly does possess,

The Vision and the Faculty divine.

One point then alone remains, but that the most important; its
examination having been, indeed, my chief inducement for the preceding inquisition.   " There neither is or can be any essential difference between the language of prose and metrical composition."
Such is Mr. Wordsworth's assertion.   Now prose itself, at least in

all argumentative and consecutive works, differs, and ought to differ, from the language of conversation; even as reading ought to differ from talking. Unless, therefore, the difference denied be that of the mere words, as materials common to all styles of writing, and not of the style itself in the universally admitted sense of the term, it might be naturally presumed that there must exist a still greater between the ordonnance of poetic composition and that of prose, than is expected to distinguish prose from ordinary conversation.

There are not, indeed, examples wanting in the history of literature, of apparent paradoxes that have summoned the public wonder as new and startling truths, but which on examination have shrunk into tame and harmless truisms; as the eyes of a cat, seen in the dark, have been mistaken for flames of fire. But Mr. Wordsworth is among the last men to whom a delusion of this kind would be attributed by any one who had enjoyed the slightest opportunity of understanding his mind and character. Where an objection has been anticipated by such an author as natural, his answer to it must needs be interpreted in some sense which either is, or has been, or is capable of being controverted. My object, then, must be to discover some other meaning for the term "essential difference" in this place, exclusive of the indistinction and community of the words themselves. For whether there ought to exist a class of words in the English in any degree resembling the poetic dialect of the Greek and Italian, is a question of very subordinate importance. The number of such words would be small indeed in our language; and even in the Italian and Greek, they consist not so much of different words as of slight differences in the forms of declining and conjugating the same words; forms, doubtless, which having been, at some period more or less remote, the common grammatic flexions of some tribe or province, had been accidentally appropriated to poetry by the general admiration of certain master intellects, the first established lights of inspiration, to whom that dialect happened to be native.

Essence, in its primary signification, means the principle of individuation, the inmost principle of the possibility of any thing, as that particular thing. It is equivalent to the idea of a thing, whenever we use the word idea with philosophic precision. Existence, on the other hand, is distinguished from essence by the superinduction of reality. Thus we speak of the essence and essential properties of a circle; but we do not therefore assert, that any thing which really exists is mathematically circular. Thus too, without any tautology, we contend for the existence of the Supreme Being; that is, for a reality correspondent to the idea. There is, next, a secondary use of the word essence, in which it signifies the point or ground of contradistinction between two modifications of the same substance or subject. Thus we should be allowed to say, that the style of architecture of Westminster Abbey is essentially different from that of Saint Paul's, even though both had been built with blocks cut into the same form, and from the same quarry. Only in this latter sense of the term must it have been denied by Mr. Wordsworth (for in this sense alone is it affirmed by the general opinion) that the language of poetry (*i. e.*, the formal construction, or architecture, of the words and phrases) is essentially different from that of prose. Now the burthen of the proof lies with the oppugner, not with the supporters of the common belief. Mr. Wordsworth, in consequence, assigns as the proof of his position, "that not only the language of a large portion of every good poem, even of the most elevated character, must necessarily, except with reference to the metre, in no respect differ from that of good prose, but likewise that some of the most interesting parts of the best poems will be found to be strictly the language of prose, when prose is well written. The truth of this assertion might be demonstrated by innumerable passages from almost all the poetical writings even of Milton himself." He then quotes Gray's sonnet:

> In vain to me the smiling mornings shine,
> And reddening Phœbus lifts his golden fire;
> The birds in vain their amorous descant join
> Or cheerful fields resume their green attire;
> These ears, alas! for other notes repine;
> *A different object do these eyes require;*
> *My lonely anguish melts no heart but mine,*
> *And in my breast the imperfect joys expire!*
> Yet morning smiles the busy race to cheer,
> And new-born pleasure brings to happier men;

The fields to all their wonted tribute bear,
To warm their little loves the birds complain.
I fruitless mourn to him who cannot hear,
And weep the more because I weep in vain;

and adds the following remark : " It will easily be perceived, that the only part of this sonnet which is of any value is the lines printed in italics. It is equally obvious that, except in the rhyme, and in the use of the single word 'fruitless' for fruitlessly, which is so far a defect, the language of these lines does in no respect differ from that of prose."

An idealist defending his system by the fact, that when asleep we often believe ourselves awake, was well answered by his plain neighbour, " Ah ! but when awake do we ever believe ourselves asleep?" Things identical must be convertible. The preceding passage seems to rest on a similar sophism. For the question is not, whether there may not occur in prose an order of words, which would be equally proper in a poem ; nor whether there are not beautiful lines and sentences of frequent occurrence in good poems, which would be equally becoming as well as beautiful in good prose; for neither the one or the other has ever been either denied or doubted by any one. The true question must be, whether there are not modes of expression, a construction, and an order of sentences, which are in their fit and natural place in a serious prose composition, but would be disproportionate and heterogeneous in metrical poetry; and, *vice versâ*, whether in the language of a serious poem there may not be an arrangement both of words and sentences, and a use and selection of (what are called) figures of speech, both as to their kind, their frequency, and their occasions, which on a subject of equal weight would be vicious and alien in correct and manly prose. I contend, that in both cases this unfitness of each for the place of the other frequently will and ought to exist.

And, first, from the origin of metre. This I would trace to the balance in the mind effected by that spontaneous effort which strives to hold in check the workings of passion. It might be easily explained likewise in what manner this salutary antagonism is assisted by the very state which it counteracts ; and how this balance of antagonists became organized into metre (in the usual acceptation of that term) by a supervening act of the will and judgment, consciously and for the foreseen purpose of pleasure. Assuming these principles as the data of our argument, we deduce from them two legitimate conditions, which the critic is entitled to expect in every metrical work. First, that as the elements of metre owe their existence to a state of increased excitement, so the metre itself should be accompanied by the natural language of excitement. Secondly, that as these elements are formed into metre artificially, by a voluntary act, with the design and for the purpose of blending delight with emotion, so the traces of present volition should throughout the metrical language be proportionally discernible. Now these two conditions must be reconciled and co-present. There must be not only a partnership, but a union; an interpenetration of passion and of will, of spontaneous impulse and of voluntary purpose. Again, this union can be manifested only in a frequency of forms and figures of speech (originally the offspring of passion, but now the adopted children of power) greater than would be desired or endured, where the emotion is not voluntarily encouraged, and kept up for the sake of that pleasure, which such emotion so tempered and mastered by the will is found capable of communicating. It not only dictates, but of itself tends to produce, a more frequent employment of picturesque and vivifying language than would be natural in any other case in which there did not exist, as there does in the present, a previous and well understood, though tacit, compact between the poet and his reader, that the latter is entitled to expect, and the former bound to supply, this species and degree of pleasurable excitement. We may in some measure apply to this union the answer of Polixenes, in the *Winter's Tale*, to Perdita's neglect of the streaked gilly-flowers, because she had heard it said:

> There is an art which in their piedness shares
> With great creating nature.
> *Pol.*   Say there be.
> Yet nature is made better by no mean,
> But nature makes that mean. So over that art,
> Which you say adds to nature, is an art

That nature makes! You see, sweet maid, we marry
A gentler scion to the wildest stock:
And make conceive a bark of baser kind
By bud of nobler race. This is an art,
Which does mend nature — change it rather; but
The art itself is nature.

Secondly, I argue from the effects of metre. As far as metre acts in and for itself, it tends to increase the vivacity and susceptibility both of the general feelings and of the attention. This effect it produces by the continued excitement of surprise, and by the quick reciprocations of curiosity still gratified and still reëxcited, which are too slight indeed to be at any one moment objects of distinct consciousness, yet become considerable in their aggregate influence. As a medicated atmosphere, or as wine during animated conversation, they act powerfully, though themselves unnoticed. Where, therefore, correspondent food and appropriate matter are not provided for the attention and feelings thus roused, there must needs be a disappointment felt; like that of leaping in the dark from the last step of a staircase, when we had prepared our muscles for a leap of three or four.

The discussion on the powers of metre in the preface is highly ingenious, and touches at all points on truth. But I cannot find any statement of its powers considered abstractly and separately. On the contrary, Mr. Wordsworth seems always to estimate metre by the powers which it exerts during (and, as I think, in consequence of) its combination with other elements of poetry. Thus the previous difficulty is left unanswered, what the elements are with which it must be combined in order to produce its own effects to any pleasurable purpose. Double and trisyllable rhymes, indeed, form a lower species of wit, and, attended to exclusively for their own sake, may become a source of momentary amusement; as in poor Smart's distich to the Welch Squire who had promised him a hare:

Tell me, thou son of great Cadwallader!
Hast sent the hare? or hast thou swallow'd her?

But for any poetic purposes, metre resembles (if the aptness of the simile may excuse its meanness) yeast, worthless or disagreeable by itself, but giving vivacity and spirit to the liquor with which it is proportionally combined.

The reference to the *Children in the Wood* by no means satisfies my judgment. We all willingly throw ourselves back for awhile into the feelings of our childhood. This ballad, therefore, we read under such recollections of our own childish feelings, as would equally endear to us poems which Mr. Wordsworth himself would regard as faulty in the opposite extreme of gaudy and technical ornament. Before the invention of printing and, in a still greater degree, before the introduction of writing, metre, especially alliterative metre (whether alliterative at the beginning of the words, as in Pierce Plouman, or at the end as in rhymes), possessed an independent value as assisting the recollection, and consequently the preservation, of any series of truths or incidents. But I am not convinced by the collation of facts that the *Children in the Wood* owes either its preservation or its popularity to its metrical form. Mr. Marshal's repository affords a number of tales in prose inferior in pathos and general merit, some of as old a date, and many as widely popular. *Tom Hickathrift, Jack the Giant Killer, Goody Two Shoes,* and *Little Red Riding Hood* are formidable rivals. And that they have continued in prose cannot be fairly explained by the assumption that the comparative meanness of their thoughts and images precluded even the humblest forms of metre. The scene of *Goody Two Shoes* in the church is perfectly susceptible of metrical narration; and among the Θαύματα θαυμαστότατα even of the present age, I do not recollect a more astonishing image than that of the "whole rookery, that flew out of the giant's beard," scared by the tremendous voice with which this monster answered the challenge of the heroic Tom Hickathrift!

If from these we turn to compositions universally, and independently of all early associations, beloved and admired, would the *Maria*, the *Monk*, or the *Poor Man's Ass* of Sterne, be read with more delight, or have a better chance of immortality, had they, without any change in the diction, been composed in rhyme, than in their present state? If I am not grossly mistaken, the general reply would be in the negative. Nay, I will confess, that in Mr. Wordsworth's own volumes, the *Anecdote for Fathers, Simon Lee,*

Alice Fell, the *Beggars*, and the *Sailor's Mother*, notwithstanding
the beauties which are to be found in each of them where the poet
interposes the music of his own thoughts, would have been more
delightful to me in prose, told and managed as by Mr. Wordsworth
they would have been, in a moral essay or pedestrian tour.

Metre in itself is simply a stimulant of the attention, and therefore excites the question, Why is the attention to be thus stimu-
lated ? Now the question cannot be answered by the pleasure of
the metre itself : for this we have shown to be conditional, and
dependent on the appropriateness of the thoughts and expressions
to which the metrical form is superadded. Neither can I conceive
any other answer that can be rationally given, short of this : I
write in metre, because I am about to use a language different from
that of prose. Besides, where the language is not such, how interesting soever the reflections are that are capable of being drawn
by a philosophic mind from the thoughts or incidents of the poem,
the metre itself must often become feeble. Take the three last
stanzas of the *Sailor's Mother*, for instance. If I could for a
moment abstract from the effect produced on the author's feelings
as a man, by the incident at the time of its real occurrence, I would
dare appeal to his own judgment, whether in the metre itself he
found sufficient reason for their being written metrically?

> And thus continuing, she said
> I had a son, who many a day
> Sailed on the seas ; but he is dead ;
> In Denmark he was cast away :
> And I have travelled far as Hull to see
> What clothes he might have left, or other property.
>
> The bird and cage, they both were his ;
> 'T was my son's bird ; and neat and trim
> He kept it : many voyages
> This singing bird hath gone with him ;
> When last he sailed he left the bird behind ;
> As it might be, perhaps, from bodings of his mind.
>
> He to a fellow-lodger's care
> Had left it, to be watched and fed,
> Till he came back again ; and there

> I found it when my son was dead;
> And now, God help me for my little wit!
> I trail it with me, Sir! he took so much delight in it.

If disproportioning the emphasis we read these stanzas so as to make the rhymes perceptible, even trisyllable rhymes could scarcely produce an equal sense of oddity and strangeness, as we feel here in finding rhymes at all in sentences so exclusively colloquial. I would further ask whether, but for that visionary state into which the figure of the woman and the susceptibility of his own genius had placed the poet's imagination (a state which spreads its influence and colouring over all, that coexists with the exciting cause, and in which

> The simplest, and the most familiar things
> Gain a strange power of spreading awe around them *) —

I would ask the poet whether he would not have felt an abrupt down-fall in these verses from the preceding stanza?

> The ancient spirit is not dead;
> Old times, thought I, are breathing there!
> Proud was I, that my country bred
> Such strength, a dignity so fair!
> She begged an alms, like one in poor estate;
> I looked at her again, nor did my pride abate.

It must not be omitted, and is besides worthy of notice, that those stanzas furnish the only fair instance that I have been able to discover in all Mr. Wordsworth's writings of an actual adoption, or true imitation, of the real and very language of low and rustic life, freed from provincialisms.

* Altered from the description of Night-Mair in the *Remorse*.

> Oh Heaven! 't was frightful! Now run down and stared at,
> By hideous shapes that cannot be remembered:
> Now seeing nothing and imagining nothing:
> But only being afraid — stifled with fear!
> While every goodly or familiar form
> Had a strange power of spreading terror round me.

N.B. Though Shakespeare has for his own all-justifying purposes introduced the Night-*Mare* with her own foals, yet Mair means a Sister, or perhaps a Hag.

Thirdly, I deduce the position from all the causes elsewhere assigned, which render metre the proper form of poetry, and poetry imperfect and defective without metre. Metre therefore having been connected with poetry most often and by a peculiar fitness, whatever else is combined with metre must, though it be not itself essentially poetic, have nevertheless some property in common with poetry, as an intermedium of affinity, a sort (if I may dare borrow a well-known phrase from technical chemistry) of *morda[u]nt* between it and the superadded metre. Now poetry, Mr. Wordsworth truly affirms, does always imply passion : which word must be here understood, in its most general sense, as an excited state of the feelings and faculties. And as every passion has its proper pulse, so will it likewise have its characteristic modes of expression. But where there exists that degree of genius and talent which entitles a writer to aim at the honours of a poet, the very act of poetic composition itself is, and is allowed to imply and to produce, an unusual state of excitement, which of course justifies and demands a correspondent difference of language, as truly, though not perhaps in as marked a degree, as the excitement of love, fear, rage, or jealousy. The vividness of the descriptions or declamations in Donne, or Dryden, is as much and as often derived from the force and fervour of the describer, as from the reflections, forms, or incidents which constitute their subject and materials. The wheels take fire from the mere rapidity of their motion. To what extent, and under what modifications, this may be admitted to act, I shall attempt to define in an after remark on Mr. Wordsworth's reply to this objection, or rather on his objection to this reply, as already anticipated in his preface.

Fourthly, and as intimately connected with this, if not the same argument in a more general form, I adduce the high spiritual instinct of the human being impelling us to seek unity by harmonious adjustment, and thus establishing the principle, that all the parts of an organized whole must be assimilated to the more important and essential parts. This and the preceding arguments may be strengthened by the reflection, that the composition of a poem is among the imitative arts ; and that imitation, as opposed to copying, consists either in the interfusion of the same throughout the radically different, or of the different throughout a base radically the same.

Lastly, I appeal to the practice of the best poets, of all countries and in all ages, as authorizing the opinion (deduced from all the foregoing) that in every import of the word essential, which would not here involve a mere truism, there may be, is, and ought to be, an essential difference between the language of prose and of metrical composition.

In Mr. Wordsworth's criticism of Gray's *Sonnet*, the reader's sympathy with his praise or blame of the different parts is taken for granted rather perhaps too easily. He has not, at least, attempted to win or compel it by argumentative analysis. In my conception at least, the lines rejected as of no value do, with the exception of the two first, differ as much and as little from the language of common life, as those which he has printed in italics as possessing genuine excellence. Of the five lines thus honourably distinguished, two of them differ from prose even more widely than the lines which either precede or follow, in the position of the words:

> *A different object do these eyes require;*
> My lonely anguish melts no heart but mine;
> *And in my breast the imperfect joys expire.*

But were it otherwise, what would this prove but a truth of which no man ever doubted ? — videlicet, that there are sentences, which would be equally in their place both in verse and prose. Assuredly it does not prove the point which alone requires proof; namely, that there are not passages, which would suit the one and not suit the other. The first line of this sonnet is distinguished from the ordinary language of men by the epithet to morning. (For we will set aside, at present, the consideration, that the particular word "smiling" is hackneyed, and — as it involves a sort of personification — not quite congruous with the common and material attribute of shining.) And, doubtless, this adjunction of epithets for the purpose of additional description, where no particular attention is demanded for the quality of the thing, would be noticed as giving a poetic cast to a man's conversation. Should the sportsman exclaim, " Come boys ! the rosy morning calls you up," he will be supposed to have some song in his head. But no one suspects this when he says, " A wet morning shall not confine us to our beds." This then is either a defect in poetry, or it is not. Whoever should decide in the affirmative, I would request him to re-peruse any one poem of any confessedly great poet from Homer to Milton, or from Æschylus to Shakespeare ; and to strike out (in thought I mean) every instance of this kind. If the number of these fancied erasures did not startle him, or if he continued to deem the work improved by their total omission, he must advance reasons of no ordinary strength and evidence, reasons grounded in the essence of human nature. Otherwise I should not hesitate to consider him as a man not so much proof against all authority as dead to it.

The second line,

> And reddening Phœbus lifts his golden fire,

has indeed almost as many faults as words. But then it is a bad line, not because the language is distinct from that of prose, but because it conveys incongruous images, because it confounds the cause and the effect, the real thing with the personified representative of the thing ; in short, because it differs from the language of good sense. That the " Phœbus " is hackneyed, and a schoolboy image, is an accidental fault, dependent on the age in which the author wrote, and not deduced from the nature of the thing. That it is part of an exploded mythology, is an objection more deeply grounded. Yet when the torch of ancient learning was rekindled, so cheering were its beams, that our eldest poets, cut off by Christianity from all accredited machinery, and deprived of all acknowledged guardians and symbols of the great objects of nature, were naturally induced to adopt, as a poetic language, those fabulous personages, those forms of the supernatural in nature, which had given them such dear delight in the poems of their great masters. Nay, even at this day what scholar of genial taste will not so far sympathize with them, as to read with pleasure in Petrarch, Chaucer, or Spenser, what he would perhaps condemn as puerile in a modern poet ?

I remember no poet, whose writings would safelier stand the test of Mr. Wordsworth's theory, than Spenser. Yet will Mr.

Wordsworth say, that the style of the following stanzas is either undistinguished from prose, and the language of ordinary life? Or that it is vicious, and that the stanzas are blots in the *Faëry Queen?*

> By this the northern waggoner had set
> His sevenfold teme behind the stedfast starre,
> That was in ocean waves yet never wet,
> But firme is fixt and sendeth light from farre
> To all that in the wild deep wandering arre.
> And chearfull chaunticleer with his note shrill
> Had warned once that Phœbus' fiery carre
> In hast was climbing up the easterne hill,
> Full envious that night so long his roome did fill.

Book I, Canto 2, stanza 1.

> At last the golden orientall gate
> Of greatest heaven gan to open fayre,
> And Phœbus fresh as brydegrome to his mate,
> Came dauncing forth, shaking his deawie hayre,
> And hurl'd his glist'ring beams through gloomy ayre;
> Which when the wakeful elfe perceived, streightway
> He started up, and did him selfe prepayre
> In sun-bright armes, and battailous array;
> For with that pagan proud he combat will that day.

Book I, Canto 5, stanza 2.

On the contrary, to how many passages, both in hymn books and in blank verse poems, could I (were it not invidious) direct the reader's attention, the style of which is most unpoetic, because, and only because, it is the style of prose? He will not suppose me capable of having in my mind such verses as

> I put my hat upon my head
> And walked into the Strand;
> And there I met another man,
> Whose hat was in his hand.

To such specimens it would indeed be a fair and full reply, that these lines are not bad because they are unpoetic, but because they are empty of all sense and feeling; and that it were an idle attempt to prove that "an ape is not a Newton, when it is evident that he is not a man." But the sense shall be good and weighty, the language correct and dignified, the subject interesting and treated with feeling; and yet the style shall, notwithstanding all these merits, be justly blameable as prosaic, and solely because the words and the order of the words would find their appropriate place in prose, but are not suitable to metrical composition. The *Civil Wars* of Daniel is an instructive, and even interesting work : but take the following stanzas (and from the hundred instances which abound I might probably have selected others far more striking):

> And to the end we may with better ease
> Discern the true discourse, vouchsafe to shew
> What were the times foregoing near to these,
> That these we may with better profit know.
> Tell how the world fell into this disease;
> And how so great distempertaure did grow;
> So shall we see with what degrees it came;
> How things at full do soon wax out of frame.
>
> Ten kings had from the Norman conqu'ror reign'd
> With intermixt and variable fate,
> When England to her greatest height attain'd
> Of power, dominion, glory, wealth, and state;
> After it had with much ado sustain'd
> The violence of princes with debate
> For titles, and the often mutinies
> Of nobles for their ancient liberties.
>
> For first the Norman, conqu'ring all by might,
> By might was forced to keep what he had got;
> Mixing our customs and the form of right
> With foreign constitutions, he had brought;
> Mastering the mighty, humbling the poorer wight,
> By all severest means that could be wrought;
> And making the succession doubtful, rent
> His new-got state and left it turbulent.
>
> Book I, stanzas 7, 8, 9.

Will it be contended, on the one side, that these lines are mean and senseless ?   Or on the other, that they are not prosaic, and for that reason unpoetic ?   This poet's well-merited epithet is that of the "well-languaged Daniel"; but likewise and by the consent of his contemporaries no less than of all succeeding critics, the "prosaic Daniel." Yet those, who thus designate this wise and amiable writer from the frequent incorrespondency of his diction to his metre in the majority of his compositions, not only deem them valuable and interesting on other accounts, but willingly admit that there are to be found throughout his poems, and especially in his *Epistles* and in his *Hymen's Triumph*, many and exquisite specimens of that style which, as the neutral ground of prose and verse, is common to both. A fine and almost faultless extract, eminent as for other beauties so for its perfection in this species of diction, may be seen in Lamb's *Dramatic Specimens, etc.*, a work of various interest from the nature of the selections themselves (all from the plays of Shakespeare's contemporaries), and deriving a high additional value from the notes, which are full of just and original criticism, expressed with all the freshness of originality.

Among the possible effects of practical adherence to a theory that aims to identify the style of prose and verse (if it does not indeed claim for the latter a yet nearer resemblance to the average style of men in the *vivâ voce* intercourse of real life) we might anticipate the following as not the least likely to occur. It will happen, as I have indeed before observed, that the metre itself, the sole acknowledged difference, will occasionally become metre to the eye only. The existence of prosaisms, and that they detract from the merits of a poem, must at length be conceded, when a number of successive lines can be rendered, even to the most delicate ear, unrecognizable as verse, or as having even been intended for verse, by simply transcribing them as prose : when if the poem be in blank verse, this can be effected without any alteration, or at most by merely restoring one or two words to their proper places, from which they had been transplanted * for

---

* As the ingenious gentleman under the influence of the Tragic Muse contrived to dislocate, "I wish you a good morning, Sir! Thank you, Sir, and I wish you the same," into two blank-verse heroics :

> To you a morning good, good Sir! I wish,
> You, Sir! I thank: to you the same wish I.

In those parts of Mr. Wordsworth's works which I have thoroughly studied, I find fewer instances in which this would be practicable than I have met in

no assignable cause or reason but that of the author's convenience; but if it be in rhyme, by the mere exchange of the final word of each line for some other of the same meaning, equally appropriate, dignified and euphonic.

The answer or objection in the preface to the anticipated remark "that metre paves the way to other distinctions," is contained in the following words : — "The distinction of rhyme and metre is voluntary and uniform, and not like that produced by (what is called) poetic diction, arbitrary and subject to infinite caprices, upon which no calculation whatever can be made. In the one case the reader is utterly at the mercy of the poet respecting what imagery or diction he may choose to connect with the passion." But is this a poet, of whom a poet is speaking? No, surely — rather of a fool or madman, or at best of a vain or ignorant phantast! And might not brains so wild and so deficient make just the same havoc with rhymes and metres as they are supposed to effect with modes and figures of speech? How is the reader at the mercy of such men? If he continue to read their nonsense, is it not his own fault ? The ultimate end of criticism is much more to establish the principles of writing than to furnish rules how to

many poems, where an approximation of prose has been sedulously and on system guarded against. Indeed, excepting the stanzas already quoted from the *Sailor's Mother*, I can recollect but one instance : *viz.* a short passage of four or five lines in the *Brothers*, that model of English pastoral, which I never yet read with unclouded eye. " James, pointing to its summit, over which they had all purposed to return together, informed them that he would wait for them there. They parted, and his comrades passed that way some two hours after, but they did not find him at the appointed place, *a circumstance of which they took no heed :* but one of them going by chance into the house, which at this time was James's house, learnt there that nobody had seen him all that day." The only change which has been made is in the position of the little word " there " in two instances, the position in the original being clearly such as is not adopted in ordinary conversation. The other words printed in italics were so marked because, though good and genuine English, they are not the phraseology of common conversation either in the word put in apposition, or in the connection by the genitive pronoun. Men in general would have said, " but that was a circumstance they paid no attention to, or took no notice of," and the language is, on the theory of the preface, justified only by the narrator's being the Vicar. Yet if any ear could suspect that these sentences were ever printed as metre, on those very words alone could the suspicion have been grounded.

pass judgment on what has been written by others; if indeed it were possible that the two could be separated. But if it be asked, by what principles the poet is to regulate his own style, if he do not adhere closely to the sort and order of words which he hears in the market, wake, high-road, or plough-field? I reply, by principles, the ignorance or neglect of which would convict him of being no poet, but a silly or presumptuous usurper of the name! By the principles of grammar, logic, psychology! In one word, by such a knowledge of the facts, material and spiritual, that most appertain to his art, as, if it have been governed and applied by good sense, and rendered instinctive by habit, becomes the representative and reward of our past conscious reasonings, insights, and conclusions, and acquires the name of taste. By what rule that does not leave the reader at the poet's mercy, and the poet at his own, is the latter to distinguish between the language suitable to suppressed, and the language which is characteristic of indulged, anger? Or between that of rage and that of jealousy? Is it obtained by wandering about in search of angry or jealous people in uncultivated society, in order to copy their words? Or not far rather by the power of imagination proceeding upon the all in each of human nature? By meditation, rather than by observation? And by the latter in consequence only of the former? As eyes, for which the former has predetermined their field of vision, and to which, as to its organ, it communicates a microscopic power? There is not, I firmly believe, a man now living, who has from his own inward experience a clearer intuition than Mr. Wordsworth himself, that the last mentioned are the true sources of genial discrimination. Through the same process and by the same creative agency will the poet distinguish the degree and kind of the excitement produced by the very act of poetic composition. As intuitively will he know, what differences of style it at once inspires and justifies; what intermixture of conscious volition is natural to that state; and in what instances such figures and colours of speech degenerate into mere creatures of an arbitrary purpose, cold technical artifices of ornament or connection. For even as truth is its own light and evidence, discovering at once itself and falsehood, so is it the prerogative of poetic genius to distinguish by parental instinct its proper offspring from the changelings, which the gnomes of vanity or the fairies of fashion may have laid in its cradle or called by its names. Could a rule be given from without, poetry would cease to be poetry, and sink into a mechanical art. It would be μόρφωσις not ποίησις. The rules of the imagination are themselves the very powers of growth and production. The words, to which they are reducible, present only the outlines and external appearance of the fruit. A deceptive counterfeit of the superficial form and colours may be elaborated ; but the marble peach feels cold and heavy, and children only put it to their mouths. We find no difficulty in admitting as excellent, and the legitimate language of poetic fervour self-impassioned, Donne's apostrophe to the Sun in the second stanza of his *Progress of the Soul :*

> Thee, eye of heaven ! this great soul envies not:
> By thy male force is all we have begot.
> In the first East thou now beginn'st to shine,
> Suck'st early balm and island spices there;
> And wilt anon in thy loose-rein'd career
> At Tagus, Po, Seine, Thames, and Danow dine,
> And see at night this western world of mine:
> Yet hast thou not more nations seen than she,
> Who before thee one day began to be,
> And thy frail light being quenched, shall long, long outlive thee.

Or the next stanza but one :

> Great Destiny, the commissary of God,
> That hast marked out a path and period
> For ev'ry thing ! Who, where we offspring took,
> Our ways and ends see'st at one instant: thou
> Knot of all causes ! Thou, whose changeless brow
> Ne'er smiles or frowns ! O ! vouchsafe thou to look,
> And shew my story in thy eternal book,
>   etc.

As little difficulty do we find in excluding from the honours of unaffected warmth and elevation the madness prepense of pseudo-poesy, or the startling hysteric of weakness over-exerting itself, which bursts on the unprepared reader in sundry odes and apostrophes to abstract terms. Such are the Odes to Jealousy, to Hope, to Oblivion, and the like, in Dodsley's Collection and the magazines of that day, which seldom fail to remind me of an Oxford copy of verses on the Two Suttons, commencing with :

> Inoculation, heavenly maid ! descend !

It is not to be denied that men of undoubted talents, and even poets of true though not of first-rate genius, have, from a mistaken theory, deluded both themselves and others in the opposite extreme. I once read to a company of sensible and well-educated women the introductory period of Cowley's preface to his Pindaric odes, written in imitation of the style and manner of the odes of Pindar. "If," says Cowley, " a man should undertake to translate Pindar, word for word, it would be thought that one madman had translated another ; as may appear when he that understands not the original reads the verbal traduction of him into Latin prose, than which nothing seems more raving." I then proceeded with his own free version of the second Olympic, composed for the charitable purpose of rationalizing the Theban Eagle :

> Queen of all harmonious things,
> Dancing words and speaking strings,
> What God, what hero wilt thou sing?
> What happy man to equal glories bring?
> Begin, begin thy noble choice,
> And let the hills around reflect the image of thy voice.
> Pisa does to Jove belong,
> Jove and Pisa claim thy song.
> The fair first-fruits of war, th' Olympic games,
> Alcides offer'd up to Jove ;
> Alcides too thy strings may move !
> But oh ! what man to join with these can worthy prove?
> Join Theron boldly to their sacred names ;
> Theron the next honour claims ;
> Theron to no man gives place ;
> Is first in Pisa's and in Virtue's race ;
> Theron there, and he alone,
> Ev'n his own swift forefathers has outgone.

One of the company exclaimed, with the full assent of the rest, that if the original were madder than this, it must be incurably mad. I then translated the ode from the Greek, and as nearly as possible word for word ; and the impression was, that in the general movement of the periods, in the form of the connections and transitions, and in the sober majesty of lofty sense, it appeared to them to approach more nearly than any other poetry they had heard to the style of our Bible in the prophetic books. The first strophe will suffice as a specimen :

Ye harp-controlling hymns ! (or) ye hymns the sovereigns of harps !
What God ? what Hero ?
What Man shall we celebrate ?
Truly Pisa indeed is of Jove.
But the Olympiad (or the Olympic games) did Hercules establish,
The first-fruits of the spoils of war.
But Theron for the four-horsed car,
That bore victory to him,
It behoves us now to voice aloud :
The Just, the Hospitable,
The Bulwark of Agrigentum,
Of renowned fathers
The Flower, even him
Who preserves his native city erect and safe.

But are such rhetorical caprices condemnable only for their deviation from the language of real life ? and are they by no other means to be precluded, but by the rejection of all distinctions between prose and verse, save that of metre ? Surely, good sense and a moderate insight into the constitution of the human mind would be amply sufficient to prove that such language and such combinations are the native produce neither of the fancy nor of the imagination; that their operation consists in the excitement of surprise by the juxtaposition and apparent reconciliation of widely different or incompatible things. As when, for instance, the hills are made to reflect the image of a voice. Surely no unusual taste is requisite to see clearly that this compulsory juxtaposition is not produced by the presentation of impressive or delightful forms to the inward vision, nor by any sympathy with the modifying powers with which the genius of the poet had united and inspirited all the objects of his thought; that it is therefore a species of wit, a pure work of the will, and implies a leisure and self-possession both of thought and of feeling, incompatible with the steady fervour of a mind possessed and filled with the grandeur of its subject. To sum up the whole in one sentence : When a poem, or a part of a poem, shall be adduced, which is evidently vicious in the figures and contexture of its style, yet for the condemnation of which no reason can be assigned, except that it differs from the style in which men actually converse, then, and not till then, can I hold this theory to be either plausible or practicable, or capable of furnishing either rule, guidance, or precaution, that might not, more easily and more safely, as well as more naturally, have been deduced in the author's own mind from considerations of grammar, logic, and the truth and nature of things, confirmed by the authority of works whose fame is not of one country, nor of one age.

WORDSWORTH'S REAL OBJECT

It might appear from some passages in the former part of Mr. Wordsworth's preface, that he meant to confine his theory of style, and the necessity of a close accordance with the actual language of men, to those particular subjects from low and rustic life, which by way of experiment he had purposed to naturalize as a new species in our English poetry.   But from the train of argument that follows, from the reference to Milton, and from the spirit of his critique on Gray's *Sonnet*, those sentences appear to have been rather courtesies of modesty than actual limitations of his system. Yet so groundless does this system appear on a close examination, and so strange and overwhelming in its consequences, that I cannot, and I do not, believe that the poet did ever himself adopt it in the unqualified sense in which his expressions have been understood by others, and which indeed, according to all the common laws of interpretation, they seem to bear.   What then did he mean ?   I apprehend that, in the clear perception, not unaccompanied with disgust or contempt, of the gaudy affectations of a style which passed too current with too many for poetic diction (though, in truth, it had as little pretensions to poetry as to logic or common sense), he narrowed his view for the time ; and feeling a justifiable preference for the language of nature and of good sense, even in its humblest and least ornamented forms, he suffered himself to express, in terms at once too large and too exclusive, his predilection for a style the most remote possible from the false and showy splendour which he wished to explode. It is possible that this predilection, at first merely comparative, deviated for a time into direct partiality. But the real object which he had in view was, I doubt not, a species of excellence which had been long before most happily characterized by the judicious and amiable Garve, whose works are so justly beloved and esteemed by the Germans, in his remarks on Gellert, from which the following is literally translated : — " The talent that is required, in order to make excellent verses, is perhaps greater than the philosopher is ready to admit, or would find it in his power to acquire ; the talent to seek only the apt expression of the thought, and yet to find at the same time with it the rhyme and the metre. Gellert possessed this happy gift, if ever any one of our poets possessed it ; and nothing perhaps contributed more to the great and universal impression which his fables made on their first publication, or conduces more to their continued popularity. It was a strange and curious phenomenon, and such as in Germany had been previously unheard of, to read verses in which everything was expressed, just as one would wish to talk, and yet all dignified, attractive, and interesting ; and all at the same time perfectly correct as to the measure of the syllables and the rhyme. It is certain that poetry, when it has attained this excellence, makes a far greater impression than prose. So much so indeed, that even the gratification which the very rhymes afford, becomes then no longer a contemptible or trifling gratification."

However novel this phenomenon may have been in Germany at the time of Gellert, it is by no means new, nor yet of recent existence in our language. Spite of the licentiousness with which Spenser occasionally compels the orthography of his words into a subservience to his rhymes, the whole *Faëry Queen* is an almost continued instance of this beauty. Waller's song, " Go, lovely Rose," etc., is doubtless familiar to most of my readers ; but if I had happened to have had by me the poems of Cotton, more but far less deservedly celebrated as the author of the *Virgil Travestied*, I should have indulged myself, and I think have gratified many who are not acquainted with his serious works, by selecting some admirable specimens of this style. There are not a few poems in that volume, replete with every excellence of thought, image, and passion, which we expect or desire in the poetry of the milder muse, and yet so worded that the reader sees no one reason either in the selection or the order of the words why he might not have said the very same in an appropriate conversation, and cannot conceive how indeed he could have expressed such thoughts otherwise, without loss or injury to his meaning.

But in truth our language is, and from the first dawn of poetry ever has been, particularly rich in compositions distinguished by this excellence.

Examples, interesting in themselves, follow out of poets from Chaucer downwards through Herbert and others to Wordsworth himself. The thread may be taken up as follows. Coleridge has passed to the vindication of the *special* qualities of Wordsworth's style.

The words themselves in the foregoing extracts are, no doubt, sufficiently common for the greater part. (But in what poem are they not so ? if we except a few misadventurous attempts to translate the arts and sciences into verse ?) In *The Excursion* the number of polysyllabic (or what the common people call dictionary) words is more than usually great. And so must it needs be, in proportion to the number and variety of an author's conceptions, and his solicitude to express them with precision. But are those words in those places commonly employed in real life to express the same thought or outward thing ? Are they the style used in the ordinary intercourse of spoken words ? No; nor are the modes of connections : and still less the breaks and transitions. Would any but a poet—at least could any one without being conscious that he had expressed himself with noticeable vivacity—have described a bird singing loud by, "The thrush is *busy* in the wood" ? Or have spoken of boys with a string of club-moss round their rusty hats, as the boys "*with their green coronal*" ? Or have translated a beautiful May-day into "*Both earth and sky keep jubilee*" ? Or have brought all the different marks and circumstances of a sea-loch before the mind, as the actions of a living and acting power ? Or have represented the reflection of the sky in the water as, "*That uncertain heaven received into the bosom of the steady lake*" ? Even the grammatical construction is not unfrequently peculiar; as, "The wind, the tempest roaring high, the tumult of a tropic sky, might well be *dangerous food to him*, a youth to whom was given," etc. There is a peculiarity in the frequent use of the ἀσυνάρτητον (*i.e.*, the omission of the connective particle before the last of several words, or several sentences used grammatically as single words, all being in the same case and governing or governed by the same verb), and not less in the construction of words by apposition (*to him, a youth*). In short, were there excluded from Mr. Wordsworth's poetic compositions all that a literal adherence to the theory of his preface would exclude, two-thirds at least of the marked beauties of his poetry must be erased. For a far greater number of lines would be sacrificed than in any other recent poet; because the pleasure received from Wordsworth's poems being less derived either from excitement of curiosity or the rapid flow of narration, the striking passages form a larger proportion of their value. I do not adduce it as a fair criterion of comparative excellence, nor do I even think it such; but merely as matter of fact. I affirm, that from no contemporary writer could so many lines be quoted, without reference to the poem in which they are found, for their own independent weight or beauty. From the sphere of my own experience, I can bring to my recollection three persons, of no every-day powers and acquirements, who had read the poems of others with more and more unalloyed pleasure, and had thought more highly of their authors, as poets; who yet have confessed to me, that from no modern work had so many passages started up anew in their minds at different times, and as different occasions had awakened a meditative mood.

REMARKS ON THE PRESENT MODE OF CONDUCTING CRITICAL JOURNALS

(I have been in two minds as to the inclusion of this chapter. It is measurably on a lower level than its context. But it is valuable and true.)

Long have I wished to see a fair and philosophical inquisition into the character of Wordsworth, as a poet, on the evidence of his published works; and a positive, not a comparative, appreciation of

their characteristic excellences, deficiencies, and defects. I know
no claim that the mere opinion of any individual can have to weigh
down the opinion of the author himself; against the probability of
whose parental partiality we ought to set that of his having thought
longer and more deeply on the subject. But I should call that
investigation fair and philosophical, in which the critic announces
and endeavours to establish the principles, which he holds for the
foundation of poetry in general, with the specification of these in
their application to the different *classes* of poetry. Having thus
prepared his canons of criticism for praise and condemnation, we
would proceed to particularize the most striking passages to which
he deems them applicable, faithfully noticing the frequent or
infrequent recurrence of similar merits or defects, and as faithfully
distinguishing what is characteristic from what is accidental, or a
mere flagging of the wing. Then if his premises be rational, his
deductions legitimate, and his conclusions justly applied, the reader,
and possibly the poet himself, may adopt his judgment in the light
of judgment and in the independence of free agency. If he has
erred, he presents his errors in a definite place and tangible form,
and holds the torch and guides the way to their detection.

I most willingly admit, and estimate at a high value, the services
which the *Edinburgh Review*, and others formed afterwards on the
same plan, have rendered to society in the diffusion of knowledge.
I think the commencement of the *Edinburgh Review* an important
epoch in periodical criticism; and that it has a claim upon the
gratitude of the literary republic, and indeed of the reading public
at large, for having originated the scheme of reviewing those books
only, which are susceptible and deserving of argumentative criticism. Not less meritorious, and far more faithfully and in general
far more ably executed, is their plan of supplying the vacant place
of the trash or mediocrity wisely left to sink into oblivion by their
own weight, with original essays on the most interesting subjects of
the time, religious or political; in which the titles of the books or
pamphlets prefixed furnish only the name and occasion of the disquisition. I do not arraign the keenness or asperity of its damna-
tory style, in and for itself, as long as the author is addressed or
treated as the mere impersonation of the work then under trial. I

have no quarrel with them on this account, as long as no personal allusions are admitted, and no recommitment (for new trial) of juvenile performances, that were published, perhaps forgotten, many years before the commencement of the review : since for the forcing back of such works to public notice no motives are easily assignable, but such as are furnished to the critic by his own personal malignity; or what is still worse, by a habit of malignity in the form of mere wantonness.

> No private grudge they need, no personal spite :
> The *viva sectio* is its own delight !
> All enmity, all envy, they disclaim,
> Disinterested thieves of our good name ;
> Cool, sober murderers of their neighbour's fame !
>
> S. T. C.

Every censure, every sarcasm respecting a publication which the critic, with the criticised work before him, can make good, is the critic's right. The writer is authorized to reply, but not to complain. Neither can any one prescribe to the critic how soft or how hard, how friendly or how bitter, shall be the phrases which he is to select for the expression of such reprehension or ridicule. The critic must know what effect it is his object to produce ; and with a view to this effect must he weigh his words. But as soon as the critic betrays that he knows more of his author than the author's publications could have told him, as soon as from this more intimate knowledge, elsewhere obtained, he avails himself of the slightest trait *against* the author, his censure instantly becomes personal injury, his sarcasms personal insults. He ceases to be a critic, and takes on him the most contemptible character to which a rational creature can be degraded, that of a gossip, backbiter, and pasquillant : but with this heavy aggravation, that he steals the unquiet, the deforming passions of the world, into the museum ; into the very place which, next to the chapel and oratory, should be our sanctuary, and secure place of refuge ; offers abominations on the altar of the Muses ; and makes its sacred paling the very circle in which he conjures up the lying and profane spirit.

This determination of unlicensed personality, and of permitted and legitimate censure (which I owe in part to the illustrious

Lessing, himself a model of acute, spirited, sometimes stinging, but always argumentative and honourable criticism) is, beyond controversy, the true one; and though I would not myself exercise all the rights of the latter, yet, let but the former be excluded, I submit myself to its exercise in the hands of others, without complaint and without resentment.

Let a communication be formed between any number of learned men in the various branches of science and literature; and whether the president or central committee be in London, or Edinburgh, if only they previously lay aside their individuality, and pledge themselves inwardly, as well as ostensibly, to administer judgment according to a constitution and code of laws; and if by grounding this code on the two-fold basis of universal morals and philosophic reason, independent of all foreseen application to particular works and authors, they obtain the right to speak each as the representative of their body corporate; they shall have honour and good wishes from me, and I shall accord to them their fair dignities, though self-assumed, not less cheerfully than if I could enquire concerning them in the herald's office, or turn to them in the book of peerage. However loud may be the outcries for prevented or subverted reputation, however numerous and impatient the complaints of merciless severity and insupportable despotism, I shall neither feel nor utter aught but to the defence and justification of the critical machine. Should any literary Quixote find himself provoked by its sounds and regular movements, I should admonish him, with Sancho Panza, that it is no giant, but a windmill; there it stands on its own place and its own hillock, never goes out of the way to attack any one, and to none, and from none, either gives or asks assistance. When the public press has poured in any part of its produce between its mill-stones, it grinds it off, one man's sack the same as another, and with whatever wind may then happen to be blowing. All the two-and-thirty winds are alike its friends. Of the whole wide atmosphere, it does not desire a single fingerbreadth more than what is necessary for its sails to turn round in. But this space must be left free and unimpeded. Gnats, beetles, wasps, butterflies, and the whole tribe of ephemerals and insignificants, may flit in and out and between; may hum, and buzz, and jar; may shrill their tiny pipes, and wind their puny horns, unchastised and unnoticed. But idlers and bravados of larger size and prouder show must beware how they place themselves within its sweep. Much less may they presume to lay hands on the sails, the strength of which is neither greater or less than as the wind is which drives them round. Whomsoever the remorseless arm slings aloft, or whirls along with it in the air, he has himself alone to blame; though when the same arm throws him from it, it will more often double than break the force of his fall.

Putting aside the too manifest and too frequent interference of national, party, and even personal predilection or aversion, and reserving for deeper feelings those worse and more criminal intrusions into the sacredness of private life, which not seldom merit legal rather than literary chastisement, the two principal objects and occasions which I find for blame and regret in the conduct of the review in question are, first, its unfaithfulness to its own announced and excellent plan, by subjecting to criticism works neither indecent or immoral, yet of such trifling importance even in point of size, and, according to the critic's own verdict, so devoid of all merit, as must excite in the most candid mind the suspicion either that dislike or vindictive feelings were at work; or that there was a cold prudential predetermination to increase the sale of the *Review* by flattering the malignant passions of human nature. That I may not myself become subject to the charge, which I am bringing against others, by an accusation without proof, I refer to the article on Dr. Rennell's sermon in the very first number of the *Edinburgh Review* as an illustration of my meaning. If in looking through all the succeeding volumes the reader should find this a solitary instance, I must submit to that painful forfeiture of esteem which awaits a groundless or exaggerated charge.

The second point of objection belongs to this review only in common with all other works of periodical criticism; at least, it applies in common to the general system of all, whatever exception there may be in favour of particular articles. Or if it attaches to the *Edinburgh Review*, and to its only co-rival, the *Quarterly*, with any peculiar force, this results from the superiority of talent, acquirement, and information which both have so undeniably displayed,

and which doubtless deepens the regret though not the blame.   I
am referring to the substitution of assertion for argument; to the
frequency of arbitrary and sometimes petulant verdicts, not seldom
unsupported even by a single quotation from the work condemned,
which might at least have explained the critic's meaning, if it did
not prove the justice of his sentence.   Even where this is not the
case, the extracts are too often made without reference to any general
grounds or rules from which the faultiness or inadmissibility of the
qualities attributed may be deduced, and without any attempt to
show that the qualities are attributable to the passage extracted.   I
have met with such extracts from Mr. Wordsworth's poems, annexed
to such assertions, as lead me to imagine that the reviewer, having
written his critique before he had read the work, had then pricked
with a pin for passages wherewith to illustrate the various branches
of his preconceived opinions.   By what principle of rational choice
can we suppose a critic to have been directed (at least in a Christian
country, and himself, we hope, a Christian) who gives the following lines, portraying the fervour of solitary devotion excited by
the magnificent display of the Almighty's works, as a proof and
example of an author's tendency to downright ravings, and absolute
unintelligibility ?

> O then what soul was his, when on the tops
> Of the high mountains he beheld the sun
> Rise up, and bathe the world in light!   He looked —
> Ocean and earth, the solid frame of earth,
> And ocean's liquid mass, beneath him lay
> In gladness and deep joy.   The clouds were touched,
> And in their silent faces did he read
> Unutterable love!   Sound needed none,
> Nor any voice of joy: his spirit drank
> The spectacle!   sensation, soul, and form,
> All melted into him.   They swallowed up
> His animal being: in them did he live,
> And by them did he live: they were his life.
>
> *The Excursion.*

Can it be expected that either the author or his admirers
should be induced to pay any serious attention to decisions which
prove nothing but the pitiable state of the critic's own taste and

sensibility? On opening the *Review* they see a favourite passage, of the force and truth of which they had an intuitive certainty in their own inward experience, confirmed, if confirmation it could receive, by the sympathy of their most enlightened friends, some of whom perhaps, even in the world's opinion, hold a higher intellectual rank than the critic himself would presume to claim. And this very passage they find selected as the characteristic effusion of a mind deserted by reason; as furnishing evidence that the writer was raving, or he could not have thus strung words together without sense or purpose! No diversity of taste seems capable of explaining such a contrast in judgment.

That I had overrated the merit of a passage or poem, that I had erred concerning the degree of its excellence, I might be easily induced to believe or apprehend. But that lines, the sense of which I had analyzed and found consonant with all the best convictions of my understanding, and the imagery and diction of which had collected round those convictions my noblest as well as my most delightful feelings; that I should admit such lines to be mere nonsense or lunacy, is too much for the most ingenious arguments to effect. But that such a revolution of taste should be brought about by a few broad assertions, seems little less than impossible. On the contrary, it would require an effort of charity not to dismiss the criticism with the aphorism of the wise man, *in animam malevolam sapientia haud intrare potest.*

What then if this very critic should have cited a large number of single lines, and even of long paragraphs, which he himself acknowledges to possess eminent and original beauty? What if he himself has owned that beauties as great are scattered in abundance throughout the whole book? And yet, though under this impression, should have commenced his critique in vulgar exaltation with a prophecy meant to secure its own fulfilment? With a " This won't do!" What if after such acknowledgments, extorted from his own judgment, he should proceed from charge to charge of tameness and raving, flights and flatness; and at length, consigning the author to the house of incurables, should conclude with a strain of rudest contempt, evidently grounded in the distempered state of his own moral associations? Suppose, too, all this done without a single leading principle established or even announced, and without any one attempt at argumentative deduction, though the poet had presented a more than usual opportunity for it, by having previously made public his own principles of judgment in poetry, and supported them by a connected train of reasoning!

The office and duty of the poet is to select the most dignified as well as

The gayest, happiest attitude of things.

The reverse, for in all cases a reverse is possible, is the appropriate business of burlesque and travesty, a predominant taste for which has been always deemed a mark of a low and degraded mind. When I was at Rome, among many other visits to the tomb of Julius II, I went thither once with a Prussian artist, a man of genius and great vivacity of feeling. As we were gazing on Michael Angelo's Moses, our conversation turned on the horns and beard of that stupendous statue; on the necessity of each to support the other; on the superhuman effect of the former, and the necessity of the existence of both to give a harmony and integrity both to the image and the feeling excited by it. Conceive them removed, and the statue would become *un*-natural, without being *super*-natural. We called to mind the horns of the rising sun, and I repeated the noble passage from Taylor's *Holy Dying*. That horns were the emblem of power and sovereignty among the Eastern nations, and are still retained as such in Abyssinia; the Achelous of the ancient Greeks; and the probable ideas and feelings that originally suggested the mixture of the human and the brute form in the figure by which they realized the idea of their mysterious Pan, as representing intelligence blended with a darker power, deeper, mightier, and more universal than the conscious intellect of man, than intelligence; all these thoughts and recollections passed in procession before our minds. My companion, who possessed more than his share of the hatred which his countrymen bore to the French, had just observed to me, "A Frenchman, sir, is the only animal in the human shape that by no possibility can lift itself up to religion or poetry"; when, lo! two French officers of distinction and rank entered the church! "Mark you," whispered the Prussian, "the first thing which those scoundrels will notice (for they will begin by instantly noticing the statue in parts, without one moment's pause of admiration impressed by the whole) will be the horns and the beard. And the associations which they will immediately connect with them will be those of a he-goat and a cuckold." Never did man guess more luckily. Had he inherited a portion of the great legislator's prophetic powers, whose statue we had been contemplating, he could scarcely have uttered words more coincident with the result; for even as he had said, so it came to pass.

In *The Excursion* the poet has introduced an old man, born in humble but not abject circumstances, who had enjoyed more than usual advantages of education, both from books and from the more awful discipline of nature. This person he represents as having been driven by the restlessness of fervid feelings and from a craving intellect to an itinerant life, and as having, in consequence, passed the larger portion of his time, from earliest manhood, in villages and hamlets from door to door :

> A vagrant merchant bent beneath his load.

Now whether this be a character appropriate to a lofty didactic poem, is perhaps questionable. It presents a fair subject for controversy ; and the question is to be determined by the congruity or incongruity of such a character with what shall be proved to be the essential constituents of poetry. But surely the critic who, passing by all the opportunities which such a mode of life would present to such a man; all the advantages of the liberty of nature, of solitude, and of solitary thought; all the varieties of places and seasons, through which his track had lain, with all the varying imagery they bring with them ; and lastly, all the observations of men,

> Their manners, their enjoyments and pursuits,
> Their passions and their feelings,

which the memory of these yearly journeys must have given and recalled to such a mind — the critic, I say, who from the multitude of possible associations should pass by all these in order to fix his attention exclusively on the pin-papers, and stay-tapes, which might have been among the wares of his pack : this critic, in my opinion, cannot be thought to possess a much higher or much healthier state of moral feeling than the Frenchman above recorded.

WORDSWORTH'S POETRY, ITS DEFECTS AND BEAUTIES — THE FORMER FOR THE MOST PART CHARACTERISTIC OF HIS THEORY ONLY

(The long and interesting twenty-second chapter contains a thorough examination of Wordsworth, from which the most remarkable parts are here sifted out.)

If Mr. Wordsworth has set forth principles of poetry which his arguments are insufficient to support, let him and those who have adopted his sentiments be set right by the confutation of those arguments, and by the substitution of more philosophical principles. And still let the due credit be given to the portion and importance of the truths which are blended with his theory : truths, the too exclusive attention to which had occasioned its errors, by tempting him to carry those truths beyond their proper limits. If his mistaken theory has at all influenced his poetic compositions, let the effects be pointed out, and the instances given. But let it likewise be shown how far the influence has acted; whether diffusively, or only by starts; whether the number and importance of the poems and passages thus infected be great or trifling compared with the sound portion; and lastly, whether they are inwoven into the texture of his works, or are loose and separable. The result of such a trial would evince beyond a doubt, what it is high time to announce decisively and aloud, that the supposed characteristics of Mr. Wordsworth's poetry, whether admired or reprobated; whether they are simplicity or simpleness; faithful adherence to essential nature, or wilful selections from human nature of its meanest forms and under the least attractive associations : are as little the real characteristics of his poetry at large, as of his genius and the constitution of his mind.

In a comparatively small number of poems, he chose to try an experiment; and this experiment we will suppose to have failed. Yet even in these poems it is impossible not to perceive that the natural tendency of the poet's mind is to great objects and elevated conceptions. The poem entitled *Fidelity* is for the greater part written in language as unraised and naked as any perhaps in the two volumes. Yet take the following stanza and compare it with the preceding stanzas of the same poem:

> There sometimes does a leaping fish
> Send through the tarn a lonely cheer;
> The crags repeat the raven's croak
> In symphony austere;
> Thither the rainbow comes — the cloud,
> And mists that spread the flying shroud;
> And sunbeams; and the sounding blast,
> That if it could would hurry past,
> But that enormous barrier holds it fast.

Or compare the four last lines of the concluding stanza with the former half:

> Yet proof was plain that since the day
> On which the traveller thus had died,
> The dog had watched about the spot,
> Or by his master's side:
> *How nourished there for such long time*
> *He knows who gave that love sublime,*
> *And gave that strength of feeling, great*
> *Above all human estimate.*

Can any candid and intelligent mind hesitate in determining which of these best represents the tendency and native character of the poet's genius? Will he not decide that the one was written because the poet would so write, and the other because he could not so entirely repress the force and grandeur of his mind, but that he must in some part or other of every composition write otherwise? In short, that his only disease is the being out of his element; like the swan, that having amused himself, for a while, with crushing the weeds on the river's bank, soon returns to his own majestic movements on its reflecting and sustaining surface.

. . . .

The first characteristic, though only occasional defect, which I appear to myself to find in these poems is the inconstancy of the style. Under this name I refer to the sudden and unprepared transitions from lines or sentences of peculiar felicity (at all events striking and original) to a style, not only unimpassioned but undistinguished. He sinks too often and too abruptly to that style which I should place in the second division of language, dividing it into the three species : first, that which is peculiar to poetry; second, that which is only proper in prose; and third, the neutral or com-mon to both.   There have been works, such as Cowley's *Essay on Cromwell*, in which prose and verse are intermixed (not as in the *Consolation* of Boetius, or the *Argenis* of Barclay, by the insertion of poems supposed to have been spoken or composed on occasions previously related in prose, but) the poet passing from one to the other as the nature of the thoughts or his own feelings dictated. Yet this mode of composition does not satisfy a cultivated taste. There is something unpleasant in the being thus obliged to alternate states of feeling so dissimilar, and this too in a species of writing, the pleasure from which is in part derived from the preparation and previous expectation of the reader.   A portion of that awkwardness is felt which hangs upon the introduction of songs in our modern comic operas; and to prevent which the judicious Metastasio (as to whose exquisite taste there can be no hesitation, whatever doubts may be entertained as to his poetic genius) uniformly placed the *aria* at the end of the scene, at the same time that he almost always raises and impassions the style of the recitative immediately pre-ceding.   Even in real life, the difference is great and evident between words used as the arbitrary marks of thought, our smooth market-coin of intercourse with the image and superscription worn out by currency, and those which convey pictures either borrowed from one outward object to enliven and particularize some other ; or used allegorically to body forth the inward state of the person speaking; or such as are at least the exponents of his peculiar turn and unusual extent of faculty.   So much so, indeed, that in the social circles of private life we often find a striking use of the latter put a stop to the general flow of conversation, and by the excite-ment arising from concentred attention produce a sort of damp and interruption for some minutes after.   But in the perusal of works of literary art, we prepare ourselves for such language; and the business of the writer, like that of a painter whose subject requires unusual splendour and prominence, is so to raise the lower and neutral tints, that what in a different style would be the command-ing colours, are here used as the means of that gentle degradation requisite in order to produce the effect of a whole.   Where this is not achieved in a poem, the metre merely reminds the reader of his claims in order to disappoint them; and where this defect occurs frequently, his feelings are alternately startled by anticlimax and hyperclimax.

Examples follow : *Resolution and Independence* being selected as " especially characteristic " both of Wordsworth's defects and of his excellences.

The second defect I could generalize with tolerable accuracy, if the reader will pardon an uncouth and new-coined word. There is, I should say, not seldom a *matter-of-factness* in certain poems. This may be divided into, first, a laborious minuteness and fidelity in the representation of objects, and their positions, as they appeared to the poet himself; secondly, the insertion of accidental circumstances, in order to the full explanation of his living characters, their dispositions and actions : which circumstances might be necessary to establish the probability of a statement in real life, where nothing is taken for granted by the hearer, but appear superfluous in poetry, where the reader is willing to believe for his own sake. To this accidentality, I object, as contravening the essence of poetry, which Aristotle pronounces to be σπουδαιότατον καὶ φιλοσοφώτατον γένος, the most intense, weighty, and philosophical product of human art; adding, as the reason, that it is the most catholic and abstract. The following passage from Davenant's prefatory letter to Hobbes well expresses this truth : " When I considered the actions which I meant to describe (those inferring the persons) I was again persuaded rather to choose those of a former age than the present; and in a century so far removed as might preserve me from their improper examinations, who know not the requisites of a poem, nor how much pleasure they lose (and even the pleasures of heroic poesy are not unprofitable) who take away the liberty of a poet, and fetter his feet in the shackles of an historian. For why should a poet doubt in story to mend the intrigues of fortune by more delightful conveyances of probable fictions, because austere historians have entered into bond to truth ? An obligation, which were in poets as foolish and unnecessary, as is the bondage of false martyrs, who lie in chains for a mistaken opinion. *But by this I would imply, that truth, narrative and past, is the idol of historians (who worship a dead thing) and truth operative, and by effects con-tinually alive, is the mistress of poets, who hath not her existence in matter, but in reason."*

Instances and discussion, chiefly from *The Excursion*, follow; and Cole-ridge meets Wordsworth full in the following.

Is there one word, for instance, attributed to the pedlar in *The Excursion*, characteristic of a pedlar? One sentiment, that might not more plausibly, even without the aid of any previous explana-tion, have proceeded from any wise and beneficent old man of a rank or profession in which the language of learning and refinement are naturally to be expected? Need the rank have been at all parti-cularized, where nothing follows which the knowledge of that rank is to explain or illustrate? When on the contrary this information renders the man's language, feelings, sentiments, and information a riddle, which must itself be solved by episodes of ancedote? Finally, when this and this alone, could have induced a genuine poet to inweave in a poem of the loftiest style, and on subjects the loftiest and of the most universal interest, such minute matters of fact, not unlike those furnished for the obituary of a magazine by the friends of some obscure " ornament of society lately deceased " in some obscure town, as

> Among the hills of Athol he was born.
> There on a small hereditary farm,
> An unproductive slip of rugged ground,
> His Father dwelt ; and died in poverty :
> While he, whose lowly fortune I retrace,
> The youngest of three sons, was yet a babe,
> A little one — unconscious of their loss.
> But ere he had outgrown his infant days
> His widowed mother, for a second mate,
> Espoused the teacher of the Village School;
> Who on her offspring zealously bestowed
> Needful instruction.
>
> From his sixth year, the Boy of whom I speak,
> In summer tended cattle on the hills ;
> But through the inclement and the perilous days
> Of long-continuing winter, he repaired
> To his step-father's school,

etc.

The Excursion Bk. I

For all the admirable passages interposed in this narration, might, with trifling alterations, have been far more appropriately, and with far greater verisimilitude, told of a poet in the character of a poet; and without incurring another defect which I shall now mention, and a sufficient illustration of which will have been here anticipated.

Third [*1, Inequality of style ; 2, Matter-of-factness*]; an undue predilection for the dramatic form in certain poems, from which one or other of two evils result. Either the thoughts and diction are different from that of the poet, and then there arises an incongruity of style; or they are the same and indistinguishable, and then it presents a species of ventriloquism, where two are represented as talking, while in truth one man only speaks.

The fourth class of defects is closely connected with the former; but yet are such as arise likewise from an intensity of feeling disproportionate to such knowledge and value of the objects described, as can be fairly anticipated of men in general, even of the most cultivated classes; and with which therefore few only, and those few particularly circumstanced, can be supposed to sympathize : in this class, I comprise occasional prolixity, repetition, and an eddying instead of progression of thought. As instances, see pages 27, 28, of the *Poems*, vol. i,* and the first eighty lines of the Sixth Book of *The Excursion*.

Fifth and last; thoughts and images too great for the subject. This is an approximation to what might be called mental bombast, as distinguished from verbal : for, as in the latter there is a disproportion of the expressions to the thoughts, so in this there is a disproportion of thought to the circumstance and occasion. This, by-the-by, is a fault of which none but a man of genius is capable. It is the awkwardness and strength of Hercules with the distaff of Omphale.

It is a well-known fact, that bright colours in motion both make and leave the strongest impressions on the eye. Nothing is more likely too, than that a vivid image or visual spectrum, thus originated, may become the link of association in recalling the feelings and images that had accompanied the original impression. But if we describe this in such lines, as

> They flash upon that inward eye,
> Which is the bliss of solitude !

* The *Anecdote for Fathers*.

in what words shall we describe the joy of retrospection, when the images and virtuous actions of a whole well-spent life, pass before that conscience which is indeed the inward eye : which is indeed "the bliss of solitude ? " Assuredly we seem to sink most abruptly, not to say burlesquely, and almost as in a medley, from this couplet to

> And then my heart with pleasure fills,
> And dances with the daffodils.
>
> Vol. i p. 320.*

.   .   .   .

To these defects which, as appears by the extracts, are only occasional, I may oppose with far less fear of encountering the dissent of any candid and intelligent reader, the following (for the most part correspondent) excellences. First, an austere purity of language both grammatically and logically ; in short a perfect appropriateness of the words to the meaning. Of how high value I deem this, and how particularly estimable I hold the example at the present day, has been already stated : and in part too the reasons on which I ground both the moral and intellectual importance of habituating ourselves to a strict accuracy of expression. It is noticeable, how limited an acquaintance with the masterpieces of art will suffice to form a correct and even a sensitive taste, where none but masterpieces have been seen and admired : while on the other hand, the most correct notions, and the widest acquaintance with the works of excellence of all ages and countries, will not perfectly secure us against the contagious familiarity with the far more numerous offspring of tastelessness or of a perverted taste. If this be the case, as it notoriously is, with the arts of music and painting, much more difficult will it be, to avoid the infection of multiplied and daily examples in the practice of an art, which uses words, and words only, as its instruments. In poetry, in which every line, every phrase, may pass the ordeal of deliberation and deliberate choice, it is possible, and barely possible, to attain that *ultimatum* which

---

* The poem commencing " I wandered lonely as a cloud." [Here Coleridge may be thought to be hypercritical. Some who are by no means Wordsworthians see no burlesque, but a real Shakespearean poetry, here. Something of a cavil, too, follows at *The Ode*. It may be not uncharitably suspected that Coleridge felt his philosophic province invaded.]

I have ventured to propose as the infallible test of a blameless style, namely, its untranslatableness in words of the same language without injury to the meaning.

. . . .

The second characteristic excellence of Mr. Wordsworth's works is : a correspondent weight and sanity of the thoughts and sentiments, — won, not from books, but — from the poet's own meditative observation. They are fresh, and have the dew upon them. His muse, at least when in her strength of wing, and when she hovers aloft in her proper element,

> Makes audible a linked lay of truth,
> Of truth profound a sweet continuous lay,
> Not learnt, but native, her own natural notes !
>
> S. T. C.

Even throughout his smaller poems there is scarcely one, which is not rendered valuable by some just and original reflection.

. . . .

Both in respect of this and of the former excellence, Mr. Wordsworth strikingly resembles Samuel Daniel, one of the golden writers of our golden Elizabethan age, now most causelessly neglected : Samuel Daniel, whose diction bears no mark of time, no distinction of age, which has been, and as long as our language shall last will be, so far the language of the to-day and for ever, as that it is more intelligible to us, than the transitory fashions of our own particular age.   A similar praise is due to his sentiments.   No frequency of perusal can deprive them of their freshness.   For though they are brought into the full daylight of every reader's comprehension, yet are they drawn up from depths which few in any age are privileged to visit, into which few in any age have courage or inclination to descend. If Mr. Wordsworth is not equally with Daniel alike intelligible to all readers of average understanding in all passages of his works, the comparative difficulty does not arise from the greater impurity of the ore, but from the nature and uses of the metal.   A poem is not necessarily obscure, because it does not aim to be popular. It is enough, if a work be perspicuous to those for whom it is written, and

> Fit audience find, though few.

. . . .

Third (and wherein he soars far above Daniel) the sinewy strength and originality of single lines and paragraphs : the frequent *curiosa felicitas* of his diction, of which I need not here give specimens, having anticipated them in a preceding page. This beauty, and as eminently characteristic of Wordsworth's poetry, his rudest assailants have felt themselves compelled to acknowledge and admire.

Fourth : the perfect truth of nature in his images and descriptions as taken immediately from nature, and proving a long and genial intimacy with the very spirit which gives the physiognomic expression to all the works of nature. Like a green field reflected in a calm and perfectly transparent lake, the image is distinguished from the reality only by its greater softness and lustre. Like the moisture of the polish on a pebble, genius neither distorts nor false-colours its objects ; but on the contrary brings out many a vein and many a tint, which escape the eye of common observation, thus raising to the rank of gems what had been often kicked away by the hurrying foot of the traveller on the dusty highroad of custom.

. . . .

Fifth : a meditative pathos, a union of deep and subtle thought with sensibility; a sympathy with man as man; the sympathy indeed of a contemplator, rather than a fellow-sufferer or co-mate (*spectator, haud particeps*), but of a contemplator, from whose view no difference of rank conceals the sameness of the nature ; no injuries of wind or weather, of toil, or even of ignorance, wholly disguise the human face divine. The superscription and the image of the Creator still remain legible to him under the dark lines, with which guilt or calamity had cancelled or cross-barred it. Here the man and the poet lose and find themselves in each other, the one as glorified, the latter as substantiated. In this mild and philosophic pathos, Wordsworth appears to me without a compeer. Such he *is:* so he *writes.*

. . . .

Lastly, and preëminently, I challenge for this poet the gift of Imagination in the highest and strictest sense of the word. In the play of fancy, Wordsworth, to my feelings, is not always graceful, and sometimes recondite. The likeness is occasionally

too strange, or demands too peculiar a point of view, or is such
as appears the creature of predetermined research, rather than
spontaneous presentation. Indeed his fancy seldom displays itself
as mere and unmodified fancy. But in imaginative power, he
stands nearest of all modern writers to Shakespeare and Milton;
and yet in a kind perfectly unborrowed and his own. To employ
his own words, which are at once an instance and an illustration,
he does indeed to all thoughts and to all objects —

—— add the gleam,
The light that never was on sea or land,
The consecration, and the poet's dream.

Elegiac Stanzas on a Picture of Peele Castle.

The preceding criticism will not, I am aware, avail to overcome
the prejudices of those who have made it a business to attack and
ridicule Mr. Wordsworth's compositions.

Truth and prudence might be imaged as concentric circles. The
poet may perhaps have passed beyond the latter, but he has confined himself far within the bounds of the former, in designating
these critics, as too petulant to be passive to a genuine poet, and
too feeble to grapple with him ; — "men of palsied imaginations, in
whose minds all healthy action is languid ; — who therefore, feel
as the many direct them, or with the many are greedy after vicious
provocatives."

Let not Mr. Wordsworth be charged with having expressed himself too indignantly, till the wantonness and the systematic and
malignant perseverance of the aggressions have been taken into
fair consideration. I myself heard the commander-in-chief of this
unmanly warfare make a boast of his private admiration of Wordsworth's genius. I have heard him declare, that whoever came into
his room would probably find the *Lyrical Ballads* lying open on
his table, and that (speaking exclusively of those written by Mr.
Wordsworth himself) he could nearly repeat the whole of them by
heart. But a Review, in order to be a saleable article, must be
personal, sharp, and pointed : and, since then, the poet has made
himself, and with himself all who were, or were supposed to be,
his friends and admirers, the object of the critic's revenge — how ?

by having spoken of a work so conducted in the terms which it deserved! I once heard a clergymen in boots and buckskin avow, that he would cheat his own father in a horse. A moral system of a similar nature seems to have been adopted by too many anonymous critics. As we used to say at school, in reviewing they make believe being rogues : and he who complains is to be laughed at for his ignorance of the game. With the pen out of their hand they are honourable men. They exert indeed power (which is to that of the injured party who should attempt to expose their glaring perversions and mis-statements, as twenty to one) to write down, and (where the author's circumstances permit) to impoverish the man, whose learning and genius they themselves in private have repeatedly admitted. They knowingly strive to make it impossible for the man even to publish * any future work without exposing himself to all the wretchedness of debt and embarrassment. But this is all in their vocation : and bating what they do in their vocation, " who can say that black is the white of their eye ? "

So much for the detractors from Wordsworth's merits. On the other hand, much as I might wish for their fuller sympathy, I dare not flatter myself, that the freedom with which I have declared my opinions concerning both his theory and his defects, most of which are more or less connected with his theory either as cause or effect, will be satisfactory or pleasing to all the poet's admirers and advocates. More indiscriminate than mine their admiration may be : deeper and more sincere it cannot be. But I have advanced no opinion either for praise or censure, other than as texts introductory to the reasons which compel me to form it. Above all, I was fully convinced that such a criticism was not only wanted ; but that, if executed with adequate ability, it must conduce in no mean degree to Mr. Wordsworth's reputation. His fame belongs to another age, and can neither be accelerated nor retarded. How small the proportion of the defects are to the beauties, I have

---

* Not many months ago an eminent bookseller was asked what he thought of ———? The answer was : " I have heard his powers very highly spoken of by some of our first-rate men ; but I would not have a work of his if any one would give it me : for he is spoken but slightly of, or not at all, in the *Quarterly Review :* and the *Edinburgh*, you know, is decided to cut him up ! "

repeatedly declared; and that no one of them originates in deficiency of poetic genius. Had they been more and greater, I should still, as a friend to his literary character in the present age, consider an analytic display of them as pure gain; if only it removed, as surely to all reflecting minds even the foregoing analysis must have removed, the strange mistake so slightly grounded, yet so widely and industriously propagated, of Mr. Wordsworth's turn for simplicity! I am not half as much irritated by hearing his enemies abuse him for vulgarity of style, subject, and conception, as I am disgusted with the gilded side of the same meaning, as displayed by some affected admirers with whom he is, forsooth, "a sweet, simple poet!" and so natural, that little master Charles, and his younger sister, are so charmed with them, that they play at Goody Blake, or at Johnny and Betty Foy!

XXVIII

HAZLITT

ON CRITICISM [IN GENERAL]

(Hazlitt, one of the very greatest of English critics, had perhaps less *reading* in criticism than any other. His coincidences with older writers (as, for instance, that noted in the contrast of Pope and Crabbe below) are all the more interesting. It has not been possible, nor for the purpose of this book would it be strictly in place, to quote his numerous and wonderful appreciations of English writers freely; that just referred to is excepted because of its *general* outshot. There is an excellent collection of his main essays in *poetic* criticism of English — he is of no authority on any other language — edited by Mr. D. Nichol Smith (Edinburgh 1901). But he is everywhere "nothing if not critical.")

Criticism is an art that undergoes a great variety of changes, and aims at different objects at different times.

At first, it is generally satisfied to give an opinion whether a work is good or bad, and to quote a passage or two in support of this opinion ; afterwards, it is bound to assign the reasons of its decision and to analyze supposed beauties or defects with microscopic minuteness. A critic does nothing nowadays who does not try to torture the most obvious expression into a thousand meanings, and enter into a circuitous explanation of all that can be urged for or against its being in the best or worst style possible. His object indeed is not to do justice to his author, whom he treats with very little ceremony, but to do himself homage, and to show his acquaintance with all the topics and resources of criticism. If he recurs to the stipulated subject in the end, it is not till after he has exhausted his budget of general knowledge ; and he establishes his own claims first in an elaborate inaugural dissertation *de omni scibili et quibusdam aliis*, before he deigns to bring forward the pretensions of the original candidate for praise, who is only the second figure in the piece. We may sometimes see articles of this sort, in which no allusion whatever is made to the work under sentence of death, after the first announcement of the title-page; and I apprehend it would be a clear improvement on this species of nominal criticism to give stated periodical accounts of works that had never appeared at all, which would save the hapless author the mortification of writing, and his reviewer the trouble of reading them. If the real author is made of so little account by the modern critic, he is scarcely more an object of regard to the modern reader; and it must be confessed that after a dozen close-packed pages of subtle metaphysical distinction or solemn didactic declamation, in which the disembodied principles of all arts and sciences float before the imagination in undefined profusion, the eye turns with impatience and indifference to the imperfect embryo specimens of them, and the hopeless attempts to realize this splendid jargon in one poor work by one poor author, which is given up to summary execution with as little justice as pity. " As when a well-graced actor leaves the stage, men's eyes are idly bent on him that enters next "— so it is here. Whether this state of the press is not a serious abuse and a violent encroachment in the republic of letters is more than I shall pretend to determine. The truth is, that in the quantity of works that issue from the press, it is utterly impossible they should all be read by all sorts of people. There must be *tasters* for the public, who must have a discretionary power vested in them, for which it is difficult to make them properly accountable. Authors, in proportion to their numbers, become not formidable, but despicable. They would not be heard of or severed from the crowd without the critic's aid, and all complaints of ill-treatment are vain. He considers them as pensioners on his bounty for any pittance of praise, and in general sets them up as butts for his wit and spleen, or uses them as a stalking-horse to convey his own favourite notions and opinions, which he can do by this means without the possibility of censure or appeal. He looks upon his literary *protégé* (much as Peter Pounce looked upon Parson Adams) as a kind of humble companion or unnecessary interloper in the vehicle of fame, whom he has taken up purely to oblige him, and whom he may treat with neglect or insult, or set down in the common footpath whenever it suits his humour or convenience. He naturally grows arbitrary with the exercise of power. He by degrees wants to have a clear stage to himself, and would be thought to have purchased a monopoly of wit, learning, and wisdom —

> Assumes the rod, affects the God,
> And seems to shake the spheres.

Besides, something of this overbearing manner goes a great way with the public. They cannot exactly tell whether you are right or wrong; and if you state your difficulties or pay much deference to the sentiments of others, they will think you a very silly fellow or a mere pretender. A sweeping, unqualified assertion ends all controversy, and sets opinion at rest. A sharp, sententious, cavalier, dogmatical tone is therefore necessary, even in self-defence, to the office of a reviewer. If you do not deliver your oracles without hesitation, how are the world to receive them on trust and without enquiry? People read to have something to talk about, and "to seem to know that which they do not." Consequently, there cannot be too much dialectics and debatable matter, too much pomp and paradox, in a review. *To elevate and surprise* is the great rule for producing a dramatic or a critical effect. The more you startle the reader, the more he will be able to startle others with a succession of smart intellectual shocks. The most admired of our Reviews is saturated with this sort of electrical matter, which is regularly played off so as to produce a good deal of astonishment and a strong sensation in the public mind. The intrinsic merits of an author are a question of very subordinate consideration to the keeping up the character of the work and supplying the town with a sufficient number of grave or brilliant topics for the consumption of the next three months!

This decided and paramount tone in criticism is the growth of the present century, and was not at all the fashion in that calm, peaceable period when the *Monthly Review* bore "sole sovereign sway and masterdom" over all literary productions.[1]

·   ·   ·   ·   ·   ·   ·   ·   ·   ·   ·

[1] Hazlitt then gives an account of this 18th-century periodical.

Neither are we less removed at present from the dry and meagre mode of dissecting the skeletons of works, instead of transfusing their living principles, which prevailed in Dryden's Prefaces,* and in the criticisms written on the model of the French School about a century ago. A genuine criticism should, as I take it, reflect the colours, the light and shade, the soul and body of a work : here we have nothing but its superficial plan and elevation, as if a poem were a piece of formal architecture. We are told something of the plot or fable, of the moral, and of the observance or violation of the three unities of time, place, and action ; and perhaps a word or two is added on the dignity of the persons or the baldness of the style : but we no more know, after reading one of these complacent *tirades*, what the essence of the work is, what passion has been touched, or how skilfully, what tone and movement the author's mind imparts to his subject or receives from it, than if we had been reading a homily or a gazette. That is, we are left quite in the dark as to the feelings of pleasure or pain to be derived from the genius of the performance or the manner in which it appeals to the imagination : we know to a nicety how it squares with the threadbare rules of composition, not in the least how it affects the principles of taste. We know everything about the work, and nothing of it. The critic takes good care not to balk the reader's fancy by anticipating the effect which the author has aimed at producing. To be sure, the works so handled were often worthy of their commentators : they had the form of imagination without the life or power; and when any one had gone regularly through the number of acts into which they were divided, the measure in which they were written, or the story on which they were founded, there was little else to be said about them. It is curious to observe the effect which the *Paradise Lost* had on this class of critics, like throwing a tub to a whale : they could make nothing of it. " It was out of all plumb — not one of the angles at the four corners was a right angle ! " They did not seek for, nor would they much relish, the marrow of poetry it contained. Like polemics in religion, they had discarded the

---

* There are some splendid exceptions to this censure. His comparison between Ovid and Virgil and his character of Shakespeare are masterpieces of their kind.

essentials of fine writing for the outward form and points of controversy. They were at issue with Genius and Nature by what
route and in what garb they should enter the Temple of the Muses.
Accordingly we find that Dryden had no other way of satisfying
himself of the pretensions of Milton in the epic style but by translating his anomalous work into rhyme and dramatic dialogue. So
there are connoisseurs who give you the subject, the grouping, the
perspective, and all the mechanical circumstances of a picture,
but never say a word about the expression. The reason is, they see
the former, but not the latter.[1]

.   .   .   .

Some kinds of criticism are as much too insipid as others are
too pragmatical. It is not easy to combine point with solidity,
spirit with moderation and candour. Many persons see nothing
but beauties in a work, others nothing but defects. Those cloy you
with sweets, and are " the very milk of human kindness," flowing
on in a stream of luscious panegyrics ; these take delight in poison-
ing the sources of your satisfaction, and putting you out of conceit
with nearly every author that comes in their way. The first are
frequently actuated by personal friendship, the last by all the vir-
ulence of party spirit. Under the latter head would fall what may
be termed *political criticism*. The basis of this style of writing is a
caput mortuum of impotent spite and dulness till it is varnished
over with the slime of servility, and thrown into a state of unnatural
activity by the venom of the most rancorous bigotry. The eminent
professors in this grovelling department are at first merely out of
sorts with themselves, and vent their spleen in little interjections
and contortions of phrase, cry *Pish* at a lucky hit and *Hem* at a
fault, are smart on personal defects, and sneer at "Beauty out of
favour and on crutches," are thrown into an ague fit by hearing the
name of a rival, start back with horror at any approach to their
morbid pretensions like Justice Woodcock with his gouty limbs,
rifle the flowers of the Della Cruscan School, and give you in their
stead, as models of pleasing pastoral style, *Verses upon Anna* —
which you may see in the notes to the *Baviad* and *Mœviad*. All

---

[1] Hazlitt here digresses to *art*-criticism, of which he was himself no mean
practitioner.

this is like the fable of the *Kitten and the Leaves*. But when they get their brass collar on and shake their bells of office, they set up their backs like the Great Cat Rodilardus and pounce upon men and things. Woe to any little heedless reptile of an author that ventures across their path without a safe-conduct from the Board of Control. They snap him up at a mouthful, and sit licking their lips, stroking their whiskers, and rattling their bells over the imaginary fragments of their devoted prey, to the alarm and astonishment of the whole breed of literary, philosophical, and revolutionary vermin, that were naturalized in this country by a Prince of Orange and an Elector of Hanover a hundred years ago.* When one of these pampered, sleek, "demure-looking, spring-nailed, velvet-pawed, green-eyed" critics makes his King and Country parties to this sort of sport literary, you have not much chance of escaping out of his clutches in a whole skin. Treachery becomes a principle with them, and mischief a conscience, that is, a livelihood. They not only *damn* the work in the lump, but vilify and traduce the author, and substitute lying abuse and sheer malignity for sense and satire. To have written a popular work is as much as a man's character is worth, and sometimes his life, if he does not happen to be on the right side of the question. The way in which they set about *stultifying* an adversary is not to accuse you of faults, or to exaggerate those which you may really have, but they deny that you have any merits at all, least of all those that the world have given you credit for ; bless themselves from understanding a single sentence in a whole volume ; and unless you are ready to subscribe to all their articles of peace will not allow you to be qualified to write your own name. It is not a question of literary discussion but of political proscription. It is a mark of loyalty and patriotism to extend no quarter to those of the opposite party. Instead of replying to your arguments, they call you names, put words and opinions into your mouth which you have never uttered, and consider it a species of misprision of treason to admit that a Whig author knows anything of common-sense or English. The only chance of putting a stop to this unfair mode of dealing would perhaps be to make a

---

* The intelligent reader will be pleased to understand that there is here a tacit allusion to Squire Western's significant phrase of *Hanover Rats*.

few reprisals by way of example.   The Court party boast some writers who have a reputation to lose, and who would not like to have
their names dragged through the kennel of dirty abuse and vulgar
obloquy.   What silenced the masked battery of *Blackwood's Magazine* was the implication of the name of Sir Walter Scott in some
remarks upon it — an honour of which it seems that extraordinary person was not ambitious : to be " pilloried on infamy's high
stage " was a distinction and an amusement to the other gentlemen concerned in that praiseworthy publication.   I was com-
plaining not long ago of this prostitution of literary criticism
as peculiar to our own times, when I was told that it was just as
bad in the time of Pope and Dryden, and indeed worse, inasmuch
as we have no Popes or Drydens now on the obnoxious side to
be nicknamed, metamorphosed into scarecrows, and impaled alive
by bigots and dunces.   I shall not pretend to say how far this
remark may be true.   The English (it must be owned) are rather
a foul-mouthed nation.

Besides temporary or accidental biases of this kind, there seem to
be sects and parties in taste and criticism (with a set of appropriate
watchwords) coeval with the arts of composition, and that will last
as long as the difference with which men's minds are originally
constituted.   There are some who are all for the elegance of an
author's style, and some who are equally delighted with simplicity.
The last refer you to Swift as a model of English prose, thinking
all other writers sophisticated and naught ; the former prefer the
more ornamented and sparkling periods of Junius or Gibbon.   It is
to no purpose to think of bringing about an understanding between
these opposite factions.   It is a natural difference of temperament
and constitution of mind.   The one will never relish the antithetical
point and perpetual glitter of the artificial prose style ; as the plain
unperverted English idiom will always appear trite and insipid to
the others.   A toleration, not a uniformity of opinion, is as much
as can be expected in this case ; and both sides may acknowledge,
without imputation on their taste or consistency, that these different writers excelled each in their way.   I might remark here
that the epithet *elegant* is very sparingly used in modern criticism.
It has probably gone out of fashion with the appearance of the Lake

School, who, I apprehend, have no such phrase in their vocabulary. Mr. Rogers was, I think, almost the last poet to whom it was applied as a characteristic compliment. At present it would be considered as a sort of diminutive of the title of poet, like the terms *pretty* or *fanciful*, and is banished from the *haut ton* of letters. It may perhaps come into request at some future period. Again, the dispute between the admirers of Homer and Virgil has never been settled, and never will : for there will always be minds to whom the excellences of Virgil will be more congenial, and therefore more objects of admiration, than those of Homer, and *vice versa*. Both are right in preferring what suits them best — the delicacy and selectness of the one, or the fulness and majestic flow of the other. There is the same difference in their tastes that there was in the genius of their two favourites. Neither can the disagreement between the French and English school of tragedy ever be reconciled till the French become English, or the English French.* Both are right in what they admire ; both are wrong in condemning the others for what they admire. We see the defects of Racine ; they see the faults of Shakespeare probably in an exaggerated point of view. But we may be sure of this, that when we see nothing but grossness and barbarism, or insipidity and verbiage, in a writer that is the God of a nation's idolatry, it is we and not they who want true taste and feeling. The controversy about Pope and the opposite school in our own poetry comes to much the same thing. Pope's correctness, smoothness, etc., are very good things and much to be commended in him. But it is not to be expected, or even desired, that others should have these qualities in the same paramount degree, to the exclusion of everything else. If you like correctness and smoothness of all things in the world, there they are for you in Pope. If you like other things better, such as strength and sublimity, you know where to go for them. Why trouble Pope or any other author for what they have not, and do not profess to give ? Those who seem to imply that Pope possessed, besides his own peculiar exquisite merits, all that is to be found in Shakespeare or Milton, are, I should hardly think, in good earnest. But I do not therefore

---

* Of the two the latter alternative is more likely to happen. We abuse and imitate them. They laugh at but do not imitate us.

see that, because this was not the case, Pope was no poet. We cannot by a little verbal sophistry confound the qualities of different minds, nor force opposite excellences into a union by all the intolerance in the world. We may pull Pope in pieces as long as we please for not being Shakespeare or Milton, as we may carp at them for not being Pope ; but this will not make a poet equal to all three. If we have a taste for some one precise style or manner, we may keep it to ourselves and let others have theirs. If we are more catholic in our notions and want variety of excellence and beauty, it is spread abroad for us to profusion in the variety of books and in the several growth of men's minds, fettered by no capricious or arbitrary rules. Those who would proscribe whatever falls short of a given standard of imaginary perfection do so not from a higher capacity of taste or range of intellect than others, but to destroy, to " crib and cabin in " all enjoyments and opinions but their own.

We find people of a decided and original, and others of a more general and versatile, taste. I have sometimes thought that the most acute and original-minded men made bad critics. They see everything too much through a particular medium. What does not fall in with their own bias and mode of composition strikes them as commonplace and factitious. What does not come into the direct line of their vision they regard idly, with vacant, " lack-lustre eye." The extreme force of their original impressions compared with the feebleness of those they receive at second hand from others, oversets the balance and just proportion of their minds. Men who have fewer native resources, and are obliged to apply oftener to the general stock, acquire by habit a greater aptitude in appreciating what they owe to others. Their taste is not made a sacrifice to their egotism and vanity, and they enrich the soil of their minds with continual accessions of borrowed strength and beauty. I might take this opportunity of observing that the person of the most refined and least contracted taste I ever knew was the late Joseph Fawcett, the friend of my youth. He was almost the first literary acquaintance I ever made, and I think the most candid and unsophisticated. He had a masterly perception of all style and of every kind and degree of excellence, sublime or beautiful, from

Milton's *Paradise Lost* to Shenstone's *Pastoral Ballad*, from Butler's *Analogy* down to *Humphrey Clinker*. If you had a favourite author, he had read him too, and knew all the best morsels, the subtle *traits*, the capital touches. "Do you like Sterne?" "Yes, to be sure," he would say; "I should deserve to be hanged if I didn't!" His repeating some parts of *Comus* with his fine, deep, mellow-toned voice, particularly the lines, "I have oft heard my mother Circe with the Sirens three," etc., and the enthusiastic comments he made afterwards, were a feast to the ear and to the soul. He read the poetry of Milton with the same fervour and spirit of devotion that I have since heard others read their own. "That is the most delicious feeling of all," I have heard him exclaim, "to like what is excellent, no matter whose it is." In this respect he practised what he preached. He was incapable of harbouring a sinister motive, and judged only from what he felt. There was no flaw nor mist in the clear mirror of his mind. He was as open to impressions as he was strenuous in maintaining them. He did not care a rush whether a writer was old or new, in prose or in verse. "What he wanted," he said, "was something to make him think." Most men's minds are to me like musical instruments out of tune. Touch a particular key, and it jars and makes harsh discord with your own. They like *Gil Blas*, but can see nothing to laugh at in *Don Quixote*: they adore Richardson, but are disgusted with Fielding. Fawcett had a taste accommodated to all these. He was not exceptious. He gave a cordial welcome to all sorts, provided they were the best in their kind. He was not fond of counterfeits or duplicates. His own style was laboured and artificial to a fault, while his character was frank and ingenuous in the extreme. He was not the only individual whom I have known to counteract their natural disposition in coming before the public, and, by avoiding what they perhaps thought an inherent infirmity, debar themselves of their real strength and advantages. A heartier friend or honester critic I never coped withal. He has made me feel (by contrast) the want of genuine sincerity and generous sentiment in some that I have listened to since, and convinced me (if practical proof were wanting) of the truth of that text of Scripture — "That had I all knowledge and could speak with the tongues of angels, yet without charity I were nothing!" I would rather be a man of disinterested taste and liberal feeling, to see and acknowledge truth and beauty wherever I found it, than a man of greater and more original genius, to hate, envy, and deny all excellence but my own — but that poor scanty pittance of it (compared with the whole) which I had myself produced!

There is another race of critics who might be designated as the Occult School — *verè adepti*. They discern no beauties but what are concealed from superficial eyes, and overlook all that are obvious to the vulgar part of mankind. Their art is the transmutation of styles. By happy alchemy of mind they convert dross into gold — and gold into tinsel. They see farther into a millstone than most others. If an author is utterly unreadable, they can read him for ever; his intricacies are their delight, his mysteries are their study. They prefer Sir Thomas Browne to the *Rambler* by Dr. Johnson, and Burton's *Anatomy of Melancholy* to all the writers of the Georgian Age. They judge of works of genius as misers do of hid treasure — it is of no value unless they have it all to themselves. They will no more share a book than a mistress with a friend. If they suspected their favourite volumes of delighting any eyes but their own, they would immediately discard them from the list. Theirs are superannuated beauties that every one else has left off intriguing with, bedridden hags, a "stud of nightmares." This is not envy or affectation, but a natural proneness to singularity, a love of what is odd and out of the way. They must come at their pleasures with difficulty, and support admiration by an uneasy sense of ridicule and opposition. They despise those qualities in a work which are cheap and obvious. They like a monopoly of taste, and are shocked at the prostitution of intellect implied in popular productions. In like manner they would choose a friend or recommend a mistress for gross defects, and tolerate the sweetness of an actress's voice only for the ugliness of her face. Pure pleasures are in their judgment cloying and insipid —

An ounce of sour is worth a pound of sweet!

Nothing goes down with them but what is *caviare* to the multitude. They are eaters of olives and readers of black-letter. Yet they smack of genius, and would be worth any money were it only for the rarity of the thing!

The last sort I shall mention are *verbal critics* — mere word-catchers, fellows that pick out a word in a sentence and a sentence in a volume and tell you it is wrong.* These erudite persons constantly find out by anticipation that you are deficient in the smallest things — that you cannot spell certain words or join the nominative case and the verb together, because to do this is the height of their own ambition, and of course they must set you down lower than their opinion of themselves. They degrade by reducing you to their own standard of merit; for the qualifications they deny you, or the faults they object, are so very insignificant, that to prove yourself possessed of the one or free from the other is to make yourself doubly ridiculous. Littleness is their element, and they give a character of meanness to whatever they touch. They creep, buzz, and fly-blow. It is much easier to crush than to catch these troublesome insects; and when they are in your power your self-respect spares them. The race is almost extinct; one or two of them are sometimes seen crawling over the pages of the *Quarterly Review!*

From *Table Talk.*

ON POETRY IN GENERAL

The best general notion which I can give of poetry is that it is the natural impression of any object or event, by its vividness exciting an involuntary movement of imagination and passion, and producing, by sympathy, a certain modulation of the voice or sounds expressing it.

In treating of poetry, I shall speak first of the subject-matter of it, next of the forms of expression to which it gives birth, and afterwards of its connection with harmony of sound.

Poetry is the language of the imagination and the passions. It relates to whatever gives immediate pleasure or pain to the human mind. It comes home to the bosoms and businesses of men; for

* The title of *Ultra-Crepidarian critics* has been given to a variety of this species.

nothing but what so comes home to them in the most general and intelligible shape can be a subject for poetry. Poetry is the universal language which the heart holds with nature and itself. He who has a contempt for poetry cannot have much respect for himself or for anything else. It is not a mere frivolous accomplishment (as some persons have been led to imagine), the trifling amusement of a few idle readers or leisure hours — it has been the study and delight of mankind in all ages. Many people suppose that poetry is something to be found only in books, contained in lines of ten syllables with like endings; but wherever there is a sense of beauty, or power, or harmony, as in the motion of a wave of the sea, in the growth of a flower that "spreads its sweet leaves to the air and dedicates its beauty to the sun," — *there* is poetry in its birth. If history is a grave study, poetry may be said to be a graver: its materials lie deeper and are spread wider. History treats, for the most part, of the cumbrous and unwieldy masses of things, the empty cases in which the affairs of the world are packed, under the heads of intrigue or war, in different states, and from century to century; but there is no thought or feeling that can have entered into the mind of man which he would be eager to communicate to others, or which they would listen to with delight, that is not a fit subject for poetry. It is not a branch of authorship; it is "the stuff of which our life is made." The rest is "mere oblivion," a dead letter; for all that is worth remembering in life is the poetry of it. Fear is poetry, hope is poetry, love is poetry, hatred is poetry; contempt, jealousy, remorse, admiration, wonder, pity, despair, or madness, are all poetry. Poetry is that fine particle within us that expands, rarefies, refines, raises our whole being: without it "man's life is poor as beast's." Man is a poetical animal; and those of us who do not study the principles of poetry act upon them all our lives like Molière's *Bourgeois Gentilhomme*, who had always spoken prose without knowing it. The child is a poet, in fact, when he first plays at hide-and-seek, or repeats the story of *Jack the Giant-killer;* the shepherd boy is a poet when he first crowns his mistress with a garland of flowers; the countryman, when he stops to look at the rainbow; the city apprentice, when he gazes after the Lord Mayor's show; the miser, when he hugs his gold; the courtier, who builds his hopes upon a smile; the savage, who paints his idol with blood; the slave, who worships a tyrant, or the tyrant, who fancies himself a god; the vain, the ambitious, the proud, the choleric man, the hero and the coward, the beggar and the king, the rich and the poor, the young and the old, all live in a world of their own making; and the poet does no more than describe what all the others think and act. If his art is folly and madness, it is folly and madness at second hand. "There is warrant for it." Poets alone have not "such seething brains, such shaping fantasies, that apprehend more than cool reason" can.

> The lunatic, the lover, and the poet, etc.

If poetry is a dream, the business of life is much the same. If it is a fiction, made up of what we wish things to be, and fancy that they are because we wish them so, there is no other nor better reality. Ariosto has described the loves of Angelica and Medoro; but was not Medoro, who carved the name of his mistress on the barks of trees, as much enamoured of her charms as he? Homer has celebrated the anger of Achilles; but was not the hero as mad as the poet? Plato banished the poets from his Commonwealth lest their descriptions of the natural man should spoil his mathematical man, who was to be without passions and affections, who was neither to laugh nor weep, to feel sorrow nor anger, to be cast down nor elated by anything. This was a chimera, however, which never existed but in the brain of the inventor; and Homer's poetical world has outlived Plato's philosophical Republic.

Poetry, then, is an imitation of nature, but the imagination and the passions are a part of man's nature. We shape things according to our wishes and fancies without poetry; but poetry is the most emphatical language that can be found for those creations of the mind which "ecstasy is very cunning in." Neither a mere description of natural objects nor a mere delineation of natural feelings, however distinct or forcible, constitutes the ultimate end and aim of poetry without the heightenings of the imagination. The light of poetry is not only a direct but also a reflected light, that, while it shows us the object, throws a sparkling radiance on

all around it : the flame of the passions, communicated to the imagination, reveals to us as with a flash of lightning the inmost recesses
of thought, and penetrates our whole being. Poetry represents forms
chiefly as they suggest other forms ; feelings, as they suggest forms
or other feelings. Poetry puts a spirit of life and motion into the
universe. It describes the flowing, not the fixed. It does not define
the limits of sense nor analyse the distinctions of the understanding, but signifies the excess of the imagination beyond the actual or
ordinary impression of any object or feeling. The poetical impression of any object is that uneasy, exquisite sense of beauty or power
that cannot be contained within itself; that is impatient of all
limit ; that (as flame bends to flame) strives to link itself to some
other image of kindred beauty or grandeur, to enshrine itself, as it
were, in the highest forms of fancy, and to relieve the aching sense
of pleasure by expressing it in the boldest manner, and by the most
striking examples of the same quality in other instances. Poetry,
according to Lord Bacon, for this reason, " has something divine in
it, because it raises the mind and hurries it into sublimity by con-
forming the shows of things to the desires of the soul, instead of
subjecting the soul to external things as reason and history do."
It is strictly the language of the imagination ; and the imagination
is that faculty which represents objects, not as they are in themselves, but as they are moulded, by other thoughts and feelings,
into an infinite variety of shapes and combinations of power. This
language is not the less true to nature because it is false in point
of fact ; but so much the more true and natural if it conveys the
impression which the object under the influence of passion makes
on the mind. Let an object, for instance, be presented to the senses
in a state of agitation or fear, and the imagination will distort or
magnify the object, and convert it into the likeness of whatever
is most proper to encourage the fear. " Our eyes are made the
fools " of our other faculties. This is the universal law of the
imagination —

> That if it would but apprehend some joy,
> It comprehends some bringer of that joy :
> Or in the night, imagining some fear,
> How easy is a bush supposed a bear !

When Iachimo says of Imogen —

> The flame o' the taper
> Bows toward her, and would under-peep her lids
> To see the enclosed lights —

this passionate interpretation of the motion of the flame to accord
with the speaker's own feelings is true poetry. The lover, equally
with the poet, speaks of the auburn tresses of his mistress as locks
of shining gold, because the least tinge of yellow in the hair has,
from novelty and a sense of personal beauty, a more lustrous effect
to the imagination than the purest gold. We compare a man of
gigantic stature to a tower; not that he is anything like so large,
but because the excess of his size beyond what we are accustomed
to expect, or the usual size of things of the same class, produces by
contrast a greater feeling of magnitude and ponderous strength than
another object of ten times the same dimensions. The intensity of
the feeling makes up for the disproportion of the objects. Things
are equal to the imagination which have the power of affecting the
mind with an equal degree of terror, admiration, delight, or love.
When Lear calls upon the heavens to avenge his cause, "for they
are old like him," there is nothing extravagant or impious in this
sublime identification of his age with theirs; for there is no other
image which could do justice to the agonizing sense of his wrongs
and his despair!

Poetry is the high-wrought enthusiasm of fancy and feeling.
As in describing natural objects it impregnates sensible impressions
with the forms of fancy, so it describes the feelings of pleasure or
pain by blending them with the strongest movements of passion
and the most striking forms of nature. Tragic poetry, which is
the most impassioned species of it, strives to carry on the feeling
to the utmost point of sublimity or pathos by all the force of comparison or contrast; loses the sense of present suffering in the
imaginary exaggeration of it; exhausts the terror or pity by an
unlimited indulgence of it; grapples with impossibilities in its
desperate impatience of restraint; throws us back upon the past,
forward into the future; brings every moment of our being or
object of nature into startling review before us; and, in the rapid

whirl of events, lifts us from the depths of woe to the highest con·
templations on human life.   When Lear says of Edgar, "Nothing
but his unkind daughters could have brought him to this," what a
bewildered amazement, what a wrench of the imagination, that cannot be brought to conceive of any other cause of misery than that
which has bowed it down, and absorbs all other sorrow in its own!
His sorrow, like a flood, supplies the sources of all other sorrow.
Again, when he exclaims in the mad scene, "The little dogs and
all, Tray, Blanch, and Sweetheart, see, they bark at me!" it is
passion lending occasion to imagination to make every creature in
league against him, conjuring up ingratitude and insult in their
least looked-for and most galling shapes, searching every thread
and fibre of his heart, and finding out the last remaining image of
respect or attachment in the bottom of his breast only to torture
and kill it!   In like manner the "So I am" of Cordelia gushes
from her heart like a torrent of tears, relieving it of a weight of
love and of supposed ingratitude which had pressed upon it for
years.   What a fine return of the passion upon itself is that in
Othello — with what a mingled agony of regret and despair he clings
to the last traces of departed happiness — when he exclaims —

> Oh, now, for ever
> Farewell the tranquil mind! etc.

How his passion lashes itself up and swells and rages like a tide in
its sounding course, when, in answer to the doubts expressed of his
returning love, he says —

> Never, Iago.   Like to the Pontic sea, etc.

The climax of his expostulation afterwards with Desdemona is at
that line —

> But there, where I have garner'd up my heart, . . .
> To be discarded thence!

One mode in which the dramatic exhibition of passion excites
our sympathy without raising our disgust is that, in proportion as
it sharpens the edge of calamity and disappointment, it strengthens
the desire of good.   It enhances our consciousness of the blessing

by making us sensible of the magnitude of the loss. The storm of passion lays bare and shows us the rich depths of the human soul: the whole of our existence, the sum total of our passions and pursuits, of that which we desire and that which we dread, is brought before us by contrast; the action and reaction are equal; the keenness of immediate suffering only gives us a more intense aspiration after, and a more intimate participation with, the antagonist world of good; makes us drink deeper of the cup of human life; tugs at the heart-strings; loosens the pressure about them; and calls the springs of thought and feeling into play with tenfold force.

Impassioned poetry is an emanation of the moral and intellectual part of our nature as well as of the sensitive — of the desire to know, the will to act, and the power to feel, — and ought to appeal to these different parts of our constitution in order to be perfect. The domestic or prose tragedy, which is thought to be the most natural, is in this sense the least so, because it appeals almost exclusively to one of these faculties, our sensibility. The tragedies of Moore and Lillo, for this reason, however affecting at the time, oppress and lie like a dead weight upon the mind, a load of misery which it is unable to throw off: the tragedy of Shakespeare, which is true poetry, stirs our inmost affection, abstracts evil from itself by combining it with all the forms of imagination and with the deepest workings of the heart, and rouses the whole man within us.

The pleasure, however, derived from tragic poetry is not anything peculiar to it as poetry, as a fictitious and fanciful thing. It is not an anomaly of the imagination. It has its source and groundwork in the common love of strong excitement.[1]

. . . .

Poetry is only the highest eloquence of passion, the most vivid form of expression that can be given to our conception of anything, whether pleasurable or painful, mean or dignified, delightful or distressing.

. . . .

Poetry is, in all its shapes, the language of the imagination and the passions of fancy and will. Nothing, therefore, can be more

[1] Hazlitt divagates somewhat on this point. The most important passage in the divagation is given above.

absurd than the outcry, which has been sometimes raised by frigid and pedantic critics, for reducing the language of poetry to the standard of common-sense and reason; for the end and use of poetry, both at the first and now, was and is "to hold the mirror up to nature," seen through the medium of passion and imagination, not divested of that medium by means of literal truth or abstract reason. The painter of history might as well be required to represent the face of a person who has just trod upon a serpent with the still-life expression of a common portrait, as the poet to describe the most striking and vivid impressions which things can be supposed to make upon the mind in the language of common conversation. Let who will strip nature of the colours and the shapes of fancy, the poet is not bound to do so; the impressions of common-sense and strong imagination — that is, of passion and indifference — cannot be the same, and they must have a separate language to do justice to either. Objects must strike differently upon the mind, independently of what they are in themselves, as long as we have a different interest in them, as we see them in a different point of view, nearer or at a greater distance (morally or physically speaking) from novelty, from old acquaintance, from our ignorance of them, from our fear of their consequences, from contrast, from unexpected likeness. We can no more take away the faculty of the imagination than we can see all objects without light or shade. Some things must dazzle us by their preternatural light; others must hold us in suspense, and tempt our curiosity to explore their obscurity. Those who would dispel these various illusions to give us their drab-coloured creation in their stead are not very wise. Let the naturalist, if he will, catch the glow-worm, carry it home with him in a box, and find it next morning nothing but a little grey worm; let the poet or the lover of poetry visit it at evening, when beneath the scented hawthorn and the crescent moon it has built itself a palace of emerald light. This is also one part of nature, one appearance which the glow-worm presents, and that not the least interesting; so poetry is one part of the history of the human mind, though it is neither science nor philosophy. It cannot be concealed, however, that the progress of knowledge and refinement has a tendency to circumscribe the limits of the imagination, and to clip the wings of poetry. The province of the imagination is principally visionary, the unknown and undefined : the understanding restores things to their natural boundaries and strips them of their fanciful pretensions. Hence the history of religious and poetical enthusiasm is much the same ; and both have received a sensible shock from the progress of experimental philosophy. It is the undefined and uncommon that gives birth and scope to the imagination ; we can only fancy what we do not know. As in looking into the mazes of a tangled wood we fill them with what shapes we please — with ravenous beasts, with caverns vast, and drear enchantments — so in our ignorance of the world about us we make gods or devils of the first objects we see, and set no bounds to the wilful suggestions of our hopes and fears.

> And visions, as poetic eyes avow,
> Hang on each leaf, and cling to every bough.

There can never be another Jacob's Dream. Since that time the heavens have gone farther off and grown astronomical. They have become averse to the imagination ; nor will they return to us on the squares of the distances, or on Doctor Chalmers's *Discourses*. Rembrandt's picture brings the matter nearer to us. It is not only the progress of mechanical knowledge, but the necessary advances of civilization, that are unfavourable to the spirit of poetry. We not only stand in less awe of the preternatural world, but we can calculate more surely and look with more indifference upon the regular routine of this. The heroes of the fabulous ages rid the world of monsters and giants. At present we are less exposed to the vicissitudes of good or evil, to the incursions of wild beasts or "bandit fierce," or to the unmitigated fury of the elements. The time has been that "our fell of hair would at a dismal treatise rouse and stir as life were in it." But the police spoils all ; and we now hardly so much as dream of a midnight murder. *Macbeth* is only tolerated in this country for the sake of the music ; and in the United States of America, where the philosophical principles of government are carried still further in theory and practice, we find that the *Beggar's Opera* is hooted from the stage. Society, by degrees, is constructed into a machine that carries us safely and

insipidly from one end of life to the other in a very comfortable
prose style.

> Obscurity her curtain round them drew,
> And siren Sloth a dull quietus sung.[1]

.   .   .   .

Poetry, in its matter and form, is natural imagery or feeling
combined with passion and fancy.   In its mode of conveyance, it
combines the ordinary use of language with musical expression.
There is a question of long standing in what the essence of poetry
consists ; or what it is that determines why one set of ideas should
be expressed in prose, another in verse.   Milton has told us his
idea of poetry in a single line —

> Thoughts that voluntary move
> Harmonious numbers.

As there are certain sounds that excite certain movements, and
the song and dance go together, so there are no doubt certain
thoughts that lead to certain tones of voice or modulations of sound,
and change "the words of Mercury into the songs of Apollo."
There is a striking instance of this adaptation of the movement
of sound and rhythm to the subject in Spenser's description of
the Satyrs accompanying Una to the cave of Sylvanus.[2]   On the
contrary, there is nothing either musical or natural in the ordinary
construction of language.   It is a thing altogether arbitrary and
conventional.   Neither in the sounds themselves, which are the
voluntary signs of certain ideas, nor in their grammatical arrangements in common speech, is there any principle of natural imitation, or correspondence to the individual ideas, or to the tone of
feeling with which they are conveyed to others.   The jerks, the
breaks, the inequalities, and harshnesses of prose are fatal to the
flow of a poetical imagination, as a jolting road or a stumbling
horse disturbs the reverie of an absent man.   But poetry makes
these odds all even.   It is the music of language answering to
the music of the mind, untying, as it were, "the secret soul of
harmony."   Wherever any object takes such a hold of the mind as

[1] Hazlitt here goes off to the contrast of Poetry and Painting.
[2] *F. Q.*, I. vi. 13, 14.

to make us dwell upon it and brood over it, melting the heart in tenderness or kindling it to a sentiment of enthusiasm ; wherever a movement of imagination or passion is impressed on the mind, by which it seeks to prolong and repeat the emotion, to bring all other objects into accord with it, and to give the same movement of harmony, sustained and continuous or gradually varied according to the occasion, to the sounds that express it — this is poetry. The musical in sound is the sustained and continuous ; the musical in thought is the sustained and continuous also. There is a near connection between music and deep-rooted passion. Mad people sing. As often as articulation passes naturally into intonation, there poetry begins. Where one idea gives a tone and colour to others, where one feeling melts others into it, there can be no reason why the same principle should not be extended to the sounds by which the voice utters these emotions of the soul and blends syllables and lines into each other. It is to supply the inherent defect of harmony in the customary mechanism of language, to make the sound an echo to the sense, when the sense becomes a sort of echo to itself — to mingle the tide of verse, "the golden cadences of poetry," with the tide of feeling, flowing and murmuring as it flows — in short, to take the language of the imagination from off the ground, and enable it to spread its wings where it may indulge its own impulses —

> Sailing with supreme dominion
> Through the azure deep of air —

without being stopped, or fretted, or diverted with the abruptnesses and petty obstacles and discordant flats and sharps of prose, that poetry was invented. It is to common language what springs are to a carriage, or wings to feet. In ordinary speech we arrive at a certain harmony by the modulations of the voice : in poetry the same thing is done systematically by a regular collocation of syllables. It has been well observed that every one who declaims warmly, or grows intent upon a subject, rises into a sort of blank verse or measured prose. The merchant, as described in Chaucer, went on his way "sounding always the increase of his winning." Every prose writer has more or less of rhythmical adaptation, except poets, who, when deprived of the regular mechanism of verse, seem to have no principle of modulation left in their writings.

An excuse might be made for rhyme in the same manner. It is but fair that the ear should linger on the sounds that delight it, or avail itself of the same brilliant coincidence and unexpected recurrence of syllables that have been displayed in the invention and collocation of images. It is allowed that rhyme assists the memory; and a man of wit and shrewdness has been heard to say that the only four good lines of poetry are the well-known ones which tell the number of days in the months of the year —

Thirty days hath September, etc.

But if the jingle of names assists the memory, may it not also quicken the fancy ? and there are other things worth having at our fingers' ends besides the contents of the almanac. Pope's versification is tiresome from its excessive sweetness and uniformity. Shakespeare's blank verse is the perfection of dramatic dialogue.

All is not poetry that passes for such ; nor does verse make the whole difference between poetry and prose. The *Iliad* does not cease to be poetry in a literal translation ; and Addison's *Campaign* has been very properly denominated a Gazette in rhyme. Common prose differs from poetry, as treating for the most part either of such trite, familiar, and irksome matters of fact as convey no extraordinary impulse to the imagination, or else of such difficult and laborious processes of the understanding as do not admit of the wayward or violent movements either of the imagination or the passions.

I will mention three works which come as near to poetry as possible without absolutely being so — namely, the *Pilgrim's Progress, Robinson Crusoe,* and the *Tales of Boccaccio.* Chaucer and Dryden have translated some of the last into English rhyme, but the essence and the power of poetry was there before. That which lifts the spirit above the earth, which draws the soul out of itself with indescribable longings, is poetry in kind, and generally fit to become so in name, by being " married to immortal verse." If it is of the essence of poetry to strike and fix the imagination, whether we will or no, to make the eye of childhood glisten with the starting tear, to be never thought of afterwards with indiffer-ence, John Bunyan and Daniel Defoe may be permitted to pass for poets in their way. The mixture of fancy and reality in the *Pilgrim's Progress* was never equalled in any allegory. His pilgrims walk above the earth, and yet are on it. What zeal, what beauty, what truth of fiction! What deep feeling in the description of Christian's swimming across the water at last, and in the picture of the Shining Ones within the gates, with wings at their backs and garlands on their heads, who are to wipe all tears from his eyes! The writer's genius, though not "dipped in dews of Castalie," was baptized with the Holy Spirit and with fire. The prints in this book are no small part of it. If the confinement of Philoctetes in the island of Lemnos was a subject for the most beautiful of all the Greek tragedies, what shall we say to Robinson Crusoe in his? Take the speech of the Greek hero on leaving his cave, beautiful as it is, and compare it with the reflections of the English adventurer in his solitary place of confinement. The thoughts of home, and of all from which he is for ever cut off, swell and press against his bosom as the heaving ocean rolls its ceaseless tide against the rocky shore, and the very beatings of his heart become audible in the eternal silence that surrounds him. Thus he says:

As I walked about, either in my hunting, or for viewing the country, the anguish of my soul at my condition would break out upon me on a sudden, and my very heart would die within me to think of the woods, the mountains, the deserts I was in, and how I was a prisoner, locked up with the eternal bars and bolts of the ocean, in an uninhabited wilderness, without redemption. In the midst of the greatest composures of my mind, this would break out upon me like a storm, and make me wring my hands, and weep like a child. Sometimes it would take me in the middle of my work, and I would immediately sit down and sigh, and look upon the ground for an hour or two together; and this was still worse to me, for if I could burst out into tears, or vent myself by words, it would go off, and the grief, having exhausted itself, would abate.

The story of his adventures would not make a poem like the *Odyssey*, it is true; but the relator had the true genius of a poet. It has been made a question whether Richardson's romances are poetry; and the answer, perhaps, is that they are not poetry because they are not romance. The interest is worked up to an

inconceivable height; but it is by an infinite number of little
things, by incessant labour and calls upon the attention, by a
repetition of blows that have no rebound in them. The sympathy
excited is not a voluntary contribution, but a tax. Nothing is
unforced and spontaneous. There is a want of elasticity and
motion. The story does not "give an echo to the seat where love
is throned." The heart does not answer of itself like a chord in
music. The fancy does not run on before the writer with breathless expectation, but is dragged along with an infinite number of
pins and wheels, like those with which the Lilliputians dragged
Gulliver pinioned to the royal palace. Sir Charles Grandison is a
coxcomb. What sort of a figure would he cut, translated into an
epic poem, by the side of Achilles? Clarissa, the divine Clarissa,
is too interesting by half. She is interesting in her ruffles, in her
gloves, her samplers, her aunts and uncles — she is interesting
in all that is uninteresting. Such things, however intensely they
may be brought home to us, are not conductors to the imagination.
There is infinite truth and feeling in Richardson; but it is extracted
from a *caput mortuum* of circumstances: it does not evaporate of
itself. His poetical genius is like Ariel confined in a pine-tree, and
requires an artificial process to let it out. Shakespeare says —

> Our poesy is as a gum, which oozes
> From whence 't is nourished; . . . our gentle flame
> Provokes itself, and, like the current, flies
> Each bound it chafes.*

I shall conclude this general account with some remarks on four
of the principal works of poetry in the world, at different periods

* Burke's writings are not poetry, notwithstanding the vividness of the
fancy, because the subject-matter is abstruse and dry: not natural, but artificial. The difference between poetry and eloquence is that the one is the
eloquence of the imagination, and the other of the understanding. Eloquence
tries to persuade the will and convince the reason: poetry produces its effect
by instantaneous sympathy. Nothing is a subject for poetry that admits of a
dispute. Poets are in general bad prose writers, because their images, though
fine in themselves, are not to the purpose and do not carry on the argument.
The French poetry wants the forms of the imagination. It is didactic more
than dramatic. And some of our own poetry which has been most admired
is only poetry in the rhyme, and in the studied use of poetic diction.

of history — Homer, the Bible, Dante, and, let me add, Ossian. In Homer, the principle of action or life is predominant ; in the Bible, the principle of faith and the idea of Providence ; Dante is a personification of blind will; and in Ossian we see the decay of life and the lag end of the world. Homer's poetry is the heroic : it is full of life and action ; it is bright as the day, strong as a river. In the vigour of his intellect, he grapples with all the objects of nature, and enters into all the relations of social life. He saw many countries, and the manners of many men ; and he has brought them all together in his poem. He describes his heroes going to battle with a prodigality of life arising from an exuberance of animal spirits : we see them before us, their number and their order of battle, poured out upon the plain "all plumed like ostriches, like eagles newly bathed, wanton as goats, wild as young bulls, youthful as May, and gorgeous as the sun at midsummer," covered with glittering armour, with dust and blood ; while the gods quaff their nectar in golden cups or mingle in the fray, and the old men assembled on the walls of Troy rise up with reverence as Helen passes by them. The multitude of things in Homer is wonderful : their splendour, their truth, their force, and variety. His poetry is, like his religion, the poetry of number and form : he describes the bodies as well as the souls of men.

The poetry of the Bible is that of imagination and of faith : it is abstract and disembodied : it is not the poetry of form, but of power; not of multitude, but of immensity. It does not divide into many, but aggrandizes into one. Its ideas of nature are like its ideas of God. It is not the poetry of social life, but of solitude : each man seems alone in the world with the original forms of nature — the rocks, the earth, and the sky. It is not the poetry of action or heroic enterprise, but of faith in a supreme Providence and resignation to the power that governs the universe. As the idea of God was removed farther from humanity and a scattered polytheism, it became more profound and intense as it became more universal, for the Infinite is present to everything : "If we fly into the uttermost parts of the earth, it is there also ; if we turn to the east or the west, we cannot escape from it." Man is thus aggrandized in the image of his Maker. The history of the

patriarchs is of this kind : they are founders of the chosen race
of people, the inheritors of the earth ; they exist in the generations
which are to come after them. Their poetry, like their religious
creed, is vast, unformed, obscure, and infinite ; a vision is upon it ;
an invisible hand is suspended over it. The spirit of the Christian
religion consists in the glory hereafter to be revealed ; but in the
Hebrew dispensation Providence took an immediate share in the
affairs of this life. Jacob's dream arose out of this intimate communion between heaven and earth : it was this that let down, in
the sight of the youthful patriarch, a golden ladder from the sky
to the earth, with angels ascending and descending upon it, and
shed a light upon the lonely place which can never pass away.
The story of Ruth again, is as if all the depth of natural affection
in the human race was involved in her breast. There are descriptions in the book of *Job* more prodigal of imagery, more intense in
passion, than anything in Homer — as that of the state of his
prosperity, and of the vision that came upon him by night. The
metaphors in the Old Testament are more boldly figurative.
Things were collected more into masses, and gave a greater
momentum to the imagination.

Dante was the father of modern poetry, and he may therefore
claim a place in this connection. His poem is the first great step
from Gothic darkness and barbarism ; and the struggle of thought
in it to burst the thraldom in which the human mind had been
so long held, is felt in every page. He stood bewildered, not
appalled, on that dark shore which separates the ancient and the
modern world ; and saw the glories of antiquity dawning through
the abyss of time, while revelation opened its passage to the other
world. He was lost in wonder at what had been done before him,
and he dared to emulate it. Dante seems to have been indebted to
the Bible for the gloomy tone of his mind, as well as for the prophetic fury which exalts and kindles his poetry ; but he is utterly
unlike Homer. His genius is not a sparkling flame, but the sullen
heat of a furnace. He is power, passion, self-will personified. In
all that relates to the descriptive or fanciful part of poetry, he
bears no comparison to many who have gone before or who
have come after him ; but there is a gloomy abstraction in his

conceptions, which lies like a dead weight upon the mind; a benumb-
ing stupor, a breathless awe, from the intensity of the impression;
a terrible obscurity, like that which oppresses us in dreams; an
identity of interest, which moulds every object to its own purposes
and clothes all things with the passions and imaginations of the
human soul, — that make amends for all other deficiencies.   The
immediate objects he presents to the mind are not much in themselves; they want.grandeur, beauty, and order; but they become
everything by the force of the character he impresses upon them.
His mind lends its own power to the objects which it contemplates,
instead of borrowing it from them.   He takes advantage even of
the nakedness and dreary vacuity of his subject.   His imagination
peoples the shades of death and broods over the silent air.   He is
the severest of all writers, the most hard and impenetrable, the
most opposite to the flowery and glittering; who relies most on
his own power, and the sense of it in others, and who leaves most
room to the imagination of his readers.   Dante's only endeavour
is to interest; and he interests by exciting our sympathy with
the emotion by which he is himself possessed.   He does not place
before us the objects by which that emotion has been created; but
he seizes on the attention, by showing us the effect they produce
on his feelings; and his poetry accordingly gives the same thrill-
ing and overwhelming sensation which is caught by gazing on the
face of a person who has seen some object of horror.   The improba-
bility of the events, the abruptness and monotony in the *Inferno*,
are excessive: but the interest never flags, from the continued ear-
nestness of the author's mind.   Dante's great power is in combining
internal feelings with external objects.   Thus the gate of hell, on
which that withering inscription is written, seems to be endowed
with speech and consciousness, and to utter its dread warning not
without a sense of moral woes.   This author habitually unites the
absolutely local and individual with the greatest wildness and
mysticism.   In the midst of the obscure and shadowy regions of
the lower world a tomb suddenly rises up with the inscription, "I am
the tomb of Pope Anastasius the Sixth"; and half the personages whom he has crowded into the *Inferno* are his own acquaintance.   All this, perhaps, tends to heighten the effect by the bold

intermixture of realities, and by an appeal, as it were, to the individual knowledge and experience of the reader. He affords few subjects for picture. There is, indeed, one gigantic one, that of Count Ugolino, of which Michael Angelo made a bas-relief, and which Sir Joshua Reynolds ought not to have painted.

Another writer whom I shall mention last, and whom I cannot persuade myself to think a mere modern in the groundwork, is Ossian. He is a feeling and a name that can never be destroyed in the minds of his readers. As Homer is the first vigor and lustihead, Ossian is the decay and old age of poetry. He lives only in the recollection and regret of the past. There is one impression which he conveys more entirely than all other poets — namely, the sense of privation, the loss of all things, of friends, of good name, of country; he is even without God in the world. He converses only with the spirits of the departed, with the motionless and silent clouds. The cold moonlight sheds its faint lustre on his head; the fox peeps out of the ruined tower; the thistle waves its beard to the wandering gale ; and the strings of his harp seem, as the hand of age, as the tale of other times passes over them, to sigh and rustle like the dry reeds in the winter's wind ! The feeling of cheerless desolation, of the loss of the pith and sap of existence, of the annihilation of the substance, and the clinging to the shadow of all things, as in a mock embrace, is here perfect. In this way the lamentation of Selma for the loss of Salgar is the finest of all. If it were indeed possible to show that this writer was nothing, it would only be another instance of mutability, another blank made, another void left in the heart, another confirmation of that feeling which makes him so often complain, " Roll on, ye dark brown years, ye bring no joy on your wing to Ossian !"

From The English Poets.

POPE AND CRABBE

Our author [Crabbe] is himself a little jealous of the prudish fidelity of his homely Muse, and tries to justify himself by precedents. He brings as a parallel of merely literal description, Pope's lines on the gay Duke of Buckingham, beginning " In the worst inn," etc. But surely nothing can be more dissimilar. Pope describes what is striking : Crabbe would have described merely what was there. The objects in Pope stand out to the fancy, from the mixture of the mean with the gaudy, from the contrast of the scene and the character. There is an appeal to the imagination ; you see what is passing in a poetical point of view.[1] In Crabbe there is no fire, no contrast, no impulse given to the mind. It is all on a level and of a piece. In fact there is so little connection between the subject-matter of Mr. Crabbe's lines and the ornament of rhyme that is tacked to them, that many of his verses read like serious burlesque, and the parodies which have been made on them are hardly so quaint as the originals.

From *The Spirit of the Age*, art. "Mr. Campbell and Mr. Crabbe."

[1] Observe the coincidence with Patrizzi *ante* (p. 88) and Hugo *post* (p. 418), almost as certainly fortuitous in the one case as in the other. It is for this, and for the remarkable unexpressed condemnation of the Wordsworthian theory, which no one so faithfully carries out as Crabbe, that the passage is quoted. To Crabbe himself it is not universally just.

XXIX

SHELLEY

DEFENCE OF POETRY

(This very interesting piece is more in the spirit of the Italian-Elizabethan apologies than anything else written so late (1821). It is, in fact, a protest in that spirit, not so much against the Puritan as against the 18th-century "good sense" view of the matter. It contains, however, as is natural, no few traces of the 18th century itself, in its generalizing assumptions about "men dancing and singing in the youth of the world," etc. And part of it is beyond all doubt directed rather against Wordsworth's doctrines, though written in a spirit almost wholly akin to Wordsworth's own. The first and last parts, amounting each to nearly a quarter of the whole, are given entire; the middle, partly historical, partly discursive-argumentative, is omitted as more controversial and less authoritative.)

According to one mode of regarding those two classes of mental action, which are called reason and imagination, the former may be considered as mind contemplating the relations borne by one thought to another, however produced; and the latter, as mind acting upon those thoughts so as to colour them with its own light, and composing from them, as from elements, other thoughts, each containing within itself the principle of its own integrity. The one is the τὸ ποιεῖν, or the principle of synthesis, and has for its objects those forms which are common to universal nature and existence itself; the other is the τὸ λογίζειν, or principle of analysis, and its action regards the relations of things simply as relations; considering thoughts, not in their integral unity, but as the algebraical representations which conduct to certain general results. Reason is the enumeration of qualities already known; imagination is the perception of the value of those quantities, both separately and as a whole. Reason respects the differences, and imagination

396

the similitudes of things. Reason is to imagination as the instrument to the agent, as the body to the spirit, as the shadow to the substance.

Poetry, in a general sense, may be defined to be "the expression of the imagination": and poetry is connate with the origin of man. Man is an instrument over which a series of external and internal impressions are driven, like the alternations of an ever-changing wind over an Æolian lyre, which move it by their motion to ever-changing melody. But there is a principle within the human being, and perhaps within all sentient beings, which acts otherwise than in the lyre, and produces not melody alone, but harmony, by an internal adjustment of the sounds or motions thus excited to the impressions which excite them. It is as if the lyre could accommodate its chords to the motions of that which strikes them, in a determined proportion of sound; even as the musician can accommodate his voice to the sound of the lyre. A child at play by itself will express its delight by its voice and motions; and every inflexion of tone and every gesture will bear exact relation to a corresponding antitype in the pleasurable impressions which awakened it; it will be the reflected image of that impression; and as the lyre trembles and sounds after the wind has died away, so the child seeks, by prolonging in its voice and motions the duration of the effect, to prolong also a consciousness of the cause. In relation to the objects which delight a child, these expressions are what poetry is to higher objects. The savage (for the savage is to ages what the child is to years) expresses the emotions produced in him by surrounding objects in a similar manner; and language and gesture, together with plastic or pictorial imitation, become the image of the combined effect of those objects, and of his apprehension of them. Man in society, with all his passions and his pleasures, next becomes the object of the passions and pleasures of man; an additional class of emotions produces an augmented treasure of expressions; and language, gesture, and the imitative arts become at once the representation and the medium, the pencil and the picture, the chisel and the statue, the chord and the harmony. The social sympathies, or those laws from which, as from its elements, society results, begin to develop themselves from the moment that

two human beings coexist; the future is contained within the present, as the plant within the seed: and equality, diversity, unity,
contrast, mutual dependence, become the principles alone capable
of affording the motives according to which the will of a social
being is determined to action, inasmuch as he is social; and constitute pleasure in sensation, virtue in sentiment, beauty in art,
truth in reasoning, and love in the intercourse of kind. Hence
men, even in the infancy of society, observe a certain order in their
words and actions, distinct from that of the objects and the impressions represented by them, all expression being subject to the laws
of that from which it proceeds. But let us dismiss those more
general considerations which might involve an enquiry into the
principles of society itself, and restrict our view to the manner in
which the imagination is expressed upon its forms.

In the youth of the world, men dance and sing and imitate
natural objects, observing in these actions, as in all others, a certain rhythm or order. And, although all men observe a similar,
they observe not the same order, in the motions of the dance, in
the melody of the song, in the combinations of language, in the
series of their imitations of natural objects. For there is a certain
order or rhythm belonging to each of these classes of mimetic representation, from which the hearer and the spectator receive an
intenser and purer pleasure than from any other: the sense of
an approximation to this order has been called taste by modern
writers. Every man in the infancy of art observes an order which
approximates more or less closely to that from which this highest
delight results; but the diversity is not sufficiently marked, as that
its gradations should be sensible, except in those instances where
the predominance of this faculty of approximation to the beautiful
(for so we may be permitted to name the relation between this
highest pleasure and its cause) is very great. Those in whom it
exists in excess are poets, in the most universal sense of the word;
and the pleasure resulting from the manner in which they express
the influence of society or nature upon their own minds, communicates itself to others, and gathers a sort of reduplication from that
community. Their language is vitally metaphorical; that is, it
marks the before unapprehended relations of things and perpetuates

their apprehension, until the words which represent them, become, through time, signs for portions or classes of thoughts instead of pictures of integral thoughts; and then, if no new poets should arise to create afresh the associations which have been thus disorganized, language will be dead to all the nobler purposes of human intercourse. These similitudes or relations are finely said by Lord Bacon to be "the same footsteps of nature impressed upon the various subjects of the world"* — and he considers the faculty which perceives them as the storehouse of axioms common to all knowledge. In the infancy of society every author is necessarily a poet, because language itself is poetry; and to be a poet is to apprehend the true and the beautiful; in a word, the good which exists in the relation subsisting, first between existence and perception, and secondly between perception and expression. Every original language near to its source is in itself the chaos of a cyclic poem: the copiousness of lexicography and the distinctions of grammar are the works of a later age, and are merely the catalogue and the form of the creations of poetry.

But poets, or those who imagine and express this indestructible order, are not only the authors of language and of music, of the dance, and architecture, and statuary, and painting: they are the institutors of laws, and the founders of civil society, and the inventors of the arts of life, and the teachers, who draw into a certain propinquity with the beautiful and the true, that partial apprehension of the agencies of the invisible world which is called religion. Hence all original religions are allegorical, or susceptible of allegory, and, like Janus, have a double face of false and true. Poets, according to the circumstances of the age and nation in which they appeared, were called, in the earlier epochs of the world, legislators, or prophets: a poet essentially comprises and unites both these characters. For he not only beholds intensely the present as it is, and discovers those laws according to which present things ought to be ordered, but he beholds the future in the present, and his thoughts are the germs of the flower and the fruit of latest time. Not that I assert poets to be prophets in the gross sense of the word, or that they can foretell the form as surely as they

* *De Augment. Scient.*, cap. I, lib. iii.

foreknow the spirit of events : such is the pretence of superstition, which would make poetry an attribute of prophecy rather than prophecy an attribute of poetry. A poet participates in the eternal, the infinite, and the one ; as far as relates to his conceptions, time and place and number are not. The grammatical forms which express the moods of time, and the difference of persons, and the distinction of place, are convertible with respect to the highest poetry without injuring it as poetry; and the choruses of Æschylus, and the book of *Job*, and Dante's *Paradise*, would afford, more than any other writings, examples of this fact, if the limits of this essay did not forbid citation. The creations of sculpture, painting, and music are illustrations still more decisive.

Language, colour, form, and religious and civil habits of action are all the instruments and materials of poetry ; they may be called poetry by that figure of speech which considers the effect as a synonym of the cause. But poetry in a more restricted sense expresses those arrangements of language, and especially metrical language, which are created by that imperial faculty, whose throne is curtained within the invisible nature of man. And this springs from the nature itself of language, which is a more direct representation of the actions and passions of our internal being, and is susceptible of more various and delicate combinations than colour, form, or motion, and is more plastic and obedient to the control of that faculty of which it is the creation. For language is arbitrarily produced by the imagination, and has relation to thoughts alone ; but all other materials, instruments, and conditions of art have relations among each other, which limit and interpose between conception and expression. The former is as a mirror which reflects, the latter as a cloud which enfeebles, the light of which both are mediums of communication. Hence the fame of sculptors, painters, and musicians, although the intrinsic powers of the great masters of these arts may yield in no degree to that of those who have employed language as the hieroglyphic of their thoughts, has never equalled that of poets in the restricted sense of the term ; as two performers of equal skill will produce unequal effects from a guitar and a harp. The fame of legislators and founders of religions, so long as their institutions last, alone seems to exceed that of poets in the restricted sense ; but it can scarcely be a question whether, if we deduct the celebrity which their flattery of the gross opinions of the vulgar usually conciliates, together with that which belonged to them in their higher character of poets, any excess will remain.

We have thus circumscribed the word poetry within the limits of that art which is the most familiar and the most perfect expression of the faculty itself. It is necessary, however, to make the circle still narrower, and to determine the distinction between measured and unmeasured language ; for the popular division into prose and verse is inadmissible in accurate philosophy.

Sounds as well as thoughts have relation both between each other and towards that which they represent, and a perception of the order of those relations has always been found connected with a perception of the order of the relations of thoughts. Hence the language of poets has ever affected a certain uniform and harmonious recurrence of sound, without which it were not poetry, and which is scarcely less indispensable to the communication of its influence than the words themselves, without reference to that peculiar order. Hence the vanity of translation ; it were as wise to cast a violet into a crucible that you might discover the formal principle of its colour and odour, as seek to transfuse from one language into another the creations of a poet. The plant must spring again from its seed, or it will bear no flower — and this is the burthen of the curse of Babel.

An observation of the regular mode of the recurrence of harmony in the language of poetical minds, together with its relation to music, produced metre, or a certain system of traditional forms of harmony and language. Yet it is by no means essential that a poet should accommodate his language to this traditional form, so that the harmony, which is its spirit, be observed. The practice is indeed convenient and popular, and to be preferred, especially in such composition as includes much action : but every great poet must inevitably innovate upon the example of his predecessors in the exact structure of his peculiar versification. The distinction between poets and prose writers is a vulgar error. The distinction between philosophers and poets has been anticipated. Plato was essentially a poet — the truth and splendour of his imagery, and the melody of his language, are the most intense that it is possible to conceive. He rejected the measure of the epic, dramatic, and lyrical forms, because he sought to kindle a harmony in thoughts divested of shape and action, and he forbore to invent any regular plan of rhythm which would include, under determinate forms, the varied pauses of his style. Cicero sought to imitate the cadence of his periods, but with little success. Lord Bacon was a poet.* His language has a sweet and majestic rhythm, which satisfies the sense, no less than the almost superhuman wisdom of his philosophy satisfies the intellect; it is a strain which distends, and then bursts the circumference of the reader's mind, and pours itself forth together with it into the universal element with which it has perpetual sympathy. All the authors of revolutions in opinion are not only necessarily poets as they are inventors, nor even as their words unveil the permanent analogy of things by images which participate in the life of truth; but as their periods are harmonious and rhythmical, and contain in themselves the elements of verse; being the echo of the eternal music. Nor are those supreme poets, who have employed traditional forms of rhythm on account of the form and action of their subjects, less capable of perceiving and teaching the truth of things, than those who have omitted that form. Shakespeare, Dante, and Milton (to confine ourselves to modern writers) are philosophers of the very loftiest power.

A poem is the very image of life expressed in its eternal truth. There is this difference between a story and a poem, that a story is a catalogue of detached facts, which have no other connection than time, place, circumstance, cause and effect; the other is the creation of actions according to the unchangeable forms of human nature, as existing in the mind of the Creator, which is itself the image of all other minds. The one is partial, and applies only to a definite period of time, and a certain combination of events which can never again recur; the other is universal, and contains within itself the germ of a relation to whatever motions or actions have place in the possible varieties of human nature. Time, which destroys the beauty and the use of the story of particular facts,

* See the *Filum Labyrinthi*, and the *Essay on Death* particularly.

stripped of the poetry which should invest them, augments that of poetry, and for ever develops new and wonderful applications of the eternal truth which it contains. Hence epitomes have been called the moths of just history; they eat out the poetry of it. A story of particular facts is as a mirror which obscures and distorts that which should be beautiful: poetry is a mirror which makes beautiful that which is distorted.

The parts of a composition may be poetical, without the composition as a whole being a poem. A single sentence may be considered as a whole, though it may be found in the midst of a series of unassimilated portions; a single word even may be a spark of inextinguishable thought. And thus all the great historians, Herodotus, Plutarch, Livy, were poets; and although the plan of these writers, especially that of Livy, restrained them from developing this faculty in its highest degree, they made copious and ample amends for their subjection by filling all the interstices of their subjects with living images.

.   .   .   .

The functions of the poetical faculty are twofold: by one it creates new materials of knowledge, and power, and pleasure; by the other it engenders in the mind a desire to reproduce and arrange them according to a certain rhythm and order which may be called the beautiful and the good. The cultivation of poetry is never more to be desired than at periods when, from an excess of the selfish and calculating principle, the accumulation of the materials of external life exceeds the quantity of the power of assimilating them to the internal laws of human nature. The body has then become too unwieldy for that which animates it.

Poetry is indeed something divine. It is at once the centre and circumference of knowledge; it is that which comprehends all science, and that to which all science must be referred. It is at the same time the root and blossom of all other systems of thought; it is that from which all spring, and that which adorns all; and that which, if blighted, denies the fruit and the seed, and withholds from the barren world the nourishment and the succession of the scions of the tree of life. It is the perfect and consummate surface and bloom of all things; it is as the odour and the colour of the rose to the texture of the elements which compose it, as the form and splendour of unfaded beauty to the secrets of anatomy and corruption. What were virtue, love, patriotism, friendship — what were the scenery of this beautiful universe which we inhabit; what were our consolations on this side of the grave — and what were our aspirations beyond it, if poetry did not ascend to bring light and fire from those eternal regions where the owl-winged faculty of calculation dare not ever soar? Poetry is not like reasoning, a power to be exerted according to the determination of the will. A man cannot say, "I will compose poetry." The greatest poet even cannot say it; for the mind in creation is as a fading coal, which some invisible influence, like an inconstant wind, awakens to transitory brightness; this power arises from within, like the colour of a flower which fades and changes as it is developed, and the conscious portions of our natures are unprophetic either of its approach or its departure. Could this influence be durable in its original purity and force, it is impossible to predict the greatness of the results; but when composition begins, inspiration is already on the decline, and the most glorious poetry that has ever been communicated to the world is probably a feeble shadow of the original conceptions of the poet. I appeal to the greatest poets of the present day whether it is not an error to assert that the finest passages of poetry are produced by labour and study. The toil and the delay recommended by critics can be justly interpreted to mean no more than a careful observation of the inspired moments, and an artificial connection of the spaces between their suggestions by the intermixture of conventional expressions; a necessity only imposed by the limitedness of the poetical faculty itself: for Milton conceived the *Paradise Lost* as a whole before he executed it in portions. We have his own authority also for the muse having "dictated" to him the "unpremeditated song." And let this be an answer to those who would allege the fifty-six various readings of the first line of the *Orlando Furioso*. Compositions so produced are to poetry what mosaic is to painting. This instinct and intuition of the poetical faculty is still more observable in the plastic and pictorial arts; a great statue or picture grows under the power of the artist as a child in the mother's womb; and the very mind which directs the hands in formation is incapable of accounting to itself for the origin, the gradations, or the media of the process.

Poetry is the record of the best and happiest moments of the happiest and best minds. We are aware of evanescent visitations of thought and feelings sometimes associated with place or person, sometimes regarding our own mind alone, and always arising unforeseen and departing unbidden, but elevating and delightful beyond all expression: so that even in the desire and the regret they leave, there cannot but be pleasure, participating as it does in the nature of its object. It is, as it were, the interpenetration of a diviner nature through our own; but its footsteps are like those of a wind over the sea, which the coming calm erases, and whose traces remain only as on the wrinkled sand which paves it. These and corresponding conditions of being are experienced principally by those of the most delicate sensibility and the most enlarged imagination; and the state of mind produced by them is at war with every base desire. The enthusiasm of virtue, love, patriotism, and friendship is essentially linked with such emotions; and whilst they last, self appears as what it is, an atom to a universe. Poets are not only subject to these experiences as spirits of the most refined organization, but they can colour all that they combine with the evanescent hues of this ethereal world; a word, a trait in the representation of a scene or a passion will touch the enchanted chord, and reanimate, in those who have ever experienced these emotions, the sleeping, the cold, the buried image of the past. Poetry thus makes immortal all that is best and most beautiful in the world; it arrests the vanishing apparitions which haunt the interlunations of life, and veiling them, or in language or in form, sends them forth among mankind, bearing sweet news of kindred joy to those with whom their sisters abide — abide, because there is no portal of expression from the caverns of the spirit which they inhabit into the universe of things. Poetry redeems from decay the visitations of the divinity in man.

Poetry turns all things to loveliness; it exalts the beauty of that which is most beautiful, and it adds beauty to that which is most deformed; it marries exultation and horror, grief and pleasure, eternity and change; it subdues to union under its light yoke all irreconcilable things. It transmutes all that it touches, and every form moving within the radiance of its presence is changed by wondrous sympathy to an incarnation of the spirit which it breathes: its secret alchemy turns to potable gold the poisonous waters which flow from death through life; it strips the veil of familiarity from the world, and lays bare the naked and sleeping beauty, which is the spirit of its forms.

All things exist as they are perceived: at least in relation to the percipient. "The mind is its own place, and of itself can make a heaven of hell, a hell of heaven." But poetry defeats the curse which binds us to be subjected to the accident of surrounding impressions. And whether it spreads its own figured curtain, or withdraws life's dark veil from before the scene of things, it equally creates for us a being within our being. It makes us the inhabitants of a world to which the familiar world is a chaos. It reproduces the common universe of which we are portions and percipients, and it purges from our inward sight the film of famil- iarity which obscures from us the wonder of our being. It compels us to feel that which we perceive, and to imagine that which we know. It creates anew the universe, after it has been annihilated in our minds by the recurrence of impressions blunted by reitera- tion. It justifies the bold and true words of Tasso — *Non merita nome di creatore, se non Iddio ed il Poeta.*

A poet, as he is the author to others of the highest wisdom, pleasure, virtue, and glory, so he ought personally to be the happi- est, the best, the wisest, and the most illustrious of men. As to his glory, let time be challenged to declare whether the fame of any other institutor of human life be comparable to that of a poet. That he is the wisest, the happiest, and the best, inasmuch as he is a poet, is equally incontrovertible: the greatest poets have been men of the most spotless virtue, of the most consummate prudence, and, if we would look into the interior of their lives, the most fortunate of men: and the exceptions, as they regard those who possessed the poetic faculty in a high yet inferior degree, will be found on consideration to confine rather than destroy the rule. Let us for a moment stoop to the arbitration of popular breath, and usurping and uniting in our own persons the incompatible characters of accuser, witness, judge, and executioner, let us decide, without trial, testimony, or form, that certain motives of those who are "there sitting where we dare not soar," are reprehensible. Let us assume that Homer was a drunkard, that Virgil was a flatterer, that Horace was a coward, that Tasso was a madman, that Lord Bacon was a peculator, that Raphael was a libertine, that Spenser was a poet-laureate. It is inconsistent with this division of our subject to cite living poets, but posterity has done ample justice to the great names now referred to. Their errors have been weighed and found to have been dust in the balance; if their sins "were as scarlet, they are now white as snow"; they have been washed in the blood of the mediator and redeemer, Time. Observe in what a ludicrous chaos the imputations of real or fictitious crime have been confused in the contemporary calumnies against poetry and poets; consider how little is, as it appears — or appears, as it is; look to your own motives, and judge not, lest ye be judged.

Poetry, as has been said, differs in this respect from logic, that it is not subject to the control of the active powers of the mind, and that its birth and recurrence have no necessary connection with the consciousness or will. It is presumptuous to determine that these are the necessary conditions of all mental causation, when mental effects are experienced unsusceptible of being referred to them. The frequent recurrence of the poetical power, it is obvious to suppose, may produce in the mind a habit of order and harmony correlative with its own nature and with its effects upon other minds. But in the intervals of inspiration, and they may be frequent without being durable, a poet becomes a man, and is abandoned to the sudden reflux of the influences under which others habitually live. But as he is more delicately organized than other men, and sensible to pain and pleasure, both his own and that of others, in a degree unknown to them, he will avoid the one and pursue the other with an ardour proportioned to this difference. And he renders himself obnoxious to calumny when he neglects to observe the circumstances under which these objects of universal pursuit and flight have disguised themselves in one another's garments.

But there is nothing necessarily evil in this error, and thus cruelty, envy, revenge, avarice, and the passions purely evil have never formed any portion of the popular imputations on the lives of poets.

I have thought it most favourable to the cause of truth to set down these remarks according to the order in which they were suggested to my mind by a consideration of the subject itself, instead of observing the formality of a polemical reply; but if the view which they contain be just, they will be found to involve a refutation of the arguers against poetry, so far at least as regards the first division of the subject. I can readily conjecture what should have moved the gall of some learned and intelligent writers who quarrel with certain versifiers; I confess myself, like them, unwilling to be stunned by the Theseids of the hoarse Codri of the day. Bavius and Mævius undoubtedly are, as they ever were, insufferable persons. But it belongs to a philosophical critic to distinguish rather than confound.

The first part of these remarks has related to poetry in its elements and principles; and it has been shown, as well as the narrow limits assigned them would permit, that what is called poetry, in a restricted sense, has a common source with all other forms of order and of beauty, according to which the materials of human life are susceptible of being arranged, and which is poetry in an universal sense.

The second part[1] will have for its object an application of these principles to the present state of the cultivation of poetry, and a defence of the attempt to idealize the modern forms of manners and opinions, and compel them into a subordination to the imaginative and creative faculty. For the literature of England, an energetic development of which has ever preceded or accompanied a great and free development of the national will, has arisen, as it were, from a new birth. In spite of the low-thoughted envy which would undervalue contemporary merit, our own will be a memorable age in intellectual achievements, and we live among such philosophers and poets as surpass beyond comparison any who have appeared since the last national struggle for civil and

[1] This Shelley did not live to write.

religious liberty.   The most unfailing herald, companion, and fol-
lower of the awakening of a great people to work a beneficial change
in opinion or institution is poetry.   At such periods there is an
accumulation of the power of communicating and receiving intense
and impassioned conceptions respecting men and nature.   The
persons in whom this power resides may often, as far as regards
many portions of their nature, have little apparent correspondence
with that spirit of good of which they are the ministers.   But even
whilst they deny and abjure, they are yet compelled to serve, the
power which is seated on the throne of their own soul.   It is
impossible to read the compositions of the most celebrated writers
of the present day without being startled with the electric life
which burns within their words.   They measure the circumference
and sound the depths of human nature with a comprehensive and
all-penetrating spirit, and they are themselves perhaps the most
sincerely astonished at its manifestations; for it is less their spirit
than the spirit of the age.   Poets are the hierophants of an unapprehended inspiration; the mirrors of the gigantic shadows which
futurity casts upon the present; the words which express what
they understand not; the trumpets which sing to battle, and feel
not what they inspire; the influence which is moved not, but moves.
Poets are the unacknowledged legislators of the world.

XXX

SAINTE–BEUVE AND VICTOR HUGO

(The influence of Sainte-Beuve, which has been enormous both directly and indirectly, was exerted rather by way of attitude and temperament than in formulated doctrines. The following passages, however, may exhibit something of its mode of exercise. The great poet who was once his friend had, on the other hand, a temperament as apparently uncritical as that of any man who ever lived; yet Shenstone's aphorism (*v. sup.*, p. 256) is justified of him also. The short question contained in the quotation given below from the Preface to *Les Orientales* (*L'ouvrage est-il bon ou est-il mauvais?*) practically " surprises by itself " the whole doctrine of modern, as opposed to ancient, criticism — put, of course, in a characteristically imperious and one-sided manner. And the passage, brief as it is, cuts forward as mightily at the Arnoldian " All depends upon the subject " as backward at the idea, then but recently championed by La Harpe, that even admitted " beauty " is not enough — that beauty has no business to be beautiful "monstrously" — out of the rules — independently of the " leading-strings and handcuffs and gags." But observe that Hugo's doctrine is not yet the later exaggeration of " Art for art *only*," though it may lead thereto. The glove thrown down is for a more catholic dogma,— Treatment and the Event against Subject and Rule.)

SAINTE-BEUVE. THOUGHTS ON CRITICISM AND CRITICS FROM CAUSERIES DU LUNDI AND NOUVEAUX LUNDIS (1849-1869)

A. DOGMATIC AND UNDOGMATIC CRITICISM

(This passage is all the more interesting because Villemain was undoubtedly Sainte-Beuve's own master, so far as he had any.)

In the kind of literary sketch, properly so called, in which he excels, and particularly in the sketch which he has given of the 18th century, I shall only take the liberty of noting one thing, of bringing out one characteristic trait, impossible to omit in speaking of the famous critic who has been the master of our age. The property of critics in general, as their very name sufficiently shows, is to judge — at need to give trenchant and peremptory judgment. Take all the eminent men to whom this title of critic has been hitherto applied — Malherbe, Boileau (both critics under the guise of poets); Dr. Johnson in England; La Harpe with us; even M. de Fontanes.[1] All these men, of authority in their day, judged matters of taste with vivacity, with too exclusive peremptoriness perhaps, but at any rate with a clear, decisive pronouncement of opinion, and without appeal. Boileau "hated a silly book," and could not help satirizing it: while, on the other hand, when he had to do with work which he thought fine, he took its side without hesitation and punished fools for their attacks on it at every opportunity. Fontanes did the same thing in his own way — he was an impassioned avenger of *Les Martyrs*,[2] so violently attacked at its first appearance, and passed the word (as it were) to admire it.

Since then things have changed greatly : criticism has turned historical, and as it were eclectic in its judgments. It has set forth much, it has understood everything,[3] but it has come to few conclusions. M. Villemain did more than any one to enter it, and keep it, in this way, which in many respects is ampler and more fertile, but which also oftentimes, by the very fact of its amplitude, comes to no definite end. Thus, in this *Literary Sketch of the 18th Century*, when he has to judge the *Henriade* he gives all the good reasons for *not* admiring it, for not giving it any rank at all among the epics which live. But when it comes to a formal conclusion, he recoils, he flinches. The judge leaves his bench, and, in half a dozen passages of sheer evasion, he tries to hope that

[1] Fontanes (1757–1821) — now much forgotten out of France, except by special students — was a poet as poets went then, a considerable rhetorician, and a not inconsiderable critic. He had political influence under the Empire and the Restoration, and used it for literature and learning. Sainte-Beuve had rather a fancy for him.

[2] Chateaubriand's rococo-Romantic romance — a real force in its time.

[3] Sainte-Beuve is almost too polite. Let our modesty substitute "tried to understand."

"the *Henriade* will traverse the ages," that " after all, it is a durable work," that it holds " a place to itself," a place of the first after really original works. He comes back to it four or five times over, instead of settling the question for good and once for all, as his own arguments entitled him to do. This is a weak spot in a mind of rare distinction. His judgments, exquisite at the outset, are hard to grasp at the conclusion — you must, as it were, catch them flying in their state of charming epigram, or disengage them for yourself from the opulent sinuosities in which he sets them forth. This is specially the case when he deals with the living. His delicacy redoubles — to the point of almost shocking mine. He loves to proceed by understandings, by allusions. In his excellent annual reports to the Academy, good judges, who can seize all the points, find nothing to desire: if we look to those who are *not* judges — to the public — these judgments want stronger relief.

C. L. i. 112–114.

B. THE "OLD MOONS" OF CRITICISM

(There is no passage in Sainte-Beuve (there are few passages in any critic) of more far-reaching wisdom than this. The truth repeats itself incessantly; and it is probably a reluctant and indignant sense of it which makes "companies of warm young men," as Dryden puts it (*v. sup.*, p. 164), affect disdain of Sainte-Beuve himself.)

The first condition of properly appreciating old critics and their journey-work, is to put oneself back in situation, and to reconstruct oneself in ideas, so as to gain the spirit of their time. The essential thing for active and practical criticism, such as that of which we speak, is not so much profound knowledge of things as a lively feeling for them, a power of inspiring taste for them, and of surrounding oneself with its atmosphere. Perhaps, from 1800 to 1814,[1] men may have been in many respects less learned, less erudite, than to-day: but, on the whole, people paid more attention to literary questions, and took more interest in them. Criticism, by itself, does nothing and can do nothing. The best of it can act

---

[1] Or, for that matter, from *abcd* to *wxyz*.

only in concert, and almost in collaboration, with public feeling. I shall venture to say that the critic is only the *secretary* of the public — though a secretary who does not wait to be dictated to, but each morning divines and redacts the general opinion. Even when he has actually expressed the thought which everybody has (or would like to have), a great and living part of his allusions, of his conclusions, and of their consequences, remains in the wits of his readers. I maintain that in reading over old papers and their most successful critiques we never find more than half the article in print — the other was written only in the reader's mind. You are to suppose a printed sheet of which we only read one side — the other has disappeared, is blank. And this other side, which would complete the thing, is the disposition of the public at the time, the office or part of *editor* which it supplied, and which sometimes was not the least intelligent or effectual part. To be just, we must effect a restoration of this disposition now, when we judge these old critics, our forerunners.

C. L. i. 372, 3.

C. THE ELUSIVENESS OF THE "CLASSICAL" QUALITY

(The whole of the *causerie* " Qu'est-ce qu'un Classique " (Oct. 21, 1850), from which this is taken, should be read, marked, learnt, and inwardly digested by any one who wishes to acquire the *ethos* of the critic. Sainte-Beuve is too seldom thus general: or rather, it is one of his greatest merits that he generalizes thus seldom. He has just given an admirable sketch of the " classics" of all nations.)

The point of importance to-day seems to me to be the maintenance of the idea, and the worship, of the " Classic," while expanding both. There is no receipt for making classics : that point might at last be recognized as proved. To believe that by imitating certain qualities of purity, sobriety, correctness, elegance, one will, independently of idiosyncrasy and inspiration, become a classic, is to believe that after Racine the father there is room for Racine the son — for that dull respectability which is, in poetry, the worst thing of all. Nay, more : it is not well to appear, too soon and too much offhand, a classic to one's contemporaries. Fontanes, in his day, seemed to his friends to be purely and simply classical : see how pale he looks to us at only five and twenty years' distance ! How many are there of these premature classics, who cannot *hold*, and are such but for a day ! You look back, some fine morning, and are quite astonished to see them no more in pride of place behind you. There was only enough of them (as Madame de Sévigné would say pleasantly) "for a sun's breakfast." In the way of classics the most unexpected are ever the best and greatest : ask, if you doubt it, the true *men* of genius who were really born immortal and to flourish perpetually. The least classical in appearance of the four great poets of Louis XIV's time was Molière. He was much more applauded than esteemed : he was relished, but without being really appreciated. The least classic after him seemed to be La Fontaine ; and see what, two centuries later, has happened to both !

The piece concludes with a brilliant plan of a new "Temple of Taste," where "nothing is to be sacrificed, depreciated, excluded," and the whole principle is to be that of "many mansions" — room for Pope, as for Shakespeare ; for Milton, as for Virgil. *C. L.* iii. 49, 50.

D. CRITICISM ACCORDING TO STANDARD

(M. Désiré Nisard, who is the direct subject of the following remarks, was the first very considerable critic who rallied "Classicism" after the rout of 1830, and gave it a new model. Sainte-Beuve explains what that model was, and, in his usual masterly way, indicates its advantages and dangers.)

Having to write on French Literature, and to follow this in its development across the ages, he has asked himself, at the very outset, "What is the French Genius?" He has made himself an idea of this to begin with ; he has worked up a kind of model of it from the most admired masters, the critics most in honour and credit ; he has presented to French readers an altogether satisfactory portrait of this French Genius seen on its best sides and in its best lights. . . . If he perhaps flatters this Genius in his general definition of it, he is not in the least flattering to particular authors.

On the contrary, by comparing and contrasting them indefatigably with this first ideal, he makes them undergo the most dangerous of tests, the hardest of examinations. More than one, even of the most famous, leaves a part of himself — the fleeting, false, ephemeral part — behind. And, as after a judgment of Minos or Rhadamanthus, only the immortal soul, the genius in whatsoever degree it has possessed goodness, purity, lasting and moral quality and wholesomeness — conformity and community with that abstract French Genius which is one of the finest representatives of human art — only *this* survives, disengages itself, and triumphs.

This is the ideal of the method. But has it always been justly applied? Could it possibly be so? Nature is full of variety — of moulds which differ: the forms of talent are infinite. Why, O Critic! insist on one pattern only? I know, of course, that your pattern is more diverse and more varied than it seems at first — that your model French Genius is manifold, complex, as elastic as this genius itself. But it is not less true that your *History* becomes of necessity a perpetual Trial-at-Bar. The critic-historian never lets himself go with the current of each writer's nature, as he meets it; he recalls it peremptorily to his own model; he forces more than one wandering stream back into the artificial channel which he has dug beforehand. If there are rebel branches, they are cut off. The French genius, in a state of Platonic and archetypal ideality, is supposed to preside in person over this *History;* according as it recognizes itself more or less in each passing writer, it distributes approval or condemnation, promotion or disgrace.

C. L. xv. 209–211.

E. THE CRITICISM OF RESEARCH

(The *causerie* (or rather lecture) from which this is taken ranks with " What is a Classic? " Its full subject is " Tradition in Literature " and it was delivered at the École Normale in April, 1858.)

Criticism and learning, guided by the historic spirit, have given themselves, of late years, up to a mighty and valuable labour, the importance and the value of which I shall take good care not to belittle. Men have contracted the taste for *origins:* have deter-mined to know everything at closer quarters, by means of documents at first hand, and, as far as may be, unpublished. . . . There has been a fancy for penetrating into the inner sanctum, the hearth and bosom, of men eloquent with tongue and pen; and, by scrutinizing their papers, their autograph letters, the first editions of their books, the testimonies of their circles of acquaintance, the journals of the secretaries [1] who knew them best, ideas of them have been obtained which are somewhat different from, and certainly more exact than, those which were furnished by the mere reading of their published works. Men of taste formerly, in judging work from the literary point of view, were a little too lazy, too fastidious, too much of fine gentlemen — they were stopped by the smallest difficulties of research, and recoiled from them as from thorns. Even professional critics, if they were of some pretensions to fashion, did not inform themselves sufficiently beforehand of whatsoever might assure to their judgments complete exactness and truth; we *know* more than they did, on many points, in subjects with which they have dealt; we have all the resources to be desired at hand. . . . This is good and advantageous: but, at a time when there is too little really synoptic and judicial criticism, certain inconveniences have not been slow to come from these proceedings; and, if I do not mis-take, they stare us in the face everywhere. . . . Let us encourage all industrious research: but let us leave in everything the crafts-mastery to talent, thought, judgment, reason, taste. . . . When I see promises of "Such and such a writer, according to unpublished documents," I am a little distrustful: — I should be quite as well contented if somebody would, for once, boldly announce "Such and such a writer According to Judicious Ideas and Views, However Old They May Be."

                                                            C. L. xv. 374–377.

[1] Curiously enough, no one has suffered more from the indiscretion or treachery of "secretaries" than Sainte-Beuve himself. I do not refer to M. Troubat.

F. THE CRITICISM OF M. TAINE

(This passage is an instance, not only of the critic's supreme acuteness
and good sense, but of that quality which not very wise persons have called
a certain *treacherousness* in him; it might be better termed a ruthless
politeness. It is curious that the bludgeoning, pistolling ways of the older
criticism seem to be less dreaded and resented than this well-bred and only
faintly ironical manner, which, while it is perfectly civil to the man, leaves
little or nothing of his theory standing.)

Now M. Taine has done nothing but try to study, methodically,
the profound differences which race, *milieu*, periods of time, cause
in the composition of minds, in the form and the bent of talents.
But, it will be said, he does not succeed sufficiently; it is in vain
that he gives us an admirable description of the race in its general
features and fundamental lines; in vain that he draws and throws
up, in his powerful pictures, the revolutions of time and the moral
atmosphere that prevails at certain epochs of history; in vain that
he disentangles, with address, the complication of incidents and
particular adventures in which the life of an individual is engaged
and as it were engeared. Still something escapes him; and what
escapes is the most living part of the man — that which brings
it about that of twenty men, or a hundred, or a thousand, subjected apparently to the same internal or external conditions, no
two are alike, and that one only of all possesses original excellence.
Nay, more. He has not attained to the very spark of genius itself
in its essential quality, and he does not show it to us in his analysis.
He has done nothing but exhibit and deduce for us, thread by thread,
fibre by fibre, cell by cell, the stuff, the organism, the *parenchyma* [1]
(if you like the word), in which this soul, this life, this spark,
when once it has entered, makes play, gives itself free (or as it
were free) variation — and triumphs.

Have I not put the objections well,[2] and do you recognize the
argument of the wisest of the enemy?   Well, what does it prove?

[1] The soft cellular tissue in plants and animals.
[2] "Too well," Taine might have said. "You have overthrown more than
my enemies."

That the problem is difficult — that it is perhaps, in final exactness, insoluble. But is it nothing, I shall ask in my turn, to state the problem as our author has done, to come so close to it, to reduce it to its simplest terms, to increase the facility of weighing and calculating all its issues? After every allowance is made for general and particular elements and circumstances, there remains place and space enough around men of talent to give them every freedom of moving and turning. Besides, however narrow the circle traced round them, each talent, each genius, by the very fact that it is in a way a magician and an enchanter, has its own secret for working miracles and producing marvels, in this circle itself.[1] I do not see that M. Taine, though he may seem to neglect this power too much, absolutely contests or denies it, though he limits it, and, in so doing, gives the opportunity of defining it better.

VICTOR HUGO. THE MAGNA CHARTA OF POETRY

FROM THE PREFACE TO LES ORIENTALES (1829)

The author of this collection is not of those who recognize the right of criticism to interrogate the poet as to his fancy, and to ask him why he has chosen such a subject, mixed such a colour, gathered from such a tree, drawn from such a fountain. *Is the work good or is it bad?* This is the whole extent of the critical province. For the rest, give us neither praise nor blame for the colours used, but only for the fashion of their using. To take a rather high view of the matter, there are in poetry no good and no bad subjects, there are only good and bad poets. Besides, everything is a subject: everything is dependent on art; everything has the franchise in poetry.[2] Ask nothing, then, about the motive for taking the subject — grave or gay, horrible or graceful, brilliant or sombre, strange or simple — rather than any other. Examine how the work

---

[1] Note that these "miracles and marvels" make the scientific restrictions nugatory and superfluous at once.

[2] Cf. (*sup.*, p. 88) Patrizzi, of whom Victor Hugo had pretty certainly never heard.

is done, not on what or why. Beyond this the critic has no right of enquiry, the poet has no account to render. Art has nothing to do with leading-strings, with handcuffs, with gags: it says "Go your ways" and lets you loose in the great garden of poetry, where there is no forbidden fruit. Space and time are the domain of the poet. Let him go where he will and do what he pleases: this is the Law.

XXXI

MATTHEW ARNOLD

PREFACE TO POEMS (1853-1854)

(This, which is almost the earliest finished and formal document of
Mr. Arnold's criticism, is also one of the best and most complete expressions of it. It contains, explicitly or implicitly, almost everything that
he said later in substance: while its form is his very best — exhibiting
his native elegance and acquired scholarship, without his later assumed
mannerism.)

ADVERTISEMENT TO THE SECOND EDITION

I have allowed the Preface to the former edition of these Poems
to stand almost without change, because I still believe it to be, in
the main, true. I must not, however, be supposed insensible to
the force of much that has been alleged against portions of it, or
unaware that it contains many things incompletely stated, many
things which need limitation. It leaves, too, untouched the question, how far, and in what manner, the opinions there expressed
respecting the choice of subjects apply to lyric poetry; that region
of the poetical field which is chiefly cultivated at present. But
neither have I time now to supply these deficiencies, nor is this the
proper place for attempting it : on one or two points alone I wish
to offer, in the briefest possible way, some explanation.

An objection has been ably urged to the classing together, as
subjects equally belonging to a past time, Œdipus and Macbeth.
And it is no doubt true that to Shakespeare, standing on the verge
of the middle ages, the epoch of Macbeth was more familiar than
that of Œdipus. But I was speaking of actions as they presented
themselves to us moderns : and it will hardly be said that the European mind, since Voltaire, has much more affinity with the times of
Macbeth than with those of Œdipus. As moderns, it seems to me,

we have no longer any direct affinity with the circumstances and feelings of either ; as individuals, we are attracted towards this or that personage, we have a capacity for imagining him, irrespective of his times, solely according to a law of personal sympathy ; and those subjects for which we feel this personal attraction most strongly, we may hope to treat successfully. Alcestis or Joan of Arc, Charlemagne or Agamemnon — one of these is not really nearer to us now than another; each can be made present only by an act of poetic imagination : this man's imagination has an affinity for one of them, and that man's for another.

It has been said that I wish to limit the Poet in his choice of subjects to the period of Greek and Roman antiquity : but it is not so : I only counsel him to choose for his subjects great actions, without regarding to what time they belong. Nor do I deny that the poetic faculty can and does manifest itself in treating the most trifling action, the most hopeless subject. But it is a pity that power should be compelled to impart interest and force to his subject, instead of receiving them from it, and thereby doubling his impressiveness. There is, it has been excellently said, an immortal strength in the stories of great actions : the most gifted poet, then, may well be glad to supplement with it that mortal weakness, which, in presence of the vast spectacle of life and the world, he must for ever feel to be his individual portion.

Again, with respect to the study of the classical writers of antiquity : it has been said that we should emulate rather than imitate them. I make no objection : all I say is, let us study them. They can help to cure us of what is, it seems to me, the great vice of our intellect, manifesting itself in our incredible vagaries in literature, in art, in religion, in morals; namely, that it is *fantastic* and wants *sanity*. Sanity — that is the great virtue of the ancient literature : the want of that is the great defect of the modern, in spite of all its variety and power. It is impossible to read carefully the great ancients, without losing something of our caprice and eccentricity ; and to emulate them we must at least read them.

In two small volumes of Poems, published anonymously, one in 1849, the other in 1852, many of the Poems which compose the present volume have already appeared.   The rest are now published for the first time.

I have, in the present collection, omitted the Poem from which the volume published in 1852 took its title.   I have done so, not because the subject of it was a Sicilian Greek born between two and three thousand years ago, although many persons would think this a sufficient reason.   Neither have I done so because I had, in my own opinion, failed in the delineation which I intended to effect. I intended to delineate the feelings of one of the last of the Greek religious philosophers, one of the family of Orpheus and Musæus, having survived his fellows, living on into a time when the habits of Greek thought and feeling had begun fast to change, character to dwindle, the influence of the Sophists to prevail.   Into the feelings of a man so situated there entered much that we are accustomed to consider as exclusively modern; how much, the fragments of Empedocles himself which remain to us are sufficient at least to indicate.   What those who are familiar only with the great monuments of early Greek genius suppose to be its exclusive characteristics, have disappeared; the calm, the cheerfulness, the disinterested objectivity have disappeared : the dialogue of the mind with itself has commenced; modern problems have presented themselves; we hear already the doubts, we witness the discouragement, of Hamlet and of Faust.

The representation of such a man's feelings must be interesting, if consistently drawn.   We all naturally take pleasure, says Aristotle, in any imitation or representation whatever : this is the basis of our love of Poetry : and we take pleasure in them, he adds, because all knowledge is naturally agreeable to us; not to the philosopher only, but to mankind at large.   Every representation therefore which is consistently drawn may be supposed to be interesting inasmuch as it gratifies this natural interest in knowledge of all kinds.   What is *not* interesting, is that which does not add to our knowledge of any kind; that which is vaguely conceived and loosely drawn; a representation which is general, indeterminate, and faint, instead of being particular, precise, and firm.

Any accurate representation may therefore be expected to be interesting; but, if the representation be a poetical one, more than this is demanded. It is demanded, not only that it shall interest, but also that it shall inspirit and rejoice the reader: that it shall convey a charm, and infuse delight. For the Muses, as Hesiod says, were born that they might be "a forgetfulness of evils, and a truce from cares:" and it is not enough that the Poet should add to the knowledge of men, it is required of him also that he should add to their happiness. "All Art," says Schiller, "is dedicated to Joy, and there is no higher and no more serious problem, than how to make men happy. The right Art is that alone, which creates the highest enjoyment."

A poetical work, therefore, is not yet justified when it has been shown to be an accurate, and therefore interesting, representation; it has to be shown also that it is a representation from which men can derive enjoyment. In presence of the most tragic circumstances, represented in a work of Art, the feeling of enjoyment, as is well known, may still subsist: the representation of the most utter calamity, of the liveliest anguish, is not sufficient to destroy it: the more tragic the situation, the deeper becomes the enjoyment; and the situation is more tragic in proportion as it becomes more terrible.

What then are the situations, from the representation of which, though accurate, no poetical enjoyment can be derived? They are those in which the suffering finds no vent in action; in which a continuous state of mental distress is prolonged, unrelieved by incident, hope, or resistance; in which there is everything to be endured, nothing to be done. In such situations there is inevitably something morbid, in the description of them something monotonous. When they occur in actual life, they are painful, not tragic; the representation of them in poetry is painful also.

To this class of situations, poetically faulty as it appears to me, that of Empedocles, as I have endeavoured to represent him, belongs; and I have therefore excluded the Poem from the present collection.

And why, it may be asked, have I entered into this explanation respecting a matter so unimportant as the admission or exclusion of the Poem in question? I have done so, because I was anxious to avow that the sole reason for its exclusion was that which has been stated above; and that it has not been excluded in deference to the opinion which many critics of the present day appear to entertain against subjects chosen from distant times and countries: against the choice, in short, of any subjects but modern ones.

"The Poet," it is said,* and by an intelligent critic, "the Poet who would really fix the public attention must leave the exhausted past, and draw his subjects from matters of present import, and *therefore* both of interest and novelty."

Now this view I believe to be completely false. It is worth examining, inasmuch as it is a fair sample of a class of critical dicta everywhere current at the present day, having a philosophical form and air, but no real basis in fact; and which are calculated to vitiate the judgment of readers of poetry, while they exert, so far as they are adopted, a misleading influence on the practice of those who write it.

What are the eternal objects of Poetry, among all nations and at all times? They are actions; human actions; possessing an inherent interest in themselves, and which are to be communicated in an interesting manner by the art of the Poet. Vainly will the latter imagine that he has everything in his own power; that he can make an intrinsically inferior action equally delightful with a more excellent one by his treatment of it: he may indeed compel us to admire his skill, but his work will possess, within itself, an incurable defect.

The Poet, then, has in the first place to select an excellent action; and what actions are the most excellent? Those, certainly, which most powerfully appeal to the great primary human affections: to those elementary feelings which subsist permanently in the race, and which are independent of time. These feelings are permanent and the same; that which interests them is permanent and the same also. The modernness or antiquity of an

---

* In the *Spectator* of April 2d, 1853. The words quoted were not used with reference to poems of mine.

action, therefore, has nothing to do with its fitness for poetical representation; this depends upon its inherent qualities. To the elementary part of our nature, to our passions, that which is great and passionate is eternally interesting; and interesting solely in proportion to its greatness and to its passion. A great human action of a thousand years ago is more interesting to it than a smaller human action of to-day, even though upon the representation of this last the most consummate skill may have been expended, and though it has the advantage of appealing by its modern language, familiar manners, and contemporary allusions, to all our transient feelings and interests. These, however, have no right to demand of a poetical work that it shall satisfy them; their claims are to be directed elsewhere. Poetical works belong to the domain of our permanent passions : let them interest these, and the voice of all subordinate claims upon them is at once silenced.

Achilles, Prometheus, Clytemnestra, Dido — what modern poem presents personages as interesting, even to us moderns, as these personages of an "exhausted past"? We have the domestic epic dealing with the details of modern life, which pass daily under our eyes; we have poems representing modern personages in contact with the problems of modern life, moral, intellectual, and social; these works have been produced by poets the most distinguished of their nation and time; yet I fearlessly assert that *Hermann and Dorothea, Childe Harold, Jocelyn, The Excursion,* leave the reader cold in comparison with the effect produced upon him by the latter books of the *Iliad,* by the *Orestea,* or by the episode of Dido. And why is this? Simply because in the three latter cases the action is greater, the personages nobler, the situations more intense : and this is the true basis of the interest in a poetical work, and this alone.

It may be urged, however, that past actions may be interesting in themselves, but that they are not to be adopted by the modern Poet, because it is impossible for him to have them clearly present to his own mind, and he cannot therefore feel them deeply, nor represent them forcibly. But this is not necessarily the case. The externals of a past action, indeed, he cannot know with the precision of a contemporary; but his business is with its essentials. The outward man of Œdipus or of Macbeth, the houses in which they lived, the ceremonies of their courts, he cannot accurately figure to himself; but neither do they essentially concern him. His business is with their inward man; with their feelings and behaviour in certain tragic situations, which engage their passions as men; these have in them nothing local and casual; they are as accessible to the modern Poet as to a contemporary.

The date of an action, then, signifies nothing: the action itself, its selection and construction, this is what is all-important. This the Greeks understood far more clearly than we do. The radical difference between their poetical theory and ours consists, as it appears to me, in this: that, with them, the poetical character of the action in itself, and the conduct of it, was the first consideration; with us, attention is fixed mainly on the value of the separate thoughts and images which occur in the treatment of an action. They regarded the whole; we regard the parts. With them, the action predominated over the expression of it; with us, the expression predominates over the action. Not that they failed in expression, or were inattentive to it; on the contrary, they are the highest models of expression, the unapproached masters of the *grand style:* but their expression is so excellent because it is so admirably kept in its right degree of prominence; because it is so simple and so well subordinated; because it draws its force directly from the pregnancy of the matter which it conveys. For what reason was the Greek tragic poet confined to so limited a range of subjects? Because there are so few actions which unite in themselves, in the highest degree, the conditions of excellence; and it was not thought that on any but an excellent subject could an excellent Poem be constructed. A few actions, therefore, eminently adapted for tragedy, maintained almost exclusive possession of the Greek tragic stage; their significance appeared inexhaustible; they were as permanent problems, perpetually offered to the genius of every fresh poet. This too is the reason of what appears to us moderns a certain baldness of expression in Greek tragedy; of the triviality with which we often reproach the remarks of the chorus, where it takes part in the dialogue:

that the action itself, the situation of Orestes, or Merope, or Alcmæon, was to stand the central point of interest, unforgotten, absorbing, principal; that no accessories were for a moment to distract the spectator's attention from this, that the tone of the parts was to be perpetually kept down, in order not to impair the grandiose effect of the whole. The terrible old mythic story on which the drama was founded stood, before he entered the theatre, traced in its bare outlines upon the spectator's mind; it stood in his memory, as a group of statuary, faintly seen, at the end of a long and dark vista : then came the Poet, embodying outlines, developing situations, not a word wasted, not a sentiment capriciously thrown in : stroke upon stroke, the drama proceeded : the light deepened upon the group; more and more it revealed itself to the rivetted gaze of the spectator : until at last, when the final words were spoken, it stood before him in broad sunlight, a model of immortal beauty.

This was what a Greek critic demanded; this was what a Greek poet endeavoured to effect. It signified nothing to what time an action belonged; we do not find that the *Persæ* occupied a particularly high rank among the dramas of Æschylus, because it represented a matter of contemporary interest : this was not what a cultivated Athenian required; he required that the permanent elements of his nature should be moved; and dramas of which the action, though taken from a long-distant mythic time, yet was calculated to accomplish this in a higher degree than that of the *Persæ*, stood higher in his estimation accordingly. The Greeks felt, no doubt, with their exquisite sagacity of taste, that an action of present times was too near them, too much mixed up with what was accidental and passing, to form a sufficiently grand, detached, and self-subsistent object for a tragic poem : such objects belonged to the domain of the comic poet, and of the lighter kinds of poetry. For the more serious kinds, for *pragmatic* poetry, to use an excellent expression of Polybius, they were more difficult and severe in the range of subjects which they permitted. Their theory and practice alike, the admirable treatise of Aristotle, and the unrivalled works of their poets, exclaim with a thousand tongues — "all depends upon the subject; choose a fitting action, penetrate yourself with the feeling of its situations; this done, everything else will follow."

But for all kinds of poetry alike there was one point on which they were rigidly exacting; the adaptability of the subject to the kind of poetry selected, and the careful construction of the poem.

How different a way of thinking from this is ours! We can hardly at the present day understand what Menander meant, when he told a man who enquired as to the progress of his comedy that he had finished it, not having yet written a single line, because he had constructed the action of it in his mind. A modern critic would have assured him that the merit of his piece depended on the brilliant things which arose under his pen as he went along. We have poems which seem to exist merely for the sake of single lines and passages; not for the sake of producing any total-impression. We have critics who seem to direct their attention merely to detached expressions, to the language about the action, not to the action itself. I verily think that the majority of them do not in their hearts believe that there is such a thing as a total-impression to be derived from a poem at all, or to be demanded from a poet; they think the term a commonplace of metaphysical criticism. They will permit the Poet to select any action he pleases, and to suffer that action to go as it will, provided he gratifies them with occasional bursts of fine writing, and with a shower of isolated thoughts and images. That is, they permit him to leave their poetical sense ungratified, provided that he gratifies their rhetorical sense and their curiosity. Of his neglecting to gratify these, there is little danger; he needs rather to be warned against the danger of attempting to gratify these alone; he needs rather to be perpetually reminded to prefer his action to everything else; so to treat this, as to permit its inherent excellences to develop themselves, without interruption from the intrusion of his personal peculiarities: most fortunate when he most entirely succeeds in effacing himself, and in enabling a noble action to subsist as it did in nature.

But the modern critic not only permits a false practice; he absolutely prescribes false aims. — "A true allegory of the state of one's own mind in a representative history," the Poet is told, "is perhaps the highest thing that one can attempt in the way of Poetry." And accordingly he attempts it. An allegory of the state of one's own mind, the highest problem of an art which imitates actions! No assuredly, it is not, it never can be so: no great poetical work has ever been produced with such an aim. *Faust* itself, in which something of the kind is attempted, wonderful passages as it contains, and in spite of the unsurpassed beauty of the scenes which relate to Margaret, *Faust* itself, judged as a whole, and judged strictly as a poetical work, is defective: its illustrious author, the greatest poet of modern times, the greatest critic of all times, would have been the first to acknowledge it; he only defended his work, indeed, by asserting it to be "something incommensurable."

The confusion of the present times is great, the multitude of voices counselling different things bewildering, the number of existing works capable of attracting a young writer's attention and of becoming his models, immense: what he wants is a hand to guide him through the confusion, a voice to prescribe to him the aim which he should keep in view, and to explain to him that the value of the literary works which offer themselves to his attention is relative to their power of helping him forward on his road towards this aim. Such a guide the English writer at the present day will nowhere find. Failing this, all that can be looked for, all indeed that can be desired, is, that his attention should be fixed on excellent models; that he may reproduce, at any rate, something of their excellence, by penetrating himself with their works and by catching their spirit, if he cannot be taught to produce what is excellent independently.

Foremost among these models for the English writer stands Shakespeare: a name the greatest perhaps of all poetical names; a name never to be mentioned without reverence. I will venture, however, to express a doubt whether the influence of his works, excellent and fruitful for the readers of poetry, for the great majority, has been of unmixed advantage to the writers of it. Shakespeare indeed chose excellent subjects — the world could afford no better than Macbeth, or Romeo and Juliet, or Othello: he had no theory respecting the necessity of choosing subjects of present import, or the paramount interest attaching to allegories of the state of one's own mind ; like all great poets, he knew well what constituted a poetical action ; like them, wherever he found such an action, he took it ; like them, too, he found his best in past times. But to these general characteristics of all great poets he added a special one of his own, a gift, namely, of happy, abundant, and ingenious expression, eminent and unrivalled : so eminent as irresistibly to strike the attention first in him, and even to throw into comparative shade his other excellences as a poet. Here has been the mischief. These other excellences were his fundamental excellences *as a poet;* what distinguishes the artist from the mere amateur, says Goethe, is *Architectonicè* in the highest sense ; that power of execution which creates, forms, and constitutes : not the profoundness of single thoughts, not the richness of imagery, not the abundance of illustration. But these attractive accessories of a poetical work being more easily seized than the spirit of the whole, and these accessories being possessed by Shakespeare in an unequalled degree, a young writer having recourse to Shakespeare as his model runs great risk of being vanquished and absorbed by them, and, in consequence, of reproducing, according to the measure of his power, these, and these alone. Of this prepondering quality of Shakespeare's genius, accordingly, almost the whole of modern English poetry has, it appears to me, felt the influence. To the exclusive attention on the part of his imitators to this, it is in a great degree owing that of the majority of modern poetical works the details alone are valuable, the composition worthless. In reading them one is perpetually reminded of that terrible sentence on a modern French poet, — *il dit tout ce qu'il veut, mais malheureusement il n'a rien à dire.*

Let me give an instance of what I mean. I will take it from the works of the very chief among those who seem to have been formed in the school of Shakespeare : of one whose exquisite genius and pathetic death render him for ever interesting. I will take the poem of *Isabella, or the Pot of Basil,* by Keats. I choose this rather than *Endymion,* because the latter work (which a modern critic has classed with the *Fairy Queen !*), although undoubtedly there blows through it the breath of genius, is yet as a whole so

utterly incoherent, as not strictly to merit the name of a poem
at all. The poem of *Isabella*, then, is a perfect treasure-house of
graceful and felicitous words and images : almost in every stanza
there occurs one of those vivid and picturesque turns of expression,
by which the object is made to flash upon the eye of the mind, and
which thrill the reader with a sudden delight. This one short
poem contains, perhaps, a greater number of happy single expressions which one could quote than all the extant tragedies of
Sophocles. But the action, the story? The action in itself is an
excellent one ; but so feebly is it conceived by the Poet, so loosely
constructed, that the effect produced by it, in and for itself, is absolutely null. Let the reader, after he has finished the poem of
Keats, turn to the same story in the *Decameron :* he will then feel
how pregnant and interesting the same action has become in the
hands of a great artist, who above all things delineates his object ;
who subordinates expression to that which it is designed to express.

I have said that the imitators of Shakespeare, fixing their attention on his wonderful gift of expression, have directed their imitation to this, neglecting his other excellences. These excellences,
the fundamental excellences of poetical art, Shakespeare no doubt
possessed them—possessed many of them in a splendid degree ;
but it may perhaps be doubted whether even he himself did not
sometimes give scope to his faculty of expression to the prejudice
of a higher poetical duty. For we must never forget that Shakespeare is the great poet he is from his skill in discerning and firmly
conceiving an excellent action, from his power of intensely feeling
a situation, of intimately associating himself with a character ; not
from his gift of expression, which rather even leads him astray,
degenerating sometimes into a fondness for curiosity of expression,
into an irritability of fancy, which seems to make it impossible for
him to say a thing plainly, even when the press of the action
demands the very directest language, or its level character the
very simplest. Mr. Hallam, than whom it is impossible to find a
saner and more judicious critic, has had the courage (for at the
present day it needs courage) to remark, how extremely and faultily
difficult Shakespeare's language often is. It is so : you may find
main scenes in some of his greatest tragedies, *King Lear* for

instance, where the language is so artificial, so curiously tortured, and so difficult, that every speech has to be read two or three times before its meaning can be comprehended. This over-curiousness of expression is indeed but the excessive employment of a wonderful gift—of the power of saying a thing in a happier way than any other man; nevertheless, it is carried so far that one understands what M. Guizot meant when he said that Shakespeare appears in his language to have tried all styles except that of simplicity. He has not the severe and scrupulous self-restraint of the ancients, partly, no doubt, because he had a far less cultivated and exacting audience : he has indeed a far wider range than they had, a far richer fertility of thought ; in this respect he rises above them : in his strong conception of his subject, in the genuine way in which he is penetrated with it, he resembles them, and is unlike the moderns : but in the accurate limitation of it, the conscientious rejection of superfluities, the simple and rigorous development of it from the first line of his work to the last, he falls below them, and comes nearer to the moderns. In his chief works, besides what he has of his own, he has the elementary soundness of the ancients; he has their important action and their large and broad manner; but he has not their purity of method. He is therefore a less safe model ; for what he has of his own is personal, and inseparable from his own rich nature ; it may be imitated and exaggerated, it cannot be learned or applied as an art; he is above all suggestive; more valuable, therefore, to young writers as men than as artists. But clearness of arrangement, rigour of development, simplicity of style — these may to a certain extent be learned : and these may, I am convinced, be learned best from the ancients, who, although infinitely less suggestive than Shakespeare, are thus, to the artist, more instructive.

What then, it will be asked, are the ancients to be our sole models ? the ancients with their comparatively narrow range of experience, and their widely different circumstances ? Not, certainly, that which is narrow in the ancients, nor that in which we can no longer sympathize. An action like the action of the *Antigone* of Sophocles, which turns upon the conflict between the heroine's duty to her brother's corpse and that to the laws of her

country, is no longer one in which it is possible that we should feel
a deep interest. I am speaking too, it will be remembered, not of
the best sources of intellectual stimulus for the general reader, but
of the best models of instruction for the individual writer. This
last may certainly learn of the ancients, better than anywhere else,
three things which it is vitally important for him to know : — the
all-importance of the choice of a subject; the necessity of accurate
construction; and the subordinate character of expression. He will
learn from them how unspeakably superior is the effect of the one
moral impression left by a great action treated as a whole, to the
effect produced by the most striking single thought or by the
happiest image. As he penetrates into the spirit of the great
classical works, as he becomes gradually aware of their intense
significance, their noble simplicity, and their calm pathos, he will
be convinced that it is this effect, unity and profoundness of moral
impression, at which the ancient Poets aimed; that it is this which
constitutes the grandeur of their works, and which makes them
immortal. He will desire to direct his own efforts towards producing the same effect. Above all, he will deliver himself from
the jargon of modern criticism, and escape the danger of producing
poetical works conceived in the spirit of the passing time, and
which partake of its transitoriness.

The present age makes great claims upon us : we owe it service, it
will not be satisfied without our admiration. I know not how it is,
but their commerce with the ancients appears to me to produce, in
those who constantly practise it, a steadying and composing effect
upon their judgment, not of literary works only, but of men and
events in general. They are like persons who have had a very
weighty and impressive experience ; they are more truly than
others under the empire of facts, and more independent of the
language current among those with whom they live. They wish
neither to applaud nor to revile their age : they wish to know
what it is, what it can give them, and whether this is what they
want. What they want, they know very well ; they want to educe
and cultivate what is best and noblest in themselves : they know,
too, that this is no easy task — χαλεπὸν as Pittacus said, χαλεπὸν
εσθλον ἔμμεναι — and they ask themselves sincerely whether their

age and its literature can assist them in the attempt. If they are endeavouring to practise any art, they remember the plain and simple proceedings of the old artists, who attained their grand results by penetrating themselves with some noble and significant action, not by inflating themselves with a belief in the preëminent importance and greatness of their own times. They do not talk of their mission, nor of interpreting their age, nor of the coming Poet; all this, they know, is the mere delirium of vanity; their business is not to praise their age, but to afford to the men who live in it the highest pleasure which they are capable of feeling. If asked to afford this by means of subjects drawn from the age itself, they ask what special fitness the present age has for supplying them : they are told that it is an era of progress, an age commissioned to carry out the great ideas of industrial development and social amelioration. They reply that with all this they can do nothing ; that the elements they need for the exercise of their art are great actions, calculated powerfully and delightfully to affect what is permanent in the human soul; that so far as the present age can supply such actions, they will gladly make use of them ; but that an age wanting in moral grandeur can with difficulty supply such, and an age of spiritual discomfort with difficulty be powerfully and delightfully affected by them.

A host of voices will indignantly rejoin that the present age is inferior to the past neither in moral grandeur nor in spiritual health. He who possesses the discipline I speak of will content himself with remembering the judgments passed upon the present age, in this respect, by the two men, the one of strongest head, the other of widest culture, whom it has produced ; by Goethe and by Niebuhr. It will be sufficient for him that he knows the opinions held by these two great men respecting the present age and its literature; and that he feels assured in his own mind that their aims and demands upon life were such as he would wish, at any rate, his own to be ; and their judgment as to what is impeding and disabling such as he may safely follow. He will not, however, maintain a hostile attitude towards the false pretensions of his age ; he will content himself with not being overwhelmed by them. He will esteem himself fortunate if he can succeed in banishing from his mind all feelings of contradiction, and irritation, and impatience ; in order to delight himself with the contemplation of some noble action of a heroic time, and to enable others, through his representation of it, to delight in it also.

I am far indeed from making any claim, for myself, that I possess this discipline ; or for the following Poems, that they breathe its spirit. But I say, that in the sincere endeavour to learn and practise, amid the bewildering confusion of our times, what is sound and true in poetical art, I seemed to myself to find the only sure guidance, the only solid footing, among the ancients. They, at any rate, knew what they wanted in Art, and we do not. It is this uncertainty which is disheartening, and not hostile criticism. How often have I felt this when reading words of disparagement or of cavil: that it is the uncertainty as to what is really to be aimed at which makes our difficulty, not the dissatisfaction of the critic, who himself suffers from the uncertainty. *Non me tua fervida terrent Dicta ; Dii me terrent, et Jupiter hostis.*

Two kinds of *dilettanti,* says Goethe, there are in poetry : he who neglects the indispensable mechanical part, and thinks he has done enough if he shows spirituality and feeling ; and he who seeks to arrive at poetry merely by mechanism, in which he can acquire an artisan's readiness, and is without soul and matter. And he adds, that the first does most harm to Art, and the last to himself. If we must be *dilettanti :* if it is impossible for us, under the circumstances amidst which we live, to think clearly, to feel nobly, and to delineate firmly : if we cannot attain to the mastery of the great artists — let us, at least, have so much respect for our Art as to prefer it to ourselves : let us not bewilder our successors : let us transmit to them the practice of Poetry, with its boundaries and wholesome regulative laws, under which excellent works may again, perhaps, at some future time, be produced, not yet fallen into oblivion through our neglect, not yet condemned and cancelled by the influence of their eternal enemy, Caprice.

INDEX OF BOOKS AND AUTHORS